THE CHEQUERED PAST:
SPORTS CAR RACING AND RALLYING
IN CANADA, 1951–1991

In the forty-year period between 1951 and 1991, Canadian sports car competition underwent a massive change, transforming itself from an amateur recreational pastime to a commercialized profession and from an individual sport to a spectacle for mass consumption. *The Chequered Past* is the story of the struggle over power and purpose within the Canadian auto sport that led to this transformation.

The first comprehensive history of sports car racing and rallying in Canada, *The Chequered Past* traces the efforts of the national governing body – the Canadian Auto Sport Clubs (CASC) – to bring its sports car competition up to a 'world class' level, and to manage the consequences of those efforts in the second half of the twentieth century. David Charters traces the social origins of the sport and the major trends that shaped it: professionalism, technological change, rising costs, and the influence of commercial sponsors. Charters argues that while early enthusiasts set the sport on a course toward professionalism that would eventually produce world-class Canadian events and racers, that course would also ultimately change the purpose of the sport: from personal recreation to mass entertainment. As technological innovations drove up the costs of competing at the top ranks, racers were forced to rely on sponsors, who commercialized and ultimately gained control of the sport. The end result, Charters argues, was the marginalization of the amateur competitor and of the CASC itself.

Based on extensive research into the CASC's records and dozens of interviews with former competitors and officials, *The Chequered Past* opens a window into the rich but virtually unknown history of the auto sport, and claims for it a place in Canadian sports history.

DAVID A. CHARTERS is a professor in the Department of History at the University of New Brunswick and an amateur sports car racer.

DAVID A. CHARTERS

The Chequered Past

Sports Car Racing and Rallying
in Canada, 1951–1991

UNIVERSITY OF TORONTO PRESS
Toronto Buffalo London

© University of Toronto Press Incorporated 2007
Toronto Buffalo London
Printed in Canada

Reprinted 2007

ISBN 978-0-8020-9093-5 (cloth)
ISBN 978-0-8020-9394-3 (paper)

Printed on acid-free paper

Library and Archives Canada Cataloguing in Publication

Charters, David Anderson, 1949–
The chequered past : sports car racing and rallying in Canada, 1951–1991 / David A. Charters.

Includes bibliographical references and index.
ISBN 978-0-8020-9093-5 (bound)
ISBN 978-0-8020-9394-3 (pbk.)

1. Sports car events – Canada – History.   2. Automobile racing – Canada – History.   3. Automobile rallies – Canada – History.
I. Title.

GV1034.15.A1C42 2007   796.720971'09045   C2006-904170-9

The cover photograph is from the historical collection of Lionel Birnbom, a photographer who covered sports car racing – mainly in Eastern Canada – from the late 1950s to the late 1980s. Mr Birnbom has said that this photograph is the favourite of his entire collection of some 40,000 photographs, as it not only captures a very significant event, but is probably the pinnacle of racing in Canada at that time.

University of Toronto Press acknowledges the financial assistance to its publishing program of the Canada Council for the Arts and the Ontario Arts Council.

University of Toronto Press acknowledges the financial support for its publishing activities of the Government of Canada through the Book Publishing Industry Development Program (BPIDP).

To my Dad,
a champion in all respects

Contents

Acknowledgments ix

Abbreviations xiii

Introduction 3

PART ONE: THE AMATEUR AGE, 1951–1960

1 The Visionaries and Their Vision: The Founding of the Canadian Automobile Sports Clubs 15

2 Canadian Club: Origins of the Sports Car Subculture, 1950–1960 23

3 Run What Ya Brung: Sports Car Competition in the Amateur Age 38

4 Rules and Regs: Professionalizing the Amateurs 56

5 Powershift: The Rise of Commercial Professionalism 72

PART TWO: GATHERING SPEED, 1961–1966

6 Behind the Wheel: Power Politics in the CASC 87

7 Trans-Canada: The Shell 4000 and the National Rally Championship, 1961–1966 101

8 Making Tracks: Commercializing Canadian Racing 119

9 Reach for the Top: Canadian Racing Driver Development in the 1960s 133

10 The Cutting Edge: Bill Sadler and the Can-Am Series 148

PART THREE: FROM SPORT TO SPECTACLE, 1967–1991

11 Coming of Age? Canadians and International Racing 163

12 Winning Formula: Formula Racing and the National Championship 173

13 Stage by Stage: Transforming the National Rally Championship 188

14 Downshift: The Crisis in Amateur Auto Sport, 1969–1975 203

15 Final Laps: The Decline and Fall of the CASC 221

Epilogue 247

Notes 261
Select Bibliography 307
Illustration Credits 321
Index 323

Illustrations follow page 144

Acknowledgments

While authors get all the credit (or blame) for the writing of a book, most will concede that they received a lot of help along the way. This book is no exception; it was, in many respects, a collective effort. I owe a special debt of thanks to the staff of the Canadian Automobile Sport Clubs National / Ontario Region office, who gave me free rein in their archives and with their photocopier. This was the essential starting point, and Jesse Hauth, Joyce Pulbrook, and Jean Noble made my work there as pleasant as it was productive. The late Robert Brockington, who initially organized the archives of both the CASC and the Canadian Motorsport Hall of Fame, was a fount of knowledge. He graciously read the first draft and set me straight where my own understanding had failed me. The Canadian Automobile Association and the Royal Automobile Club (UK) also provided useful research material, while Dr Stephen Koerner of Victoria shared with me the fruits of his research in British archives. Marcel Chichak did the same with materials from his excellent collection on the Shell 4000 rally.

But documents tell only part of the story. It would not have been possible to give this history a human face without the generosity of the many people who consented to be interviewed, who responded to letters, emails, and questionnaires, and who shared their personal papers with me. The scale of their contribution is readily apparent in the bibliography. Lionel Birnbom, the pioneer of Canadian auto sport photography, generously opened up his massive collection to me and patiently helped me select the best for this book. Bruce Buntain loaned me his Atlantic region photographs, while Tom Johnston was equally helpful with photos from western Canada. Can-Am series chronicler Pete Lyons was likewise very generous.

I am grateful to the Faculty of Arts and the History Department at the University of New Brunswick for grants that supported the research for this book and the purchase of photographs. I also benefited greatly from the encouragement I received from my colleagues in the department at every stage of this project. Phil Buckner, Ernie Forbes, Beverly Lemire, and Marc Milner all read and commented on parts of the book. Steve Turner read the whole first draft and was generous with his time and his advice.

Many others offered encouragement and help at various stages: Dr H.F. Moorhouse at the University of Glasgow, the authority on the sociology of the American 'hot rod' culture; Professor Don Davis, transportation historian at the University of Ottawa; Professor Brad Cross of St Thomas University, who shared some insights and sources on Canadian urban history; and Ed Moody at the Canadian Motorsport Hall of Fame. Jane Davidson, an old school friend and an accomplished writer herself, also read portions of the book and urged me to let the people in the story tell it in their own words. My many friends and colleagues in Atlantic Region Motor Sports helped this book more than they realized, on and off the track. I learned a great deal behind the wheel and just as much from sharing experiences with them after the events.

I should like to thank Len Husband, John St James, and the editorial staff at University of Toronto Press for patiently guiding me through the various stages of turning the manuscript into a book. Equally important, they have done so in a way that makes it accessible to scholars and enthusiasts alike. The press also deserves applause for venturing down the uncharted roads of Canadian auto sport history. They have opened the door to a new field where I hope others will follow.

This book is also something of a family affair. It has its origins more than forty years ago when my dad, whose own experiences form part of this book, was racing and rallying. I spent many weekends with him at the Connor Circuit and Mosport, and navigating in rallies on the back roads of Quebec. So, thirty years later when I broached the idea of the book, dad became my most enthusiastic supporter, putting me in touch with former competitors, sharing his recollections, and, later, reading the manuscript. But it was my son Steve's passion for watching car racing on TV that had first reignited my interest in auto sport and started me on this quest. And when I decided to compete myself, he dutifully followed my footsteps and crewed for me at Pennfield and Atlantic Motorsport Park. If, some day, he becomes the third generation in our family to compete in auto sport, he will have this book to tell him how he got there. And, to Mary and Jen, thanks for your unspoken support and for your patience while I hogged the family computer on so many evenings and weekends.

Finally, notwithstanding all the help I received, I must issue the usual disclaimer – that any errors of fact are mine alone.

Abbreviations

ACAM	l'Association des Coureurs Automobile de Montréal
ACCUS	Automobile Competition Committee for the United States
AMP	Atlantic Motorsport Park
ARCA	Automobile Racing Club of America
ASC	*Autosport Canada*
ASCC	Atlantic Sports Car Club
ASN	Autorité Sportif National (National Sporting Authority)
BARC-OC	British Automobile Racing Club – Ontario Centre
BCITF	British Columbia International Trade Fair (rally)
BEMC	British Empire Motor Club
BFG	BF Goodrich
bhp	brake horsepower
BMC	British Motor Corporation
BP	British Petroleum
CAA	Canadian Automobile Association
CAC	Canadair Auto Club
CARS	Canadian Association of Rallysport
CART	Championship Auto Racing Teams
CASC	Canadian Automobile Sport Clubs
cid	cubic inch diameter
CKF	Canadian Karting Federation
CMB	*Canadian Motorsport Bulletin*
CRCA	Canadian Race Communications Association
CRDA	Canadian Racing Drivers Association
CRRC	Canadian Road Race of Champions
CSCC	Calgary Sports Car Club

Abbreviations

CSI	Commission Sportive Internationale (International Sporting Commission)
CTT	*Canada Track and Traffic*
DAC	Deutscher Automobile Club
DIY	do it yourself
DNF	did not finish
DOT	Department of Transport
EIS	Edmonton International Speedway
EZE	Eastern Zone Endurance (championship)
F1	Formula One
F2	Formula Two
F1200	Formula 1200
FAQ	Fédération Auto-Quebec
F/Atlantic	Formula Atlantic
FIA	Fédération Internationale de l'Automobile
FISA	Fédération Internationale du Sport Automobile
FJ	Formula Junior
FOCA	Formula One Constructors Association (also F1CA)
FV	Formula Vee
GCR	General Competition Rules
GT	*Gran Turismo* (Grand Touring)
ICNSCC	International Conference of Northwest Sports Car Clubs
IMSA	International Motor Sports Association
JOA	Jaguar Owners Association
LASC	London Automobile Sport Club
MGCCT	MG Car Club of Toronto
MIV	Molson Indy Vancouver
Mk	Mark
MMGCC	Montreal MG Car Club
MMRC	Montreal Motor Racing Club
MMSC	Moncton Motor Sport Club
MRP	Motor Racing Partnership
NART	North American Racing Team
NASCAR	National Association for Stock Car Auto Racing
NBSCC	New Brunswick Sporting Car Club
NCB	National Competition Board
NKC	National Karting Committee
NTMC	North Toronto Motorsport Club
OASC	Okanagan Auto Sport Club
OLCC	Ottawa Light Car Club

PRSL	Public Relations Services Limited
RAC	Royal Automobile Club
St LAC	Saint Lawrence Automobile Club
SCC	Sports Car Club (Toronto)
SCCA	Sports Car Club of America
SCCBC	Sports Car Club of British Columbia
SCCS	Sports Car Club of Saskatchewan
SMCC	Sports Motor Car Club
TNN	The Nashville Network
TSD	Time-Speed-Distance (rally)
TSN	The Sports Network
UNBSCC	University of New Brunswick Sports Car Club
USAC	United States Auto Club
USRRC	United States Road Racing Championship
VW	Volkswagen
WOSCA	Western Ontario Sports Car Association
WRC	World Rally Championship

THE CHEQUERED PAST:
SPORTS CAR RACING AND RALLYING
IN CANADA, 1951–1991

Introduction

Hall of Fame

On a sweltering August night in 1993, the famous and not so famous of Canadian and international auto sport gathered at the Four Seasons Hotel in Toronto's trendy Yorkville area for an event that all agreed was long overdue: the inauguration of a Canadian Motorsport Hall of Fame. In a glittering ballroom awash in black satin gowns and too-tight tuxedos, a veritable who's who of former competitors, officials, sponsors, and fans mixed and mingled, many seeing old friends for the first time in decades. The distinguished guests included John Surtees, the British Formula One champion, who raced frequently in Canada in the 1960s, and Major General Lewis MacKenzie, then Canada's most famous soldier and an avid amateur Formula Ford racer. They presented medals to nine men and one corporate sponsor who had made Canadian auto sport history over the previous forty years. The ceremony was repeated in subsequent years and many of the sport's pioneers have now been honoured for their contributions.[1]

Since the early 1950s, Canadian auto sport has produced its share of 'stars,' even 'superstars,' many of whom were nominated for induction that evening. The inductees themselves constituted a remarkable 'snapshot' of Canada's auto sport past. Bill Brack, the Toronto car dealer with the dashingly handsome looks and the shy, almost self-effacing manner, was three times the Canadian driving champion in the 1970s. The towering John Cannon, a transplanted Brit and now a Texas businessman, was the only Canadian to drive to victory in the Can-Am racing series. Eppie Wietzes, a soft-spoken Dutch immigrant and, like Brack, a successful car dealer, had been one of the stable of drivers groomed by the Comstock Racing Team, winning the Canadian championship twice at the end of the 1960s.

They also honoured Bill Sadler, the racer and self-taught engineering *wunderkind* from St Catharines, Ontario, who showed his genius as a racing car designer and builder. In the early 1960s his hand-built cars were not just at the cutting edge of design, but were even ahead of their time – the prototypes of the powerful and innovative Can-Am cars of the late 1960s.

Four of the inductees had died trying to make their marks in the 'major leagues' of international auto sport. Billy Foster from Vancouver was the first Canadian to drive in the Indianapolis 500. He had come up through stock car racing, and died in 1967 practising for a race at Riverside, California. Bob McLean, a rising star from British Columbia, was killed while driving for the Comstock team in the 1966 Sebring twelve-hour endurance race in Florida. Hired by the world-famous Lotus team, Peter Ryan died in practice for a Formula 2 race at Reims, France, in 1962. And if winning in Formula One is the only true measure of racing greatness, then the greatest of them all was the diminutive, unlikely 'superstar' from Berthierville, Quebec: Gilles Villeneuve. He won his first Grand Prix in Montreal in 1978, and was killed in practice at Zolder, Belgium, in 1982. His son Jacques, not yet the Indy Car and Formula One champion that he is today, accepted the honour for his father. It was an entirely appropriate gesture; no one had done more than Gilles to bring auto racing into the hearts and minds of Canadians.

But the racers didn't do this all by themselves. They had a lot of corporate help along the way. Charles 'Chuck' Rathgeb, a giant of Canadian industry and sport, who wore his wealth with hearty amiability, was recognized for creating and running the Comstock Racing Team. Canada's first 'national' commercially sponsored team, it nurtured the careers of several Canadian champions. Imperial Tobacco was recognized for its support of Canadian auto sport that began with the first Players 200 race in 1961 and continued with its driver development programs in the 1990s. The tobacco advertising ban terminated its auto sport role in 2003, ironically just before their driver Paul Tracy won the prestigious Championship Auto Racing Teams (CART) (Indy Car) championship.[2]

Yet, most conspicuous by their absence from the list of inductees were the sport's 'founding fathers,' the eight men who – forty-two years earlier – had established Canada's first national governing body for auto sport: the Canadian Automobile Sport Clubs (CASC). Several years would pass before even one of them – Jim Gunn – was inducted. By 1993, the CASC had been deceased for two years. But unlike the four racers who died accidentally, it had succumbed to politics. It was the victim of power struggles over professionalism and commercialism, the very forces it had unleashed in its quest to raise Canadian auto sport – racing in particular – to 'world class' status. The CASC's role in the sport was always political, always controversial, and for many in the sport its demise left a sense of betrayal that was deeply personal and painful. Without the decades of work by the organization and its cadres of dedicated amateur volunteers, it is unlikely that the hall of fame would have had anyone or anything to celebrate. In fact, it might never have come into being. Consequently, the rise and fall of the CASC and its struggles to cope with the changes in and the forces influencing the sport lie at the heart of this history.

But if bitterness lingered in the hearts of any of those present, they did not allow it to mar the occasion. The summer of 1993 was an auspicious time to launch the hall of fame. Canada's international auto sport fortunes seemed to be on the rise. Scott Goodyear and Paul Tracy, both from the Toronto area, were showing great promise in the CART series. They were soon to be eclipsed by Jacques Villeneuve, who would win the prestigious Indy 500 in 1995. Other promising drivers, like Greg Moore and Patrick Carpentier, were about to break into the public eye. Major auto sport events – the Canadian Grand Prix for Formula One, the Toronto and Vancouver Indy Car races – were drawing huge crowds, massive corporate sponsorship, and worldwide TV coverage. As the century was drawing to a close, Canadian auto sport had achieved 'world class' status in every respect.

The hall of fame ceremony was a hallmark event in that process. Yet, it highlighted a simple, but striking, fact; of the nine men inducted that evening only one – Gilles Villeneuve – had achieved the status of a *national* sports hero, whose name had become a household word. Outside the ranks of true enthusiasts, the other eight were virtual unknowns.

The contrast with other sports and their halls of fame could not be more dramatic. The average Canadian ten-year-old boy probably could name half a dozen baseball hall of fame stars without even thinking. And none of them would be Canadian. The hockey hall of fame is filled with Canadian *national* heroes, from Maurice 'Rocket' Richard to Wayne Gretzky. But, would that same ten-year-old recognize the other eight names on the motorsport hall of fame list? The answer, almost certainly, is no. Although car racing attracts a huge crowd a few times a year in Canada, it simply has not captured the national imagination to the same extent as the traditional 'stick and ball' sports. The large audiences at the Toronto and Vancouver Indy Car races look less impressive when you realize that – at least up until the 1994 baseball strike – the Toronto Blue Jays had been drawing crowds of a nearly comparable size for *every* game at the SkyDome.

By contrast, in the United States, races such as the Indy 500 and the Daytona 500 are promoted, even enshrined, as *national* spectacles, complete with flags, prayers, anthems, bands, fireworks and flypasts, and, inevitably, intense commercial and media hype. The Indy 500 claims to attract the largest single-day sporting event audience in the world.

And the stars of these events past and present – such as Mario Andretti, Jeff Gordon, Richard Petty, and the late Dale Earnhardt – are treated as sports icons. Some European auto sport heroes have achieved superstar status and universal name recognition, Stirling Moss, Michael Schumacher, and Jackie Stewart among them. In Italy, Ferrari drivers – regardless of their national origin – have a devoted following, the *tifosi*, who display their exhilaration and anguish at victory and defeat with the unbridled passion of soccer fans. Until he died, Gilles Villeneuve was probably better known and more adored in Italy than in Canada.[3] In auto sport, as in so many other forms of endeavour, Canadians have had to succeed abroad before they are recognized at home. As for the rest of Canada's auto sport hall of fame inductees and the many more who have since been recognized, they laboured in comparative obscurity.

Still, they paved the track for Villeneuve's success. He could not have made it to Formula One without their vision, their work, and their competitive spirit. Some were only laying the foundation when he was born. Yet by the time he was ready to step into a racing car and show what he could do, all the pieces were in place. Thus, his success belonged to them almost as much as it did to him. By 1993 their recognition was long overdue. The hall of fame ceremony was a start, but it left most of the tale untold. This book is their story. But it is more than that. It is the story of a sport whose character changed fundamentally even as they competed in it.

A Sport Transformed

Abbotsford airport, just east of Vancouver, is famous today for its annual air show that features some of the world's most advanced high-performance aircraft. But in 1949 the airfield hosted a different kind of speed event: the first sports car race in post-war Canada. Organized by a group of car enthusiasts, part of an emerging sports car 'subculture,' it was a low-key, strictly amateur, affair. Arleigh Pilkey, who raced that day in his MG TC, recalled later that there were only seven cars and no spectators.[4] Speeds were modest – the sports cars of the day could barely reach 80 mph – and when the racing was done, they drove their cars home.

Fifty years later the tenth running of the Molson Indy Vancouver (MIV) race involved two dozen CART 'Champ Cars' that were capable of speeds well in excess of 200 mph. They looked less like the spectators' cars and more like the high-tech jet fighters that regularly dazzle the crowds at Abbotsford. The MIV competitors were members of an elite club – full-time 'professional' drivers, teams, crews, and officials – who earn their livelihoods from a sport that has been transformed into a multinational, multimillion-dollar entertainment business. And among them, centre stage that day, were the Canadians: the brash, hard-charging veteran Paul Tracy; the youthful newcomer Patrick Carpentier, who finished second in the rain-soaked event; and the rising would-be superstar the late Greg Moore – who hailed from Maple Ridge, a few miles from Abbotsford. Whereas the racers in 1949 competed to entertain themselves, the Indy racers were performing for an audience of nearly 100,000 on site and millions more watching on television all over the world or following the race on the Internet. They were also 'working' for their corporate sponsors, who bombarded the audience and viewers with a slick campaign of advertising and promotional hype that turned a simple race into a 'pop culture' spectacle.[5]

These two races mark the outer boundaries of the transformation of Canadian sports car competition in the second half of the twentieth century, from sport to spectacle, from subculture to pop culture. The question to be answered in this book is simple: how and why did this happen?

The chapters that follow will show that this dramatic change was the result of the convergence and interaction of two trends – professionalization and commercialization – a process that has occurred in most sports, starting even before the twentieth century. The former trend emerged from the desire of Canadian amateur enthusiasts and entrepreneurs to raise Canadian auto sport to 'world class' status, which necessitated 'professional' organization, standards, and regulation. The latter trend reflected changes in the nature of the international auto sport to which Canadian enthusiasts aspired. Advances in technology and the changing formats of the events themselves, including national championships, pushed up the costs of competing. This put the top levels of the sport out of reach to all but a small, select 'technocratic meritocracy' of commercially sponsored and professionally trained competitors and teams. It also meant that 'world class' events, facilities, and teams had to be run as businesses, by businesses. Once they became involved, they shaped it to promote their interests, and gradually took over the sport. Later, using television, they transformed its major events into a mass consumption spectacle.[6] The consequences of this process were serious; professional auto sport was 'commodified,' while amateur sports car competition was marginalized.

But this transformation raises a host of important questions. What is the purpose of auto sport? Is it just to provide self-gratification for the competitor? Is it to entertain an audience? Is it supposed to sell cars or other products? Is it meant to make money for promoters and to provide a living for professional participants? Who *owns* Canadian auto sport and whose interests does it serve? Does the sport belong to the competitors and the fans? Or is it the domain of the sponsors, promoters, teams, and automobile manufacturers? What is the relationship between amateurism, professionalism, and commercialism? And how did we get from the former to the latter?

Sports journalists and historians who cover the traditional 'stick and ball' sports have been grappling with similar questions for decades, and with good reason. The second half of the past century was notable for the veritable 'explosion' of commercialized professional sport, particularly in North America, but even in the international Olympic movement.[7] Baseball, basketball, football, and hockey have been transformed from locally based, local fan-oriented activities into multibillion-dollar, business-run and media-oriented cartels, whose sole purpose is simple: to make money. Television, with its almost limitless capacity for promotion and revenue generation changed dramatically the nature of professional sports – from sport into spectacle, from competition into commodity, from something one *does* to something one *buys* and *consumes*. And it often appears that many of the *owners* know or care little about the sports they control. Teams are franchised like so many fast-food outlets, and players are treated as commodities, to be traded, bought, and sold. That said, the players themselves are hardly powerless victims of this process, but willing and eager participants, since this new form of indentured servitude allows them to 'market' themselves. They are able to trade generously on their name and fame, to command enormous salaries, and to reap equally large fees from product endorsements and the sale of personalized iconography. Sports broadcaster Howard Cosell summed it up neatly years ago when he observed acerbically: 'It's all about deals.'[8]

Auto sport has moved a long way in the same direction, most noticeably in stock car racing, which has been a business since 1948. Today, it is a multi-billion-dollar entertainment industry. But the other forms of auto sport are not far behind. The agent for drag racer Kenny Bernstein once described him as a 'sellable commodity.'[9] In the mid-1990s Michael Schumacher won the Formula One (F1) championship in a car named after, produced, and raced on behalf of the upscale Italian clothing company Bennetton. Indeed, like the players in other pro sports, the top-rung auto sport competitors themselves seem to have become expendable bargaining chips to be used, marketed, traded, and discarded at the whim of their corporate team owners and sponsors. Their careers depend as much upon the performance of their owners' businesses as upon their own performance in competition. In F1, the deal making over individual drivers begins long before the season ends. One effect of this has been to impose a certain homogeneity on the sport's top teams; cars, drivers, owners, and sponsors are interchangeable from one season to the next. This and rigid design rules level the playing field, but critics say it also has made F1 racing rather dull.[10]

And it has had a 'trickle down' effect on 'amateur' – that is, recreational – auto sport. Like its professional counterpart, it is highly organized and regulated. It has also become very expensive, such that even amateur racers and some rallyists need sponsors to offset the costs of their hobby. Just like the pros', their cars have become 'rolling billboards'. Thus, even at the grass roots the lines between amateur and professional have become blurred. That said, the similarities are more apparent than real, particularly in terms of expectations and financial rewards. Nor is there today necessarily a direct career path from the one to the other. In fact, by the 1990s the gap between the two – the recreational amateur and the career professional – had become wider than ever.

The auto sport organizing bodies, such as the CASC, provide a useful lens through which to examine these changes in the sport. They took the lead – wittingly and willingly or otherwise – in raising the standards of professionalism and in attracting commercial sponsorship. And they did so at the behest of their members. But it was not a smooth or even a predetermined process. As the sport changed, the organizing bodies were not always responsive to those changes, even those they had instigated through their decisions and actions. Resistance to their authority emerged among competitors, teams, car builders, promoters, and sponsors. Struggles ensued over control of big-league international auto sport. Not surprisingly, at the heart of these disputes lay the fundamental – and linked – issues of power and money.

The Untold Story

Only very recently have auto sport historians begun to address these issues and questions. But in Canada historians have not tackled them at all. Sports history is still a small, developing field within the historical discipline here,[11] and auto sport is an orphan outside it. As one scholar has observed, 'historians have not examined the sport possibly most identified with modern technology, automobile racing, even though it is currently the most attended spectator sport.'[12] So, as the bibliography shows, there is no comprehensive history of the sport in Canada. This book is an attempt to fill that gap and to give auto sport a place in Canadian sports history.

History, my mentor Professor Toby Graham used to say, quoting the eminent Michael Howard, 'is about gaps and chaps.' That is, it fills in the unfinished parts of a story and explains the role people played in making it. He also meant that history 'happens' in the gaps, the 'stress lines and gray areas,' the points where 'the conflicting influences of politics, events, decisions, personalities, and other factors'[13] interact to produce unexpected outcomes and consequences. In Canadian auto sport history there are plenty of gaps and 'chaps' (they *are* mostly men). Until now, that history has been told only in parts, scattered through a handful of books and magazines. Mostly it has remained buried in dusty files and in the memories of those who lived the experience. This book tries to bring it all together and to make sense of the why and the how.

Using original records has made it possible to fill in some of those gaps and to explain what happened in the sport's stress lines and grey areas. But documents don't always tell the whole tale and rarely capture its full 'flavour,' especially its human dimension. The interviews with and private papers of many people have helped to put some flesh on the bare bones of the story. This has allowed me to tell it – at least in part – from the perspective of those who were involved in all aspects of the sport. If there are no real villains, there are some genuine characters and more than one hero and heroine. They give the story its drama, its humour, its triumph, and its tragedy. Many of the names will be unknown to most Canadians, but history does not belong just to the famous. It owes just as much to the 'ordinary' people who made it happen out of the limelight.

What emerges from all this is an untidy history. It is the story of a sport pushed and pulled in several directions at once, by competing agendas within and by outside influences, often beyond the control of its Canadian participants. Its founders had a vision of the future that has been very largely realized. But they did not anticipate some of its unintended consequences. And so, Canadian auto sport truly has a 'chequered past.'

PART ONE

The Amateur Age, 1951–1960

1 The Visionaries and Their Vision: The Founding of the Canadian Automobile Sport Clubs

The Visionaries

On 17 June 1951 eight men gathered at the old Frontenac Hotel in Kingston, Ontario. Two – Jack Luck and Jack Fidler – were local men; Luck was a member of the St Lawrence Automobile Club (St LAC). Three – Bert Punshon, Hugh Young, and Tom Pearce – representing the Sports Car Club (SCC), hailed from Toronto. The other three – Norm Hain, Jack Fee, and Jim Gunn – members of the Sports Motor Car Club (SMCC), were from Montreal. They met to 'explore the possibility of the formation of an Organization, National in scope, to concern itself with automobile sport' and to 'examine aspects of obtaining National and International recognition of the Organization.'[1] By the end of the day, they had founded the Canadian Automobile Sport Committee (later Clubs, CASC). They appointed themselves the provisional executive, to run the CASC until an executive could be elected. They directed the secretary, Jim Gunn, to contact the Royal Automobile Club (RAC) in Britain about asking the international governing body of motoring and auto sport (the Fédération Internationale de l'Automobile – FIA) to recognize the CASC as the Canadian auto sport authority.

The picture taken for the occasion is a snapshot of a whole other age. Gathered around a 'roadster,' and dressed in tweedy sports jackets, slacks, and sweaters, some sporting pipes and jaunty caps, the 'founders' look like refugees from some 'terribly British' expatriates club. This effect was probably deliberate. Although only two of the group (Luck and Punshon) were recent British immigrants, Canadian car clubs had many like them. They gave the clubs a distinctly British flavour and provided a solid core of enthusiasts committed to 'improving' Canadian auto sport.

Decades later, Jim Gunn added depth to that picture by providing some background on the founders. Jack Luck was a talented, award-winning industrial designer for Alcan. Fidler, described by Gunn as a 'charming, hail fellow, diamond in the rough,' ran a printing business. Bert Punshon worked for the Boosey and Hawkes musical-instruments company in Toronto. He had been involved with sports cars in Britain before emigrating to Canada after his wartime service. Only Hugh Young, the son of a reasonably wealthy stockbroker, came from a 'moneyed' background. He worked as an engineer and was a good car mechanic. Pearce, a fellow engineer, was his best friend. He owned a three-litre Sunbeam that he had bought in Britain. The remaining three were also engineers; Hain, a 'quiet man with a good sense of humour,' worked for Ford, while Fee and Gunn both worked for Northern Electric. Gunn himself came by his interest in cars early. He recalled later that during his high school days in pre-war Toronto, 'many of the kids had "foreign" cars and we used to have a lot of fun with them.'[2] After wartime service as an RCAF navigator in Lancaster bombers, Gunn returned to work in Montreal, and joined the SMCC in 1947. That kindled his interest in car rallies. And in 1951 that same interest brought those eight men together.

In the years that followed, these men laboured mostly unrecognized behind the scenes in the CASC. Jack Luck served as president from 1951 to 1954. An industrial designer by trade, he put his talent to use designing the CASC crest, still used by the Ontario Region today. Jack Fidler organized the meetings held for the first five years in Kingston, arranging accommodation and meals for the rapidly growing number of delegates, who by 1955 exceeded thirty. And Jack Fee was CASC treasurer for the first fifteen years, carefully managing assets that grew from $21.81 in petty cash in 1952 to an annual budget of nearly $10,000 ten years after the founding.[3]

Of the eight founders, however, there is no question that Jim Gunn was *primus inter pares*. He served as secretary of the CASC from 1951 to 1954, then was president during its period of greatest growth. Between 1959 and 1963 the CASC more than doubled in size, from 40 clubs to 92. One of Gunn's most notable accomplishments was persuading the British Columbia clubs to join, making the CASC a truly national organization. He convinced the FIA to recognize the CASC as the national auto sport authority through the RAC. Jim threw the CASC's weight behind the first Trans-Canada Rally in 1961, and worked for Shell Oil running the event from 1962 until 1968.[4] As such, he was the first Canadian to earn a living full-time from sports car competition. Jim Gunn's foresight and his dedication to the sport have earned him unique recognition. He is the only one of the founders to be inducted into the Canadian Motorsport Hall of Fame.

What brought these men together, what they shared in common, was their love of cars and their passion for auto sport. The sport had been born in Europe, the birthplace of the automobile, itself an end-product of that region's industrial, economic, and transportation revolutions that were reaching their apogee at the turn of the century. The first car competition was a 'trial' run from Paris to Rouen in 1894, and the following year twenty-one entries *raced* from Paris to Bordeaux and back. From these modest beginnings the sport grew and spread rapidly to Britain and America. The early reliability trials became exploratory touring events that evolved into rallying. The Monte Carlo Rally, first held in 1911, became the premier event of its kind in the world, and is still run to this day. The competitors start in several cities, follow different routes, and finish (or 'rally') at the wealthy resort-city of Monte Carlo. Grand Prix racing began in 1906 with a lavishly funded event at Le Mans, which later became the site of the famous twenty-four-hour sports car race. These early events served three functions that have remained integral to the sport: entertainment, testing the reliability of cars and their components, and promoting the cars themselves for sale to customers. Given the importance of the two latter roles, auto sport involved manufacturers from the outset. Henry Ford, who won a race in Detroit in 1901, put it bluntly: 'Winning a race or breaking a record was the best kind of advertising.'[5]

Grand Prix racing and rallying remained largely a European phenomenon – and there quite socially exclusive – until after the Second World War. In the United States, where the car was more affordable and ubiquitous, the sport became more diversified, with distinctly regional roots. In the Mid-west, car racing began on horse-racing tracks and evolved into the uniquely American tradition of oval-track racing epitomized by the Indianapolis 500, first launched in 1911. The Indy 500 set the tone for American racing: high speeds, big crashes, big crowds, and big money. In short, from the outset, it was a *spectacle*.[6]

Stock car racing emerged from the South, where its association – in myth if not in fact – with running illicit liquor gave that sport its distinctive working-class, 'outlaw' image. The 1920s saw the birth of 'hot rods' and 'drag racing' on the dry lakes of southern California. European-style racing was *imported* to the Northeast, along with its carefully cultivated aura of wealth and class. New York socialite William K. Vanderbilt inaugurated in 1904 a race for a silver cup bearing his family name. By the 1930s sports car racing was confined to the Automobile Racing Club of America (ARCA), itself an exclusive coterie of wealthy, educated young scions of the 'establishment' who deliberately emulated the European racing traditions. Their ranks included Miles Collier and Briggs Cunningham, who were instrumental in reviving and expanding sports car competition in the United States after the war.[7]

Canadian auto sport emerged from local automobile clubs, which had appeared almost as quickly as the car itself in the early 1900s. And though these were concerned mainly with everyday 'motoring' issues, such as better roads, they also organized 'sporting' activities. The first event had been a 'speed trial' between Toronto and Hamilton in 1900 (it took three hours and twenty minutes to drive the sixty kilometres). The next year, as part of the Pan Am Exhibition, the Buffalo (New York) Auto Club organized the first car race in Canada, at a horse-racing track in Fort Erie, Ontario. Over the next thirty years, there were races and gymkhanas (driving skill tests) in Toronto, Montreal, Ottawa, Winnipeg, and Calgary. The Canadian National Exhibition hosted national championship races from 1920 to 1928. These events drew sizeable crowds, but the big stars of the early years were Americans such as Barney Oldfield and Ralph de Palma, not Canadians.[8] When the sport went into decline during the Depression and the war, it left behind no known Canadian drivers, no permanent racetracks, and no national 'tradition' of auto sport. What did survive were two nascent sports car clubs, the SMCC in Montreal and the British Empire Motor Club (BEMC) in Toronto.

The SMCC had originated as the Sports Motor Cycle Club in the 1920s. By 1937 there were enough car owners in the club to form a 'light car division.' They continued as a subgroup within the club for about a year, then broke away to form a separate club, which took on its permanent name in 1939. The SMCC held its first major rally, the Night Trial, in the fall of 1938. But the war postponed further events and limited the club to social activities for its duration.[9] It was just reviving its competition activities when Jim Gunn joined the club in 1947.

The BEMC also was founded by motorcyclists. One of them, Johnny

Edmonson, recalled that they chose the rather grandiose name for the club deliberately, 'to draw to ourselves a little better type of motorcyclist who was interested in good sport and to try to improve the present conditions in the game.'[10] Since the club had included automobile owners from the outset, at an early stage it organized activities for its car-owning members, and to this day the BEMC is unique in maintaining a link to both sports. Its motorcycle races were very popular, drawing thousands of spectators to the track laid out at Wasaga Beach, on the shores of Georgian Bay. However, at the outbreak of the war the club suspended its activities, so the transformation of the BEMC into a *car* club did not occur until after the war.[11]

The BEMC resumed its activities in 1946, and automobiles were soon plentiful and popular enough that a car committee was formed in 1948. The first car competitions – a time trial and a two-day rally – were held early the next year. The club ran its first car race on 25 June 1950, at the abandoned Edenvale airport, near Stayner, Ontario. But the 'bikers' regarded the auto sport enthusiasts as a 'dissident' faction, and their desire to pursue car racing seriously caused a split in the club. In the end, the car enthusiasts – among them Tom Pearce, Bert Punshon, and Hugh Young – broke away, and on 17 May 1951 established the SCC. Exactly one month later it was that club, not the BEMC, that co-founded the CASC. What had forced their hand was the need to separate themselves from the bikers. Before leaving the BEMC, the dissidents had contacted the RAC in Britain regarding affiliation to the FIA. The RAC advised the BEMC dissidents that the FIA would not recognize *any* club associated with motorcycles, and would accept only a *national* organization concerned with all aspects of motoring. As the organization representing Canada on the FIA, the Canadian Automobile Association (CAA) was entitled to serve as the national auto sport authority. But the CAA devoted its efforts to the concerns of the everyday motorist; it had no interest in auto sport. In the absence of a Canadian auto sport body, the RAC reserved Canada's authority to itself, but told the BEMC car enthusiasts that it would delegate this power to a national body once one was formed.[12] So, at the Kingston meeting, the eight men established the CASC to do just that.

What the CASC's founders originally had wanted to do, however, was to run a winter rally along the lines of the Monte Carlo Rally. According to Gunn, this idea originated with Fred and Peter Hayes of the BEMC. Realizing this was something the club couldn't do on its own, in 1949 they contacted the SMCC and later the Ottawa Light Car

Club (OLCC), but discussions dragged on for about two years without success. By 1951 all three clubs had concluded that a national organization was needed to run an event on this scale.[13] Thus, the CASC was born out of mixed motives: the need for help in running a rally and the desire for a national auto sport authority that had to be separate from the motorcycle clubs.

In creating a national auto sport organization, these Canadians were completely in step with the times. Britain, many European countries, and the United States all had national automobile organizations that also organized and sanctioned auto sport activities. Some, like the RAC, dated back to the birth of the car. Auto sport had ceased during the Second World War, but when it revived in the early post-war period, new organizations proliferated, especially in the United States. In 1947 stock car racers established the National Association for Stock Car Auto Racing (NASCAR) to run the sport as a money-making business. Four years later the southern California 'hot rodders' founded the National Hot Rod Association to organize and regulate drag racing, largely to promote a more 'respectable' image for what was widely regarded as an 'outlaw' sport.[14]

The American body that most closely resembled the CASC was the Sports Car Club of America (SCCA). Founded in Boston in 1944 by seven wealthy men to preserve exotic and expensive 'sporting' automobiles, the SCCA was not initially intended to run auto *sport*. The SCCA's founders had expected that the ARCA would revive 'sports car' racing after the war, and thus 'had never given any thought to this type of activity when [they] formed the SCCA.'[15] But ARCA never revived; instead, its former members joined the SCCA and reshaped it to fulfil their passion for competition. They changed the club's aims to include the regulation of *competitive* events 'for amateur members' and the encouragement of 'safe and sportsmanlike conduct on public highways.' The emphasis on amateur competition and sportsmanlike behaviour was a hold-over from the so-called 'Golden Age' of amateur sport that still exerted its influence within America's wealthy elites, whose ranks included the founders of the SCCA. It was nothing if not a 'gentlemen's club,' and encouraging safe driving would help to give auto sport a 'respectable' public image. Pushed into racing by the former ARCA members who infiltrated its ranks, the SCCA organized its first major race through the streets of Watkins Glen, New York, in 1948. Within a decade it had 9000 members and was sanctioning and regulating races and rallies all over the United States. It even had

Canadian regions in the 1950s to allow Canadians to compete in the States.[16]

However, until the CASC was established, there was no comparable, Canadian auto sport organization. Thus, there was a vacuum to be filled. When those eight men met in Kingston, then, they did more than form a national auto sport organization; they founded the sport itself.

Their Vision

The future shape of Canadian auto sport is captured in the founders' vision of the purpose of the CASC. Among other things, they wanted the national organization

> To develop Automobile Sport in Canada on a National basis, along lines similar to those found in Europe ...
> To establish, for Canada, a recognized place in International Automobile Sport.
> To encourage Canadian participation in International Automobile Sport events, and to encourage International participation in Canadian events ...
> [And] to prevent ... the exploitation of Automobile Sport for purely commercial reasons.[17]

In short, they intended to make Canadian auto sport 'world class.' Over the next few decades the founders and their successors worked hard to bring this vision to life, and for the most part they succeeded. From a small nucleus of three clubs (the third one being the OLCC), the CASC grew exponentially; twenty years later, it comprised some 5800 members in over 100 clubs that spanned the country.[18] Races, rallies, and other events from amateur to international levels filled the calendar year round. Crowds of spectators, by that time numbering in the tens of thousands, flocked to major races. The world's best racing drivers competed in the Canadian events, and Canadian racers were competing in 'world class' events at home and abroad. And in 1967 the FIA recognized the CASC as Canada's national auto sport authority, in its own right. Thus, they had achieved their first three objectives, without question.

But they were unable to do so without foregoing the fourth. Their vision of a sport unsullied by commercial exploitation simply was unrealistic. Auto sport has been a business venture from the very start, and by the 1950s big-league European and American racing was becoming thoroughly commercialized. Race track owners and promoters charged admission to events, and track facilities were festooned with advertising. Even racers themselves were starting to earn a living from it, especially in the United States, where the Indianapolis 500 and NASCAR stock car races were attracting big business sponsors and large winning purses.[19] Eventually, this trend spread to all aspects of auto sport. As with baseball and hockey, a lot of people had a stake in making money out of this sport. It was already too late to turn back the clock.

If the CASC's founders were aware of that, what made them think they could swim against the tide? Perhaps the answer is simply that it is hard to discard tradition. These men were members of a generation that was deeply imbued with the ideals that infused amateur sport in Canada – especially the notion that 'gentlemen do not play for pay.' Even if such lofty ideals *never* had reflected the realities of amateur sport, they were no less influential for that.[20] In this sense, the founders shared the same vision of amateur auto sport as their counterparts in the SCCA. By the early 1960s, however, both organizations were forced to accept that aspiring to 'world class' status in auto sport meant becoming professional *and* commercial. And so, over the next forty years the founders' vision came to pass, but at a price. Amateur auto sport gradually was sidelined, and battles over professionalism and commercialism divided the organization, eventually costing the CASC its leadership role in Canadian auto sport.

In the meantime, however, auto sport clearly was a *phenomenon* of the post-war era. So how do we explain the growth of the Canadian sports car movement after the war? It is unlikely that the mere existence of a few men with a vision was sufficient by itself to 'kick start' it. As the following chapters will show, the answer seems to be this: post-war British immigrants brought the enthusiasm for auto sport, and British industry sent the cars. In Canada both found a niche within a burgeoning suburban car culture, where they tapped into a receptive 'market' among middle-class men with time and money to spare for indulgent recreational pursuits. These, in turn, created a subculture of sports car clubs that 'played' the sport and fostered its growth. And among the enthusiasts were some auto sport 'entrepreneurs' who could see the business potential if the sport became 'professional.'

2 Canadian Club: Origins of the Sports Car Subculture, 1950–1960

> While travelling ... in his new MG TC ... in the spring of 1953, [Doug Phippen] passed Jim Good driving his new Sunbeam Talbot, stopped ... ahead and flagged Jim down. They talked about their cars ... and about ... establishing the first sports car club in Western Ontario. They arranged a preliminary meeting in May ... in Sarnia.
>
> *Western Ontario Sports Car Association History*[1]

Grass Roots: The Sports Car Clubs

From that chance meeting the Western Ontario Sports Car Association (WOSCA) was founded. And that experience was repeated across the country. The London Automobile Sport Club (LASC) began in September 1956, when 'six gentlemen met together with the purpose of forming a sports car club for the London district whose members would be actively engaged in the competative [sic] aspects of the sports car fraternity.'[2] The staff of Canadair in Montreal formed a company car club. Les Stanley recalls: 'Canadair ... had an old disused hangar that they allowed us to use. This would hold six to eight cars. It was used as a repair shop.'[3] Founded in Toronto in 1958, the Canadian Racing Drivers' Association (CRDA) drew its members by invitation only from the ranks of experienced racing drivers. At the University of New Brunswick, the minute book records that on 11 February 1960 'a now regular meeting of the newly formed U.N.B. S.C.C. was held at 7:30 pm in the Jones House Library.'[4] Auto sport journalist Len Coates writes that 'from Tuesday nights in the rec' room, the cult grew. Organization came. Presidents and treasurers, and club names ...'[5] The Canadian sports car subculture was born in the 1950s, and its midwife was the sports car club.

Three clubs had founded the CASC in 1951. By 1960 the association boasted some fifty clubs,[6] with more than a thousand members among them. Where did they all come from? The answer seems to be that they grew out of the intersection of two trends: Canada's emerging suburban 'car culture' and the post-war influx of British cars and auto sport enthusiasts.

The Suburban Car Culture

The veterans and others who returned to post-war occupations expected peace to bring freedom from the financial woes of the Depression and of wartime rationing. For the most part they got their wish. The first quarter-century after the Second World War was a period of unparalleled economic growth and prosperity in Canada. Incomes increased steadily until the mid-1970s. 'White collar' professional/management occupations rapidly outstripped those in the traditional 'blue collar' and agricultural sectors. The result was the creation of a new and much larger middle class, with both discretionary income and disposable *leisure time*.[7]

This was the class that founded the car clubs and participated in auto sport in the 1950s. Few of them came from 'moneyed' families, the exceptions including Dave Greenblatt, Hugh Young, and Peter Ryan. Like the founders, most were employed in the growth sectors of the post-war economy and a large proportion was in 'white collar' positions, with incomes well above the national average. Montrealers Peter Bone, Les Stanley, and Les Chelminski, for example, worked as engineers for Canadair, while John Gallop was employed at IBM. George Chapman, a Winnipeg racer and later CASC president, was a lawyer. Jim Fergusson and Dick Shelton of Toronto were just two of the many car dealers in the sport at that time. Bob MacGregor was an active rallyist while he produced and broadcast an auto sport program for the CBC.[8] Occupation and income did not define or limit roles within the sport, only the type of car one drove at the outset.

Canada's new middle class spent its discretionary income trying to fulfil self-induced and marketing-stimulated social and economic expectations. Car ownership was one of these. Doug Owram, historian of the Canadian baby boom, writes: 'By 1945 that dream of automobile-ownership was probably only second to that of home ownership in the minds of Canadians. The automobile symbolized the good life.'[9] Or, as historian Robert Bothwell and his co-authors put it: 'Motoring was one of the fruits of victory – liberation.'[10] Canadians were *hungry* for cars, *any* cars. In 1945 they owned just over one million cars. By 1951 that number had doubled, and within a decade it had doubled again. Indeed, the car was central to the new middle-class lifestyle; it became synonymous with suburban life in particular. It was the suburbs that experienced the greatest growth in post-war Canada. The streets, housing, habits, and hobbies of suburbia featured the car as both a functional and symbolic centrepiece. It became a 'status symbol' as well as the primary means for travel to work and for family life and leisure. Suburban middle-class Canadian society was a 'car culture.'[11]

The suburban middle class disposed of its leisure time through recreational activities outside the home. This fact not only bears witness to the growing prosperity of suburbia, but also explains much of the appeal of suburban life at that time. For example, by the 1960s Montreal's relatively affluent West Island suburbs boasted yacht clubs, curling clubs, and golf courses, and most had ballparks, tennis courts, and swimming pools. These facilities were for *amateur* sport, but many were organized as clubs that provided leadership, direction, structure, funding, and a social network. And where the club-based 'leisure culture' met the 'car culture' in the suburbs of Montreal and Toronto, from towns like St-Laurent and Pointe-Claire, Quebec, to Willowdale and Don Mills, Ontario, people joined car clubs in growing numbers.[12] Like the proverbial crabgrass, the sports car subculture took root and flourished in the heartland of Canada's new middle class.

The automobile also symbolized the dominant role of technology at work, in the home, and in leisure within North American society. Many veterans, wartime industry workers, and immigrants returned from the war with enhanced technical skills, or developed them at work after the war. The ranks of auto sport enthusiasts included many engineers, mechanics, and others with technical training and employment. Because of the cost of professional home and car repair and shortages of skilled labour, the 'do it yourself' (DIY) attitude, forged out of necessity during the Depression, became a post-war suburban phenomenon. In this situation, it was probably inevitable that some people would apply their technical skills to their cars in their spare time. 'Tinkering' with the family car, either to save money on repairs or to improve handling and performance, became a common suburban pastime, and companies like Canadian Tire catered to and capitalized on the DIY auto-repair fad. Moreover, 'risk recreation,' of which auto sport was one form, became increasingly popular after the war. Thus, for a few more adventurous members of the car culture it was only a short step from daily driving and weekend tinkering to testing their results in competition. Some scholars also have suggested that this was a way for people to assert human domination over a technology that was encroaching on their lives.[13] Whatever the reason, the activities organized by sports car clubs provided an outlet for their skills and personal goals.

With an expanding network of roads and highways, rapidly rising car ownership, and a growing number of drivers with the time, money, and inclination to 'play' with their cars, post-war Canada provided a milieu in which auto sport could flourish. All that was needed was a catalyst to 'kick start' the process. The British sports car export drive and the influx of British immigrant enthusiasts did just that. They stimulated the creation and growth of sports car clubs and auto sport events and drew in like-minded Canadians. And that gave the sport the 'staying power' it had lacked in the pre-war era.

Lion Rampant: The British Invasion

If a picture is worth a thousand words, then the photo of the 1954 BEMC races at the Edenvale, Ontario, track speaks volumes. MG TCs and TDs fill the first two rows on the grid, and as automobile writer Rich Taylor put it, 'the MG-TC was just about the most lovable car ever built ... The TC said SPORTS CAR in ... British racing green.'[14] Out of the photo, the rest of the field was also dominated by British sports cars. Vern Jeffries and Hugh Sutherland were driving Jaguar XK-120s. Jerry Polivka, Jim Fergusson, and George Schon were in Austin Healeys. Bryan Rowntree, Bob Hanna, and others raced the MGs, while Bill Sadler competed in a Singer Sports. Six years later, at the Montreal MG Car Club's (MMGCC) first race of the 1960 season on the Connor Circuit, St-Eugène, Ontario, just west of Montreal, a home movie tells a similar story. As the camera pans around the crowded paddock, then follows the close action on the track, we see Ross de St. Croix's MGA twin-cam; Don Baird's Austin Mini; Graham Locke's Elva Courier; Harry Entwhistle's Lotus Elite; Jean-Guy Pilon's D-Type Jaguar; Peter Keith's AC Ace-Bristol; a flock of Austin-Healey Sprites and 3000s, Triumph TR3s, more MGs and Elvas; and a few Austin and Morris sedans. There are *other* cars as well: the sleek and powerful silver

Porsche RS60s of Francis Bradley and Peter Ryan; Dave Greenblatt's massive silver and red Corvette; a bunch of Volvos, a sprinkling of VWs, a few Porsche Carreras, and a lone Saab.[15] If images and raw numbers tell the story, then British sports cars were synonymous with the first decade of sports car racing in Canada.

And this phenomenon wasn't confined to racing. The figures for rallying are similar. From 1956 to 1958, British cars typically accounted for more than half of the entrants in the BEMC Canadian Winter Rally. In the 1958 Ladies Division Centennial Year Rally, organized by the Sports Car Club of British Columbia (SCCBC), twenty-four of the thirty-three cars that finished were British makes.[16]

Yet, in the 1950s Canadians, as a whole, owned *American* cars in overwhelming numbers, largely because the Canadian automobile industry was nothing more than a branch plant of its American counterpart.[17] So how did British sports cars manage to get a near chokehold on auto sport in a country wedded to the large and very 'unsporting' American family sedan?

Popular legend has it that returning Canadian servicemen brought back sports cars and auto sport with them from Britain and Europe at the end of the war. Like most legends, it contains a kernel of truth. MG deliberately marketed to returning *American* troops. But the production of personal vehicles had ceased in Britain during the war, and gas and tire rationing meant that few cars were on the road. Moreover, it took several years for the British auto industry to fully restart car production. There was no auto sport during the war, and it is unlikely that many *Canadian* veterans witnessed its very limited post-war revival before returning to Canada in 1946. Military pay was meagre; it is doubtful that any but a few senior officers might have been able to afford to buy a car, had there been any to buy. And servicemen returned to Canada on crowded troopships that would have had little room for cars.[18] Still, the legend is correct in one respect; the cars and the sport were largely imported in the early post-war years. But it was British manufacturers who exported the cars to Canada and British immigrants who brought enthusiasm for the sport.

The export drive wasn't a matter of chance. After the war, the British government was trying to fend off economic collapse. It provided incentives for those British industries that could export their products and earn desperately needed foreign exchange. This policy favoured the auto industry, since the demand for cars in early post-war North America vastly exceeded the Big Three automakers' ability to produce them. As a result, British car exports tripled in the first five post-war years, and by 1950 the United Kingdom had replaced the United States – temporarily – as the world's leading car exporter. In 1960 Britain exported 92,831 cars to Canada.[19]

What British car makers exported were small sedans and sports cars. In fact, after the war Britain had three of the leading mass producers of sports cars: Austin-Healey, MG, and Triumph. The specialist (limited production) sports car market also was dominated by British firms, such as AC, Allard, Aston Martin, Elva, Jaguar, Lotus, Morgan, and TVR. In 1947 the Nuffield Organization – the owners of MG – sent a sales team to survey the American market. They reported that British cars would need some kind of 'unique appeal' to break into the North American market, and that an 'open' (i.e., 'sports') car – clearly different from the typical American sedan – would be the secret to success. To American Anglophiles, especially in the Northeast where the SCCA began, British sports cars had a certain 'snob appeal.' It was the *look* of these cars that attracted the sports car enthusiast. In 1953 'the small, peppy, but mechanically tempermental MG sports car was the top import ... Partly because there really was nothing like it, but also because of the cachet it bestowed upon its owners.'[20] Between 1947 and 1959 more than 85 per cent of MG's production was exported to North America. Compared to the Big Three's output, that was just pocket change; the total production of MG cars in the 1950s did not amount to much more than a slow day in Detroit. Canadians bought only 3735 of them between 1952 and 1959. But auto industry historian Timothy Whisler insists that MG single-handedly 'created the sports car segment.' He goes on to stress that the cars were known for their handling and performance, and developed 'a subjective image through design, styling, and participation in motorsports.'[21]

The fact is they did not face much competition. The Big Three American automakers have been criticized for ignoring the small sedan and sports car market in the early post-war era, but from a business standpoint they read their market correctly. The North American 'Baby Boom' and the explosive growth of highways and suburbia favoured the large family sedan. Either by choice or in response to skilful marketing, most Americans and Canadians bought big American cars. Oriented to this market, American car manufacturers were ambivalent at best towards other sectors.[22] Indeed, the determination of the British car builders to corner the sports car market contrasts sharply with the attitudes of the Big Three. They produced only two 'sporting' cars in the 1950s, the Ford Thunderbird and the Chevrolet Corvette. But the T-Bird quickly evolved into a big luxury car, and by contrast with British sports cars, the early 'Vette was big, heavy, under-powered, and expensive. In fact, it barely survived its first two years in production. Only the challenge mounted by the early T-Bird and some fundamental changes in its design and powerplant saved it from extinction. By the late 1950s the Corvette had evolved into a more nimble and powerful sports car, if still heavier and more costly than a British one. An MGA, for example, was less than half the price of a Corvette. It was not until 1963, when the Sting Ray model was introduced, that the Corvette's production figures began to outstrip those of the leading British sports car manufacturers.[23] In fact, until the Ford Mustang heralded the advent of the mid-sixties 'muscle cars,' the giant U.S. auto industry never seriously challenged the dominance of its comparatively weak British counterpart in this segment of the car market.

Nor did the British have to fear much of a challenge from their European counterparts, who took longer to rebuild their war-damaged auto industries. The only rival to British supremacy was the Volkswagen 'Beetle,' which developed a wide appeal among auto sport enthusiasts. Thanks largely to its sturdy reliability and fuel economy, the VW was used extensively for rallying. Twenty-one of them finished the 1956 Canadian Winter Rally, and they took first and third places in the 1959 Thousand Islands Rally. The German sports cars that could match or beat MGs in racing – Mercedes and Porsches – were much more expensive. Alfa Romeos were rare in Canadian auto sport in the 1950s.[24] And you couldn't buy a Ferrari in Canada until the 1960s, even if you could afford one.[25] This left the import sports car market wide open for the British.

And MG wasn't the only British success story in North America. Nearly half of the 49,000 original Austin-Healey Sprites (1958–61) were exported to the United States, and many were sold in Canada as well. With its 'bugeye happy face' front end it rivalled the MG TC for cuteness, and it was cheap: less than $2000 Cdn. in the summer of 1960. 'Launched in 1958, the Sprite quickly became the [BMC] corporation's best selling sports car.'[26] Owners could easily turn it into a very competitive racing car. Former Montreal racer Don Baird recalls that in 1959,

> I drove home a new Sprite and consigned it to my garage. Piece by piece, ... the entire engine ... and all the major moving parts were gathered into a

box and presented to the local engine balancing shop, for improvement on the factory tolerances ... The engine balancing job ... played a considerable part in making my car the fastest stock Sprite in the Montreal area, and one to be reckoned with seriously in the sharper competition south of the border.[27]

Cheap, easy to tune, remarkably quick, and fun to drive, the Sprite quickly became a favourite among Canadian competitors. They showed up in large numbers at rallies, races, and every kind of driving skill test, and performed well. Baird beat three other Sprites to take the win in the race for sports cars up to one litre in the Tuppence Cup Races at the Connor Circuit in 1959.[28]

Of the specialist, limited production sports cars Jaguars had the highest profile, even though then as now they were really luxury cars. In Canada in 1960 the cheapest Jag was *twice* the cost of an MGA. Only the Corvette and the Mercedes were more expensive. And yet, Jags did it all in Canadian auto sport. The fact is that competition *sold* Jaguars; no other British sports car had as impressive a record in international racing in the 1950s. Jaguars won Le Mans in 1951, 1953, and 1955–7. It was no different here. In the late 1950s and early 1960s, Jaguars were dominant. Jim Rattenbury in British Columbia and Jean-Guy Pilon in Quebec won or placed regularly in their sleek D-type sports racing cars, while Ray Carter from Hamilton did the same in his rare XKSS, which was nothing more than a D-type 'for the road.' Jim Fergusson, a Toronto racer, dealer, and sponsor, dropped a gutsy XK150S engine into the rather sedate, bulbous 3.4 sedan, allowing Ed Leavens and Bryan Rowntree to walk off with their share of victories.[29]

In Canada British manufacturers found a ready market for their sports cars among the rising number of British and European immigrants. In the two decades after the war Canada received some 2,500,000 immigrants from the heartland of auto sport: Britain and Europe. Britain alone accounted for about one-quarter of them. Some of them had been exposed to auto sport in the UK and brought their enthusiasm (and their preference for British sports cars) with them. Most had left Britain for economic reasons, part of the 'Brain Drain' from Britain that populated the rapidly expanding Canadian professional and management classes. Working in Canada meant higher wages and a lower cost of living, and as Graham Locke explained, that made auto sport accessible in a way that wasn't possible back home. 'Trying to do the motorsport thing on English wages was pretty difficult. Coming here, immediately wages were roughly a three-to-one ratio ... That put us in a much more favourable position to do the thing we liked doing.'[30]

Most of them arrived and became involved during the 1950s – the formative period of Canadian auto sport. They joined Canadian car clubs in large numbers, and some of them rose to some prominence within the sport. Of the CASC's two British founders, Jack Luck served as its first president, while Bert Punshon was its first vice-president, as well as the CASC secretary from 1955 to 1958. But they were hardly unique.

Neale Johnson, the son of a pre-war motorcycle racer from Watford, became one of the original members of the Sports Car Club of Saskatchewan (SCCS) after moving to Regina in the 1950s. There he took part in all aspects of the sport, and served as race director of the SCCS. Later, Johnson returned to the UK and became manager of the BRM Formula One team. Peter Bone, of London, came to work for Canadair in 1956 and joined the Canadair Auto Club (CAC). He had first been exposed to the sport in Britain and had taken part in motorcycle rallies. While studying at De Havilland (UK), he and his fellow students worked as volunteers for Colin Chapman at the small, but up and coming, Lotus racing car firm. In Canada Peter later became Jim Gunn's co-organizer of the Shell 4000 Trans-Canada rally, and also served as CASC national racing chairman. Also from London, Roger Peart was first attracted to auto sport as a teenager reading *Motorsport* magazine. Drawn into the sport through his mechanical ability, he started out as a mechanic, working on engines for Rileys raced by future Formula One champion Mike Hawthorn. Later he formed a car club at the Farnborough aircraft establishment and organized car rallies. After coming to Canada in 1958, Peart became president of the Montreal Jaguar Owner's Association (JOA), and later designed the Circuit Gilles Villeneuve. He rose through the ranks of the CASC executive to become its president in the late 1980s, then went on to head its successor, ASN Canada, now the national authority for all FIA-sanctioned events.[31] Francis Bradley had been to a race at Brooklands at age twelve, and that hooked him for life. Like Peart, he became an avid reader of *Motorsport*, until he was old enough to drive: 'As soon as the war ended I got a motorcycle, and did quite a bit of motorcycling in the London area ... I went to a hill climb at Prescott. Saw Stirling Moss for the first time in a Cooper. I was very impressed. He was my hero from then on.'[32] Emigrating to Canada in 1954, Bradley became a Toronto bus driver, joined the BEMC, was one of the founders of the CRDA, and won the Canadian racing championship in 1962.

This pattern was repeated many times over. As a result, many Canadian sports car clubs exhibited a distinctly British character that reflected the origins of their members. The British Automobile Racing Club – Ontario Centre (BARC-OC), for example, was the Canadian affiliate of the UK club of the same name. John Gallop thinks that perhaps as many as half of Montreal's SMCC members were British, and that they 'were really the driving force, the most enthusiastic, the ones who could be counted upon to be there, and to be really supportive of the activities.'[33] Don Baird agrees that many of them were 'fresh off the boat from Britain.'[34] Les Stanley, himself born in Northern Ireland, worked for Canadair as an aeronautical engineer, and was a member of the company's car club, which 'drew on what the population was in Canadair, and Canadair had a lot of Brits.'[35] Art Moseley, former president of the BEMC, at one time belonged to Toronto's Sports Car Club (SCC), which was formed by owners of British sports cars. He recalls that the atmosphere of the club was a bit *too* British: 'I felt compelled to adopt a British accent. If you didn't you were a colonial.'[36] The evidence is compelling: a potent mix of British cars and British characters founded and defined the Canadian sports car subculture.

That said, while the British influence was dominant, European immigrants also figured prominently in the sport and in particular clubs. Eppie Wietzes, who emigrated to Canada from the Netherlands in 1950, became involved in the sport in 1958, and went on to become a national racing champion in the 1960s. Les Chelminski, proclaimed Canada's first national rally champion in 1957, was born in Poland. Montreal racer and rallyist Sam Nordell was from Sweden. The Deutscher Automobile Club (DAC), formed in Toronto in 1958, drew upon the German-Canadian and German émigré populations. The DAC was the home club of future national racing champions Ludwig Heimrath and Horst Kroll.[37] As numerous as they were, however, Europeans usually were outnumbered by 'Brits,' who gave most Canadian sports car clubs their very 'British' flavour. That, in turn, helped to define those clubs as part of a distinct subculture.

The Sports Car Subculture

While each club had its own identity, collectively they represented something more: a sports car 'subculture.' Simply put, a subculture is a 'group within a group' that forms around a specific activity. Certain attributes and behaviours define it: exclusive membership, prescribed rules and induction rites, and participation in the *rituals* that constitute the subculture's raison d'être. *Signals* and *symbols* indicate group identity, acceptance, and solidarity. Members may share a specific, exclusive *lexicon*, as well as a shared heritage of history, legends, and myths and the means to share them within the group.[38]

From the outset, the sports car milieu was a subculture in Canada. First, the vast majority of car owners did not belong to sports car clubs and probably did not even know they existed. While millions of Canadians drove cars, most of the clubs had no more than a few dozen members each. Even if one includes the thousands of fans that attended races but who were not club members, in the 1950s the sport involved only a tiny fraction of the Canadian population.

Second, members of the subculture could be identified by the cars they drove: small foreign sedans and sports cars, British ones in particular. That was part of the self-selection process that defined the sport and the subculture. Graham Locke recalls that the SMCC originally limited membership to owners of cars with a maximum engine capacity of one-and-a-half litres. 'That was deliberately designed to keep out big American cars, because it was a European car sport.'[39] In fact, there were clubs for owners of specific car makes, such as Jaguar and MG. Thus, although the auto sport enthusiasts clearly were drawn from the wider Canadian car culture, their cars identified them as a distinct and visible minority.

If numbers and car type were not enough to set the auto sport enthusiasts apart from Canadian society, it is what they *did* with their cars that clearly marked them as a true subculture. They formed car clubs *to compete in auto sport events*, which immediately rendered them a distinct minority group. Club membership was a prerequisite for acceptance into the core of the subculture, since only members of the fraternity could participate in its primary *rituals* (racing, rallying, and solo events). In one sense, then, as later racing champion Bill Brack put it, 'clubs were a means to an end: getting on the track.'[40]

Doing this through organized clubs helped to legitimize these activities, which were 'frowned upon' by the public. And so, car club constitutions explicitly promoted safe, lawful, and courteous driving, and required members to be 'of good character' and to abide by regulations, procedures, and hierarchies. Applicants had to be sponsored and introduced by an existing member; all members were to be notified of the application. Paying dues completed the initiation process. Recruiting and attracting members took a variety of forms. Many drifted into the sport through a general interest in cars that led them into competition. Others were introduced to it by friends who were already involved. Alvin Ashfield was walking through the UNB student centre when fellow student and avid rallyist Dwight Scott 'dragged him' into a UNBSCC meeting.[41] Roy McLaughlin was working in advertising for the Rootes Motors distributor in Toronto when BEMC president Ron White approached him to ask if the club could use their car lot as the starting point for the Winter Rally. Once that was agreed, White said, 'You could be helpful to the club ... you could do PR ... Why don't you join, which I did,' recalls McLaughlin. 'He immediately made me PR officer. So, I stepped right into the executive.' The club was socially inclusive; all that was required was enthusiasm: 'If you were interested, you were in.'[42]

Elected executives ran the clubs and represented them in the CASC. Most clubs held regular monthly meetings, which were usually run in a formal, business-like manner. Ross de St. Croix recalls that members were 'very competitive' in meetings, causing long debates, with 'obscure regulations being used to nail somebody down.'[43] Peter Bone agrees: 'There were more arguments about *Robert's Rules of Order* than I can remember.'[44]

Once a person joined, the clubs performed 'socializing' functions that imbued members with a sense of belonging to an exclusive group. Enthusiasts developed *signals* and *symbols* to acknowledge other members and be recognized themselves. For example, in the early years when the Volkswagen still was relatively rare in North America, VW drivers often waved or flashed their headlights at each other. The clubs also designed their own distinctive badges and decals, which members mounted on their cars' bumpers or coachwork.[45] The subculture also had its own language. It had borrowed terms like steward, paddock, pole, *grand prix*, *écurie*, and *scuderia* (stable – for team) from horse racing, while others, such as pits, 'blower,' 'full bore,' 'drift,' GT (*Gran Turismo*), and 'Le Mans start' emerged from the sport itself. Enthusiasts shared an exclusive repertoire of stories, heroes, legends, myths, and humour. These were transmitted both orally and through club newsletters available only to the membership. The newsletters also recorded news, event results, and the social side of club life, which included awards banquets, Christmas parties, tours, picnics, and 'Concours d'élégance' ('show and shine' car displays). Races and rallies usually finished up with informal social gatherings, such as the infamous binge-drinking 'boat races' at the bars in Rigaud, Quebec, after racing at St-Eugène. Fred Motton recalls that in the early 1950s after club meetings in downtown Montreal SMCC members would run the 'Decarie Grand Prix' – an informal street race up Decarie Boulevard to the Windsock Restaurant in the suburb of Cartierville. By contrast, year-end banquets could be quite elaborate. Ross de St. Croix says that the MMGCC claimed to have 'the biggest and best banquets. We would rent a major room at the Queen Elizabeth Hotel in Montreal and we'd all go in black tie, and the girls would all go in long dresses.'[46]

This last image begs a larger question: what was the role and place of women in the sport in the early years? Like the mainstream 'stick and ball' sports, auto sport generally was (and largely still is) an overwhelmingly *male* activity. The Canadian sports car subculture was no different; men dominated both organization and competition. Nevertheless, there was significant female participation in a sport where the prevailing gender and social obstacles might have allowed very little. From the outset, women took part in almost all of its aspects, albeit in relatively small numbers. It was common for one or two to serve on car club executives, most frequently in the position of secretary and/or treasurer and as social convenor. For example, Yvonne Hamerton was the secretary of the Hamilton Motor Sport Club when it joined the CASC in 1956, while Mrs G. Riley filled that position for the BARC-OC in 1960. These were, of course, comparable to roles commonly assigned at that time to women in wider Canadian society, both in business and in the community. So at auto sport events women tended to be confined to secondary roles as organizers, clerks, and timers.[47]

But not all women were content to play supporting roles. Alice Fergusson, wife of racer/sponsor Jim Fergusson, was probably the first woman to compete in post-war sports car racing. In June 1950 she drove a Fiat 500 in the inaugural BEMC Spring Trophy Races. In the same event five years later Vivian Petura of Toronto placed second in the modified sedan race. What is notable is that these were not 'ladies only' races, the so-called 'powder puff derbies' that were part of the Canadian racing scene at that time. As journalist and fellow competitor Heather Wilson noted in 1959, 'the general attitude of most people, especially the men, towards the ladies race – it was a joke.'[48] She agreed with Alice, who argued that women should compete with the men on an equal footing. Along with Petura and Wilson, Fergusson showed that they could.

By contrast, because rallies required a two-person crew in each car, women competed regularly in rallying in the 1950s. Wives and husbands often entered together. There were at least five husband and wife teams and one all-women team in the 1956 Canadian Winter Rally. The SCCBC's 1958 Centennial Year Rally and 1959 Ladies Rally featured couples and all-women teams. Grant and Frances McLean competed in the 1959 Thousand Islands Rally, while John and Nancy Gallop and John and Ruth Searle were among the seven couples who entered the SMCC's first Evening Rally in 1960.[49]

Several factors explain both the extent and the limits of women's participation in auto sport in this formative period. The car club provided a setting for women to become involved in the sport with their husbands or boyfriends. Likewise, the sport's need for a large infrastructure of supporting officials offered further opportunities for participation. Car racing does not require the size and brute strength of many 'stick and ball' sports. So why did relatively few compete?

Those who wanted to had to overcome a number of barriers to their participation. First, even in the 1950s, the sport required some discretionary income. As veterans returned after the war, they displaced women in the workplace, who left it en masse to become homemakers and to raise families. Those who remained in the workforce suffered discrimination in salaries and promotion. Even those who worked part-time had little or no disposable income of their own. Consequently, many women were financially dependent on their husbands and family expenses consumed their 'allowances.' That situation did not begin to change until the 1960s.[50]

Second, and closely related to this, was the problem of women's access to automobiles. The two-car family did not become the norm for several decades, so many women in the 1950s shared a car with their husband. Above all, the car has been seen as a *male* technology. Sports cars, in particular, have been promoted as 'toys for boys.' So, women had to overcome a persistent mindset about how they relate to cars and to technology in general. A recent study suggests that the male 'love affair with technology' is considered so unexceptional that it does not warrant any further discussion. However, the classic kind of father-son bonding activity, such as working on a car together, is not usually shared with daughters. Thus, 'boys are more likely than girls to be socialized into hands-on tinkering with mechanical devices,' and deriving pleasure from technology 'appears to be more legitimate for adult men ... than for adult women.'[51] Historian Jane Jenkins, herself a former auto slalom racer, shares this view: 'It's a cultural impression ... that cars are a guy thing, that men are more capable with cars ... And it's also just the whole notion of a big machine. Women are ... deemed to be inept around machinery, and cars are big machines, so women culturally are not supposed to ... feel comfortable with them or feel accomplished around them.'[52]

Finally, prevailing attitudes about women in society and in sport threw up other informal obstacles. Gender stereotyping discouraged female athleticism or channelled it only into those sports, such as figure skating, that were deemed appropriately 'feminine' and did not challenge men on their own turf.[53] And so Canada's sports car subculture included women, but not quite as equals.

A Significant Subculture

The car club subculture was *the* formative influence on Canadian sports car competition during its first decade. It provided a means for enthusiasts to pursue their passion. The clubs organized and funded the competitive events and the related activities. They also served as the structural base of the CASC; it was an association of clubs, and derived its national authority from them.[54] In short, the car clubs *created* Canadian auto sport. Nevertheless, while the subculture drew mainly from the Canadian middle class, by its very nature it was a deviation from the mainstream. In a country enamoured of hockey as its national sport, auto sport was a minority activity. In its formative years it clearly was an 'imported' sport with a British flavour. Finally, it was almost exclusively male. Initially, these factors probably limited its appeal among francophone Quebecois and women. In the 1950s, that left the sport in the hands of a small number of men, some of whom were determined to professionalize it. But, as the next chapter shows, at the outset at least they competed for fun.

3 Run What Ya Brung: Sports Car Competition in the Amateur Age

In those days the sport was fun ... It was almost a hell of a big social event with races for daytime activity ... There was a high percentage of guys drove their car to the track. And they drove them to work on Monday morning too!

Roy McLaughlin[1]

The founders of the CASC may have had a grand 'vision' of the future of Canadian auto sport, but Roy McLaughlin's recollections capture neatly the spirit of the sport in the 'Amateur Age' of the 1950s: 'Run what ya brung' and have fun. It was strictly amateur, accessible, and affordable. As a result, the sport grew rapidly. In 1954 six CASC clubs in Quebec and Ontario organized thirty-seven events. Five years later, thirty clubs from the Maritimes to the Prairies were running 125 races, rallies, and other competitive activities.[2] There was an event for every enthusiast, every kind of car, and every budget, throughout the year.

A Day at the Races

The BEMC races held 26 June 1954 at Edenvale, an airport circuit west of Barrie, Ontario, were typical of the era. Among the three dozen drivers (all men) competing that day were several who became fixtures during the first decades of Canadian racing: Bob Hanna, Jim Fergusson, Al Pease, Jerry Polivka, Bryan Rowntree, Bill Sadler, and Hugh Sutherland. Hanna doubled as racer and scrutineer, while Peter Hayes served as chief marshal. The seven races were short: three each of five laps and eight laps respectively, and the closing event, a sixteen-lap 'Grand Prix' for sports cars.

The racing cars were almost all British, with six Jaguars and six MGs dominating the field. The lap speeds around the 1.75-mile course were slow by today's standards: about 35 mph for the small sedans and about 50 mph for the fastest sports cars (the Jaguars). In the feature race, Vern Jeffries's Jag XK-120 beat Fred Allen's MG Special by only 4/10 of a second at the checkered flag. Several other races were decided by a similar margin. There was only one 'incident'; in the second race Les Varley rolled his car, causing extensive damage, but suffering no injuries. Jim Gunn, who critiqued the event for the CASC, felt that the standard of competition was 'very high, the best I have seen. Driving was excellent except in one or two cases.' He complimented the club on the scrutineering, marshalling, and lap scoring, but was critical of several other aspects of the event: pit location and crowd control there; 'haphazard' time-keeping; excessively 'dicey' practice; and punctuality. He also felt that the race announcer's commentary 'stunk.' Finally, Gunn criticized the race organizers for allowing Bill Sadler to bend the car classification rules. He observed caustically that 'a Hillman that has had a can opener taken to it and a V-8 "60" inserted, is *not* a production car.'[3] As will be discussed later in this book, Sadler's Hillman was just the first of his specials that 'pushed the outside of the envelope' of racing car design.

Mere words undoubtedly fail to capture fully the atmosphere of a race, which assaults the senses with a miasma of colours, noises, and aromas. But the Edenvale event probably provides a fairly accurate 'snapshot' of a typical Canadian sports car race in the mid-1950s. Most competitors raced their own cars, which they drove to the track, so car preparation was minimal. Graham Locke recalls that 'the first time I raced at all was in a '55 Triumph TR2. I drove it to Edenvale, stripped off the windshield ... raced it, put everything back together ... and drove back.'[4] The races had no prize money, sponsorship, or TV coverage. There were few spectators. And clubs ran the events themselves, with racers, their friends, wives, and girlfriends providing the volunteer staff. Since there usually were no restaurants on site, picnics were the norm. There would be some kind of prize-giving ceremony at the day's end, often followed by less formal and more rowdy celebrations. Roy McLaughlin recalls: 'The banquet ... for presenting trophies was just a big party. When you went back to the motels after the day's practice or whatever, there was a party.'[5]

The Canadian climate imposed a relatively short regular racing season, but ice racing allowed die-hard enthusiasts to pursue their summer hobby in winter. All they needed was a frozen surface large enough to lay out a track and thick enough to support the cars. The Muskoka Motor Sports Club of Huntsville, Ontario, held the first 'Dice on Ice' in 1951 and the BEMC followed suit in 1954. By the 1960s ice races were regular features for many clubs, and they usually attracted several dozen racers and thousands of spectators, drawn to the hilarious spectacle of wildly spinning cars vanishing into clouds of snow. The inevitable collisions encouraged racers to use older (and cheaper) cars, so ice racing was not usually a venue for 'hot machinery.' Rather, it featured the agile and sure-footed European sedans – VWs, Minis, Renaults, NSUs, DKWs, and Citroens. But the usual British sports cars raced as well and frequently won.[6] Ice racing sorted out the true racing *fanatics* from the 'fair weather' racers. The only thing that could spoil an ice racing event or season was a bout of mild weather.

Ice racing symbolized the amateur spirit of 1950s auto sport: rudimentary organization, minimal safety precautions, loose rules, and a lot of fun. Racing was also cheap then; a five-dollar entry fee and a single tank of gas could get you through the day. These features made the sport accessible and appealing to many racers for whom self-gratification was sufficient. But as will be discussed later, by the late 1950s the purpose of racing had begun to change – to audience entertainment and sponsor promotion. The character of race tracks changed with it.

Flat Out: Airport Race Tracks

The first challenge facing would-be Canadian racers in the 1950s was finding places to compete. When the sport revived in Europe after the war, racers there returned to established pre-war circuits. American sports car enthusiasts started racing through the streets of Watkins Glen and Bridgehampton, New York.[7] But, in Canada (as in Great Britain), for the first decade and more, enthusiasts raced mostly on airfields left over from the Second World War.

> Where once the air vibrated with the thunder of aero engines as the Commonwealth strove to supply the desperate need for crews to man combat planes, the end of the war rendered these airstrips useless ... As the interest in ... racing grew in post-war Canada, the discovery of these mouldering airfields was like finding gold in the Yukon.[8]

Fortunately for the racers, there were plenty of them; at least fifteen were used in the 1950s. The Abbotsford, BC, airfield was the first.

Ontario racers originally used Edenvale, then later moved to Harewood and Greenacres. The Montreal clubs found no airfields available locally, so they raced just across the border at the Connor Circuit in St-Eugène, Ontario, starting in 1954, while Ottawa racers ran at Carp for a few years in the 1950s. Western enthusiasts like Lou Kennedy, 'Slim' Routliffe, and George Chapman started racing at tracks in Claresholm, Alberta, Davidson, Saskatchewan, and Dauphin and Netley, Manitoba. Most airfield tracks had only a short lifespan, as they deteriorated rapidly with age and use. The military had abandoned or sold most of these airfields after the war, so the clubs had to lease or rent them from the new owners, invariably farmers like Russ Hare or Doug Connor, for whom tracks were named. According to Len Coates, the farmer who owned Edenvale took the view that 'if the damn fools can afford to pay the rent, why should I care if they want to break their necks?'[9]

The airfields were roughly triangular in shape, usually consisting of one or two long runways connected to shorter taxiways and aprons. It took some imagination, and a lot of oil drums and hay bales, to lay out an interesting circuit. Even then, they were hardly ideal. Most were in poor condition, with weeds splitting the concrete or asphalt. Worse, they were 'flat, uninviting places, devoid of trees or brush, swept by wind, bleached by sun and, invariably, situated far from any creature comforts.'[10] The facilities were primitive, and the paddock and pit areas were open, unprotected from rain, dust, or snow. But they offered real advantages to the fledgling sport: cheap, ready-made concrete or asphalt circuits, surrounded by flat fields (into which a racer could spin safely), far from towns where people might complain about the noise.

Still, Canadian racers yearned for something better. In its inaugural 1959 issue *Canada Track and Traffic* magazine stated bluntly that the 'racing circuits in existence in Canada are hopelessly inadequate, both in quality of circuit and spectator facilities. Everybody in the sport realizes this.'[11] By the time that article appeared, however, the problem already was being addressed in British Columbia.

Built-to-Purpose: Westwood Motorsport Park

In 1957 the Department of National Defence had transferred the Abbotsford airfield to the Department of Transport for use by civilian air traffic. The SCCBC ran their last race there in March 1958. In the meantime, the club had found a site in a large clear-cut owned by the province on a plateau above Port Coquitlam, *'only 15 miles from Downtown Vancouver.'*[12]

The club negotiated an initial ten-year lease (later extended to thirty) with the province, paying a nominal annual rent, with the option to buy the property (about 480 acres) when the lease ran out. To finance the $82,500 project the SCCBC authorized the sale of $50,000 in debentures, with the balance to come from club revenues. Based on experience, the club felt it would make a modest profit on every race, and it planned to use those profits to pay down the debt. With 445 members the SCCBC was a large and comparatively wealthy club. Thus, it was confident it could afford to launch what *Canada Track and Traffic* magazine described as 'probably the most ambitious undertaking ever attempted by a sports car club.'[13]

The first notice to members had predicted optimistically that the track would be ready for racing in 1958, but in fact clearing the site did not begin until the fall of that year and continued into the following spring. Ambitiously, the SCCBC originally visualized a track for Formula One cars, but that proved beyond their means. Still, they brought in Stirling Moss as a consultant, and using topographic maps and aerial surveys, he and the club laid out a course 1.8 miles long, roughly triangular in shape, designed with both the competitor and the spectator in mind. The natural contours of the land ensured exciting driving and viewing, against a backdrop of dramatic mountain scenery. The start/finish/pit straight was followed by a series of turns that descended to the half-mile-long back straight, which climbed then dropped dramatically after the crest at 'Deer's Leap,' where fast cars would become airborne. A very tight hairpin brought cars into a steep climb through the 'Esses' back to the start. In 1983, driving a Formula Atlantic Ralt RT4, Michael Andretti set the track record: 58.795 seconds. Jim Maddin, who raced an Alfa there in the 1960s, recalls that 'it was a really fun course to drive.'[14]

The track's name, so evocative of the location itself, actually was chosen to honour Earle Westwood, the provincial minister of conservation and recreation who had approved the club's acquisition of the property. It was supposed to open in June 1959, but bad weather and money problems delayed construction and paving, which was not completed until a few hours before the first race. The cost increased to $100,000 and the debentures did not sell as well as expected. The club had to turn to some of its wealthier members to guarantee the payment of the construction bills, and to the club membership generally for the balance of the costs. In mid-July 1959 members were warned that if they didn't 'kick in' their share, 'the Club will not be able to complete "Westwood" and the whole project will collapse.'[15]

The appeal worked, and the track opened on 26 July 1959 in bright sunshine amid much celebration: a ribbon cutting, a band, and an RCAF fly-past. A capacity crowd of 10,000 was on hand, and almost as many were turned away at the gate for lack of parking space. The audience was treated to seven races, with at least seventy entries from the SCCBC, other BC clubs, and the United States. The sports car had changed dramatically in the decade since the first Abbotsford race. A few MG TCs and TDs were the hangovers from that era, in a field now dominated by the next generation: MGAs, TR3s, Austin-Healey Sprites, Porsches, Corvettes, and AC Bristols. There was a sizeable entry of modified sports cars, including five Lotuses, two Ferrari 250 *Testa Rossas*, and a D-type Jaguar. Driving the Jag, the SCCBC's Jim Rattenbury held off Americans George Keck (in a Ferrari) and Tom Luce (Corvette) to win his class in the sixth race, but Keck came back to dominate the final event. Bob McLean, destined for both triumph and tragedy later in his racing career, rolled his MG, but walked away.[16]

The SCCBC had every reason to be proud of its achievement, and clubs in the East soon followed its lead. Even so, Westwood was a 'cautionary tale' in two respects. First, it showed that building a 'world class' track was not a job for part-time amateurs. Second, because it required professional construction, it was a costly, financially risky project for a club. Westwood quickly ran into financial problems, discussed later in this book. Eastern clubs soon confronted the same harsh reality. It was one thing to build a track; it was quite another to make it pay.

Rally Around

Lacking in its early days the high drama and the visceral visual appeal of wheel-to-wheel circuit racing, rallying – a point-to-point competition at legal speeds – was long considered its 'poor cousin.' But whereas there were only twenty circuit races on the CASC calendar in 1959, there were seventy rallies: a more than three-fold increase over the number five years earlier.[17] How do we explain this glaring discrepancy in the relative levels of activity?

The appeal of rallying, shown by its growth in this period, can be explained in a number of ways. First, unlike racing, which required a closed track and a variety of safety measures, rallies used public roads, ostensibly within the speed limit. Thus, they could be run anywhere, on any kind of road, and generally were quite safe. Even though cars frequently went off the road – especially in winter rallies – injuries or fatalities in rallying were rare. Second, while racing was confined largely to summer (ice racing being the exception), rallying was a year-round activity. Third, although rallies required organization, people, and planning, any club could run one, at very little cost. Fourth, in the early years, participants did not require a highly prepared car or special equipment; the family car was quite adequate. That made it affordable. Finally, rallying offered variety and challenge for driver and navigator – interesting roads and complex problem solving. In fact, it might be described as the 'thinking man's auto sport.' Former Montreal rallyist John Gallop recalls that 'every event was different ... You never knew what you were going to be expected to encounter and cope with. It was an intellectual challenge, and [had] some physical exhilaration.'[18] Cheap, safe, easy to run, and anyone could do it; for the average car club member, rallying was a very attractive form of auto sport. Like early racing, the main purpose of rallying in the 1950s was to have fun. And that applied to organizers and competitors alike.

Although the types of rallies described below posed different degrees of challenge to the competitors, *initially* they all shared a common characteristic: navigation by following instructions. The 'time-speed-distance' (TSD) 'navex' (navigational) rally was the quintessential car club activity of the 1950s. In TSD rallies, competitors starting at timed intervals follow a route guided by a set of instructions of varying degrees of complexity, at set legal speeds on public roads to a destination unknown to them at the start. Performance is measured, not by speed, but by staying on route and on time (neither early nor late) through a series of checkpoints until the competitor reaches the finish. Penalty points are assessed for being early, late, or off route. A book from the period stressed that being on time at the right place was more important than being fast: 'The rally ... is in no sense a speed event ... It is designed to test the entrants' skill in finding their way around a route that is not disclosed until the rally starts ... while maintaining average speeds which also are not revealed until the instruction sheets are issued just before the starting time.'[19] Put another way, in a navigational rally 'you don't know the way and you don't know when you're expected [to arrive], but you must be there on time.'[20] Former Fredericton sports broadcaster Dave Morrell later summed up what he called 'the three *commandments* of rallying – stay on the road, stay on the right road and stay on time, if you have time.'[21] Indeed, the challenge of confronting and overcoming the unknown captures the essence of Canadian rallying in the amateur age.

TSD rallies varied widely in terms of difficulty. At the most basic level was the social, fun rally, whose purpose was closer to the original meaning of the term 'rally,' 'to assemble or to reunite.' They could take the form of a tour to a restaurant, or a 'treasure hunt' (looking for clues en route). Since these events, which were used to recruit new members, were often a competitor's first contact with the sport, they were intended to be easy.[22]

By far the most common event in this period was the navex. In 1958 they constituted three-quarters of the rallies in the CASC calendar. Using mostly unpaved roads, they also offered the greatest variety: from beginner to expert, from a few hours to twenty-four hours in length. Navexes usually consisted of a series of sections or 'legs,' each with its own set of instructions. To ensure that the crews stayed on course, the organizers would place along the route a number of 'checkpoints': usually a marked vehicle, whose crew would record the time in and out for each competitor. Missing a checkpoint would result in penalty points. Each leg had to be completed within a certain amount of time, based on the distance involved, and the speeds given in the instructions; usually the speeds would vary considerably and frequently, even within a leg, just to make it more challenging for the driver.

But a navex was primarily a test of the navigator. Indeed, it was the most 'intellectual' of all auto sports, with the variety of instructions limited only by the imagination of the organizers. They might be presented in written form, as diagrams, or as a map. They could be straightforward (e.g., 'at 1.4 miles, turn right at tee; at 1.6, bear left'), or deliberately complex and tricky, based on riddles, rhymes, conversations, or songs, or arranged out of sequence. For some sections, calculations or measurement might be required. There usually were random route questions (e.g., 'what is the date on the covered bridge at 2.75 miles?'). Mileages might be cumulative for a whole section, or non-accumulative (the odometer would be zeroed at each instruction). Almost every rally had a map section; some (referred to as 'Map Runs') were run entirely from maps (usually topographic), using grid references, landmarks, and compass bearings (including magnetic deviations). The challenge for the navigator was increased by the time factor. Receiving the instructions only minutes before the start, he/she would have to work through them 'on the fly,' using every spare moment to read ahead into the next section and figure out the route before they reached it.[23]

The equipment required for navexes depended on their level of difficulty; a beginner rally would require nothing more than a watch, a ruler, a pencil, and perhaps a compass. By the end of the first decade, an experienced crew entering an expert-level navex would have a fully equipped cockpit. Typically that included a map board with a night light, a Curta Calculator, a Halda Speedpilot (a mini-computer run off the wheels, whose gauges indicated elapsed times and the car's proximity to set average speeds), highly accurate timepieces, compasses, slide rules, and other measuring devices. Spares and safety and repair equipment usually were mandatory.

The Lower Canada Motor Club's Triskaidekaphobia Rally was typical of the most demanding navexes. It was notable for complex instructions, involving map reading, compass bearings, line diagrams, mathematical calculations, logic problems, and letter/number substitution codes. The 'Triska' always started on Friday the thirteenth, and the instructions made liberal use of the number thirteen. Of the twenty-three starters in the 1959 event, only two did not finish. But the penalty points tell the real story. The winning car accumulated only sixty, while the last-place car had earned 1136; sixteen others had between 400 and 950.[24]

Organizing a major rally involved considerable time-consuming, detailed planning and rehearsal. As John Charters explains: 'You'd have to cover every piece of territory a number of times by car, measuring mileages, deciding where to put checkpoints, what average speeds you could do, writing instructions ... months of organization, but not every night or every weekend.'[25] Fortunately, for some enthusiasts the real attraction was in *organizing* a challenging event. Les Stanley was one. As he explains:

> Canadair Auto Club was a rallying type of club, because the people behind it were engineers ... the sort of people who were interested in composing [and] solving navigational problems. That first Quebec Rally that they organized [in 1956] ... was watertight... There wasn't a mistake in the whole damn thing. This reflected the meticulous planning, starting with research of major English rallies, precise rules and regulations, and concise course instructions checked and double checked.[26]

Press on Regardless: Endurance Rallying

Navexes, with their varying degrees of complexity, appealed to the broad base of amateur rally enthusiasts, and it was not unusual for club navexes to attract large entry fields, even from other clubs. But for some organizers and competitors, European-style, driver-oriented, *endurance* rallies represented the acme of rallying. It was the desire to run such an event that had brought the CASC's founders together in the first place. From the outset, endurance rallies attracted the most committed rallyists, and soon thereafter, commercial sponsors. By the end of the 1950s they were changing the face of Canadian rallying.

Many years later, Les Stanley recalled an incident that neatly encapsulates the essence of the endurance rally, doing all it takes to reach the finish:

> Chelminski and I left Montreal as the first car on a Thousand Islands Rally with Peter Bone as 'Clerk of the Course' driving about 30 minutes ahead of us. Less than 40 minutes out of Montreal our generator failed so we drove all night (dark and raining) with no headlights or windshield wipers, saving the battery to keep the engine running. Every meal stop we would catch up with Bone and while Chelminski would keep him looking the other way, I would switch his VW battery for ours!! So we always had a freshly charged one! Bone never could understand why *we* had to give him a push start![27]

These rallies were intended to be 'a test of man's endurance and of the reliability of his motor vehicle.'[28] In fact, the punishment they inflicted on cars, through a combination of bad roads and bad weather, earned them an appropriate nickname: 'car breakers.' But they appealed to the truly dedicated rallyist like Peter Bone who found TSD rallies 'boring, boring, boring.'[29]

In Europe, the long-distance endurance event dominated championship-level rallying. The Monte Carlo Rally was the first and the most famous of these, and was emulated throughout the world. While it originally was a competitive 'tour' across Europe, as cars became faster and more reliable it began to resemble a road 'race'; speed became a key factor. In fact, high-speed rallies eventually replaced racing on roads, which disappeared for safety reasons. The SCCA staged the first such event in North America – the Press On Regardless Rally – in 1949. Initially conceived as a scenic but competitive tour of upper Michigan, it evolved into a Monte Carlo–style event, covering 1200 miles of rough roads over four nights.[30]

The Thousand Islands Rally was the first endurance rally run in Canada, and was the only competitive event ever organized by the

CASC itself. The concept of the rally (which consciously emulated the Monte) was that the competitors would start simultaneously from Toronto, Ottawa, or Montreal and travel about 200 miles to finish at Gananoque, Ontario. Forty competitors entered the first rally in October 1952, which the CASC called an unqualified success. For 1953, the daytime section was extended to 450 miles. The event the following year showed that the CASC still had a lot to learn about running rallies; a month after the event the results were still only provisional. At the November 1954 CASC meeting the rally was the subject of considerable controversy and discussion. Several members wanted to declare it 'no contest.' That idea was defeated, but the competition chairman took control of the 1955 event.[31]

Apparently that change did not solve the problem, so the 1955 rally was cancelled. The CASC decided to 'sub-contract' the 1956 rally to the Kingston-based St Lawrence Automobile Club (St LAC), while retaining final authority over the event. The St LAC shortened the rally to a single day, starting and finishing it in the Kingston area, with part of the route run in the United States. The result was a generally satisfactory event, and the club was given the 'green light' to run it again. In 1957 the St LAC aimed to make it longer and tougher, so the rally returned to its original format, with multiple midnight start locations and a common finishing point, twenty-one hours and 700 miles later (at Alexandria Bay, New York). The demanding nature of the event apparently caught the entrants by surprise; only seventeen of thirty cars finished. The main criticism was that the average speeds could not be maintained safely on the roads used.[32]

In February 1958 the CASC decided to withdraw completely from organizing events, so the rally was turned over permanently to the St LAC. The CASC later criticized the 1958 rally and warned that it could be removed from the calendar if there was no improvement. The club apparently got the message; the 1959 event seems to have gone smoothly. It attracted thirty-three entries (including two dealer-sponsored teams), starting from Montreal, Toronto, and Ottawa. The organizers also persuaded businesses, such as Carling Breweries, to support it.[33]

Intent aside, the Thousand Islands Rally was not a truly European-style endurance rally. Rather it was a compromise, designed to appeal to a wide spectrum of rallyists. Although the CASC's guidelines de-emphasized navigation in endurance rallies, in practice the early events usually combined driving skill with challenging instructions. The guidelines also suggested that lumbering, farming, and very rough rural roads should not be used. But, given the poor state of most Canadian secondary roads in the period, rough roads were unavoidable; endurance rallies used mostly unpaved roads, some little more than tracks or cowpaths. One thousand miles was supposed to be the minimum distance, since 'anything less than this would not constitute a test of the endurance of either man or machine.'[34] However, most endurance rallies were only between 600 and 800 miles long. Even so, two days – over a weekend – was the norm for such events. Often starting on a Friday evening and finishing Sunday, they usually involved a significant amount of night driving. Crew members took turns driving, navigating, and sleeping whenever possible.

Still, if emulation is the measure of success, then enthusiasts must have seen endurance rallies as the 'wave of the future'; the CASC calendar soon was filled with them. The Calgary Sports Car Club (CSCC) ran its first Loop Rally in 1955. Initially a scenic but demanding twenty-four-hour drive through the Rockies and the high prairie, each year it became tougher and oriented more towards driving rather than navigation.[35] From its first run in 1956, the Canadair Auto Club's Quebec Rally was a 'tougher than average' endurance rally. It was a two-day, two-night event, with three sections covering about 1000 miles in all. The first began in Montreal, and took crews up the Ottawa valley, through the Gatineau area to the Mont Laurier region, then down to the Eastern Townships. Section two, nearly 300 miles of straightforward navigation, went from Magog to Quebec City. The final part took rallyists back to Montreal. Co-organizer Les Stanley, later explained how the Volkswagen team tried to outsmart the organizers by taking a shortcut:

> This occurred on a navigational section. Competitors had to get from ... [the] starting point ... [the] finish of section, while being *not permitted* to travel along certain roads ... They were 'boxed in' and penalized if found on the forbidden roads by either checkpoints or spotters. The VW team, unable to solve the puzzle, took to driving up a boulder strewn dried-up river bed to get past a checkpoint. This required considerable push, shove and jacking cars over the boulders![36]

Icy Does It: Winter Endurance Rallies

Part of rallying's appeal was that it was a year-round sport, and it didn't take long for some 'die hard' enthusiasts to combine the concept of endurance rallies with winter conditions. All endurance rallies were meant to test car and crew. But for sheer *punishment*, there was nothing to match the BEMC Canadian Winter Rally. Only the SMCC's Rallye Des Neiges came close. When it came to 'car breakers,' these two rallies were in a class by themselves.

Eve White credits BEMC members Fred Hayes and Neil Bryson with the inspiration for the Winter Rally, born of concern that club members had few competitive events to occupy them during the winter. And so in January 1953 they ran the first Winter Rally, which remained an annual event for the next twenty-three years. That first one set a pattern for many of those that followed; unpredictable weather took its toll on the crews and of the forty-one entrants, only nineteen finished. It started in rain, which continued for thirty hours. In Quebec, the rain poured off high snow banks and into all parts of the cars, then froze. Chuck Stockey, one of the winners that year, recalled that 'some cars which had been abandoned had water up over the tires which froze solid and in the morning the drivers had to chop their cars free.'[37]

That first event started in Toronto, circled Lake Ontario to Watertown, New York, then moved on to Montreal, Maniwaki, and back to Toronto via Peterborough and Huntsville. Crossing the border proved problematic, however, so the American section was dropped for 1954. For the next five years, the rally ran through Ontario and Quebec. Between 1955 and 1958 it had two start points: Toronto plus Ottawa or Montreal. Over the next two years, it was confined to Ontario, starting and ending in Toronto with an overnight stop in North Bay. Typically, the rally covered 1200 to 1300 miles over forty-eight hours and used many of the same roads each year. In 1957 the BEMC created separate race and rally committees, and the following year Jim Plumley, a Winter Rally veteran, took on the task of organizing the event. He placed greater emphasis on accurate route navigation and timing, but without diminishing the challenge for the driver, since the rally was intended to be a test of the winter driving abilities of both car and driver. It made extensive use of demanding country roads, so like a European event it demanded 'a high degree of skill on the part of the driver as well as the navigator.'[38]

Road conditions determined the extent to which it was a 'driver's rally,' but the weather shaped those conditions, and thus exerted the most powerful influence on the character of each event. Even without bad weather the roads usually were challenging. Cars ended up in ditches and snowbanks, lost windshields, exhausts, springs and shocks, oil pans, and gas tanks, while other parts simply froze up or failed. In the 1960 rally the heater in John Charters's Corvair failed on the first night and the windshield froze over. But he and his partner forged on, scraping continuously and peering out the open side windows with goggles on. They arrived at the finish with the interior covered in a thick coating of frost. From the rally organizers' perspective, good weather was bad news. Still, bad weather played havoc with the route, timings, and results. During its final hours the 1960 event was hit by a severe blizzard that forced the highway department to pull its snowplows off the secondary roads in order to keep the highways open. Up to that point only twenty cars had dropped out; the storm claimed fifty-one more. Barely half of the entries completed the rally. The dramatic finish garnered front-page headlines in the *Globe and Mail*. As one later report put it: 'It was at Lindsay that the rally met the storm and the storm won.'[39]

The Winter Rally had attracted factory- and dealer-sponsored teams as early as 1956. Two years later it became the first Canadian auto sport event to be granted international status, and thus to be listed in the FIA calendar.[40] A rally that popular and successful was bound to find imitators. Moreover, the BEMC's decision to confine the Winter Rally to Ontario after 1958 left a gap in the calendar for Montreal-area competitors. Montrealers who wanted to compete in the rally faced almost a day's driving each way to and from Toronto over and above the 1000-plus miles of the rally itself. Thus, the SMCC decided to offer a national championship–calibre event comparable to the Winter Rally for rallyists in the Quebec region. It launched the Rallye Des Neiges in 1959, and it quickly became the club's premier event.[41]

Like the Winter Rally, the Rallye Des Neiges was from the outset 'primarily a driver's rally' designed 'to test driving skill and navigational ability as well as vehicle reliability, under severe Winter conditions, over a route which lies chiefly in the Laurentian mountains.'[42] Initially it covered 600 to 700 miles over a twenty-four-hour period. The balance of driving to navigation varied from year to year. In the early events, the navigational instructions were uncomplicated. Timing was to the nearest minute, and average speeds were set to match the road conditions. The Rallye Des Neiges was an instantly popular event, although it never matched the BEMC rally either for toughness or for the number of competitors. Weather did not wreak havoc to same degree as it did on the Winter Rally, probably because for many years the SMCC ran it in early March, when the weather was starting to improve.

By the mid-1950s there were enough major rallies to establish a championship series. In 1955, to honour the late CASC co-founder Jack Fidler, the national body approved the awarding of the Fidler Memorial Trophy to the champion rally driver. However, the championship was not established officially until 1957, when the CASC approved a plan drafted by the North Toronto Motorsport Club (NTMC). The aim of the series was to promote rally and navigational driving by increasing the motivation of, participation in, and quality of rallies. Points were awarded to driver and navigator equally, for participation in series events, for finishing events of specified distances, and for finishing in the top three places. The championship calendar for the first year included the 1000 Islands Rally, the Quebec Rally, seventeen other endurance rallies, navexes, and regularity runs. Two driving-skill test events and a 'day of dicing' (see below) rounded out the series.[43]

The selection of events looks a bit curious in retrospect. The BEMC Winter Rally was excluded from the 1957 series because the championship was not created until after the event had been run. The 'day of dicing' (which involved pairs of cars doing timed laps around a racetrack) was completely at odds with the purpose of a rally championship; rallies were non-speed events. Finally, the series hardly could be considered national when all of the events were confined to Ontario and Quebec. This regional bias, of course, reflected a reality that shaped the early years of national auto sport; the majority of CASC-affiliated clubs were in those two provinces, and travel by road to and from events elsewhere in the country was still difficult.

The 1957 series got off to a rough start; had the CASC discounted every rally about which complaints were filed, there would have been no championship at all that first year. Apparently, 1958 was no better; the CASC directors were highly critical of the quality of events. In 1959 the CASC eliminated all driving-skill tests, since they were 'not in keeping with the purposes and principles of the rally championship.' Moreover, consistent with its status as an amateur sport body, the CASC decided in 1960 to discourage 'the use of monetary awards for any competition held on public highways, i.e. rallies.' The first four years of the championship were dominated by a handful of people: the team of Les Stanley and Les Chelminski in 1957, Chelminski with several others in 1958, and the team of Art Dempsey and Bill Silvera in 1959 and 1960.[44]

In less than ten years Canadian rallying had grown from a local-club social activity to a national championship sport. Thus, it had been firmly established as one of the two central pillars of Canadian auto sport. But the emergence of endurance rallies showed it was evolving into a more demanding sport. As will be discussed in later chapters, that required a more serious, professional approach and commercial sponsorship. Just as 'commercial professionalism' changed the character of Canadian racing, in the next decade it would change rallying and marginalize the amateur rallyist.

Solo Pursuits: Slaloms and Hill Climbs

For those who found rallying too tame and circuit racing too risky or expensive, 'solo' racing (slaloms and hill climbs) offered alternative outlets for the 'need for speed.' In solo events the cars compete singly and are timed individually over a prescribed course. Slaloms evolved from gymkhanas (also called driving skill tests), which have a pedigree as long as that of racing and rallying. Typically, the early gymkhanas combined slaloms, braking tests, driving in reverse, precise parking, and 'gimmicks' such as plucking balloons off pylons. Penalty points would be awarded for hitting markers, going off course, or other errors. Skill, more than speed, was of the essence.

In 1958 the CASC defined the rules for gymkhanas, eliminating the gimmicks and re-emphasizing the driver's control of the car. They were open to any licensed driver, and did not require a specially prepared vehicle; any type of family car was quite suitable. Of all auto sports, they were the easiest and cheapest to organize, requiring nothing more than an open space (such as a parking lot), some markers, and a stopwatch. Their low cost, simplicity, and accessibility made gymkhanas popular, and often they were the first events run by a new car club. The WOSCA held its first one six days after the first club elections in July 1953. Since demonstrating safe driving helped to legitimize auto sport, the St Catharines Motor Club invited the local police to participate in their first gymkhana in July 1958. The force entered a VW that took third place.[45]

Like gymkhanas, hill climbs have a long history. They were part of the earliest car 'trials' in Britain.[46] In the United States, the Mount Washington hill climb dates from 1908 and the Pike's Peak event predates the Second World War. But unlike gymkhanas, they were more clearly speed events. The car that reached the top of the hill in the shortest time was the winner.

Hill climbs were slightly more difficult to organize, if only because they required a road on a hill. This meant using either private property or a section of road closed to traffic, which required the cooperation of landowners, the police, and highway departments. Not surprisingly, hill climbs were always in a minority among solo events. Nonetheless, a number of clubs organized them on a regular basis. Toronto's BEMC and SCC began running theirs as early as 1954, at Hockley Valley (near Orangeville) and Rattlesnake Point (near Milton), respectively. That same year in Quebec the Laurentian Autosport Club held the first hill climb up the steep road to the ski lodge at the top of Mont Gabriel, north of Montreal. In 1958 the Jaguar Owners Association took it over and it became a regular fixture on the Quebec region schedule. The Okanagan Auto Sport Club (OASC) ran its first annual one in 1955. The courses varied in length and difficulty; Rattlesnake was the shortest, at less than four-tenths of a mile. The OASC's Westbank course was the longest: one and a half miles. The most challenging of the early courses was the Calgary Sports Car Club's Groeneveld farm site: a twisty dirt road up the side of the Bow Valley, with twelve turns and a rise of 350 feet in seven-tenths of a mile, and drops of 50 to 100 feet along the edge. Fifty-four entries, in everything from VWs and Minis to MGs, Alfas, Triumphs, and a Daimler, turned out for the first climb in the autumn of 1960. Dick Draper earned fastest time of the day (FTD) (1 min., 10.4 sec.) in his MGA twin-cam. But the 'comeback of the day' was by Paul Dyson, who drove his Triumph over the road's edge at high speed during practice, coming to rest against a tree fifty feet below. After being winched back up, he went on to win his class and claim second FTD (1 min., 13.7 sec.). Back in the East, the entry lists for the Hockley and Rattlesnake events included many of the well-known Ontario track racers, such as Bradley, Hanna, Polivka, and Sadler. But it was Don Haddow, driving a motorcycle-engined, open-wheeled 'Jordan Special,' who was 'king of the hill' at both locations in 1959–60.[47]

The popularity of solo competition is readily discernible in the growth of the sport. The number of events on the CASC calendar more than quadrupled in seven years: from five hill climbs and six gymkhanas in 1954 to nineteen hill climbs and twenty-nine gymkhanas in 1960. That year, thirty clubs from coast to coast organized solo events; fully one-third of the events were in the West. The participation level was high; fifteen of the 1960 events averaged more than twenty-eight entries each.[48] Although solo lacked racing's prestige and its audience-drawing capacity, it was not a marginal form of auto sport. Racing was not accessible to everyone for a variety of reasons, location being prominent among them; it was concentrated at a few tracks close to the major cities. Yet many car clubs had emerged in areas far from those circuits, the Atlantic Sports Car Club (ASCC) being a case in point. In those more remote areas solo racing filled a void. At a time when the CASC was trying to build an auto sport community in all parts of the country, solo gave the sport an important national presence.

In the decade after the founding of the CASC, Canadian auto sport experienced dramatic growth in all its forms and in all parts of the country. Canadian races were attracting larger crowds and eventually commercial sponsors. Clubs were starting to build permanent race tracks. All of this had been achieved by a subculture of amateurs. But the price of success was change, from a fun amateur hobby pursued for self-gratification to a more serious, 'professional' sport with a different purpose: entertainment and promotion. The next two chapters show how the quest for 'world class' status pushed Canadian auto sport into more organized, regulated 'commercial professionalism.' By the end of the first decade, this trend would merely confirm what many enthusiasts already suspected and desired: that the 'amateur age' was over.

4 Rules and Regs: Professionalizing the Amateurs

> For those who find death alluring ... the world now provides three sports that offer the penalty of a splendid exit for the slightest mistake ... bullfighting, mountain climbing, and car racing – and the most violent and bloody of the three is racing.
>
> June Callwood[1]

Death in the Fast Lane

Frame by frame in a grim photo sequence, the racing accident that prompted Callwood's bitter tirade unfolds at the head of her 1960 *Maclean's* article. Tapped from behind entering the twisting chicane at the Harewood race track, Ted Pope's modified Triumph TR3 swerves, then rolls over three times. Trapped in the open cockpit, a fixed metal tonneau cover preventing him from ducking down into the passenger compartment, Pope – a CBC television producer and the senior driver for the CBC Car Club racing team known as Group Three – is fatally injured.[2]

Pope's death outraged Callwood. Calling it a 'blood sport,' she castigated racers for their cavalier attitudes towards risk and death. Noting that the new Westwood and Mosport tracks would be faster than the airport circuits, she predicted that 'despite precautions and regulations to make racing in Canada as safe as the nature of the sport permits, no one doubts that drivers will die on the new tracks.' And, in a passage that proved eerily prophetic, she quoted an unnamed 'authority' who said that Canada's then rising star, Peter Ryan, would be good enough to race with the best in Europe, 'if he lives.'[3]

Ted Pope was not the first Canadian racer to be killed in competition; that dubious distinction belongs to Ed Purdy, who had died the previous year in a crash at the Connor Circuit.[4] Nor was Pope the last. Racing accidents would claim the lives of some of Canada's best drivers: Ryan, Billy Foster, Bob McLean, Wayne Kelly, Gilles Villeneuve, and Greg Moore. Only Kelly died on a Canadian track, but Callwood was fundamentally correct; in racing, death is a fact of life.

But while the risk is real, it would be misleading to overstate it. When compared to the many thousands of races run worldwide since her article was published, the number of drivers killed has been remarkably small. Accident statistics for Formula One races show that in spite of increasing speeds F1 racing has become safer and fatalities fewer, thanks largely to changes in racing car design.[5] Racing also has become safer for spectators; casualties are very rare. As will be discussed below, Canadian race organizers and the CASC were forced to take safety seriously at an early stage. Ironically, Pope's and Purdy's deaths occurred several years *after* the CASC had started to introduce and enforce regulations to protect both racers and spectators. These were part of a larger process of setting higher standards of behaviour and performance for the sport and its participants. That, in turn, represented a conscious effort to meet the 'world class' status to which the founders aspired. The end result was to impose a greater degree of professionalism on what had begun simply as an amateur pastime.

CASC Expansion and Authority

Before it could impose professionalism on the sport, however, the CASC first had to establish its authority as the governing body of a growing national organization. By the end of its first decade the CASC had expanded from the three founding clubs to more than fifty, with nearly 4000 members. In 1952 the provisional executive approved a process for affiliating other clubs to the CASC. Clubs had to send a copy of their constitution and/or by-laws, state their total membership, and provide a list of club officers. The two most important criteria were that the club would have to pass a resolution stating that it would abide by the rules and regulations of the CASC, and that it would pay a fee to join. Once all these conditions were met, the executive would approve affiliation. A member club then would be able to send voting delegates to all national meetings.[6]

These procedures established two important principles: first, that local clubs would accept and submit to the national authority of the CASC; and second, that the CASC would be run and funded by its membership. Accepting the first principle was particularly important because the CASC's authority was entirely self-created – a kind of legal fiction. After all, only three clubs initially had agreed to establish the national body, which now imposed itself on all the others. Having done so, however, the CASC became dependent upon them, constitutionally and financially. At the outset, then, the structure was inherently democratic; the CASC derived its authority from its member clubs, and 'taxation' granted them representation. There was a simple division of labour; the CASC made the rules, and the clubs ran the events according to the rules.

Thus, the CASC never was a monolithic body, but rather a coalition of like-minded groups. That worked well enough in the early years, but was to become a source of problems later as the organization grew and the sport changed. At a relatively early stage the CASC was confronted with a dilemma: how to balance efficiency with fair 'national' representation. The problem was that club growth was distributed unevenly; by the end of the decade more than 60 per cent of affiliated clubs were in Ontario. Sheer numbers, therefore, meant there was a risk that the CASC could become simply an Ontario/Toronto-centric organization, with clubs elsewhere acting as minor appendages. Indeed, power in the CASC naturally tended to gravitate to Ontario and Toronto just as it did in other sports. Quebec was the only region that could rival their influence. This 'centre versus periphery' problem was, of course, not unique to the CASC. Regionalism has bedevilled Canadian politics and all 'national' organizations and activities for most of the nation's history.[7]

Of the Toronto clubs – and perhaps among all the clubs in the early years – the BEMC was *primus inter pares*. With 579 members in 1957, it was larger than most of the Toronto area clubs put together. Art Moseley, a member in the 1950s and later president, recalls that the meetings were always crowded. 'There was a time, if you didn't get there early you didn't get in the room. There was 3–400 people, and they all came.'[8] The BEMC gradually shrank in size as it spawned several other clubs, including the SCC and the CRDA. It founded and ran several of the major competitive events: the Winter Rally, the Indian Summer Trophy Races, and later the Canadian Grand Prix for Sports Cars (which became one of the Can-Am Series races). It also created the race tracks at Edenvale and Harewood and was the driving force that built

Mosport. Former president Roy McLaughlin recalls that in its heyday the club was running almost an event a week, from club to international level, year round, and each one had a committee. 'It was run almost like a very large company in those days ... I was attending meetings constantly.'9

Consequently, the club had a large number of the most active competitors and officials, and thus exercised an almost disproportionate influence on the CASC and on the direction of the sport. It was BEMC members Fred and Peter Hayes who came up with the idea of a Monte Carlo–style rally that was the catalyst for creating the CASC. They were also among the founders of the CRDA. Peter later served as CASC Ontario Region director and as its steward, and Fred was an outspoken advocate for professional racing. Al Sands served as the national competition chairman (1959–63). Tom Gilmour was a founder and the first president of the CRDA, and a force for professionalism. Bob Hanna served as executive director of the CASC for nearly twenty years. Moseley would give at least as much weight to George Moss, whom he described as 'Mr. Motor Racing in Canada.' Moss was secretary of CASC in 1959, and vice-chairman of the Ontario Region (1960–1). 'George's ultimate goal was to bring Formula One to Canada.' To that end, he was one of the key organizers of both the first Canadian Grand Prix for Sports Cars and the CRDA's Player's 200 in the early 1960s, and later helped to launch the Can-Am Series. The CRDA was, in Moseley's words, 'a club of racing drivers, not a club of organizers,' but Moss was 'a great organizer and team leader,' and so he, Moseley, and others from BEMC ran the 200 for them. He also gained an enviable reputation for working well with the top foreign racers; he may have been unique in his ability to get along with irascible Luigi Chinetti, the manager of Ferrari's North American Racing Team (NART). But George's dedication to the sport took a toll on his career. Altogether 'he had lost five or six jobs ... to help motorsport in Canada.'10

The BEMC was not the only Toronto area or Ontario club represented at the top levels of the sport in its first decade. Lawrence Bateman of the SCC was vice-president of the CASC from 1955 to 1964, and J.C. Carrothers of the OLCC served as a director from 1957 to 1964. But the prominence of BEMC members in the sport and in the CASC speaks for itself. The CASC's national committee/directors continued to meet regularly in the Kingston-Belleville area until 1957. The following year the meetings moved to Toronto, which made sense from the standpoint of administrative efficiency since most of the national committee lived in or near that city. The national office was established there in 1961. The group's AGMs, however, rotated between Montreal and Toronto.[11] When the CASC marked its tenth anniversary, Torontonians held three of the top executive positions: Jim Gunn (President), Bateman (VP), and Peter Lighthall (Secretary). In addition, rally chairman Art Dempsey and the licensing and marshalling chairs (George Grant and Harry Johnson) were also from the Toronto area. Sands was from suburban Thornhill, and national steward Mike Grinstead lived in Oakville. Furthermore, Toronto-area residents dominated the CASC Ontario Region executive. Given the social base of the subculture and the BEMC's central role, it probably was inevitable that Toronto would dominate the CASC.

To be fair, the founders and their successors recognized the problem at a relatively early stage and attempted to organize the CASC in a way that would offset the growing influence of Toronto and Ontario. In November 1955 the directors observed astutely that '[i]t appears that Canadian geography dictates a regional type of organization governed by a national body.'[12] They also noted that Quebec and Ontario were developing regional structures and felt that a western region should be encouraged. The by-laws drafted the next month stated, 'Regional centres may be established ... consisting of a group of Member Clubs in a geographic area.'[13] The regions would be represented at national meetings, just as clubs were. The region chairman and committee, elected by the clubs, would be responsible for conducting the business of the region.

However, the exact structure and powers of regions remained a matter for debate. The national directors felt that if regional matters could be dealt with locally, that would leave them free to focus only on 'national' issues. In May 1957 Burt Punshon presented them with a draft plan for regional organization and powers. It proposed a relatively simple division of responsibility. The national committee would establish national policies, rules, and standards. It would issue licences and permits for international events, publish the annual calendar, and look after insurance. The committee would represent the interests of the sport to national and international authorities, serve as the final court of appeal for disputes, and would organize the AGM. The regions would implement and enforce the policies, rules, and standards, represent the interests of their clubs to the national body, issue 'junior' licences, and handle regional administration. The regional executive would roughly parallel that of the national (chair, secretary, treasurer, competition director, and chief steward). Punshon also suggested that regions be limited to one delegate on the national executive, to 'avoid undue bias being imposed upon the national scene by the larger Regions.'[14] Whether he realized and intended it or not, Punshon had designed a federal system. The national committee approved the plan in principle, and directed Quebec and Ontario clubs to establish regions on an experimental basis to test its viability. In February 1958 the division of responsibility was amended slightly to clarify national and regional roles in licensing and permits. Regional representation at national meetings was also increased to two delegates, to ensure attendance. By May, both the Quebec and Ontario regions were fully operational, and at the AGM in December a Western (Prairie) region was formed. The AGM decided that a minimum of three clubs, with at least twenty members each, was required to constitute a region. As a result, the only affiliated club in the Maritimes at that time – the ASCC – was assigned temporarily to the Quebec region.[15] The Atlantic and BC regions were not created until 1963. Until then, the CASC was a national organization in name only; its power was concentrated in Quebec and Ontario, and their agendas drove the sport.

The late formation of the BC region was not for lack of clubs or activity. Canadian sports car racing had revived first in BC after the war, and it was the SCCBC that built Canada's first real road course: Westwood. And so it was not a question of capabilities; it was all about attitudes. Former SCCBC president Bob Randall put it bluntly: 'As far as sport on the West Coast is concerned it's north and south, not east and west.'[16] He was not being merely parochial; he was stating a reality based on the simple facts of geography. The mountains and the coast *defined* BC's identity and shaped its outlook, in auto sport as in everything else. The SCCBC was already affiliated to a regional auto sport association. The fact of the matter was that the CASC needed the BC clubs more than they needed the CASC. To be recognized by the FIA as Canada's auto sport authority, the CASC *had* to be national. Thus, a courtship was both inevitable and necessary. But the CASC's leaders had no idea how difficult it was going to be.

The process began in November 1955 when the CASC directed the chairman to contact the Vancouver Motor Club, at that time the only BC club affiliated to the CASC, to urge it to form a western regional centre. But that and subsequent letters yielded no response. And so in January 1957 Burt Punshon wrote to the SCCBC, stating, 'We would welcome – that is the understatement of the week – the setting up of a West Coast region of CASC, and there is obviously no other Club than your own which could possibly be expected to lay the foundation of such an organisation.' Punshon emphasized that the BC clubs would not jeopardize their autonomy by joining the CASC, since the region would govern its own competition. The CASC, he pointed out, 'has always been, and will continue to be a thoroughly democratic organisation whose only object is the development of the Sport, and the fostering of coordination and closer ties ... That's where we are going. Won't you come too?'[17]

In some respects Punshon's assurances on regional autonomy were premature, since the CASC had not yet finalized the exact terms of reference for regions. His appeal, in any case, apparently elicited no response. The following year, he wrote again, noting wistfully, 'We have never quite been able to understand why you have remained aloof.'[18]

Punshon's efforts finally yielded an answer, although not the one he sought. In his reply SCCBC club secretary Robert Sayle praised the CASC for its service to the sport, but went on to explain: 'It is only the geographical distances that make it difficult for us to associate with you in full ... This club has associated with the Northwest Conference ... In joining this we are simply being practical because our chaps race a lot down there and we rely on their competitors coming up here.'[19] He had put his finger on the nub of the matter: geography. For BC enthusiasts, it was easier to compete in Washington than in Alberta, let alone in the rest of Canada. So the SCCBC had joined the International Conference of Northwest Sports Car Clubs (ICNSCC). Formed in 1957, it comprised clubs from Alaska, Idaho, Washington, Oregon, and BC. Sayle proposed that the SCCBC affiliate with the CASC on an 'associate' basis; in return for paying a modest fee it would represent the CASC in the province. But he rejected any CASC control of their events.[20] Punshon hastened to assure them that the national body had not asked for that. 'It has not been, and will not be our intention to interfere in any way with the manner in which our member clubs conduct their events ... unless they are national or International when the existing F.I.A. rules and classifications have to apply.'[21] He suggested that the SCCBC consider dual affiliation: to the CASC and the ICNSCC. Finally, he hinted that the CASC might be willing to subsidize the travel costs for a BC delegate to attend national meetings. Despite this and the fulsome praise Punshon heaped upon the BC club, the discussions effectively ended there, and the issue remained unresolved for another five years.

While a regional structure made administrative sense for the CASC, it solved one problem while creating another. The regions soon became more influential than the clubs whose interests they were supposed to represent. This eventually changed the character of the CASC from an association of clubs to one of regions. The kind of 'bottom-up' democracy that the clubs represented was gradually supplanted by a 'top-down' approach wherein the national body tried to impose its will on and through the regions.

The Rule-Makers

In the meantime, the CASC had recognized at an early stage the need to regulate the sport to keep it safe and fair. That imposed changes on the structure of the organization itself. The first was the appointment in 1953 of a competition chairman (Fred Mallard being the first), whose initial task was to adapt the RAC's General Competition Rules (GCR) to Canadian conditions.

But it was during Bob Evis's tenure – he served for nearly four years – that the CASC made the greatest strides towards professionalizing the sport in the 1950s. Under his direction, the CASC formed the competition committee, which by 1957 was responsible for event permits and results, insurance, and the issuing of more than 1100 licences and for supervising the board of stewards. The latter was a major task, as a steward had to be present at every event and had to submit a report on it. By the second half of the decade, this meant collating reports on dozens of events each year. The committee also heard appeals and protests arising from events. In February 1957, about a year after taking up his post, Evis warned the CASC executive that his committee actually had no authority to make rules or changes, which seriously hampered its work. The executive then amended the constitution to read that 'the Competition Board is empowered to interpret standing rules and regulations and to introduce further standing rules and regulations.'[22]

The following year, the chairman's position was re-titled director of the competition department, but more important, in recognition of the expanding nature of the position, it was redefined. The director was to be responsible for coordinating, reporting on, and maintaining detailed records of all competition matters. By the 1958 AGM Evis had more than sixty people working for the competition board, and had formed a committee to codify regulations. In 1959 that committee expanded, and the duties and powers of the national chief steward were clarified. These included calling meetings of a board of referees, keeping a roster of national and regional stewards, appointing them to supervise all national events, enforcing all rules and regulations made by the rules committee, imposing discipline in general, and handling national level appeals. The paperwork and meetings this generated really demanded a full-time staff, not volunteers. By the end of that year, the work of coordinating all of this had overwhelmed Evis and he resigned, to be succeeded by Al Sands.[23] But Evis's legacy was a professional structure to oversee the sport.

The CASC did not make rules for their own sake; they were supposed to ensure fair competition. In theory, the simplest way to achieve that was to regulate car classifications and modifications, so that all cars would compete against other cars of similar characteristics and performance capabilities. In practice, creating and applying a standard of classes and modifications proved far more difficult. Broadly speaking, the FIA grouped cars by type, then by engine displacement. As of 1958, it recognized five types of cars (apart from open-wheel formula cars) and nine engine displacement classes: first, series production touring cars (sedans) – e.g., Volkswagen; second, 'Grand Touring' (GT) limited-production high performance sports cars – e.g., Ferrari coupe; third, special-series production touring cars (performance modified by manufacturer or owner) – e.g., MGA Twin-Cam; fourth, series production sports cars – e.g., Triumph TR3; and finally, limited-production sports cars modified according to specific FIA rules – e.g., Lotus XI. Within these groups, engine displacement classes ranged from A (eight litres) to I (350–500 cc). In addition, the FIA had approved 'Performance' classes, which could be applied to production sports cars competing in any non–International Calendar events. Originally developed by the SCCA, these classes grouped together cars with similar performance capabilities (e.g., power-to-weight ratio) rather than by engine displacement. They were arranged in decsending order from the most to the least powerful. Class B included the Corvette, the Ferrari Berlinetta and California, and the Aston Martin DB4. Class H had the Fiat Abarth 750 GT Coupe and the stock Austin-Healey Sprite.[24]

The FIA also permitted national bodies to modify the rules to suit local conditions. The CASC had interpreted this to allow the establishment of several special car classes unique to Canada. The first, established in 1958, was 'Canada Class,' a category created for racers who wanted to design and build their own open-wheel racing cars. The second was 'Modified Production,' created the following year. It had arisen out the need to end disputes over what constituted production and modified cars. The FIA rules notwithstanding, the definition of what was (or was not) a production car was quite unclear and controversial, and when the CASC had tried to settle the issue in 1955 the debate was so heated that the matter had to be put aside. So the category was left open, the source of endless post-race protests. The rules for Modified Production specified that it could be a touring, GT, or sports car, in which anything could be modified except the original chassis, engine block, transmission, axle housings, and external appearance. This class was meant to accommodate innovators like Bill Sadler and other racers who just liked to tinker with their cars. As Bill Brack said, 'Part of the whole thing that I really enjoyed about racing was ... the things you could do to the car to make it better than the next guy's car.'[25]

It was one thing for the FIA and the CASC to write the rules; it was quite another thing to enforce them. Club race organizers adapted rules to suit local conditions. The result was a patchwork application of improvised class rules. In July 1958, for example, the BEMC's 8th annual sports car races at Harewood had classes for Formula Libre (undefined in Canadian rules), Formula 3 (a one-litre entry-level class), and Canada class. Production MGs and a separate class of MG T-series cars had their own race, as did 'Century Class,' which was not defined in the rules but was used in Ontario Region for cars capable of reaching 100 mph. This included Austin-Healey 100s, Triumphs, Jag XK120s, Porsche 1500s, and Morgans, which under FIA rules would not normally compete against each other. Finally, there were races for production sports cars, for modifieds, and for touring cars listed as 'Not Necessarily Production' – a classification left unexplained. By contrast, the SCCS used only the FIA displacement classes for its races at Davidson airport in May 1960. The SCCBC initially used the ICNSCC class rules, an amalgam of FIA and local rules with three broad classes: production, modified, and unrestricted sports cars. The production-car class rules were almost identical to those of the FIA/CASC, and their group classifications were similar to the SCCA performance classes, but they included sedans as production *sports* cars. By 1960, however, the club apparently was using the FIA displacement classes (A–I) for its races.[26]

The problem with this uneven application of class rules was twofold.

First, car design and performance was not static; cars changed and improved from year to year, even if they retained the same engine specifications. Arguing the case for performance-based classes, Al Sands pointed out that having two cars with the same engine displacement did not guarantee equal performance: 'To quote our Secretary, "A driver is able to buy his roses." A driver in a given class can offset a driving deficiency with money ... [and] buy a faster car. Is it fair for the average enthusiast to flog his MG 1500 or 1600cc against cars costing twice as much but having the same engine displacement that are able to "walk away" from him?'[27] Second, a racer competing in different provinces could not be certain that his/her car would compete against exactly the same types of cars in every event. This conferred an unfair advantage on some drivers and cars and almost certainly guaranteed post-race protests. Nevertheless, the car-class rules issue remained unresolved and subject to constant tinkering well into the next decade.

Playing It Safe

'It scares me to death to think of the chances we took,' Bob Hanna recalled about racing in the 1950s. The racer and CASC executive director, who later represented K & K Insurance (which insures major auto sport events in Canada), went on to add, 'No crash helmets, roll bars, no seat belts – just hop in the car and race it.'[28] But that was the norm. Racers often competed in short sleeve shirts and slacks – there were no fireproof racing suits – and with no more head protection than a polo helmet, if that. It was this 'devil-may-care' attitude that Callwood had decried in the wake of Pope's death.

Even so, from the outset Canadian race organizers and the CASC were forced to take safety seriously. They introduced and enforced regulations to protect both racers and spectators. The CASC discussed driver safety equipment first in 1954, and the following year decided that safety belts and helmets would be required for all 'speed events' (races, sprints, hill climbs, and gymkhanas). However, some competitors simply ignored the ruling, so in 1956 several Montreal area racers asked for a new ruling to enforce the use of safety belts for all races. Three years later, however, the rules still were being flouted; so Quebec Region introduced motions at the national AGM to make roll bars (for open cars) and the wearing of crash helmets mandatory for all speed events. In response, the CASC struck a safety committee in 1960 under Al Sands to study the issues and make recommendations. The committee ruled that roll bars and quick-release safety belts were required for all open and removable-hard-top cars taking part in speed events on a race track. It also reaffirmed the mandatory use of crash helmets in all speed events. The Bell company had introduced the first helmet designed specifically for car racing in 1954. Two years later, after American racing driver Charlie Snell died of head injuries, the Snell Foundation was established to test and set standards for race helmets. The SCCA decided in 1958 that only those helmets recommended by Snell would be accepted in their races. In 1960 the CASC followed the SCCA's lead; drivers of open and removable-hard-top cars could wear only those helmets approved by Snell or the British Standards Institute.[29] Today, 'Snell Approved' is the certification standard for helmets throughout the sport.

Yet in spite of Purdy's and Pope's deaths, there still was some opposition to the CASC's rulings. The lack of enforced standard specifications for roll bars only made the problem worse; usually they were not high enough or strong enough to protect the driver properly during a high-speed rollover. Some racers complained about the cost of installing them and the depreciation effect on the resale value of their cars.[30] Nevertheless, the ruling gave scrutineers the power to decide whether a car would be allowed on the track. Adequate or not, roll bars were in and, on balance, drivers were safer for it.

Canadian racing also got an early reminder that drivers were not the only ones who needed protection. On 27 August 1955, during an OLCC race at Carp airport near Ottawa, a Morris Minor special, driven by novice Vic Stiles, went out of control when its steering failed. The car ploughed into a crowd of spectators, killing two and injuring eleven more, including Les Stanley. Stiles himself survived the crash without injury – he *was* wearing a crash helmet and seat belts. The spectators had been warned to stay well back, but were standing only about ten feet from the edge of the track. Without a fence between them and the track, they were totally unprotected.[31]

The FIA's International Sporting Code delegated the authority to control auto sport within a country to each national body, which would draft or adopt a set of rules (subject to approval by the FIA). Lacking at the time the authority of an FIA-sanctioned body, the CASC had started adapting the RAC's GCRs for use in Canada. These rules specified minimum safe distances for spectators at race tracks: forty feet from the track along straights, and one hundred feet at corners (unless protected by a substantial barrier, ditch, or hill). Since the

CASC had not completed the redrafting of the GCRs by 1955, however, it is unlikely that the OLCC was aware of this standard. Still, like the daredevil attitude of the racers themselves, such a laissez-faire approach to rules, and to crowd control in general, was quite common at the time. During the early SCCA road races at Bridgehampton, Elkhart Lake, and Watkins Glen, crowds stood right on the edge of the circuits. In response to the tragedy at Carp, the CASC quickly issued new rules for the control of races. These confined spectators to a designated area of the infield, restricted their access to other areas, and kept them at least one hundred feet from the edge of the track. The rules specified that a 'medical officer' and an ambulance be present. Finally, they made scrutineering (technical inspection) of racing cars mandatory prior to practice on the track, with particular emphasis on the security and strength of vital components, such as steering, brakes, and wheels. Even so, for legal reasons (undoubtedly related to concerns about liability) the federal Department of Transport decided in 1956 not to permit any further racing at Carp airport, and indicated that this prohibition would apply to all airports under its jurisdiction.[32] But at those airport circuits where racing continued into the 1960s, spectator restraint and protection remained no more substantial than a thin line of wooden snow fencing – which was virtually no protection at all.

Control of every aspect of a race event rested on the shoulders of volunteers, amateurs all and most without any formal training. They gained the necessary skills through trial and error experience. As some early race reports indicated, the standards of efficiency and effectiveness sometimes were inadequate. This included the work of the marshals, who were responsible for on-track safety, in particular, for the system of coloured flags used to warn the drivers of problems and danger on the track. By 1958 the CASC rules committee had become convinced that the quality of marshalling had to be improved. It instituted a course to train and certify marshals in the use of the flags, fire extinguishers, emergency first aid, and communications equipment, all of which would be required at each race track corner. The following year a group of marshals formed the Canadian Race Communications Association (CRCA), consisting of CASC-accredited marshals, whose purpose was 'to provide a marshalling and communications service, and to promote safety at all C.A.S.C. sanctioned SPEED EVENTS.'[33] These initiatives went a long way to standardize and improve race control, safety, and rescue procedures at the race tracks.

The CASC also tried to make racing safer by controlling the on-track behaviour of drivers through regulations and licensing. The process of adapting the RAC's GCRs to Canadian use took much longer than expected, and so in 1957 the rules committee was established to draft standing regulations for each type of event. The CASC's first yearbook, published for the 1958 season, contained a compendium of the approved rules. It stated unambiguously that safety was the highest priority in organizing auto sport events, not least because '[t]he future of motor sport depends upon its safety record. It is the duty of all organizers to ensure that every possible precaution for the safety of spectators, drivers and officials has been taken.'[34] It devoted more than twenty pages to detailed safety rules, as well as explaining the duties of stewards at competition events, laying out procedures for timing and scoring and the requirements for organizing permits, racing licences, waivers, and insurance. Except with regard to racing licences, the yearbook did not specify any penalties for failure to follow the rules. Apparently some chose to exploit that gap, so the following year the CASC decided to impose fines on clubs that did so. During the discussion of disciplinary action, the CASC executive emphasized that 'the whole organization of C.A.S.C. is based upon the declared willingness of member clubs to be bound by Rules and Regs. established by the National Committee ... *All* C.A.S.C. Rules and Regs ... are binding until they are either rescinded or superceded.'[35]

Of all the regulatory issues, licensing proved to be the most complex and controversial. The CASC decided in 1952 to develop a licensing system for competitors, and the following year it copied the RAC system and instituted a novice licence for new race drivers. No skill test was involved; all that was required was a valid driver's licence. The awarding of a full licence was to be at the discretion of the CASC competition committee, an arbitrary system that the committee tried to refine further. It decided that licences subject to annual renewal would be required for all speed events, and a competition record would be kept for each competitor. It also established procedures for suspension and appeal. In 1956, then, Bob Evis proposed a 'graded' licensing system with novice, intermediate, and senior levels. A medical certificate would also be required for all competitors. To obtain a novice licence an applicant had to produce a certificate of good health and fitness, pass a colour-blindness test (to ensure flag recognition), and sign a statement that he/she had read the RAC/CASC rules. This licence would allow a novice to gain experience in competition. After competing in two speed events (one of which had to be a track race) and two long-distance rallies, or in four races – without being criticized by marshals or organizers – the novice could be awarded an intermediate licence, valid for all national events. Finally, a senior licence could be awarded to the few competitors 'who have had an impressive competition career and have proven themselves to be sportsmen of a high calibre.'[36]

Evis's proposal was discussed at length in November 1956 and sent back for revision, but the issue was not settled until the end of 1960, when a simplified three-stage system was finally approved. Under this scheme there would be a basic licence for all events (including novice races), a national licence good for all events in Canada beyond the novice level, and an FIA licence, required for all Canadian, SCCA, or FIA-sanctioned international speed events held in Canada.[37]

At the same time, efforts were under way to improve the racing skills of new drivers. Until the late 1950s, racers were essentially self-taught, learning by 'the seat of their pants.' But if the graded licences were to have any meaning, the CASC needed a way to determine whether a driver was qualified for a higher licence. And so in 1958, at the Harewood circuit, the nascent CRDA ran the first racing drivers' school, which became an annual event. Seventy drivers attended the April 1960 course, where they learned cornering and braking techniques, gridding procedures, and Le Mans starts (where drivers run to their cars), then practised what they had learned in a series of short races. Experienced Canadian drivers like Bill Sadler, Jerry Polivka, Fred Hayes, and Bryan Rowntree served as instructors for the CRDA courses. Occasionally, well-known American drivers such as George Constantine served as instructors. The idea caught on quickly; the Ontario and Quebec Regions quickly established their own schools. The national executive was impressed with the concept, and by 1961 attending a racing school had become one of the requirements for a national licence, the others being participation in a club or novice race and successful completion of a written exam on flags and CASC competition rules.[38] From this point on, *all* Canadian racers would at least start with a similar basic standard of training. How much further they developed would depend largely on their individual talent and effort.

Mission Accomplished?

All of these decisions and regulations were intended to improve racing safety and to ensure fair competition, but collectively they represented something more. First, they were the most practical demonstrations – and tests – of the CASC's authority as the governing body of the sport. Although the CASC drew its authority from the clubs, it had to be able to show that it could enforce its writs over them. Ultimately, it passed the test, but not without encountering some resistance from certain clubs and from individual competitors. As later chapters will show, these were not the last challenges to the CASC's authority from within. Second, the increased regulation of the sport represented a change in its character. The efforts to standardize car classification, safety, and licensing illustrate this clearly. Step by step, rule by rule, the CASC was moving Canadian auto sport away from unregulated amateurism and towards regulated professionalism. Ironically, at this very point, when the CASC had proved its ability to govern the sport through regulation, a competing trend – 'commercial professionalism' – had begun to emerge from within, and almost immediately it encroached upon and challenged the CASC's control of auto sport.

5 Powershift: The Rise of Commercial Professionalism

Clubs just cannot expect to draw competitors with good equipment to come a great distance, race their cars and return home with only the prospect of a silver cup for their efforts. There are now a number of good professional races being staged in the U.S. ... over better courses than those found here. Why then remain an amateur?

Fred Hayes[1]

The CRDA's Pro Races, 1959–1960

In the brilliant sunshine the line of colourful cars, parked side-by-side for the Le Mans start, stretches as far as the eye can see. The silver and red Gorries-sponsored Corvette is in the foreground, but most of the entries are British sports cars – Triumphs, MGs, and Austin-Healeys. There are a handful of 'specials': built-to-purpose race-only cars. In the background, across the wide tarmac of the Harewood airport circuit, the crowd of 10,000 – huge by the standards of the day – waits expectantly for the start. It is May 1959, and they are about to witness a 'first' in Canada: a 'professional' sports car race, *for money*.

The CRDA, barely a year old, staged the 135-lap, 500-km event. Ray Carter and Craig Hill won the race, sharing the drive in a Jaguar XKSS. The CRDA paid out almost $4000 in prize money, refunded the drivers' entry fees, and banked a 'tidy profit.' The following year it attracted a brewery as the major sponsor, renamed the race the Carling 300, spent over $30,000, increased the purse to $6000, and brought in some international racing 'stars,' including European Formula One driver Olivier Gendebien and a promising young American, Roger

Penske. This time the main event was run as a 'Formula Libre' ('unrestricted') race, which pitted open-wheel formula cars against closed-wheel sports-racing cars. The starters included Carter's Jag, Peter Murdoch's Formula One Connaught, the Sadler specials of Bill Sadler and Dave Greenblatt, Harry Entwhistle and Jerry Polivka in Lotuses, and the Porsche RS's of Penske, Gendebien, Francis Bradley, Jim Muzzin, and a relatively unknown but impressive young Canadian, Peter Ryan. The record crowd of 14,500 witnessed some fine racing, with Ryan challenging Penske for a virtual 'photo finish' in the final heat. The day belonged to Porsche; Penske was the winner, with Ryan second and Gendebien third. The Belgian driver was sufficiently impressed to tell CRDA president Tom Gilmour, 'Get your event on the international calendar now ... I will tell my friends to come with me next year.'[2]

These two races were significant, because they pointed the way to the future of racing in Canada. First, in the 1960 race, specialized racing cars dominated the feature event. Production sports cars and sedans – the staple of Canadian racing through the first decade – were relegated to the supporting races. Second, Canadian racing had 'matured' to the point where it could attract international drivers and draw a bigger crowd than the 'local heroes' could on their own. Finally, the big-name racers with the best cars *would* come, *if* they could 'run for money.' That required commercial sponsorship. In short, racing had begun to serve new and different purposes: audience entertainment and sponsor promotion. And the money involved raised a tantalizing prospect – that competitors and others might earn a living from it, rather than just gaining some personal satisfaction. Pushed towards 'commercial professionalism' by the CRDA, Canadian racing was becoming a business, and that changed and raised the stakes. Once racing involved money, it was never the same again.

Together these facts raised a fundamental question: Who is racing for? This question initiated a debate about the purpose of the sport and posed a dilemma for the CASC. On the one hand, the CRDA races fulfilled part of the founders' vision: making Canadian racing 'world class' by bringing top international racers to Canada. On the other, the CASC was committed to *amateur* auto sport. Moreover, the CASC was an association of clubs made up of amateur competitors, organizers, and enthusiasts. Commercial professionalism could marginalize the clubs, undercutting the CASC's power base. For the next thirty years, the CASC wrestled with the task of squaring the amateur/professional/ commercial circle. It never fully resolved the problem, which eventually tore the organization apart. In the meantime, as far as the CRDA was concerned, the 'Run What Ya Brung' era was a thing of the past.

Runnin' for Money: The American Experience

The commercial professionalism movement had both international and local roots. At this time few racers could earn a living from the sport; even Formula One 'stars' like Stirling Moss had to supplement their meagre race winnings with a 'day job' and product endorsements. However, the NASCAR example suggested that a racing career was feasible, given proper organization and commercial sponsorship. NASCAR *made* money – for racers and promoters alike. That lesson was not lost upon American sports car racers. The pro-am debate emerged within the SCCA as early as 1951 and continued for more than a decade. Throughout the 1950s the SCCA stuck resolutely to its 'amateur-only' policy, and revoked the licences of members who competed in races for money.

But the best American drivers, including Carroll Shelby, Phil Hill, and Masten Gregory, defied the ban, raced in Europe – where there was prize money, albeit in small amounts – and lobbied hard for professional racing. Even in the United States, major team owners like Briggs Cunningham paid their 'amateur' drivers 'under the table,' and the SCCA, which could not afford to alienate such big names, was forced to look the other way. The rival United States Auto Club (USAC) – which ran the lucrative Indy 500 – began to organize road-racing events and offered cash prizes (in 1959 the USAC sports car series awards totalled $100,000). The first USAC race at Lime Rock, Connecticut in September 1958 drew 7000 spectators and offered a purse of $2750. One month later the USAC and the FIA sanctioned a Grand Prix for sports cars at the new track at Riverside, California, with the Times-Mirror Corporation as the sponsor and promoter. The race attracted 70,000 spectators, fulfilling the prediction of John Fitch (former racer turned Lime Rock track manager): 'Road racing in the United States, released from the suffocating hobble of amateurism, will now take its rightful place as a major spectator sport.'[3]

The tide was running against the SCCA. To survive as the governing body of sports car racing in the US, it had to adapt to the changing currents in the sport. Beginning in 1959, it changed its policy by stages, gradually allowing its members to race in pro events without penalty, and eventually launched its own pro-racing series, the US Road Racing Championship, in the 1960s. The SCCA continued to run amateur racing at the club level, but it had grudgingly accepted that commercial professionalism was part of auto sport.[4]

The CRDA and the Auto Sport Entrepreneurs

Developments south of the border did not go unnoticed in Canada. In the fall of 1957, a group of about twenty Canadian drivers who had been racing in semi-professional events in the United States discussed the idea of forming an association of racing drivers 'to promote international racing in Canada and to improve the quality of Canadian racing and Canadian drivers.'[5] In January 1958 they met at the Toronto home of Tom Gilmour and founded the CRDA. Its founders included many of the best racers in eastern Canada: Gilmour, Bradley, Peter and Fred Hayes, Bryan Rowntree, Jim Fergusson, and Bob Hanna. As Bradley recalls, they decided that 'it would be a good idea to get a little professionalism in the sport ... to get sponsorship, to get money into the sport.'[6]

So why were these men pushing commercial professionalism? In his study of American drag racing, sociologist H.F. Moorhouse identified several layers of participants, each with their own interests and agendas. At the centre there are both amateur and professional enthusiasts. The former see themselves as upholding the 'core values' of the sport, while the latter include competitors and others who are trying to make a living from the sport. Beyond the centre are the 'interested public' – individuals, businesses, the media, and others who seek something from it. Over time, people move between these layers and categories, playing different roles in the sport.[7] Some of the CRDA's founders, who would shape the destiny of the sport in Canada, acted in just that fashion. They were auto sport *entrepreneurs*, that is, both competitors *and* businessmen. Most were sports- or imported-car dealers; others were suppliers of 'aftermarket' performance parts. They used their businesses as a way to get into the sport, competing themselves and/or sponsoring others, and they used the sport to promote their businesses. Some became quite influential at the highest levels of Canadian auto sport.

Jim Fergusson was typical of the enthusiast entrepreneurs of the early period. He owned a sports car dealership: Jim Fergusson Motors. Round of face and form, with moustache, glasses, and trademark bow tie, he was not only one of the founders of the CRDA, but also a fixture at CASC meetings. Fergusson was a regular columnist in the early issues of *Track and Traffic*, and an advertiser in the CASC's yearbook. He raced, rallied, and sponsored cars and drivers, such as Ed Leavens and Bryan Rowntree, with enviable success. Len Coates writes: 'They say if Jim Fergusson was managing your team in a long-distance race, there was little else to do but listen carefully to everything he told you, then show up to collect the awards.'[8]

Fergusson was hardly unique. Dick Shelton, co-owner of Shelton-Mansell Motors in the Toronto suburbs of Willowdale and Richmond Hill, was a sponsor and competitor in the late 1950s and early 1960s. He was a member of the CRDA and was CASC competition chairman from 1963 to 1967, when the Can-Am series and the Canadian Grand Prix for Formula One were established. Burke Seitz, son of the owner of Gorries Downtown Chevrolet in Toronto, raced and rallied frequently. Known as 'Canada's Corvette Headquarters,' Gorries sponsored Leavens and Greenblatt driving their Corvettes and then Sadler and Greenblatt in the Corvette-engined Sadler specials. The Montreal area had its share of sponsor/competitors. Louis O'Neill of Automobiles Renault was an active racer and later the manager of the successful factory-sponsored Renault rally team. Alec Budd of Budd and Dyer Ltd – importer and distributor of Jaguar and Alfa Romeo – was a rallyist and a sponsor. Les Barrell was both a competitor and a dealer/sponsor. Ross Brander, owner of The Pit Stop – an 'aftermarket' sports car accessories shop – was active as a competitor and as both a CASC Quebec Region and national director. Peter Broeker – racer, racing car builder, and founder of the Stebro performance exhaust company – explicitly linked his racing and his business, saying, 'I am in racing to promote my product.'[9]

Yet none of them had the lasting influence on Canadian auto sport of Bob Hanna. The slight and slender redhead with the serious demeanour started his auto-industry career as a partner in a 'speed shop' in Cooksville, Ontario. Later he became the national service manager for Canadian Motor Industries, the Toyota importer and rally team sponsor. A racer since the early 1950s, Hanna made his mark as an organizer. As a member of the BEMC, he was instrumental in building the Harewood track. He was also one of the founders of the CRDA, serving as its president in 1967. The following year he was appointed the first executive director of the CASC, holding the full-time position until 1985. In that capacity Bob Hanna became the most powerful man in Canadian auto sport. After his official role in the sport came to an end, his career fit Moorhouse's 'model'; he moved to the outer layer, remaining active in the sport through K & K Insurance. Throughout his auto sport career Hanna's was a strong voice in favour of commercial professionalism, which he was instrumental in bringing about.[10]

'Win on Sunday, Sell on Monday'

This symbiotic relationship between competition and commerce in auto sport was neither new nor unique to Canada. As noted earlier, it had existed from the very start of the sport in Europe. By the mid-1950s, convinced that victory in stock-car and drag racing sold cars, the Big Three had adopted the slogan 'Race on Sunday, Sell on Monday.'[11] Anecdotal evidence seemed to support that proposition in sports car competition as well. MG and Jaguar used their success in competition to enhance the reputation of their cars and thus to increase sales. In her *Maclean's* article, June Callwood claimed that when Ed Leavens won a race driving an MG at Sebring, Florida, on a Saturday in 1957, Toronto dealers sold thirteen MGs on Monday. The next year, she says, 'when an Austin A-40 won the Winter Rally ... the sales of Austins jumped forty-five percent the following month. 'That's not coincidence,' remarked British Motor Corporation's Ian Paterson.'[12] However, Martin Chenhall, racer and former director of GM Canada's motorsport program, cautions that it has always been hard to measure any direct relationship between racing and sales, because there are so many other factors at work in the car market. Indeed, economists have found it difficult to establish a clear cause-and-effect link between advertising, sponsorship, increased sales, and profits.[13] However, there was obviously enough profit to convince some businesses that it was worthwhile sponsoring auto sport activities. On the other hand, it might be argued that by supporting auto sport the car industry was simply 'reclaiming' from the amateurs the sport it had created.

Few of the Canadian auto sport entrepreneurs were as explicit about the racing/sales linkage as was Peter Broeker. But they undoubtedly could see the marketing opportunities the sport offered through visibility at the track, via ads in *Track and Traffic*, and by word of mouth. The interlocking roles they played as competitors, sponsors, and sport officials make it easy to conclude that many of them favoured professionalizing the sport purely for their own commercial benefit.

Yet it probably would be a mistake to overstate this matter. For the most part, these men ran small businesses in a limited market. They weren't likely to get rich selling only to other auto sport enthusiasts. Except for a bigger firm like Gorries, where the sale of one or two Corvettes might cover their sponsor costs for a season, the financial returns on sponsorship probably would be small. Thus, profit alone cannot explain or justify the commitment of time and money that participating in the sport demanded of these men, even at the amateur level. In short, we must acknowledge that they were enthusiasts themselves. It's one thing to be a passive sponsor, merely supporting someone else's racing; it's quite another to be a competitor as well. For Jim Fergusson and others like him, being in the car business provided an entry into an activity *they* wanted to do *for themselves* anyway. Racing, it is said, 'is not a profession; it's an obsession.'[14] Eventually, commercial professional racing would make money and a living – for *somebody*; that much was clear. In the meantime, as Fred Hayes's chapter-opening quote suggests, what the CRDA racers wanted initially was much less – simply some return on the cost of competing.

Selling Professionalism

If pro racing was the CRDA's goal, however, it was carefully disguised in their constitution, which committed the club to promoting and encouraging Canadian sports car races, developing new racers, and advising race organizers. It did not mention prize money or sponsorship. In fact, it stated explicitly that the CRDA would 'operate entirely independently of any policy influence from manufacturers, dealers or others who might bias the operation of this organization.'[15] Since some of its founders and early members were intimately involved in the auto industry, however, that phrase appears somewhat disingenuous. The founders probably felt they had to insert it to ensure affiliation to the CASC. It was left to Gilmour and Hayes to explain the CRDA's position.

They fired their opening volley in the inaugural issue of *Canada Track and Traffic*. In the 'CRDA Report,' Gilmour laid out the group's vision of a 'first class' race event, which, he argued, required proper organizational procedures, strict adherence to the schedule, sufficient practice time, and a hard surface paddock (with enough space for tow vehicles and trailers) that was 'not liable to become a quagmire should the rains descend.'[16] Without saying so directly, he was criticizing the current, amateurish state of club racing. In that sense, his critique was also a broadside against the CASC itself. Furthermore, he made it clear that the CRDA ran things differently.

The staff of the magazine joined the debate in the same issue in an article entitled 'Is Professional Motorsport Here to Stay?' Not surprisingly, since *Canada Track and Traffic* earned its living from the auto sport business, they came down firmly on the side of commercial professionalism. The writers relied heavily on the views of Gilmour and Hayes, the only people quoted in their text. To their credit, they confronted the money issue head on, but in doing so they also had to examine the *purpose* of racing and who should run it. They pointed out that even for the amateur, the cost of racing was getting higher. This had brought the sport 'face to face with a serious dilemma: should it continue as a sport of the amateur enthusiast or should it be placed on a professional footing with prize money for winners?'[17]

Amateurs, they said, argued that by offering money to drivers 'the sport as such will be ruined ... [and] the sporting aspect of motor racing will be lost,' and that 'eventually motor racing would become nothing more or less than a commercial spectacle, in line with stock car racing.'[18] The voices for commercial professionalism asserted that offering prize money to bring the best racers and cars was the only way to develop the sport. Their reasoning was logical, if circular. The financial success of a race depends on spectators, but they will only come if they get value for money. 'This means putting on events with interesting cars and drivers who will provide the spectator with the thrills he expects ... How can we interest them – and interest them we have to if the sport is to grow – in coming out to racing events. There is only one way: provide them with a spectacle and make it attractive for them to attend.'[19] The authors were not concerned about attracting the enthusiast, who would attend anyway. Rather, they wanted to capture the non-enthusiasts whose presence would make the difference between financial success and failure. Unless they got their money's worth in the form of an exciting spectacle, however, they might never attend another race.

The recipe for success was simple: good cars, drivers, tracks, and organization. But since racing was becoming more expensive, the good drivers and cars would come only if some of their costs were covered. Furthermore, as noted earlier, the airport circuits were seen as completely inadequate, for racers and spectators. Finally, there was the organizational issue: 'If ... professional racing is a necessity, then the question of control becomes paramount. There has to be a strong national governing body which can exercise control and institute rules and regulations for the safety and benefit of the competitors and public alike.'[20] While acknowledging that this was the CASC's role, the writers questioned 'whether or not this body can exert the necessary authority ... At the moment, the C.A.S.C. is undergoing heavy criticism for lack of direction and initiative.'[21] The alternative, they pointed out, was the CRDA, which had already shown it could run a quality professional event (the 500-km race). They argued that Canadian racing would benefit from the entry of 'professional promoters': 'Putting on a good sports car race is an expensive business, and generally speaking the races organized by professionals are of a far higher calibre, both driving and spectator wise, than those put on by amateurs. They have to be if they are going to pay.'[22] The authors left the last word to Tom Gilmour, who issued a stern warning to the clubs: 'The only way in which clubs can successfully organize events is to run them on a competent business footing. It is no longer practical to rely on amateur unpaid labour for the highly technical functions so necessary to the success of an event.'[23]

The magazine also enlisted the authoritative voice of *the* international racing star of the day, Stirling Moss. Asked if he would race in Canada if there were a suitable circuit, he replied:

> Yes, I would ... if there was the competition. But you have to make it attractive to the driver ... If you run a sports car race with plenty of money behind you and at the right time of year, you could get the big drivers over for very little ... If people are going to pay to see racing then I think they ought to get their money's worth. They must see good racing and for this you've got to bring in good people. But they won't come unless it's attractive to do so.[24]

Apart from decrying amateurism and promoting professionalism, there were two themes running through this carefully orchestrated assault. The first was a not-so-thinly-disguised attack on the CASC. In what amounted to a 'warning shot across the bow,' the CRDA was issuing a direct challenge to its authority; if the national body did not 'get its act together,' and run racing 'properly,' the CRDA was prepared to take over national-level racing. The second theme went straight to 'the heart of the matter' – who is racing for? On this the CRDA and *Track and Traffic* were unanimous: races are mounted for the benefit of the *audience*. And what the audience wanted, in the CRDA's view, was a 'spectacle.' The implications were clear. Canadian racing had to offer the best cars and the best drivers, who would come only if there was a financial reward.

The CASC rose to the CRDA's challenge. In the next issue, competition chairman Bob Evis took issue with the notion, attributed by the *Track and Traffic* staff writers to Fred Hayes, that sports car clubs were fattening their bank accounts at the expense of the racers. Evis replied: 'Some drivers have been quoted as saying ... that it was about time that clubs with rich bank accounts shared some of the gravy with the drivers. The truth of the matter is that there are no rich clubs and there has been very little gravy.'[25] Evis went on to add that the clubs had long recognized that competing was expensive, and would like to be able to reimburse the racers, but their earnings so far were too small to be worthwhile. He also pointed out that many club members, who did not compete, voluntarily put in long hours to organize races, for which they received no recognition. He praised their dedication for making the sport a success and, in a dig at the pro-racing lobby, suggested that the real enthusiast would be 'more concerned with the success of his own club than with any personal glory he may accumulate.'[26]

But Evis then effectively disarmed the CASC's critics by agreeing with them. Without conceding that races ought to be 'spectacles,' he quoted them back to themselves. 'Worthwhile prize money must depend on the size of the gate and this in turn depends upon giving the public the type of event that will hold their interest and ensure their attendance at the next event.'[27] In effect, he lobbed the ball back into the CRDA's court, suggesting that – at least in part – it was up to *them* to provide the kind of racing that would draw a large audience. And on this matter the CRDA was open to criticism. In fact, there was a debate among CRDA members over that very issue.

The debate focused on 'endurance' races. Many of the better racers preferred long endurance races, because of the greater challenge they imposed on the car and the driver. By way of comparison, the feature race at the BEMC 1955 Indian Summer Trophy Races (held at Edenvale) had been only twenty laps; at the 1958 event – at the Harewood circuit – it lasted one hour. The following year the CRDA 500 was more than four hours long. The longest and toughest Canadian endurance race, by far, was the six-hour Sundown Grand Prix, launched in 1959 by the North Toronto Motorsport Club (NTMC). Considered Canada's 'little Le Mans,' it was a gruelling affair that started in daylight and ended in darkness; time took its toll on cars and drivers alike.[28]

But endurance racing did not appeal to all spectators, and making sure they came back and paid to watch races was at the heart of the CRDA's case. While the Carling 300 attracted nearly 15,000 people, the 1960 Sundown Grand Prix drew only 3000. In the first issue of *Canada Track and Traffic*, Stirling Moss was vehement on this point: 'Nobody wants to watch a six-hour race ... It's downright confusing to watch. To keep spectator interest you should keep the time of races down under four hours and have only one driver per car.'[29] He was not alone in his opinion. CRDA co-founder and future national champion Francis Bradley wrote:

> I may be sticking my neck out in saying that the majority of spectators get bored, lose interest and don't follow ... the races ... [but] looking at racing from the spectator angle, I'd suggest that the organizing clubs change their feature race to a 20 or 25 lap race in place of a 1-hour, 25 laps ... would hold the interest of the crowd far more than a 1-hour.[30]

John Hatch echoed Bradley's sentiments in a subsequent letter, noting:

> The '500' proved only one thing, that the public does not want to see long races. A large number of the record-breaking crowd left before the race was half over because there [sic] were fed up with watching a procession of cars going around and around the track ... The majority of spectators ... want to see ... as much excitement as possible, the type produced by short races with comparatively evenly matched cars competing with each other and not the clock.[31]

These criticisms did not deter the NTMC from running its 1960 Sundown Grand Prix for the full six hours. But the small audience turnout may have made the point just as well; the club did not run it again until 1964. The CRDA, by contrast, apparently got the message; the Carling 300 consisted of three 30-lap heats, interspersed with shorter supporting races. Subsequent major races, such as the Player's 200, followed that pattern.

The exact form of the sport aside, the CASC could hardly oppose pro racing. It had not objected when its competition chairman Fred Mallard announced in 1954 that he would be competing as a representative of the auto industry. To subsidize the costs of its yearbook, the CASC itself sold ad space to auto-industry firms.[32] And, of course, it had sanctioned the CRDA's first pro race. By 1960 dealer sponsors such as Gorries and Eglinton-Caledonia Motors were discreetly putting their names on the bodies of the cars they sponsored. That violated FIA rules, but the CASC chose to ignore those infractions. And so, little by little, the CASC had accepted these changes, which were transforming sports car competition in Canada – as elsewhere – from a sport into a business.

Powershift

In his address to the CASC's tenth anniversary AGM in December 1961, then president Jim Gunn highlighted the role of commercial sponsors:

> Interest by commercial organizations (and I think this is very significant) including automobile manufacturers ... has grown in one year from a very minor participation to a healthy and knowledgeable recognition that motorsport is here to stay. Their support is required for continued growth, and from all indications there will be greater commercial interest in the future. Oil companies, cigarette companies, press, radio, and television are all making an important contribution.[33]

However, it is not clear whether those involved with the issue understood its wider implications – that commercializing the sport inevitably would involve sharing *power* with business, and lead to a consequent loss of control over the sport. The CASC assumed it could exercise control through the regulation and sanctioning of events; the CRDA made a similar assumption, based on its ability to organize events and provide quality competitors. What neither group seems to have considered is that sponsoring major events actually put *business* 'in the driver's seat.' It was one thing for a car dealership to lend its name and a few dollars to a car or a team; it was quite another for a major corporation to invest tens of thousands (and later, millions) of dollars in a high-profile event. That was a business decision; if the event did not earn money for the firm, the company could leave, and the loss of a major sponsor could kill an event, as happened later to the Shell 4000 car rally. Likewise, keeping the sponsor satisfied and the money flowing meant allowing them to change events to suit their needs. In short, accepting commercial professionalism meant surrendering a degree of control over the sport.[34] However, this result was not immediately apparent in the early 1960s.

By contrast with the acrimonious battle south of the border, the CASC's embrace of commercial professionalism seems to have happened with relatively little internecine debate. So why was the Canadian situation different? While the CASC shared the SCCA's views about the inherent value of amateur sport, it was not so wedded to the ideal. After all, it did not share the SCCA's 'blue blood' social origins; in fact, it was very middle class. Its founders and those in the CRDA were businessmen as well as enthusiasts. For them, auto sport and the auto business were a natural fit, and their mutual benefit so obvious that it scarcely warranted comment. In fact, Peter Lighthall and Lawrence Bateman suggested that the CASC issue a policy statement to the effect that they saw 'no need in Canada for distinction between amateur and professional racing.'[35] Moreover, the CASC was well aware of the divisive impact of the pro-am debate within the SCCA. Perhaps recognizing the limits of its own authority and the relative weakness of the sport in Canada, the CASC was not prepared to divide it, and jeopardize its own leadership role, over the issue. In the end, everyone accepted that money would bring the best competitors to Canada. That, in turn, would open the doors for the best Canadians to rise to world status themselves. Even if they hadn't fully grasped the commercial implications, this was what the founders had intended for the sport.

PART TWO

Gathering Speed, 1961–1966

6 Behind the Wheel: Power Politics in the CASC

You cannot run ... CASC ... as a democratic organization. You have to run it as a benevolent dictatorship when it comes to dealing with professional aspects of the sport.

Milton J. Wright[1]

At six feet tall and two hundred and twenty-five pounds Milt Wright was one of the giants of Canadian auto sport, and more than in just physical stature. He was the CASC president during the turbulent mid-1960s, when Canada was breaking into professional international racing in a major way. As the quote above suggests, he put his stamp on the CASC during this period, asserting its leadership role, but not without some controversy. Wright had joined the BEMC in 1954 and was later involved with the Twin Lakes Motor Club and the Burlington Autosport Club. From 1957 to 1961 he raced a powerful Austin-Healey 3000 known as 'The Boomer,' and later the home-built 'Makins Special.' Wright was the CASC national racing chairman from 1962 to 1964 before becoming president by acclamation. Although officially he left the sport in 1968, he simply moved from its inner core to the outer layer. He continued to play an indirect role through Imperial Tobacco, whose Player's division was Canada's major auto sport sponsor.[2]

The major question during the first half of the 1960s was summed up in Wright's quote: Who *runs* Canadian auto sport? In short, the issue was *power*. At this time, the most serious challenge to the CASC's national authority came from within. The seeds of conflict had been sown with the creation of regions during the late 1950s. As the CASC continued to grow in the next decade, power shifted away from the clubs and their members, and there ensued a struggle for control of the sport between the regions and the national body.

From Sea to Sea

If Jim Gunn had accomplished nothing else during his four-year tenure as CASC president (1960–3), he still would be remembered for expanding it into a *national* organization. The number of member clubs more than tripled in that period, from thirty in 1959 to ninety-two in 1963. By the time Gunn stepped down, the CASC stretched from sea to sea.[3]

Creating a British Columbia region proved the most difficult task. Between 1960 and 1963, four BC clubs affiliated to the CASC. That was enough to form a region, but the SCCBC – the largest and most influential of the BC clubs – postponed its decision to join, delaying that final step. In the fall of 1961 Gunn and Doug Wilson (a CASC director who lived in BC) met with the SCCBC, who now indicated that they wished to affiliate to the national body. They did not, however, want to associate with the other BC clubs and or help to establish a CASC region, and so the negotiations stalled. The logjam finally was broken by Wilson and CASC general manager Don Stewart, who met with the BC clubs in 1962 and 1963, while Stewart was helping to organize the Shell 4000 (Trans-Canada) rally.[4] As he told the CASC in March 1963: 'It is obvious that interest in the Shell 4000 has contributed beyond any reasonable doubt more to motorsport in out-of-the-way areas than any other factor. Fortunately, the association of the C.A.S.C. with this event has resulted in much of this good will being bounced toward C.A.S.C.'[5] The rally persuaded the BC clubs to see their activities as part of something more than local. By drawing them in, it succeeded where the CASC had failed in eight years of trying. But the creation of a twelve-club BC region in 1963 made the CASC the rally's principal beneficiary.

By contrast, the clubs in the Maritimes had been only too eager to join the CASC. The Atlantic Region, comprising the ASCC, the St John's Motor Club, the Moncton Motor Sport Club (MMSC), and the New Brunswick Sporting Car Club (NBSCC), was formed in August 1963. By mid-decade, one more club – the UNBSCC – had joined them.[6] It was then, and remained, the smallest region in the CASC, but through sheer enthusiasm it was able to punch above its weight.

But when Gunn took office there still was one noticeable gap in the CASC ranks: Quebec francophone clubs. Anglo-Canadians and British and European immigrants dominated the sport in Quebec. Relatively few Quebecois had achieved a high profile there, the exceptions being Jean-Guy Pilon and Jacques Duval. These competitors tended to join the Anglo clubs, because that's all there was. And English was the language of the sport at that time. At the start of the decade, only one francophone club existed. The Club de Voitures Sport Cerf-Québec had been formed in Quebec City in 1959, but did not affiliate to the CASC until 1962. By the mid-1960s, the number of clubs had expanded to ten, a dramatic increase in a short period of time. Ironically, according to Jacques Duval, it was an Anglo – Norm Namerow – who was most influential in promoting racing among Quebecois. To encourage them, he even joined L'Association des Coureurs Automobile de Montréal (ACAM) upon its founding in 1963.[7] The growth of clubs and members in Quebec continued into the 1970s.

It is striking – and is probably no accident – that the 'explosion' of Quebecois auto sport in the 1960s coincided with that period of dramatic political, social, and economic change in Quebec known as the 'Quiet Revolution.' The same factors that drove the expansion of the car culture and auto sport elsewhere in Canada – urbanization and modernization – were rapidly reshaping the province.[8] But where the Anglo clubs were concentrated in the Montreal area, the francophone clubs emerged in the heartland of nationalist Quebec: the smaller cities, from Sherbrooke to Chicoutimi, Trois-Rivières to Rimouski. Nor is it a coincidence that auto sport in francophone Quebec experienced its greatest growth *after* the opening in 1964 of Le Circuit, the first purpose-built, permanent road-racing course in Quebec.[9] Having a first-class track in Quebec made all the difference. No more would francophone racers be limited to racing in Ontario. Nor would their fans, who flocked to Le Circuit in numbers never seen at St-Eugène. Enthusiasm for sports car racing may have come late to most Quebecois, but when they discovered it, they embraced it with a passion unmatched anywhere else in Canada. Embracing the Quebecois made the CASC truly *national*.

National Authority versus Regional Power

By 1960 the CASC had achieved another of the founders' major goals, affiliation to the FIA – albeit through Britain's RAC. This meant that the international governing body recognized the CASC as Canada's national auto sport authority. Reaching this goal had taken much longer than expected, simply because it took the CASC a long time to organize itself. For example, the constitution was not approved until 1960, and required further amendment before incorporation in 1964. The quest for FIA recognition had begun at the CASC's founding meeting. It was not until 1959, however, that the CASC had fulfilled two of the principal criteria required by the RAC: creation of a national organization with regional centres and appointment of a board of stewards to ensure standards and adjudicate disputes. When Dean Delamont, manager of the RAC's Competition Department, visited in late 1959 he said that the RAC was ready to recognize the CASC. In fact, it was prepared to support direct affiliation to the FIA. However, since this would have imposed high costs, such as affiliation fees and sending delegates to meetings in Paris, the CASC decided to affiliate through the RAC. The agreement was concluded in October 1960. Since the RAC sat on the all-important Commission Sportive Internationale (CSI), the CASC indirectly had a seat and a voice at the 'top table' of the FIA.[10]

Armed with a constitution and international recognition, the CASC endeavoured to assert its authority over its constituency. The constitution stated that the CASC was a federation of automobile clubs and other organizations. It was responsible for developing all aspects of auto sport, establishing and enforcing rules and regulations, and cooperating with other national and international auto sport bodies.[11] The by-laws defined the organization's structure and powers, providing for an elected board of directors and a national committee (including the president, vice-president, secretary, treasurer, competition director, and regional representatives), elections and terms of office, meetings and club representation for voting at meetings, dues, and discipline. The board was the supreme authority of the CASC, with the power to make or change rules and by-laws, appoint and approve the actions of committees, approve club affiliations, and conduct financial business. Since the membership was virtually identical, the national committee was, in effect, a subcommittee of the board, responsible for the ongoing administration of the CASC.[12]

With this power in mind, one of Al Sands's first initiatives as chair of the competition department had been to appoint separate chairs and committees for racing and rallying. This made sense, since both had grown considerably. Each was demanding increasing amounts of time from the department, which by 1962 consisted of the chairman, chairs for racing and rallying, the licensing registrar, the chief marshal, and the chief steward. Over the next two years it was expanded to include a secretary, a scorer, and a medical director, and was officially renamed the National Competition Board (NCB).[13] The NCB brought together in one body all the people with the national authority to oversee and regulate competition. Its clearly defined powers amounted to an all-encompassing and uncompromising statement of national authority:

> The Competitions Board shall authorize and supervise Club sports car events; make and construe rules for, and render decisions concerning them, grant, refuse, or withdraw licenses, approve and appoint officials, impose and remove penalties for violations of its Rules, establish standards of eligibility for participation in these competitions; establish rules for its own procedures; do any and all things which in its judgment are conducive to the well being of the conduct of motor sport events held under the sanction of the Canadian Automobile Sport Club.[14]

Nonetheless, the regions did not let this assertion of national authority go unchallenged. Based on the strength of their member clubs, they asserted their own power, and taxed the patience of the CASC. They demanded and got representation on the national board of directors. Finance was an ongoing bone of contention, as both the national and regional organizations felt that they needed more funds to run their activities properly. So long as funding came primarily from membership levies this conflict could not be solved, since the costs of running more and larger events and supporting the national organization rapidly outpaced the meagre revenues from clubs and regions.[15] While the money problem was never fully resolved, eventually it was alleviated by funding from sponsors.

The first major national versus regional dispute occurred in 1965. In January the NCB approved a change of date for the Player's Quebec race at Le Circuit in September. This caused a conflict with the Canadian Grand Prix for Sports Cars at Mosport, as the two races, which were intended to attract many of the same spectators, were now only a week apart. That might reduce the audience – and revenues – for both events. When it could not get the date changed, Ontario Region issued a bulletin and sent letters to the FIA and other international auto sport bodies stating that the national bulletin announcing the original date change was illegal. Furious, the national committee, meeting in May, censured the region's executive, stating that 'they willfully and knowingly acted contrary to ... the CASC National Constitution in corresponding directly with the SCCA, RAC, ACCUS and FIA and in a manner contrary to the best interests of Canadian Motorsport at the international, national, regional and club levels.'[16]

Prior to this dispute the national office had circulated a memo delineating the powers of the NCB and the regions as they pertained to authorizing and scheduling national and international events. After the May meeting the CASC issued a series of bulletins reminding race organizers and promoters, regions, clubs, and competitors that only the national committee had the authority to deal with other FIA-affiliated sanctioning bodies and also explaining the process for setting and amending the competition schedule. Ontario Region had no choice but to accept the date change, and the matter was closed. But they were proved right; the Mosport race suffered from poor attendance, which may well have resulted in part from the close proximity of the two events.[17] The first round had gone to national, but it was not the end of the sparring.

The following year the CASC felt it had to assert its authority once again. In August 1966 general manager Don Stewart issued a memo noting that clubs tended to forget that they had agreed to abide by the rules and regulations passed by the national body. 'In other words,' he wrote, 'the sport is run by CASC – not the individual clubs.' He added:

> It has been customary, in the past, to follow democratic principles and to encourage proposals and suggestions from the clubs. Unfortunately this policy has resulted in many decisions to the detriment of the sport generally, and the mistaken belief that the right to make changes rests solely within the Regions and the Clubs. It is my personal belief that democracy has been overdone. Both RAC and SCCA operate a mild form of dictatorship. It is evident that this is more successful.[18]

While the memo went out under Stewart's name, it summarized president Milt Wright's views exactly, and would not have been sent without his approval. Stewart followed up with a bulletin that, in gentler terms, reminded clubs that the regions were responsible for running the sport according to policies established by the NCB, and that 'authority is delegated from the top down through the various levels of our organization.'[19] The memos are significant because they clearly reversed the original philosophy of the CASC, which was one of 'bottom-up' democracy, the national organization deriving its authority from the clubs. At the 1966 AGM Wright endorsed this new approach, asserting that 'there is no strength in individual Members, individual Clubs or individual Regions, but rather only as a United National Body can we really move on.'[20]

These shifts in the locus of power – and the disputes that arose as a consequence – had occurred quite quickly. In part they were the result of the CASC's rapid growth and the changes the organization itself had initiated – such as the creation of regions – to cope with that growth. It could not continue to operate as if it was a small, informal gentlemen's club. International recognition imposed an obligation of professionalism in its approach to running the sport. The CASC had to become more 'business-like,' run 'top-down' rather than 'bottom-up.' Thus, among other things, it had opened a national office and appointed a full-time manager. Moreover, as the following chapters demonstrate, the sport itself was growing and changing, becoming more professional and more commercial. Races and rallies were becoming big, crowd-drawing, sponsored events. This, too, drove change in the organization and in its operating style. Since more was at stake, money in particular, decisions mattered more. And where decision-making power and money intersected, disputes were inevitable. The simple fact was that the sport and the CASC were outgrowing their roots. In the first half of the 1960s the sports car subculture was 'maturing' into something quite different – more than a hobby, but not yet a profession.

Second-Generation Racers

The changes at the top of Canadian auto sport accompanied changes at the grass roots. The first half of the 1960s saw the emergence of a new generation of racers: both drivers and cars. The influx of new drivers was the result of the growing popularity of the sport, while the new cars reflected shifting trends in automobile marketing and in racers' preferences.

The Weekend Warriors

As the 'Run What Ya Brung' generation took control of the sport's levers of power, they were replaced behind the wheel by the second wave of competitors, who came into a sport that was better organized, safer, and often sponsored. In the first half of the 1960s amateur events still boasted large fields and close racing. The final race at the Connor Circuit in 1963 – a national championship event – drew 137 entries and 4100 spectators.[21] Quebec Region produced more than its share of talented new drivers: George Brocklehurst, Jacques Couture, Ernie Devos, Hugh Dixon, Jacques Duval, François Favreau, Peter Keith, Peter Lerch, Gary Ross, John Sambrook, and John Spencer-Nairn. Prominent among Ontario's many new amateurs were Bill Brack, Gunther Decker, Louis Donolo, George Eaton, Max Nerriere, and Charlie Wilkinson. Racing enthusiasts on the Prairies watched Doug Bateman, Peter Brand, Phil Goodhall, Graham Lowden, and Herb Petras, among others. BC's local heroes included John Hall, Terry Nilsson, John Razelle, and G.B. Sterne.[22] Either by choice or because of the higher costs of national events and series, many of these new drivers rarely competed beyond the regional level, so their names remained unknown outside the small circle of enthusiasts in their home provinces. Yet it was their commitment to the sport that kept amateur racing vibrant in early 1960s. And at this point, amateur racing was still the foundation upon which national series and national champions were being built.

Fast Women

But these men did not have the tracks to themselves. Following the lead of Alice Fergusson and her contemporaries, more women joined the ranks of amateur racers. Wendy Keith, wife of Peter Keith, initially was the only woman racing in Quebec. She was joined later by Toni Ramsey (wife of racer Stuart Ramsey) and Nicole Martin, who married – and raced successfully against – François Favreau.[23] Stephanie Ruys de Perez drove for the Toronto-based Comstock Racing Team – Canada's first commercially sponsored team. In 1962, Janet Sharp took a fourth-place finish at Bon Accord, Alberta, while Fran Hamilton won the women's section of a novice ice race run by the Saskatoon Sports Car Club.[24] Out on the West Coast, Diana McColl of Vancouver was a frequent winner in the early 1960s in her H Production Austin-Healey Sprite.[25] Hilda Randall raced a hot Fiat Abarth in the SCCBC and American-based International Conference events for several years in the 1960s, with some success. She got started while waiting for her son John at the go-kart track. 'I wasn't the knitting type, so I got bored, and they bought me a go-kart.'[26] When John moved up to racing cars, so did she. Similarly, Karen Hall followed her husband onto the track in BC and began winning races in a Mustang.[27]

Among women racers at that time, however, Toronto's Diana Carter was in a league of her own. A product of the burgeoning suburban car culture, she was taught to drive by her father. A friend took her to a race, where she crewed for Jerry Polivka. He taught her how to race, and she won her first novice event at the Connor Circuit. Her victory made national news: 'Imagine ... "a girl had beaten the guys in auto racing." So, now I was really hooked. A checkered flag will do that to you.'[28] Soon Carter was working with Polivka for *Canada Track and Traffic*, was involved in the construction of Mosport, and was racing regularly. She was as thoroughly committed to the sport as any male racer. 'I was very serious about my capabilities on the track; concentrated on winning and drove to the best of my abilities with the equipment I had. I think that this ethic earned me respect and helped me to be "just one of the guys" around the track.'[29]

Often the only woman competing, her results proved that point. Diana won the touring class (sedan) championship in 1963 and the production car class in a three-hour endurance race at Mosport in 1964, sharing the drive in a Mini Cooper with Shirley Bowles. 'Highly regarded by the men competitors as a fast, smooth driver,'[30] she drew praise from her employer: 'Diana's performance also proved a point. That the Toronto girl should not be considered a "woman driver" as she has shown she deserves the respect given to everyone who races a car.'[31] By this time as well, the CASC had done away with 'powder puff derbies.' Little by little, then, racings' gender barriers were crumbling, at least among the 'weekend warriors' who made up grass-roots racing.

From Minis to Muscle Cars

While the faces of Canadian racing were changing, so were the cars. On the surface, the cars racing in the first half of the 1960s looked little different from those of the late 1950s. For example, most of the races at the MMGCC's opening meet of the 1962 season at St-Eugène featured 'traditional' sports cars: Corvettes, Jaguars, MGs, Porsches, and Sprites. But it was the sedan race that showed one emerging trend. Rod Campbell described it as a veritable 'David and Goliath' clash that pitted Grant Clark's tiny Austin Mini Cooper against Craig Fisher's massive Pontiac Catalina. 'The lead had see-sawed back and forth most of the race, Fisher ploughing ahead on the straights and Clark nipping past on the corners, only to be hauled down on the next direct stretch.'[32] Clark won, while Fisher ended up in the hay bales. The duel was replayed many times over through 1962 and in the next season, with the crowds thrilled and the victories shared.

The significance of that clash was that a race between *sedans*, rather than sports cars, proved to be a real crowd-pleaser. British sports cars, the very foundation of the sport itself, reached their apogee in the first half of the 1960s, with the advent of some of Britain's most popular cars: the MGB, Sunbeam Alpine, and Triumph TR4 and Spitfire. During the second half of the decade, however, they were well in decline, plagued by the full range of problems afflicting the British automobile industry as a whole, and vastly outstripped in sales by the cheap and highly competitive Mini.[33] By that time, as well, they largely had been displaced in many North American races, first by modified sports-racing cars and then by American 'muscle car' sedans.'[34]

The latter trend represented a major shift by the Big Three auto makers. In 1957, due to political criticism of the 'horsepower race,' which was blamed for the rising death toll on American highways, the Automobile Manufacturers Association had banned corporate involvement in car racing. But the Big Three continued to support racing sub rosa.[35] Finally, in 1962, asserting that the ban was ineffective, Ford formally announced its return to auto sport. Benson Ford dressed up the policy to emphasize the value of racing and rallying as a testing ground for the everyday automobile, but even he had to acknowledge that racing appealed to the consumer's 'gut instincts': 'Racing is stimulating passion for automobiles within the general public ... Americans are beginning once again to harken to the deep, full-throated music of a fine-tuned engine pouring it on, the whine of the gearbox, the squeal of hot rubber on asphalt.'[36]

In fact, it was *all* about marketing. Prodded by the irrepressible Lee Iacocca, Ford was trying to shed its stodgy image. Its 'Total Performance' marketing theme was designed to attract buyers among the emerging 'Baby Boomer' generation of younger drivers. For this market Ford introduced in 1964 the Mustang, a sedan that *looked* like a sports car. It was an overnight success; by 1966 it had captured 6 per cent of the new car market and had launched the 'Muscle Car Revolution' in the North American car culture. Chrysler and GM quickly followed suit with their own 'sports sedans': the Plymouth Barracuda and the Chevrolet Camaro / Pontiac Firebird. Ford's Mercury Division then introduced the Cougar, and even struggling American Motors entered the fray with its Javelin AMX line. By 1967 sports sedans accounted for more than 10 per cent of new car sales in North America.[37]

Inevitably, the competition for market share spilled onto the track. Ford saw racing as the best way to sell the Mustang and the Total Performance image:

> Our racing program is a prudent business investment ... sales records can be attributed to many factors ... racing is one of them ... Ford's participation in motor racing is 'widely publicized proof of the performance we are ... putting into the vehicles we build, and proof of the confidence we have in our ability to put it there. Nothing does more to sell a vehicle than ... enthusiasm for it, and we believe that nothing generates enthusiasm for a car faster than winning in flat-out competition' ... We are in business to sell automobiles, not to win races but that chequered flag is ... more exciting than a ten-day sales report.[38]

In that regard, Ford had a leg up on the competition even before it launched the Mustang. It had tried to get into racing by buying the Ferrari firm, but the deal foundered because Enzo Ferrari was unwilling to relinquish the very thing Ford had wanted most: his company's racing program. In the meantime, a retired racer from Texas was putting Ford's name into racing with his own hybrid sports car: the Cobra. Forced out of racing by a heart condition, Le Mans winner Carroll Shelby was scraping out a living selling tires and running a racing school in Los Angeles. But he was a man with a vision: to marry American horsepower to a British sports car. With no more collateral than his fame and a grin as wide as the Rio Grande is long, he persuaded Ford to give him a V-8 engine, which he then shoehorned into a borrowed AC Ace. Thus was born in 1962 the Shelby Cobra. The next year, running under the slogan 'Powered by Ford,' a Cobra won the SCCA road racing championship. Ford didn't need any more convincing. Two years later it 'upped the ante' in sports-sedan marketing by licensing Shelby to produce Mustangs tuned for racing. Shelby delivered; in 1966 a Shelby GT-350 Mustang, using the same 289 cid engine as the Cobra, beat the Corvette Sting Rays to win the SCCA B Production class championship.[39]

That same year, the SCCA launched a series that specifically featured American sports sedans: the Trans-American Sedan Championship, known simply as the 'Trans-Am.' It quickly evolved into a highly competitive, factory-supported series, popular with spectators and manufacturers alike because – unlike traditional sports car racing – it showcased cars that the everyday driver might buy. Two years later, it came to Canada, and Canadian racers went on to excel in the series. The first of these was Craig Fisher, who placed fourth overall in 1968, driving a Camaro and a Firebird for Penske Racing.[40]

Open Wheels

There were, however, a few 'purists' who yearned to emulate Formula One. They felt, as Peter Broeker did, that 'the quickest way around a course is in a single seater open-wheel car.'[41] As noted earlier, Canada Class had been created to allow these enthusiasts to build their own open-wheel racers. However, it was quickly overtaken by Formula Junior (FJ), which was launched in Europe in 1958. Recognized by the FIA as an international class the following year, FJ was instantly popular but lasted only until 1963. By that time it had become too costly, and changes in rules made other formula classes more accessible. FJ appealed to the few who could afford to buy a racing car 'off the shelf.' British makes – Cooper, Lola, and Lotus – dominated, and were scaled-down versions of the Formula One cars produced by those firms. Unlike Canada Class cars, which always looked 'home-built,' foreign-made FJs were constructed professionally to rigid specifications.[42]

Broeker was a man a little ahead of his time in Canadian racing. The Montrealer designed and built his Stebro rear-engine FJ so that it could be upgraded for Formula One, and to the cheers of thousands of Canadian fans he drove it to seventh place overall in the 1963 US F1 Grand Prix at Watkins Glen. His design was so versatile that he was able to race the car in FJ, Formula Two, Formula B, and Formula Libre races. By 1968, however, Broeker could not modify the car further to accept the more powerful engines and wider tires that were now the standard. And so he retired from racing and returned to his performance exhaust business.[43] It appears that Broeker built only four FJ models, and while he was not the only FJ builder or racer in Canada, the class did not expand the base of Canadian open-wheel racers.

Rather, it was Formula Vee that captured the hearts of many amateur Canadian racers in the mid-sixties, offering a cheap entry into open-wheel racing. Based on the abundant VW engines and components, the cars were easy and relatively cheap to build and run. 'That was part of the appeal,' says Tony Short, who raced a Vee in the 1970s. 'It was something that I could afford and something that I could do.'[44] In popularity, it rapidly outstripped both Canada Class and FJ. Whereas those classes had often struggled to field more than two or three cars for a race, it was not uncommon to see a grid with a dozen or more FVs. By 1966 it had become the largest class in the CASC and the SCCA.[45]

Horst Kroll lays claim to being Canada's FV pioneer. Born in Germany, he was sent to Canada by Porsche to service their cars and that got him into racing. He built his own FV in 1963 with the engine, transmission, front suspension, wheels, and brakes from a wrecked VW, all mounted on a tubular frame enclosed in a fiberglass body. It cost him about $1700 plus the cost of the wreck. That was a bargain even by 1960s standards. Horst won the class championship that year and again in 1965 and 1966. He recalls his first Vee fondly. 'I competed that car all over North America ... I was very successful ... My car was the first Canadian-built [FV] in Canada.'[46]

But it was Kroll's close friend Wayne Kelly who emerged as the most prolific FV constructor in Canada. A Nova Scotia native, Kelly took up racing while stationed in Germany as an RCAF radar technician. Driving his own Porsche 1600 coupe he came second in his first race. Impressed by Wayne's driving, Porsche invited him to take a course at the factory and then sold him a Carrera at cost for racing. Kelly rewarded their confidence with two spectacular seasons in 1959 and 1960: five wins, one second, and three third-place finishes in nine races. Returning to Canada, he later built the Kelly-Porsche sports-racing car, which Kroll drove to win the 1968 Canadian racing championship – the last for closed-wheel sports racing cars. Since the six-year-old two-litre car was up against newer and much more powerful Lola and McLaren Can-Am cars, Kelly said, 'it was a case of the turtle beating the hares.'[47]

After seeing Vees racing in Nassau during the 1963 Speed Weeks, Kelly decided to build one. He then went on to found an FV industry. Over the next four years he built twenty Vees and sold them in Canada and the United States; the Kelly Vee dominated the class in Canada from 1965 to 1969, while Kelly himself won two class championships. Learning from the 'harrowing experience' of crashing his Kelly-Porsche, he focused on making his cars strong and reliable. He strived in his cars to emulate the stringent specifications applied to aircraft construction. 'Reliability ... is the key factor in the success of my cars,' he said. 'If anyone has any doubts about the workmanship on them, I wouldn't sell any. Word spreads very quickly in this sport.'[48] And the word from the 'pros' was good. Viewing the Kelly Vee in the paddock at Le Circuit, Bruce McLaren described it as 'a very professional job,' and Colin Chapman of Lotus said, 'It's alright, that car.'[49] That was high praise indeed from those very much in the know. Wayne Kelly had a dream: to become the 'McLaren of Canada,' building racing cars for the whole world. But before that dream could be realized, his promising career and life came to an end in a crash during a preliminary race at the Canadian Grand Prix in September 1971.[50]

The examples of Broeker and Kelly show that Canada did not lack for talented formula car designers and builders. But they were few in number and their efforts were always on a small scale. They could never fulfil even the relatively modest domestic demand for their open-wheel cars. And as popular as they were, Vees were no match for the performance of European formula cars. At heart Formula Vee remained the hobby-racer's formula; it did not groom future Canadian national formula racing champions like Bill Brack or Gilles Villeneuve. But few other formula cars were competing in Canada before 1967. The absence of such cars meant that Canadian racers trying to break into F1 had to do so without the benefit of appropriate driving experience. And it showed when they first tried to break into Formula One.

7 Trans-Canada: The Shell 4000 and the National Rally Championship, 1961–1966

The Shell 4000 really put Canada on the world rally map.

Robin Edwardes[1]

Renault's Finest Hour: The Shell 4000, 1962

It was not supposed to end like this, sixty miles from Vancouver and the finish of the 1962 Shell 4000 'Trans-Canada' car rally. Not with the Manufacturer's Team Award in their grasp. The other factory teams – the Studebaker Larks, the Hillmans, and the Volvos – had lost at least one car each, so they were no longer eligible. But the first two Renault team cars had completed the rally. All that John Charters and his navigator Ian Worth had to do was to reach the finish, and the prize would belong to Renault. But as they lifted the rear hood on their Dauphine 1093, they could see the prize slipping through their fingers. The main engine bearings had seized. There was nothing they could do. Their rally was over. The award would go begging.

Or would it? At the sound of an approaching truck, they looked up. 'It's our mechanic!' said John. Remi Leber, the factory mechanic driving the team service truck, had followed the three cars on their week-long journey from Montreal, servicing them whenever the rules permitted. But would he be able to save them now, when it mattered most? Sent directly to Canada from the Renault factory in France, Leber spoke no English. Charters and Worth, both Anglo-Montrealers, spoke virtually no French. 'Le moteur,' John said, using his hands to mimic the motion of a crankshaft, 'c'est jammé, ça.' Leber shrugged, collected his tools from the truck, jacked up the car on rocks, and started to work.

Changing engine bearings at the side of the road is no easy task. While Remi worked methodically, Charters and Worth anxiously watched the time tick away. Even if they got going again, they had to reach the finish within their allotted time. It was going to be close. After an hour, the job was done. Charters climbed into the driver's seat, turned the key, and the car coughed to life. With the service truck following, they headed for Vancouver, where the rest of the team paced the finish line with sinking hopes.

After about twenty miles, however, the engine began to make grinding noises again. Damaged during the first seizure, it was leaking oil profusely. They drained the crankcase and refilled it with extra-heavy-grade 'goop.' Too thick to leak out, it kept the bearings lubricated while Charters and Worth nursed their car to the finish. They arrived with less than two minutes to spare. 'Worth leaped from the car to punch the time clock, while Charters sat behind the wheel grinning broadly. 'Bearings!', he yelled. 'We're on our second set and they're going too.' Jumping up and down with excitement, team member Sam Nordell exclaimed, 'I knew they were good, I knew they would make it. But there's always that doubt until they get here.' The only team with all of its cars finishing, Renault took home the manufacturer's award. The team presented the trophy to Leber.[2]

It was perhaps the most dramatic finish in the eight-year history of the Shell 4000 and certainly Renault's finest hour in Canadian rallying. For Louis O'Neill, Renault's wiry and fiery competition manager who had forged the team, the win was a personal victory. He had set a new standard for rally teams. In the 4000s that followed, other manufacturers' teams copied the Renault support model. Today's Canadian pro-rally teams that travel with a phalanx of service vehicles and mechanics are simply continuing what Renault started. With this kind of participation by major auto makers and the infusion of funding from a big business firm, the Shell 4000 heralded a major change in Canadian rallying.

Origins of the Shell 4000

The idea of running a cross-Canada rally had been raised first in 1956 by the St LAC, after learning that a similar event had been held in Australia. But the initiative to organize one in Canada came from outside the sport. In 1959, as it was developing plans to promote the 1961 BC International Trade Fair (BCITF), the British Columbia government broached the idea of running such a rally, which would reach Vancouver in time to coincide with the opening of the fair. The British trade commissioner in BC asked the RAC about organizing an event, and in turn, it passed the inquiry on to the CASC. At the 1959 AGM, CASC members asserted that 'such a rally would much more likely be successful and a credit to the sport if organized under the direction of the C.A.S.C.'[3] After meeting with the BCITF general manager, Don Mollison, in May 1960 Doug Wilson (acting as the CASC's West Coast representative) concluded that Mollison had seriously underestimated the scale of the task. Wilson suggested that the best option might be to 'drop the whole thing into the hands of a competent club such as BEMC and leave it to them to contact the various clubs across Canada.'[4]

In the end, the BCITF board decided to organize it themselves and persuaded Shell Oil to sponsor it. The CASC agreed to sanction the event, approved the rules and regulations, and contacted clubs across the country to urge them to provide assistance along the route, from Montreal to Vancouver. It also appointed Graham Locke as rally steward and provided a protest/appeals committee. The BCITF designated Wilson as rally manager (clerk of the course), and he laid out the route. The clubs provided officials to look after organization in their respective areas. According to Jim Gunn, Shell had been 'astounded' when they first learned what was required to organize a rally on that scale.[5] But the appointment as rally officials of experienced competitors and organizers such as Locke, Wilson, Ross Brander, and George Moss helped to lift some of the burden from Shell's shoulders, while ensuring that the event would be run to the standards the CASC expected of an international-calibre rally.

And so, at 7 am on an overcast and chilly 30 April 1961, G.J. Ellison and W. Ripley's factory-sponsored Hillman Minx rolled down the starting ramp at the Jean Talon Street Shell station in Montreal to begin the week-long, 4000-mile trek to Vancouver that was the inaugural Trans-Canada Rally. It was followed at two-minute intervals by 104 others, ranging from tiny Austin Minis to a magisterial 1937 Rolls Royce. Following a detailed route book, those first crews endured rough roads, bad weather, accidents and damage, a series of driving-skills tests, unclear instructions, delays, and fatigue. A serious collision near Port Arthur (now Thunder Bay), Ontario, claimed the life of Montrealer Bill Roscoe and injured his navigator, Ken Withers. Ninety-three cars reached the finish, but the rally ended in a blizzard of protests, which began as soon as some of the crews stepped out of their cars.

104 Part Two: Gathering Speed, 1961–1966

Computer errors in the scoring meant that only the first five positions were confirmed by the time of the awards banquet. In fact, the first four cars were tied in points, so their final positions were decided on the basis of the driving-skill test results. The overall winners were Jack Young and Reg Hillary of Toronto, who drove a factory-sponsored Studebaker Lark. All the difficulties and the protests notwithstanding, most of the competitors were eager to do it again; some even demanded that the rally be made tougher.[6]

Known thereafter as the Shell 4000, the rally became a fixture on the national auto sport calendar for the next seven years. It was notable for three features: professional organization, commercialism, and the introduction of European-style special speed sections that attracted international competitors. By redefining what Canadian endurance rallying was, these features transformed it from an amateur hobby into a commercial professional competition. They also set the stage for changes that completely reshaped the national rally championship in the 1970s.

Gunn and Bone: Professional Organizers

That first event taught the organizers a great deal. The steward reported that Doug Wilson 'was shamefully overworked to the point of mental and physical exhaustion brought about by lack of sleep and too many varied tasks.'[7] Thus, Shell Oil hired Jim Gunn to organize the event on a full-time basis from 1962 on. Two years later, Gunn asked Peter Bone to join him; he agreed willingly: 'To get the opportunity to do professionally the thing that you love to do ... it comes only once in a lifetime. I would have *paid* to do that job!'[8] Gunn and Bone worked together on five Shell 4000s. 'We would do a preliminary run in ... September [or] ... early October ... using a tape recorder, recording the route directly as we went. We'd transcribe that, and then go out again, maybe a month later, and re-run it, and sort of refine it, fine-tune the directions.'[9] Altogether they would take about 100 pages of notes. They actively recruited from the car clubs along the route to staff the checkpoints and provide other local assistance. Bone says, 'We couldn't have done it at all without the club people ... so we'd appoint a club coordinator for each area.'[10] Closer to the event Gunn and Bone did a lot of public-relations work with the news media to promote the rally. Then in the spring they would do a final run with an observer to make sure that there weren't any problems, such as misleading instructions. Still, the weather, which varied considerably over the course of a week and over such a distance, could close roads, requiring last-minute route changes. Bone recalls: 'If there was anything that was wrong, you had to do some very creative, some very rapid, re-routing. We didn't have too many of those, because the club people, if there were problems, would call us up. You had to have an alternate [route], you had to have a driver's meeting, new instructions ... We carried literally a full-scale office with us.'[11] All rallies require thorough organization, but up to that point no Canadian rally had required or received preparation on the scale of the Shell 4000.

The Business of Rallying: Sponsors and Teams

Obviously, for Shell Oil the rally was first and foremost a business promotion. The rules and regulations made no secret of the fact that the purpose of the rally was marketing, both of the BC trade fair itself and of Shell products. The cars displayed the Shell logo on rally bumper plates and on large number stickers on their doors. Vasey Ash, the president of Shell Oil of Canada, stated: 'We are confident that the trans-Canada car rally will prove to be an event of international interest.'[12] When Shell hired Jim Gunn to run the rally, he saw it as an opportunity to 'marry commercial sponsorship with the sport.'[13]

From a marketing standpoint, the rally was a big success. It attracted daily news coverage during the event, and extensive post-event reportage and paid advertising. According to Shell, the 1962 rally garnered over fifty-seven hours of radio coverage, almost five hours on TV, and more than 10,000 column inches in daily newspapers, as well as space in other print media in Canada, the United States and overseas – *over and above* the advertising. Factory-sponsored teams from Studebaker, Volvo, Mercedes-Benz, GM-Chevrolet, Rootes, and Ford (UK) entered the 1961 event. The following year Renault joined the fray, as did Chrysler in 1963. Manufacturers, such as Studebaker (overall winners in 1961 and 1962), were quick to feature the rally in ads to promote their cars. With its logo so prominent on the cars, Shell received a secondary boost from their ads.[14]

But it was an expensive commitment. Shell supplied gas and oil for all the participants and, in addition to trophies, awarded cash prizes ranging in that first year from $50 to $500. This violated CASC policy that banned monetary awards for rallies, but it waived the rule for this truly *national* rally, the first in Canada ever fully sponsored by a business. The company spent $100,000 on the 1962 rally (including Gunn's salary, but excluding advertising fees). Those costs continued to grow and by 1966 Shell wanted to reduce its share of the costs.[15]

But that did not discourage other companies from tapping into the rally market. In 1965 Dow Breweries became the sponsor of the Quebec rally, offering cash prizes of at least $1000 and paying for a post-rally reception. In return the Canadair Auto Club renamed the event the Dow Quebec Rally.[16] Shell had set an example that would be followed by others.

Factory-sponsored rally teams were not new to rallying in the 1960s. The first Alpine Rally, held in Europe in 1928, had attracted thirteen manufacturers' teams.[17] But according to Graham Robson, until the 1950s manufacturers largely ignored rallying: 'Having stubbornly written off rallying as a minority interest, they let private owners, or ... their dealers, enter the cars. If the right sort of result came along, the makers reaped the rewards, but they rarely agreed to pay the bills.'[18]

In the post-war era, Britain's Rootes Group was the first manufacturer to enter rallying in a big way. They established a competition department in 1948 and entered a three-car team in the 1949 Monte Carlo Rally. For more than a decade, the Rootes team was dominant. By the late 1950s many other European car manufacturers, such as Renault, had followed the Rootes example. Since that time, factory teams have remained in the forefront of European rallying.[19]

Manufacturers had entered Canadian rallying as early as 1956, when Ford, Rootes, Standard (Triumph), and Volkswagen sponsored teams in the Canadian Winter Rally. But until the early 1960s, dealer sponsors generally outnumbered the factory teams. Toronto dealers Jim Fergusson Motors, Shelton-Mansell Motors, and Werner Ornstein British Motors, as well as Cook-Toledo Motors and Budd and Dyer from Montreal, provided varying degrees of support to their teams. The Canadian Renault distributor provided a car to Les Chelminski one year, while Chevrolet dealer Harold Cummings gave him a car and paid expenses during another event. Les Stanley, who won the 1955 Winter Rally in a VW, recalls that Volkswagen serviced his car for free before an event, and 'used the results in advertising in Europe, not in Canada. You'd find out in the European papers, Volkswagen won the Canadian Winter Rally.'[20]

But the breakthrough for factory teams in Canadian rallying came in 1961, when the Big Three American car makers began to provide direct factory support, fielding multiple-car teams. It probably was no coincidence that they entered rallying in a big way at the very time when they were launching their new 'compact' cars, which were intended to recapture market share lost to European imports. The onslaught began when thirteen factory teams entered the 1961 Winter Rally. The GM- and Ford-sponsored teams took five of the top six places, with a Chevrolet Corvair the overall winner. Ford, which actually entered its British-built Anglias, took the manufacturers' team award. A few months later, Ford, GM, and Studebaker were among the five manufacturers competing in the first Trans-Canada Rally. Surprisingly, to many, the Studebaker Larks took the top two places, and they repeated their victory the following year.[21]

By the time Renault decided to launch a major team effort in Canadian rallying in 1962, it was well prepared. The firm had created a factory team in the 1950s and its Dauphine sedans won the 1958 Monte Carlo Rally outright. Louis O'Neill, a Renault racer himself, had been lobbying the French factory for a year, urging them to field a Canadian team. After all, auto sport was a marketing tool, and a significant proportion of the Canadian public was buying small foreign cars. From an auto industry perspective, the first Trans-Canada rally had been an advertising 'gold mine.' Yet there had been only a lone privately entered Renault in the field of 105 cars. O'Neill's persistence paid off. He later told auto sport writer-broadcaster Rod Campbell, 'The main reason for the excellent factory support this year is European awakening to motorsport activity in Canada.'[22]

For the 1962 rally season Renault introduced the Dauphine 1093; the cars were, in O'Neill's words, 'designed strictly for competition purposes and are very potent.'[23] Charters explained later that they had 'better suspension, a different exhaust system ... rally equipment, two Halda Speedpilots, spotlights.'[24] Renault shipped three of them, painted in French racing colours (white with twin blue stripes), to Montreal, where O'Neill went 'head-hunting' to create a winning rally team. Jim Van Vliet of the Montreal *Gazette* wrote:

> I hereby issue fair warning to the rallying team managers and sponsors that there lurks on the Montreal scene a modern day Jean Lafitte. This present day model of the famous French pirate ... has successfully scuppered the plans of Volkswagen and Volvo for the coming year. How? He has just stolen some of the leading rallyists in the country and formed a most formidable team.[25]

O'Neill selected three drivers and three navigators from among the top Quebec rallyists. Noted filmmaker Grant McLean had rallied a Volvo and an aging Bentley. His navigator, Bill Leathem, was a recent immigrant from Ireland. Sam Nordell, from Sweden, was an avid racer as well as rally driver. Born in England, Robin Edwardes had rallied since moving to Canada. Montrealer John Charters had rallied and raced his family VW and was president of the SMCC. Ian Worth from Lachine was his navigator. They all shared one thing: proven rally-winning talent. Between them they had claimed third through fifth places in the inaugural Trans-Canada Rally, while McLean and Leathem had won the 1961 Quebec rally championship. The team was allotted its own space in Renault's Montreal headquarters and its own staff of mechanics to work on the cars. Renault paid the team members a small stipend for every event they entered and covered their rally expenses. O'Neill planned to enter the team in thirty-four events in 1962, but he had a more ambitious goal in mind: 'taking a Canadian Renault team over to the big events in Europe by 1964.'[26]

He never saw that ultimate goal fully realized. But, at least in the short term, O'Neill was not to be disappointed. In addition to their victory in the Shell 4000, the Renaults took the factory team award in the Rallye des Neiges, and placed second in the factory team standings in the BEMC Canadian Winter Rally. During the rest of 1962 the team captured the team awards in events throughout Eastern Canada, such as the Nova Scotia Highlands Rally. During the Shell 4000 they had shown how teamwork paid off; they sacrificed points by keeping all three cars together. That proved to be a sound strategy when they encountered the thick prairie mud (known to the rallyists as 'gumbo') that lay across part of the rally route. Robin Edwardes says: 'We had ... decided what we're going to do about "gumbo" when we hit it ... It was really a matter of manhandling, having six crew members there, with the three cars together, to get those cars out of the "gumbo."'[27] In the national rally championship standings, the team members took places four through nine, and the Charters/Worth crew also won the 1962 Quebec rally championship.[28] Had there been a national manufacturers' team championship that year, Renault would have won it hands down.

The following year the team received the new R-8, but they did not fare as well. While they repeated their victory in the Rallye des Neiges, they were relegated to third place in the Winter Rally and in the Shell 4000. In that event the Ford factory Falcon Futura Sprints won the team award, with the Chrysler team second. VW won the first national manufacturers' championship that year; Renault was fourth. Nordell and McLean entered a single R-8 in the Monte Carlo Rally, but did not place well. According to Peter Bone, who knew them both, the experience of driving at high speed through the Alps 'absolutely scared Grant speechless.'[29]

By the end of 1963 the team had undergone personnel changes. John Charters had retired after a rollover racing at Mosport and a crash rallying on icy roads that, in his words, 'shortened the car substantially.'[30] Robin Edwardes left the team early in 1963 and navigated for a variety of drivers thereafter. Sam Nordell went back to Europe where, Edwardes recalls, 'he was certainly getting noticed.'[31] But, practising in a Vauxhall for the 1964 Monte Carlo Rally, he plunged over a cliff in the Alps and was killed. Phil Bailey and Doug Gallop, and Marcel and Roland Rainville joined the team to fill vacancies during the year. They all proved to be talented rallyists, but the team never again achieved the dominance of its first season. It was seventh among the factory teams in 1964 and tenth in 1966. Nevertheless, Renault had proved the value of a well-managed and supported factory team. Edwardes later reflected on the reasons for their success: 'The hand-picked crews ... the fact that there was a team manager ... and a certain amount of support ... Particular members of the team ... were seeing to it that Renault provided the preparation that was appropriate ... The expertise of the crews saw that the cars were properly prepared ... The crews were the key to that.'[32]

Where Renault led, other manufacturers and their teams followed. When Ford USA officially returned to international competition, their approach was thoroughly professional. They entered the 1963 rally season with a team of Falcon Futura Sprints specially prepared by Ford's stock-car associates Holman and Moody. They had lightweight body panels, the 260-cid V-8 used in the first Shelby Cobras, close-ratio gearboxes, and front disc brakes. And just as Renault had done, Ford hired the best teams they could find. They won their class in the Monte Carlo Rally that year and in 1964 their top driver, Bo Ljungfeldt of Sweden, brought a Falcon to second overall. For the 1963 Shell 4000, the Falcon crews were selected from among the best in the Toronto area, including Paul MacLennan, Art Dempsey, Lloyd Howell, and Bill Silvera. The crews and the cars were the winning formula that brought Ford the manufacturers' award.[33]

After a scoring fiasco in 1965 cost Ford the overall victory, the company helped their Canadian affiliate – the Comstock Racing Team – secure the 1966 team award. They assembled three experienced crews: Edwardes and British rallyist Roger Clark; MacLennan and John Wilson; Brent Davies and racer Eppie Weitzes, guided by factory 'strategist' and British rallyist Henry Taylor. Meticulously prepared by mechanic Paul Cooke, the team's Ford Lotus Cortinas took first, third, and ninth overall, bringing Ford its second team prize in the rally.[34]

In an effort to 'level the playing field' between the factory, sponsored, and private teams for the 1964 event, Gunn and Bone ordered that the engine head and sump, transmission, and drive axle be sealed, with points to be deducted if the seals were broken. They also reduced the repair time allowed at the end of each day from one hour to fifteen minutes. The following year, they combined the sponsored and manufacturers team categories. Even so, the factory- and dealer-sponsored teams continued to dominate the Shell 4000. The statistics tell the story. The number of entries dropped dramatically after the first year, to only forty-two in 1962; of these about two dozen were private entries, compared with forty-five in 1961. Only twenty privately entered cars competed in the 1963 event, out of a total of forty-seven entries. For the next few years, entries increased into the sixties, with private entries ranging between thirty and forty. But the factory- or dealer-sponsored teams won overall every year and with few exceptions took the top five places. The fact that the '4000' became tougher and faster over the first five years favoured these teams because they had the best crews and the most through car preparation and servicing.[35] Just as in European rallying, the increasing emphasis on both endurance and speed in the '4000' and in the national rally championship seemed to mark 'the beginning of the end' for the amateur 'privateer.'

'Car-breakers,' Speed, and the National Championship

The first step in this direction was the CASC's effort to impose some standards on the national championship. By the early 1960s, the term 'national' had become rather vague. A club could simply place any of its events on the national calendar, and it would qualify automatically as a championship event. The result was something of a hodge-podge. The 1961 calendar listed thirty-four 'national' rallies that spanned the full range in levels of difficulty. It included, at one end, relatively undemanding events such as the Columbian Canyon Rally in BC and WOSCA's Auto-Mapic Marathon. At the other were the car- and crew-testing endurance rallies: the Winter Rally, the Rallye des Neiges, and the Trans-Canada Rally. In between were navexes of varying degrees of difficulty. And the championship was hardly 'national'; only four of the events took place in the West, and there were none in Manitoba or Atlantic Canada.[36]

The situation began to change in 1962. The number of championship events was reduced to thirty. The CASC decided that all of them would have to be run under national rules. Jim Plumley (rally chairman on the NCB) proposed a number of changes to those rules. First, only the NCB would have the power to classify events as national championship rallies. Second, to qualify for that status they would have to be a minimum of 500 miles in length, with straightforward instructions. For 1963 the NCB got the power to select the championship events, but not the 500-mile minimum length. Instead, the championship points system was altered. Through 1962, points had been awarded for starting and finishing events of varying distance (from under 200 to over 1000 miles). Championship contenders counted their five best events. Under the new rules, points would be awarded only for the top six finishers, with rallies of 500 miles or less being worth the fewest points. The five best events would count towards the championship, but now – in an effort to make the championship more national in scope – one of those would have to be outside the competitor's home province. Since factory-sponsored teams represented a significant portion of the entries and usually were the winners, the CASC also introduced a national championship for manufacturers, using the same points system. Finally, instructions for national rallies had to be designed so that there was 'no reasonable doubt' as to their meaning;[37] in short, simple instructions for fast driving. While these rules did not *exclude* navexes from the championship, they obviously were biased towards endurance rallies and 'professional' (sponsored) teams.

Just as the introduction of endurance events had generated debate over the purpose of racing, a similar debate developed in rallying when the Trans-Canada rally was being launched. The losses caused by the combination of speed, weather, and road conditions that gave endurance rallies their reputation as 'car-breakers' began to change the character of national championship rallying. In some events, just finishing was regarded as a major accomplishment. Consider, for example, the experience of Simca crew Rasche and Grimshaw in the 1965 Winter Rally: 'A bad frost heave ... threw the car up into the air. The wheelplay was so limited by ice build-up that when it came down again they lost control, hit a snowbank, flipped over onto the roof and caroomed off into the woods. Undeterred, the two then winched it back onto the road, turned it right side up, and went on to a class win and 16th overall.'[38] Indeed, the statistics from the Winter Rally read like the toll from some dreadful battles: 1960 – 163 entrants, only 92 finishers; 1962 – 182 entrants, 89 finishers; 1965 – 132 entrants, 23 finishers.[39] With attrition rates like that, it is hardly surprising that some rallyists began to question for whose benefit these events were being run. John Searle, club rallyist and editor of the *Exhaust* – the SMCC's newsletter – voiced concern in 1961 about the rising toll from endurance rallies:

> Not too long ago, it was most unusual for a car to be damaged during the course of an event, and rallyists would complain bitterly about certain events being 'car breakers' simply because the route crossed rough terrain. Now the position has changed to such an extent that the term 'car wrecker' could well be applied in many instances, and events which pass without taking considerable toll from competing cars are a comparative rarity. Obviously something is wrong somewhere.[40]

He specifically singled out the Quebec Rally as an example of the problem. It always had a reputation as a tough rally, and about 30 per cent of the entries did not finish the 1961 event, which emphasized driver skill and car reliability at higher speeds over rough roads. Searle conceded that, as a national championship endurance rally, it was designed to challenge the best rallyists,

> but examination of the casualty list must surely make us realize that an event which is tough for the experienced competitor can be little less than murderous to novice ... Canadian rallying is a young, amateur sport ... Very few of us can genuinely afford to damage our cars ... A continuation of the appalling record of accidents which have recently occurred could very easily lead to the end of rallying completely.[41]

Without coming out and saying so directly, he was probably referring to the fatal crash in the first Trans-Canada Rally, which had cast a pall over that event. But Searle's comments did generate some discussion within the SMCC about the relative merits of endurance rallying, in particular a debate over daytime versus nighttime events. The proponents of night rallies argued the case for safety: less traffic, fewer police, simpler navigation, and lower speeds without loss of driver interest. Those, like club president and Renault team driver John Charters, who were opposed, pointed to the changing pattern of endurance rallies, especially the increased speeds and the risks associated with them:

> Personally, there is nothing I enjoy more than a fast run over rough roads – I feel this is a real test of car and driver ... The very nature of the sport demands that the driver make every attempt to maintain the set average – before he knows it, he is at his limit, with his navigator urging him ever onwards. It takes a strong will to deliberately lose points in the interest of safety; not every driver knows his limit ... The endurance rally's main requirement is the ability to remain awake for long hours at the wheel ... If we must have this kind of rally, I suggest it also be confined to daylight hours. It is easier to remain awake during the day, and far safer ... Long over-night events, with no navigation or driving challenge to keep one awake ... can be most dangerous, as the fatal accident on last year's Trans Canada proved ... High speed events ... are far safer ... if held at night ... Slow night rallies, and high speed day rallies are equally dangerous.[42]

Overshadowed, but not completely obscured, in this debate was a more fundamental issue. For whose benefit were rallies to be run: the average, amateur club members or the 'hard-bitten' semi-professionals who were beginning to emerge at this time? Searle clearly favoured the former; Charters and Ian Worth – his navigator and Searle's successor as newsletter editor – represented the latter. Peter Bone weighed into the debate on the side of 'progress,' arguing that Canadian rallying had matured to an international standard. He felt that organizers had to maintain high standards, even when catering to the average competitor. He also asserted that rallies should be challenging and accurate, but that honest grading and advertising of events would allow the average club member to enter those rallies for which their ability was best suited. While conceding that perhaps the factory team 'professionals' could be banned from small club events, Bone asserted that 'the sport needs these professional teams and SMCC should be proud that it can provide crews of the required calibre.'[43]

Despite concern about 'car breakers,' the speed/endurance enthusiasts predominated. This encouraged rally organizers to take the second step towards changing the national championship: the introduction of special speed sections, which moved Canadian rallying closer to the European model.

During its first few years, the Shell 4000 was mostly a test of car reliability. In the first event, the instructions were straightforward, without the 'tricks' common to a navex. In many places the navigator needed only a standard highway map to plot the most direct route to reach the next control within the allotted time. But times were generous and even the driving was not too difficult. The absence of alternate routes around Lake Superior confined the rallyists to a long stretch of highway, though some of it was still under construction. Thus, it was not surprising that 90 per cent of the starters finished the rally, four of them tied in points.

By contrast, the 1962 event was a 'car-breaker.' The weather and road conditions of early April left the route strewn with wrecked cars and lost parts. There were rollovers and collisions (none fatal); in BC one crew hit a deer, which cost them points for body damage. The rally's most costly section was 'a snaking, potholed, inundated little stinker of a road.'[44] near Housey's Rapids, Ontario. There the Pontiac Acadian of Tony Wilson and Red Lemieux lost its gas tank in a water-filled wallow. Before they could retrieve it, the Studebaker Lark of Alice Fergusson and Mary Clark flattened the sunken tank. But all was not lost; the Martin Chenhall / John Wilson Acadian soon came along and dropped its tank in the same spot. Equipped with a spare they drove on unaware of their loss. Lemieux and Wilson attached the dropped tank to their car, and continued the rally, finishing twelfth overall, only two places behind Chenhall and Wilson.[45]

In 1963 the rally was added to the RAC world rally championship for manufacturers, a first for a Canadian rally. Consequently, whereas in the first two years the rally had been billed as a test of skill on the part of the driver and *navigator*, the 1963 regulations referred to the crew members as first and second *drivers*. Despite the emphasis on *driving* skill, the organizers also tried to make *navigation* more challenging. However, the event that year, which ran from Vancouver to Montreal, did not match the first two for toughness. All of the instructions were in correct order, with cumulative mileages. This and the lack of difficult roads or bad weather made the 1963 rally too easy. 'The total point loss for the first five cars added together wouldn't come close to that of the winner in a good European rally.'[46]

The next year, however, Gunn and Bone introduced the European-style 'special stages' into the '4000' for the first time. These were sections of road closed to public traffic, where the rallyists had to drive 'against the clock'; in short, speed was everything. Peter Bone had tried this feature as an experiment in an earlier Quebec Rally, where the route crossed into the United States: 'We found a beautiful little piece of road, and we figured, well, don't think anybody's going to use *that* at two o'clock in the morning. We didn't close it. We, in effect, ran a closed section and crossed our fingers that nobody would come the other way!'[47] Likewise, the Calgary Sports Car Club's 1962 Loop Rally included a 56-mile stretch through the Logan Pass where drivers could go as fast as the road permitted. One section of forestry road seventeen miles long had to be driven in no more than thirty minutes, with penalties for seconds late. 'Straights were little more than a hundred yards long and the road climbed twice to a height of four hundred feet.'[48] A Renault Gordini finished the stretch in twenty-three minutes.

The addition of the special stages, inclusion in the world championship, and the resulting entry of more European rallyists changed the character of the '4000.' Veteran rallyist Diana Carter, who won the Coupe des Dames in a Volvo, wrote that in the 1964 event '[t]here were no ambiguous instructions ... no navigational tricks ... just good hard rallying.'[49] Swiss driver Jean-Jacques Thuner, driving a factory-sponsored Triumph TR4 sports car, covered the first special section, 33.79 miles of winding gravel roads through BC's Cascade Mountains, in a remarkable 44.38 minutes. Bo Ljungfeldt from Sweden, who had won every special stage in the Monte Carlo Rally that year, was forced out of the '4000' after he crashed his Falcon during the speed section at Camp Wainright, Alberta.[50] Belgian Formula One racer Olivier Gendebien, who had first entered in 1962, placed fourth in 1964. He said the rally was 'an enormous improvement' over previous years, 'a challenge truly worthy of its world championship classification.'[51] *Track and Traffic* concurred: 'Competitors and observers alike agreed that it was the toughest, truest test of cars and drivers in the four-year history of the event, elevating it to realistic world-championship calibre.'[52]

The introduction of special stages put a premium on accurate timing, so the organizers employed the same Longines Printogines punch clocks as used in European rallies. Still, Peter Bone recalls, the distances involved posed challenges for timing:

> We had two lead cars an hour [ahead of the competitors] ... We brought the clock and the Longines guy set it up ... he did the final adjustment with the national time signal. Then, we'd leap in the car and go off. Well, we started off an hour ahead of everybody, but you run twelve-, fifteen-hour routes, you wanna believe that you're *five* minutes ahead of the lead car by the time you get to the end![53]

Although the rally began using more time controls, they could not get more clocks. Airline flight schedules didn't fit the rally, Bone explains, so they used a truck with 'a couple of demon rally drivers ... These clocks would be gathered up by the "sweep car" [following the last entry] ... [H]e'd bring them in, they'd load them on the truck, then they'd dash off.'[54]

For the special sections in 1964, crews had been penalized one point for each *minute* they were slower than the fastest car in their class. The next year, Gunn and Bone added more special sections, and tightened up the timing and scoring. Crews would lose one point for every *six seconds* they were behind the fastest car. The more demanding rally attracted more high-profile foreign drivers, among them Mexican racer Pedro Rodriguez and British rallyist Henry Taylor, who proved to be the 'star of the show.' Paired with Robin Edwardes in a Ford Cortina GT, Taylor won every special section. It was his impressive run on the narrow, twisting trail through the Cascades special section that showed his European rally experience. He lightened the car by removing extra fuel, spares, and luggage and ran the thirty-eight-mile section in 50.54 minutes, two minutes faster than Paul McLennan's Ford Mustang, which had twice the horsepower. Edwardes commented: 'Paul and Scott Harvey [who was driving a Plymouth Valiant] were fast uphill, but it was in those frightening downhill runs that Henry won.' At the closing banquet Taylor, who finished third overall, praised the '4000' saying, 'I enjoyed it more than any rally I've driven for some time.'[55]

Less than half of the sixty entries finished the 1966 rally. The steward felt the rally was better than earlier events, but most of the regular '4000' participants felt it was *not* as difficult as in previous years and that the dropouts could be attributed to poor car preparation rather than the route. Certainly, the special sections were no more demanding than in previous events.[56]

The changing character of the Shell 4000 refocused attention on the national rally championship. CASC rally chairman Robin Wright told the regions in 1966 that the NCB was not satisfied with the quality of several national-level rallies and with the low number of entries in them. The remedy, he felt, was limit the number of events in any one year. The total for 1967 was to be twenty. The BC and Atlantic regions would have three each, Quebec and the Prairies four, and Ontario six. Wright requested that regions ensure that 'these events cover at least 400-500 miles and present a real challenge to competitors.'[57] National competition chairman Dick Shelton explained why the NCB was reducing the number of events and setting a minimum distance standard:

> In the last few years it has become quite obvious that rallying is not holding its own as a major part of the sport, and the sport, as a whole, is suffering because of it ... National Championship Rallies have become so unimportant as to be of little interest to the competitor – note the lack of entries in most of them – and of less interest to the Sponsors. Therefore, the National Competition Board ... decided to attempt to upgrade the National Championship by reducing the quantity but improving the quality of Championship events ... We might add that due, no doubt, to the rising costs of car insurance and/or car repairs, 'car busting' rallies are of little or no interest to any competitor.[58]

The smaller number of entries in the Shell 4000 validated his last point. While its special stages covered only a fraction of the total distance, the potential for damage they promised was discouraging private entries. However, the rally had taken its toll on Shell too, and the firm bowed out after the 1968 event. Run in June from Calgary to Halifax, the last Shell 4000 offered neither the weather nor the road conditions to seriously challenge the crews.[59]

Jim Gunn organized one last 'Trans-Canada' Rally (without Shell) in 1971. Run by his own company (the International Motorsport Association of Canada), the British Columbia Centennial Car Rally covered a tough 5000 miles from Ottawa to Victoria. Only eighteen of the thirty-eight entries finished the rally, which was won by Haydn Gozzard and David Grundy in a Renault Gordini. The event, however, was poorly promoted and was never revived again.[60]

By Canada's centennial year, the rally championship had become truly national, with about half the events taking place in the West and the Atlantic region. Moreover, the '4000' institutionalized the stage rally concept in Canada. By the mid-1970s, Canadian championship rallies would be indistinguishable from their European counterparts: races on roads in everything but name. And so the '4000' was a precedent-setting event. However, the increasing financial and mechanical cost of commercialized endurance rallying was winnowing out the amateur 'privateers,' who simply could not afford to compete – or expect to win – in this league. National rallying, like national racing, was 'going pro.'

8 Making Tracks: Commercializing Canadian Racing

The Player's 200 as a race was humdrum; the Player's 200 as a spectacle was a glittering success.

Canada Track and Traffic, 1961[1]

It Was a Very Good Year

If 1961 was notable for marking the tenth anniversary of the CASC and the launching of the Trans-Canada Rally, it was also a banner year in Canadian racing. Simultaneously in June it saw the opening of the Mosport race track in Ontario, the first Player's 200 international sports car race, and the debut of the first commercially sponsored national racing team and their remarkable Canadian-built racing car. A few months later, Canada's most promising driver won the inaugural Canadian Grand Prix for Sports Cars. In short, it was a year of superlatives. How it all came together, where it led, and what it meant is explored in this and the next two chapters.

Becoming Players

The twenty-fourth of June 1961 was the day the CASC's founders had dreamed of for ten years: the best drivers in the world competing against the best Canadians, on a brand-new, built-to-purpose, Canadian race track – Mosport – with 40,000 Canadian racing fans looking on. For many in the audience it was their first opportunity to see three of the most famous European racers of the day: Joakim Bonnier, Olivier Gendebien, and Stirling Moss. This wasn't just a race, but a spectacle.

Indeed, the feature race was hardly exciting. Broken into two 100-mile (forty-lap) heats, it had only eighteen starting entries. Apart from the three Europeans, most were Canadians. Only a handful of Americans showed up; the SCCA had banned its members from entering because the race offered appearance and prize money. Even Canadian Peter Ryan withdrew rather than risk losing his SCCA licence. Bonnier and Gendebien, driving Porsche RS61s, were completely outclassed by Moss's Lotus 19. The newly formed Comstock Racing Team entered its cutting-edge Sadler Mk. Vs, driven by Bill Sadler and Grant Clark. The rest of the field included many of the big names of Canadian racing in that era: Ludwig Heimrath and Jim Muzzin in Porsches; Francis Bradley in a Lola; Harry Entwhistle in a Lotus 15; Nat Adams in a Jaguar XKSS; Dave Greenblatt in the Sadler Mk. IV; and Fred Hayes, Oliver Clubine, and Milt Wright in a variety of homebuilt specials. Moss drove away from the pack easily. Heimrath was the top Canadian, in fourth place. Both Comstock cars suffered gearbox problems, but Clark managed to claim fifth place overall and tied Moss for the fastest lap. For the organizers, the sponsors, and perhaps even the audience, the fact that the first Player's 200 was a rather dull race probably didn't matter. That it happened at all made it a success.[2]

The second major race at Mosport that year was the Canadian Grand Prix for Sports Cars, held in September. Organized by the BEMC and sponsored by Pepsi Cola, it was in many ways simply a carbon-copy of the Player's 200: famous drivers, specialist cars, and a large crowd. By this time, however, the SCCA had lifted its ban on 'pro' races, so the Grand Prix boasted a better field of twenty-five drivers and cars. Moss and Gendebien returned in Lotus 19s. Thanks to the patience and tenacity of race organizer George Moss and $7500 in appearance money, Luigi Chinetti provided six factory-sponsored Ferraris. His North American Racing Team (NART) drivers included the famous Mexican racers Pedro and Ricardo Rodriguez. A mixture of cars, including the Sadler Mk. Vs, filled out the rest of the grid. Peter Ryan, driving his Comstock-sponsored Lotus 19, headed the field of Canadian drivers, who included the usual 'local heroes.'

Moss and Gendebien dominated the 100-lap race, exchanging the lead twenty-six times. But it was Peter Ryan's day. Good driving, superior power, an extra fuel tank, and 'gremlins' that plagued some of the opposition allowed him to overcome an off-track excursion and a sixty-second penalty to take the win: the first for a Canadian in a major international race. Pedro Rodriguez was second, and Moss third.

Canadians Heimrath and Bradley finished fifth and eighth respectively. As a *race*, it was much more competitive and exciting than the Player's 200. The audience was the sole disappointment for the organizers; the turnout was only about 25,000.[3]

These two events remained as *the* fixtures on the Canadian racing calendar until they merged with the Can-Am series in the mid-1960s. The '200' grew in popularity, drawing a record crowd of 58,312 in 1965. The Grand Prix, often plagued by cool, wet September weather, never matched the audience of the '200.' Except for Ryan's win, foreign drivers dominated. Masten Gregory from the United States, driving a Lotus 19, won both races in 1962. Pedro Rodriguez, in NART Ferraris, won the GP in 1963 and 1964. New Zealander Bruce McLaren won the '200' in 1964 and 1966, taking the latter victory in one of the first cars to bear his name. American Jim Hall won the 1965 GP in his own Chaparral 2, and British world champion John Surtees drove a Lola T70 to victory in the 1965 '200.' The Canadian entries included every national champion of the decade.[4]

The two races rivalled attendance records for Canadian sports events. Only the Grey Cup had drawn a bigger crowd than the first Player's 200, which attracted nearly *three times* as many spectators as the Carling 300 race the previous year. Some fans showed up as much as fourteen hours before the racing began. Traffic jams clogged the country roads around the track for hours before and after the race. In fact, the audience so exceeded the organizers' expectations that the gates ran out of tickets. The cash flow overwhelmed CRDA officials Barry Morton and Doug Sellers, who knew almost nothing about gate procedures:

> We really didn't know what the hell we were doing. We were collecting money in bags and throwing it in the trunk of Doug's car. The idea was that we would run it down to Bowmanville where R.M. Hollinshead had an office, where we could stick it in a safe ... During the middle of the night Doug Sellers locked his keys in the trunk with all the money.[5]

Morton remembers that they had to remove the back seat and crawl into the trunk to find the keys among the cash. They finally drove to the Hollinshead office with a police escort, lights flashing and sirens blaring.

Len Coates believes that the first Player's 200 gave car racing a place in Canadian sports. Bill Wordham, then executive editor of *Canada*

Track and Traffic, noted: 'After years of doling out token recognition at best, the Toronto press unleashed a barrage of race coverage. It's pretty hard for any newspaper to ignore 40,000 potential customers.'[6]

The size of the crowd was no accident. The '200' sponsor – Imperial Tobacco – had launched a major promotion effort through the firm Public Relations Services Limited (PRSL), and clearly it paid off. But the tobacco company's entry into race sponsorship was almost serendipitous. The race organizers (the CRDA) originally had counted on Carling Breweries as the sponsor. But the Ontario liquor board had decided to reduce high-profile advertising of beer, thus barring the company from the sponsorship role. According to Milt Wright, who at the time was working for one of Imperial Tobacco's subsidiaries, Carling's loss coincided with his firm's search for new ways to promote their cigarettes. Player's product manager Edmund Ricard thought car racing would be a perfect promotional vehicle to upgrade its brand image to appeal to a younger audience.[7] It must have worked; Player's remained one of the principal sponsors of Canadian racing for the next forty years.

Art Moseley recalls that the total cost of the sports car Grand Prix was about $80–90,000. Of that, Pepsi Cola would contribute about $10,000–15,000 in cash, as well as paying for the advertising. The rest had to be generated from gate receipts, because there was no guarantee that Pepsi would make up any shortfall. For events on this scale, major commercial sponsorship was both desirable – for publicity purposes – and essential, to cover costs. Without the appearance and prize money the sponsors provided, it would have been difficult to attract some of the world's best drivers to these events.[8]

The '200' and the Grand Prix solidified the changes in Canadian racing initiated by the CRDA in 1959, and set the pattern for nearly two decades. The racers competed on purpose-built racetracks instead of airport circuits. Specialist racing cars dominated the feature races, which in turn showcased famous international drivers. And their fame attracted the large audiences and major media coverage that began the process of turning a sport into a spectacle.

The Mosport Saga, 1958–1966

For racers, however, the Mosport track itself was a drawing card. Moss, who denied any hand in designing the corner named in his honour, was nonetheless fulsome in his praise for Mosport, calling it 'one of the best and most challenging tracks in the world.' Gendebien said it was one of the best driver's courses he had ever seen. 'If you can drive well on this course, you can drive on any track in Europe.' Bonnier echoed those sentiments: 'It is definitely a long way above average ... You hear so much about race tracks you have never seen and then when you get there you are disappointed. Mosport is an exception.'[9] Even Chinetti, who had a reputation for being hard to please, was impressed. 'It's one of the best courses in North America,' he said. 'You have good pits and safety for spectators. We go to only a few big races a year but I like the course and the people here, and I will be back next year.'[10]

Like Westwood before it, the creation of Mosport was a club effort that eventually outgrew its humble origins. Roy McLaughlin recalls that the BEMC had long wanted to have a proper race course. So after a lot of talk at club meetings they struck a committee to find some property. What they found was a parcel, known locally as Walter's Place, near Peterborough, Ontario. It offered '450 acres of beautiful rolling country, well studded with fine trees ... opening up prospects of a race track over three miles long ... All this within one hour's comfortable drive of Toronto.'[11]

The committee had visions of an auto sport 'resort,' but was stunned by the financial implications. The land alone would cost $31,000, and the whole facility was estimated initially at $250,000. Clearly, this was more than one club could handle. And so, to raise the funds to buy the property, in November 1958 the BEMC founded a company – Mosport Limited – that sold $25 shares to members of the eastern Canadian sports car clubs. Then, the following spring, the company bought the land. To build the track it copied Westwood's example by selling $100 debentures. John Wilson, a Presbyterian minister and auto sport enthusiast, pitched them to the Ontario sports car clubs. By 1960 the shareholders included virtually every one of them, as well as the Canadian Motorcycle Association.

Seeing Mosport as a national asset, the CASC agreed in May 1960 to buy $1000 in debentures. But Quebec Region director Ross Brander was opposed, because his region saw the effort as national support for an Ontario project. In fact, only one Quebec club (the Jaguar Owners Association of Montreal) bought shares in the track. This failure to involve the Quebec clubs violated one of the principles established by company president Dick Byatt: that 'control of the venture must be vested in the "Sport" as a whole.'[12] Quebec's reluctance probably had more to do with resentment that by 1960 the real power in Canadian auto sport was already concentrated in Ontario. Regionalism – the bane of Canadian unity – was rearing its ugly head in auto sport, just as it did elsewhere in Canadian life. Later, it would have serious implications for Mosport and for the sport itself.

Mosport Limited reflected the professionalism and commercialism that were creeping into the sport by the end of the 1950s. But the scale of this project made a business approach indispensable. Indeed, financial concerns took on a greater sense of urgency over time. In August 1960 Wilson told the shareholders that the sale of debentures had raised over $43,000 and that he expected sales to reach their targets. By the end of January 1961, however, once construction was under way, the situation looked grim. The company faced a deficit of more than $50,000, while the cost estimate for the whole project had skyrocketed to over $500,000, without any prospect of long-term funding. Financial shortfalls at various stages delayed work on the track. Bulldozing, grading, and filling were not finished until the end of 1960. Poor weather delayed paving until shortly before the track opened in June 1961. Track historian the late Robert Brockington says:

> The planners wanted a ... course much like a winding country road with many up-and-down hill sections, fast sweeping turns, a tight turn, and a long back straight where cars could use their power. They also wanted a track that was equal to European Grand Prix tracks ... that would challenge the driver. It also had to meet current track standards in the hopes of one day hosting a Formula One Grand Prix ... With the exception of the pits the paying customer could go anywhere they wanted to see all the action.[13]

The original design was altered several times, but when it was completed, Mosport was a first-class track. Following the natural shape of the land, it was two and a half miles long, with ten turns and a long (0.8-mile) back straight, making it both a driver's and a spectator's course. In spite of his denials, the official history of the track still credits Stirling Moss for the design of the hairpin turn that bears his name.[14] The course had closed pit buildings and, later, a timing tower. But the absence of the originally intended clubhouse and pool reflected the harsh financial realities that placed the track's future in jeopardy from the moment it opened.

After its initial success, Mosport's lustre wore off quickly. The Grand Prix in September 1961 and the 1962 Player's 200 attracted audiences only in the 20,000 range, and the 1962 Peterborough International stock car race drew a paltry 5600. Mosport shared the profits and the losses with the event organizers, and was soon in trouble. Chuck McLaren says:

> The financial bath from the Peterborough International happened in the face of the crushing debt load that resulted from the cost overruns on the original construction. By itself the loss from the stock car race could have been absorbed, but added together, the two factors were another story ... It was the red ink from Mosport's best-ever race that pushed the operation over the brink and caused the management to call in the receivers.[15]

And so, barely a year and a half after opening, Mosport was bankrupt and facing closure. Fortunately, the receiver – National Trust – allowed racing to continue. In 1963 George Moss and Jim Fergusson from the BEMC joined forces with Bob Hanna and Bryan Rowntree from the CRDA, along with Harry Johnson, creating the Motor Racing Partnership (MRP) to rent the track and run the races. This was the group that 'saved Mosport,' and kept it going for the next three years. Growing crowds eventually brought in more money, but MRP made little headway against the track's massive debt.[16]

The problem, Roy McLaughlin explains, was that drivers demanded all their money up front. Once they were paid, the modest profit – perhaps a few hundred dollars – did not even begin to reduce the debt. He recalls that the races ran on the fine edge of solvency:

> Art and I would be signing cheques for up to $50,000, and we didn't have a dime in the bank. We had paid all these guys [drivers] with cheques that would bounce unless they [people] came through the gate on the day of the event ... We made money on that day, we paid everybody off on that day. And we sat the next day and said, 'Gee, that's great, we've got fifty cents left.' But we went through a hundred thousand the day before.[17]

Years later, *Canada Track and Traffic* magazine editor Frank Orr lauded their intentions while gently chiding them for falling short:

> When Mosport went belly-up in '62 and fell into the clutches of a huge, impersonal trust company, love poured in from all angles ... People love the underdog, and Mosport played that role well, battling along in the face of incredible odds ... her lessee operators wearing 'Preserve Racing' buttons like life belts to prevent their drowning in a sea of red ink....

Mosport was easy to love in those days, easy to overlook the shortcomings of her operation such as lack of sound financing, business acumen and promotional savvy ... The men who called the shots in those days where [sic] old shoe guys who did it because of their love of the sport, a motivation that tends to make things lose their focus.[18]

But Muriel Knap, long-time executive secretary of CASC Ontario Region, who lived at the track and was known to many racers as 'Mother Mosport,' was less charitable. At age eighty-two she was characteristically blunt: 'At the beginning, Mosport belonged to the sport. It was the sport that organized it ... [but] was not astute enough on running a business ... They had fun and frolic and loved it ... and lost money, hand over fist.'[19]

MRP ran the races at Mosport until April 1966, when National Trust sold it to Cantrack Motor Racing Ltd – a subsidiary of *Canada Track and Traffic* magazine. National Trust tried but failed to bring the two groups together. Roy McLaughlin says that MRP was hoping it could stall the sale long enough to raise the funds to buy the track, but the receiver decided to sell to the group that had 'cash in hand.' The Cantrack team included two well-known racers: Peter Lerch and Jerry Polivka, who was by then managing editor of the magazine. The new president of Mosport, Dr Irwin Fineberg, was a brother-in-law of Norm Namerow, who had died the previous year. But the real power players within the group were Harvey Hudes and Bernard Kamin, respectively the accountant and the lawyer for Cantrack. Neither of these two men had been involved with the sport previously; they knew nothing about it. Thus, they relied on experienced club organizers to run races. Yet as track chronicler Chuck McLaren suggests, it was not a comfortable alliance. Hudes and Kamin did not really understand racing, while the clubs were suspicious of the business interests that had taken over 'their' racetrack. McLaughlin feels the new owners came in with the attitude that, 'since I own the ball and bat, you'll play the game my way.'[20] In the short term that attitude was to cost them dearly. But at least Mosport was now back on a sound financial footing – as a business.

Quebec Follows Suit: Le Circuit

As with Westwood, the Mosport story should have served as a cautionary lesson for enthusiasts in Quebec. They were well aware of

Mosport's problems, but that did not deter them from building a track of their own. Sadly, after a promising start and several successful seasons, the outcome was even worse.

Ironically, the story of Le Circuit really begins in Ontario. Unable to find a locale in Quebec in the 1950s, Montreal racers had competed at the Connor airfield circuit just across the border in St-Eugène, Ontario. The Laurentian Autosport Club ran the races there until, according to Coates, the club treasurer skipped town with the gate receipts. At that point, racer Norm Namerow stepped in and ran the track for about a year and a half until he could convince the Montreal MG Car Club (MMGCC) to take over the operation. From 1957 to 1963, MMGCC ran a series of races there that attracted the biggest names in Eastern Canadian racing. But the primitive facilities attracted only small crowds, and by the early 1960s the track itself was 'literally falling apart.' In a telling 1962 race report that explicitly imposed professional standards on an amateur club–run race, Rod Campbell commented that the small crowd (2200) indicated

> that Montreal motorsport enthusiasts aren't going to bother going to an event and put up with second-rate facilities. They've no doubt been somewhat spoiled by the wonderful Mosport set-up. And further, the four and five hours of traffic-congested driving back to Montreal and the muddy mess at two events last year (still fresh in many minds) really stretched the spectators' patience. A new race circuit closer to Montreal is definitely needed and may be the only solution to poor attendance figures.[21]

The Connor Circuit needed to be re-paved and improved to bring it up to a usable standard. But even that would only postpone its inevitable demise, at great cost to the club. And it would still be just an airport track. What the clubs really wanted was a track *in Quebec* that would rival Mosport. As John Ross, one of Le Circuit's founders, later put it: 'It would be difficult to overemphasize the importance we placed on coming up with something better than Ontario had.'[22]

The MMGCC had begun lobbying for a new track in the Montreal area in the summer of 1962. Club spokesman Bob MacGregor used his own CBC radio show to push the idea. At one point the club considered creating a circuit on Île Ste-Hélène. In light of what transpired sixteen years later, it was a visionary concept. But the club could not build a track on its own, and initial approaches to investors fell flat. Then fate intervened in the form of St-Jovite businessman Leo Samson. He knew nothing of the club's dreams, but had long had one of his own: to create a racetrack as a tourist attraction for the ski resort area during the summer season. Samson also knew Peter Ryan and had seen racing at Watkins Glen. But his efforts to win over other local businessmen to his idea had failed. Then, at an ice race in Ste-Agathe in the winter of 1963 Samson met CKVL radio reporter Jacques Duval, considered by some 'the foremost racing commentator in Canada in the 1960s.' Former MMGCC president Ross de St. Croix credits Duval – a racer himself – with seizing the opportunity: 'Jacques ... came to our club one day and said, "Look, you guys are the only club who I believe can put this package together ... I've got a bunch of guys at St. Jovite who want to build a racetrack ... They need some people to help them."'[23]

Samson and the MMGCC met and drafted a proposal for prospective investors. John Ross, André Ouellette, de St. Croix, and then club president John Spencer-Nairn presented it to a meeting of St-Jovite area businessmen. John Ross remembers that they went into the meeting committed to persuading the town that car racing was a tourist attraction too good to pass up. Despite the hard sell, they had no takers. But Samson refused to give up. He bought some land, formed the Mont Tremblant Circuit Corporation with his local business partners, including ski resort manager Maurice Paquin, and kept up the lobbying. By the spring of 1964, after two bad ski seasons in a row, the locals were more receptive to Samson's idea. Facing a two-week decision deadline, Samson convinced fifty local investors to pledge $1000 each. The club – now renamed the Montreal Motor Racing Club (MMRC) – put up $6000. In all they raised $89,000, just enough to construct the track. They agreed that the club would organize the races, while the company would run the track as a business. The MMRC formed a track design committee, including de St. Croix, MacGregor, Namerow, Paquin, Ross, and – at the urging of sponsor British Petroleum (BP) – former racer John Fitch, who owned and ran the Lime Rock track in Connecticut. Armed only with topographic maps and some advice on design from the RAC, they tramped the woods and sketched out the track plan. Then, in stark contrast to the experience of Westwood and Mosport, they turned the design into a race-ready track in three months and three days. It opened on time for the first race on 3 August 1964.[24]

That first event attracted 16,800 spectators and – even more important – big corporate sponsors. Prodded by Ross and Campbell, Labatts lent its name to the feature race (won by Heimrath in the Comstock team's King Cobra) and paid for a bridge over the track to allow spectators to drive into the infield. BP covered the cost of building the control tower, estimated at $30,000. And Player's came on board to sponsor the next race. Held in September the Player's Quebec featured only one major international driver (Pedro Rodriguez in a Ferrari), but drew 35,000 fans (21,000 paying). That was about seven times larger than the biggest crowd at St-Eugène, and more than any previous sports event in Quebec. And the MMRC made a profit.[25] Le Circuit, it seemed, had got it right.

The next season Pepsi Cola added its name to the race sponsor list. The fans were treated to battles between Ferraris, Lolas, McLarens, and Chaparrals, the exotic, powerful machines on the cutting edge of the car racing 'revolution.' From the outset, however, experienced drivers had complained that the track was too short, too tight, and too slow to show off these cars at their best. And so in September 1965 it was extended by another mile. Even so, Le Circuit remained a challenging circuit with demanding corners, few level spots, and an infamous 'jump,' where high-speed cars sometimes got airborne. Yet, while it seemed to go from success to success, hosting the inaugural Can-Am series race in 1966, Le Circuit was facing a crisis. Just as at Westwood and Mosport, it all came down to money. In a 1964 editorial, *Canada Track and Traffic* had praised the Samson-MMRC alliance for financing and constructing the track intelligently and economically:

> The businessmen provided most of the funds required, with the Montreal car club also participating financially while ... carrying out much of the early leg work efficiently and effectively. The two groups complement one another almost ideally ... the businessmen providing the corporate and financial know-how and the club, as partners, contributing racing knowledge and promotional enthusiasm. As a result, the circuit was built with sound planning, no unnecessary capital expenditures ... It carries no outstanding debt.[26]

If only that had been true. In fact, the track had cost almost $400,000, *eight times* the club's original estimate. The corporation had mortgage and construction bills to pay, but the MMRC got most of the profits from the races. Ross de St. Croix feels the club got in over its head:

> We [MMRC] were twelve per cent owners of St-Jovite, before it went bankrupt. And I guess we were still naive enough not to really know all

the intricacies of business ownership ... We cleaned out our bank account to buy our share of the business ... Then we were told one day that our investment was of little value. We had an accountant who could never get to the bottom of it; financial statements were lost. It was a terrible mess ... I believe to this day that we got screwed out of our ownership.[27]

A lawsuit and an out-of-court settlement followed. The track and the club then asked the CASC to mediate, but when the track refused to accept the arbitration committee's binding decision, the CASC refused to sanction any events at Le Circuit for 1967. In the meantime, due to poor promotion because of the dispute, the national championship race at the track in July 1966 had lost $43,000 and the sponsor (Pepsi Cola) promptly pulled out of auto sport. When the dust finally settled in early 1967, Samson and the MMRC were out, and Le Circuit was in the hands of a holding company: Gestion Laurentide.[28]

Business First: Edmonton International Speedway

Successful or not, Mosport and Le Circuit were too remote to benefit Prairie Region racers. A small, widely dispersed population, a large area, and a short season meant that racing on the Prairies in the early 1960s displayed a distinctly amateur flavour. Region clubs continued to use airport circuits simply because there was no alternative. Only diehard enthusiasts, who were prepared to travel long distances to race, kept the sport alive. For example, in September 1961 the Lethbridge Sports Car Club's race at the Pinetree airport circuit, at Pearce, Alberta, drew drivers from across the region. Joe Hamilton from Saskatoon won two races in his Austin-Healy 3000. Doug Bateman of Winnipeg raced a Triumph TR3. Len Cook from High River, Alberta drove an MGA twin-cam, and Phil Goodhall brought his Canada Class special from Calgary. The seven-race event drew 2200 spectators. The entire Prairie Region season that year consisted of only four races – the Pearce event, two at Carberry, Manitoba, and one at Davidson, Saskatchewan – which forced Peter Brand, the CASC regional steward, to travel 3500 miles to supervise.[29]

The need for a proper racetrack on the Prairies finally was met by Reginald and Percy Booth. The owners of an Edmonton construction company, they also operated Breckenridge Speedway, a stock car oval on the outskirts of the city. According to Coates, when an over-zealous employee left them with a set of architect's track plans and a $41,000 bill, they saw an opportunity where others might have seen only a problem. With some encouragement from Tommy Fox, who was both a racer and a prominent businessman, the Booths used the plans to build Edmonton International Speedway (EIS) at a cost of $1.3 million.

EIS differed from the earlier purpose-built tracks in three important ways. First, it was a business venture from the outset; it was built *to make money*. To that end, its second key feature was its integrated, multi-use layout, intended to attract the full range of auto sport enthusiasts – and their money. EIS included a two-mile, eight-turn road-racing circuit, which was tied into a drag strip and one of two stock car ovals. It had grandstand seating for 10,000, thirty covered pit buildings, and a control tower that also housed a press centre, clubhouse, lounge, restaurant, and banquet rooms. Finally, it was only a fifteen-minute drive from downtown Edmonton.[30] The road course opened in 1968 and was an immediate success, hosting a wide range of regional, national, and international events for the next fifteen years. Its close proximity to the downtown of a major city was an advantage that would be sought later by race promoters elsewhere. Ironically, however, it eventually would lead to the demise of EIS.

Left in the Dust

For the amateur 'weekend warriors,' tracks like Westwood and Mosport represented a quantum leap in quality. A smoothly paved racing surface was a vast improvement on the rough airport tracks that had taken their toll on cars, tires, and drivers alike. But airport racing did not end with the opening of the new tracks. The London Auto Sport Club (LASC) took over Harewood from BEMC in 1963, repaved the track and held races – including national championship events – there until it closed in 1970.[31] On the Prairies, there was no alternative to airport racing until EIS opened. But, whether on a 'real' racetrack or an airport course, club racing in the first half of the 1960s looked little different from that in the 1950s. It featured 'local heroes,' small crowds, production sports cars, and sedans.

By the middle of the decade, however, the trend towards commercialized racing that the CRDA had started was firmly established. The new tracks and the major races they hosted highlighted two significant changes in the sport. First, they validated the CRDA's view that the *purpose* of pro racing was to attract and entertain a crowd large enough that the event could pay for itself and even turn a profit. That said, at this stage the profits were not large and the question of whom they belonged to was a matter of some dispute. What was clear is that racing was becoming a business and – just as the advocates of pro racing had argued in 1959 – the clubs were out of their depth in this milieu. Their travails over financing and running the new race tracks made that point abundantly clear.

The second change was in who made up that audience and what they expected from racing. Through the 1950s small crowds, drawn from the equally small sports car subculture, watched amateur club races featuring 'local heroes' because that's all there was. But, once events like the Player's 200 offered the chance to see famous drivers and cars, even these diehard fans all but abandoned club racing. Moreover, the much larger crowds that flooded Mosport and later Le Circuit represented a new fan base that extended well beyond the subculture. And it was the famous European drivers and their exotic cars, not the Canadian amateurs, whom this new audience came to see. They were attracted by celebrity rather than by fascination for the finer points of racing. Art Moseley later derided them as little more than 'event groupies' who knew nothing about the sport. 'They go to be part of a big event ... just so they can say they were there.'[32] That probably was true, but in the 1960s, before televised race coverage expanded the audience and the sponsor's promotional market, their gate fees paid the bills. Without them, races like the Player's 200 simply would not have been possible.

Thus, in the wake of the watershed year of 1961, Canadian racing exhibited a kind of 'dualistic' character, both embracing change *and* seeing it pass by. Professional and amateur racing were developing separate and diverging tracks, and as a result the amateurs were being 'left in the dust.' But those who followed the professional route quickly found themselves confronted with a steep learning curve and an exponential leap in the cost of staying competitive.

9 Reach for the Top: Canadian Racing Driver Development in the 1960s

> There seems to be a feeling that Canadians can't do well enough to win in international competition ... I say nuts to that.
>
> 'Chuck'Rathgeb, Jr[1]

'Young Man in a Hurry'

What does it take to be a racing superstar? If it takes good looks, charm, and a raw, unbridled talent for driving – then Peter Ryan had it all in spades. And in the fall of 1961 at Mosport, the blond-haired, blue-eyed boy from Mont Tremblant, Quebec, won the first Canadian Grand Prix for Sports Cars. Beating the likes of European stars Olivier Gendebien and Stirling Moss, Ryan served notice on the racing world that he was on his way to the top. More than fifteen years before Gilles Villeneuve burst upon the Formula One scene, the world sat up and took note of a young Canadian racer. But less than a year later, he was killed in a racing accident in Europe. It was a hard lesson for all Canadian racers in the early 1960s. To 'reach for the top' they needed professional development.

Growing up at the famous ski resort established by his father, Peter was a natural athlete and a top ski racer. Barred from the Canadian Olympic ski team because he had been born in the United States, he found a new direction in life after trying a friend's sports car. He bought a Porsche Spyder 550, took a lesson from John Fitch at his Lime Rock track, then practised on the roads that twisted around the ski hill. Peter's racing debut at the Greenacres airport circuit in May 1959 was a humbling experience; he over-revved the engine and blew it up. Frustrated, he said later, 'I nearly cried, sitting there watching the other cars go around.'[2]

Still, in racing Peter had found his calling. 'It is the biggest thrill you can get out of life, the biggest in the world,' he remarked. 'You live in a higher way during a race. Everything is duller afterward.'[3] His potential impressed Porsche, and for the 1960 season they sold him one of the two low-slung, sleek, silver RS60 sports-racing cars provided to Canadian racers. Francis Bradley, Peter's fiercest rival on the track, raced the second one for a Toronto Porsche/VW dealer. While trying to pass Bradley in the chicane at the CRDA championship race on the Connor circuit, Peter went into it too fast, left his braking too late, and ended up in the hay bales. 'Peter did the only gentlemanly thing when he took to the hay,' Bradley said later, 'for he could have smashed into me and probably put both of us out of the meet.'[4] Bradley won that race, but Peter picked up two other victories that day. 'Speed doesn't bother me,' he said between races. 'The only worry I have is reaching the finish line – ahead of everyone else.'[5]

Another rival, but also perhaps his closest friend, was Roger Penske, a young American driver who since has become one of the most successful and influential men in auto racing. They shared the drive and the victory in the 1960 Sundown Grand Prix at Harewood, beating the second-place RS60 driven by Bradley and Heimrath by almost a full minute. This achievement prompted CRDA president Tommy Gilmour to remark, '[Ryan] shows, without qualification, the greatest potential of attaining international status of anyone we've ever seen in Canada.'[6]

Peter lived up to that billing in 1961, which proved to be his banner year. Although he had never driven a Formula Junior before, Peter showed his mettle in a borrowed Lotus 20, winning the August 1961 Vanderbilt Cup FJ race at Bridgehampton, New York – the most important race for the class in North America – and earning headlines in the *New York Times*.[7]

Rathgeb Goes Racing: The Comstock Racing Team

About a month before his victory in the Canadian Grand Prix for Sports Cars Peter had bought a Lotus 19 sports-racing car. Needing a sponsor, he turned to 'Chuck' Rathgeb, who had just established the Comstock Racing Team. 'Ryan came [to me] and said, "You know, I can drive well." And I said, "I know you can. You're a damned good driver." And he said, "Why don't I give you my car ... and you paint it in Comstock's colours, and you do the mechanical work, and I'll drive."'[8] And so the deal was struck, and Canada's best racer joined Canada's first 'national' racing team: the personal creation and fiefdom of 'Chuck' Rathgeb, a wealthy, white-haired, cigar-smoking giant of a businessman, and an avid sportsman. Rathgeb didn't set out to create Canada's first 'racer nursery,' but in that de facto role the Comstock team left an indelible mark on Canadian auto sport.

Born in 1921 in Trois-Rivières, Quebec, Charles Rathgeb Jr discovered his passion for sport during his school days at Upper Canada College, in Toronto. Following a stint in the Royal Canadian Mounted Police, wartime service in the navy, and business studies at the University of Toronto, Chuck joined the family firm, Canadian Comstock Company. The Toronto-based engineering construction firm that worked on 'megaprojects' like the St Lawrence Seaway and the trans-Sahara gas pipeline showed the young Rathgeb how to think big and succeed. And that success afforded him the time and money to indulge his competitive spirit. His sporting accomplishments include climbing the Matterhorn, big game hunting, managing a successful stable of thoroughbreds, and coaching the 1964 Olympic gold medal–winning Canadian bobsled team. Furthermore, Rathgeb was an unabashed nationalist when it came to sports. Speaking as the team readied the Comstock-Sadler racing cars for their inaugural season, he asserted: 'I believe it's possible for Canadians to compete in Canadian cars in North American racing and do well.'[9]

Like many good ideas, the Comstock Racing Team owed its origins partly to chance. Travelling regularly to the company plant in St Catharines, Ontario, in the fall of 1960, Rathgeb spotted Bill Sadler's racing shop there and out of curiosity stopped in to visit. Sadler was building the first of his two innovative rear-engined Mk. V sports-racing cars, but was short of money. At about the same time Grant Clark, who wanted to move up in racing, took Rathgeb out to the site of the new Mosport track, which was then under construction. Impressed by the possibilities for big-league racing that Mosport offered, Rathgeb decided to form a team, with Sadler building the cars, Clark driving, and Comstock funding the effort. The company paid for one of the Mk. Vs; never one to think small, Rathgeb mused that 'perhaps we can produce other [racing] cars for sale.'[10] The fit between construction and car racing was not a natural or obvious one, but except for the beer and tobacco firms Rathgeb was ahead of his time. Comstock's effort presaged by nearly two decades the entry of non-auto-related racing sponsors.

The team fielded three Sadler cars for the 1961 season: the two Mk. Vs and an FJ. The Mk. Vs were the first cars to carry the team colours: white with two dark green stripes, the firm's logo, and a green maple leaf with 'Canada' emblazoned across it. But it was Ryan, driving his Lotus 19 dressed in team colours, who brought the team its first victory, winning the first Canadian Grand Prix for Sports Cars in September 1961. A Canadian driving for a Canadian team beating the world's best on a Canadian track made for an immensely popular victory. Ryan was mobbed by the crowds after the race, and received a standing ovation at the victory banquet. Rathgeb recalled the win with great pride: 'We knew we had one heck of a driver in young Ryan, but we were facing some of the biggest name drivers of the era, people like Stirling Moss and Olivier Gendebien. There was no way we expected to win. We were ecstatic.'[11]

Ryan's Reach

The victory augured well for the future of the Comstock team, but in fact heralded a series of changes. Ryan's departure was the first. Colin Chapman, the founder, builder, and driving force behind Britain's Lotus racing cars, had an eye for talent that would take his team to seven Formula One constructors' championships. He offered Peter the chance of a lifetime: to drive for the Lotus team. 'Peter was thrilled,' his sister Seddon Ryan Wylde recalls. 'He wanted to go to Europe because he knew that is where the best racing was taking place, and he wanted to see how he could do against the best.'[12]

The seeds had been sown immediately following the Vanderbilt Cup race, when Ryan's local sponsor contacted the Lotus factory about possible support. After the win at Mosport, Chapman invited Peter to drive a Formula One Lotus in the US Grand Prix at Watkins Glen in October, which made him the first Canadian to compete in an F1 car in a world championship race. Despite the fact that he was driving an older model plagued by carburetor and gear problems, Ryan managed to finish ninth, respectably in the middle of the pack. A few hours after the race, Chapman made his formal offer to Peter.[13]

After his stellar 1961 season, Ryan's move to England the next spring proved to be something of a let-down. Chapman had signed him to a three-year contract, but for the first year assigned him to the Lotus FJ team. Peter's sister remembers that he was very disappointed: 'He thought he belonged in Formula One. Despite his young age he ... thought that Chapman was making him waste a year by not allowing him to run Formula One ... It was no doubt a wise decision, but Peter didn't see it that way. He was very impatient.'[14] Ryan also received a shock when he saw his racing car for the first time – in pieces. Believing that his drivers should know their cars inside out, Chapman told Peter he had to build it himself. He did so in less than two weeks, and in one of his earliest races in the 1962 season at Mallory Park he beat Peter Arundell, who had been the British FJ champion the previous year. He was also only marginally slower than the track lap record set by John Surtees in an F1 Lola. The British auto sport press described Ryan enthusiastically as 'an exciting new Formula One prospect.'[15]

Ryan's only race at Le Mans, France, was less inspiring. Luigi Chinetti, the manager of Ferrari's NART, hired Ryan to co-drive a *Testa Rossa* in the famous twenty-four-hour endurance race, sharing the ride with American John Fulp. He was having a great dice with Ricardo Rodriguez, but went into Mulsanne hairpin too fast, lost control, and ploughed into a sandbank at over 50 mph. After hours of digging, Peter gave up and watched the rest of the race from the Ferrari pits. Veteran Ferrari driver Bob Grossman told him, 'Don't let it get you down. Plenty of drivers with a lot more experience than you have gone off the course in the same spot. It's nothing to be ashamed of.' But British driver [Sir] John Whitmore was a little less sympathetic. 'Every time I came around the track I saw you digging in the sand with your hands ... You were a very sorry sight.'[16]

When a friend had once remarked to Peter that he might get killed racing, he simply shrugged and said, 'When your number comes up, you're going to get it. But meanwhile, you're enjoying yourself.'[17] Peter's number came up a few weeks after Le Mans. In the Formula Junior Grand Prix at Rheims, France, at the beginning of July, he was dicing for the lead with British driver Bill Moss when the two cars touched or locked wheels. Peter's car flipped over and Moss's car ran over it, crushing Ryan underneath. After thirty hours in a coma, Peter died in a Paris hospital. He was buried at Mont Tremblant alongside his father. Amid an outpouring of grief unmatched in Canadian auto sport until Gilles Villeneuve's death twenty years later, Chuck Rathgeb noted prophetically, 'It'll be a long time before the sport sees another man of his calibre again.'[18]

Following Ryan's Lead

Almost unnoticed in the enthusiasm over Ryan's success and the sorrow over his death was the fact that at the same time other Canadians were trying to break into Formula One. In April 1962, as a reward for winning the 1961 CRDA championship, Player's sponsored Ludwig Heimrath's entry in a non-points F1 race at Pau, France. Driving a factory Porsche he qualifed twelfth in a field of eighteen, less than four seconds behind F1 star Joakim Bonnier, also in a Porsche. In the race itself Heimrath ran in the top ten before he crashed, owing to either a locked brake or oil on the track. Nevertheless, his driving impressed his fellow competitors and the world's racing press: 'He proved able to lap very quickly indeed in very exalted company.'[19] However, Heimrath never competed in F1 again.

Peter Broeker raced his versatile FJ for six seasons, winning more than a hundred races in North America. While he was considered 'the father' of Canadian formula car racing,[20] his car was outclassed in European Formula Two events. And so, as with Heimrath, no F1 teams came knocking.

Powered by Ford ... and Chuck

In the meantime, the Comstock Racing Team had endured more changes. Even before Ryan's Mosport victory, Bill Sadler had fallen out with Rathgeb and left the team. Sadler later reflected, 'It started out a pretty good relationship, but unfortunately he [Rathgeb] made decisions over and above my decisions ... and I quit.'[21] The Mk. Vs were sold and, bucking the Sadler-led trend, the team built a new front-engined car: the EXP, which was powerful, but hard to drive. As Rathgeb said at the time, 'We can't blame him [driver Fred Hayes] for losing faith in the car; after all, the suspension broke three times and the wheel fell off once. That's enough to shake any driver.'[22] The EXP's problems reflected the period, when racing cars were becoming more complex. Development required constant testing in competition. But, as Rathgeb explained, the EXP never got the necessary testing because 'the short Canadian season, with only two professional races, influenced the development speed, which should have been tempered by the benefits of day-to-day racing ... Amateur events don't offer the chance to recoup some of the expenses.'[23]

The team's fortunes turned the following year, thanks to the Ford Motor Company. Coincidentally, at this time Comstock was doing a lot of construction work for Ford of Canada. Aware that Ford was getting back into racing, Chuck met with Carl Scott, president of Ford of Canada, and said, 'Why don't you and I start? ... It'll be good for the Ford business in Canada and he agreed ... So he got in touch with the States, they said okay ... What they would do is provide the cars, the engines, the parts, and I would provide the [team garage] space, the mechanics, and the drivers.'[24] The Comstock Racing Team was back in business.

They opened 1963 in splashy style at the Toronto auto show, with an array of cars on display including their new pride and joy: a Shelby Cobra. All of the cars were painted in the team colours and carried the 'Powered by Ford' logo. It was a banner start to a banner year. The team claimed eighteen overall victories and thirty-five class wins. They finished the season in dramatic style at the Canadian GP. Driving two Cobras, Torontonian Eppie Wietzes and Ken Miles (who was on loan to Comstock from Shelby American Racing) carried on a hair-raising duel that had the crowd on its feet as Wietzes beat Miles to the line.[25]

The year 1964, however, got off to a rough start. Comstock had purchased two $20,000 Cooper-Fords (also known as King Cobras) from Shelby. These low-slung and sleek sports-racing cars had an expanded Cooper Formula One body with the Cobra's Ford 289 V-8 in the rear. The team transported them out to the Westwood track for the Player's Pacific race. Wietzes was to drive one of the cars and Ludwig Heimrath the other. But during practice Eppie crashed and destroyed one of the new cars, suffering a broken leg and cracked ribs. Rathgeb remembers:

> Somebody saw a flash of silver ... going through the trees and reported an airplane had crashed ... It was him [Eppie]. It was a sad state of affairs ... We'd just got them. We'd hauled them all the way. Stopped at tracks along the way, demonstrated them for Ford dealers from all over.[26]

Eppie's recollection, if slightly different, is understandably more vivid:

> The car was ... approaching Deer's Leap, and ... just veered left and went down in the hole ... hit a big rock and it went straight up ... and I landed in the trees upside down ... They had to chop all the trees down to get the car out. It took them over two and a half hours ... Weber carburetors, they were cleaned right off; the cylinder head – a whole chunk of it was broken off. And they never did find the battery ... that broke my leg.[27]

In the race itself, however, Heimrath recouped some dignity for the team by taking third place. After that discouraging start, 1964 proved to be another great year for the team. Heimrath won several races and claimed the Canadian racing driver's championship.[28]

They also dominated production sedan racing that year, fielding an array of Ford Cortinas, Falcons, and Mustangs. To promote the Falcon, Ford sent up a pair of race-prepared cars from the United States. The team painted them in Comstock colours and raced them in Canadian events. Driving one in the three-hour Canada Touring Trophy endurance race at Mosport, team crew chief Paul Cooke 'steamed to the front at the start and managed to lap all opposition but the second and third place finishers'[29] Teammate Ron Goldsack, driving a Cortina, was fourth.

The team had bought one of the first production Mustangs, which became the first one raced anywhere in the world. Nominally it was a sedan, but with four Weber carburetors on its 384-bhp engine it was no more than a thinly disguised sports car that left all other sedans eating its dust. Team driver Craig Fisher remembers the car: 'I got a homemade [GT] 350. I think actually my car was probably quicker [than the Shelby 350], but I didn't know how to drive it.'[30] In August 1965 Fisher and Wietzes, driving the team's Shelby Mustang, overcame fading brakes and a fifteen-second penalty to win the six-hour Sundown Grand Prix endurance race at Mosport. Comstock's early success with the Mustang impressed Ford in the United States and strengthened the team's relations with the company. Realizing they had a winning product, Rathgeb says, Ford would send people up every time the team raced them. 'They'd want to know what broke ... what did our mechanics think ... were the weak spots in the car.'[31] Racing tests cars to their limits, and as Ford executive vice-president Charles Patterson explained:

> When we say 'racing improves the breed,' we don't just mean the mechanical aspects of our motor vehicles. We also mean it improves the breed of engineers, designers and manufacturing people who adapt these improvements ... From this work on racing cars, these specialists know more about automobiles – faster and sometimes more painfully – than they could ever have learned otherwise.[32]

All of this stood the Comstock team in good stead to join Ford's assault on the World Sports Car Championship in 1966. After being rebuffed in its effort to buy Ferrari, Ford had decided to beat them where they were most dominant: Le Mans. Starting with a design by Eric Broadley – the British builder of Lola racing cars – Ford poured millions into the development of a prototype sports-racing car, which became known as the GT40. The car's first two Le Mans outings – in 1964 and 1965 – began with promise but ended in failure. While the Fords were faster than the Ferraris, they suffered from a variety of mechanical problems and failed to finish the gruelling twenty-four-hour race. Only Shelby's Cobras kept the Ford name in the top ten.

By 1966 Ford had a reliable car: the GT40 Mk. II, powered by a 427-cid (seven-litre) engine. The Comstock team was invited to join Ford's Le Mans effort, starting with the twelve-hour endurance race at Sebring, Florida. Rathgeb selected four top drivers for the event: Wietzes and Fisher, both from Ontario, Jean Ouellette from Quebec, and national champion Bob McLean from British Columbia, giving the team a national flavour. Comstock took delivery of two brand new GT40s, powered by the smaller 289-cid engine rather than the 427. A month before the race, the team went down to Sebring. Craig Fisher recalls feeling that they were a little out of their league:

> Here we were, a relatively unknown Canadian concern, up against the factory teams with all the big name drivers. Our cars had been freshly delivered from Ford and weren't set up yet. We didn't even have time to paint them in our colours. During one session it rained and I remember losing it and spinning onto the grass. We had to figure it out ourselves, but eventually we did get the cars set up properly ... I wasn't happy driving the GT40. It didn't feel safe.[33]

His concerns were borne out in the race, which for the Comstock team ended as a tragic baptism by fire. About a third of the way into the race, approaching the hairpin, probably at high speed under heavy braking, a wheel locked and McLean lost control. The car flipped over three times and hit a utility pole. That ruptured the gas tank, the gas was ignited by the red-hot disk brakes, and the car exploded. McLean died instantly. Wietzes was driving the other team car: 'When I came around to the hairpin there were yellow flags everywhere and I saw this burning wreck. It never even occurred to me that it could be Bob. A few laps later Chuck was leaning over the pit wall motioning for me to come in. It was only then that I realized what had happened. We immediately withdrew from the race.'[34]

McLean's death shocked the team and the Canadian racing community. The modest, slender thirty-two-year-old Australian-born mechanic was immensely popular among BC racing fans. He had won the 1965 Canadian championship in an under-powered Lotus 23B, travelling thousands of miles to race in five provinces, and earning the victory – and a mere $5261 – by sheer hard work. When he died he left behind a wife and two young children. Asked during an interview at Sebring why he made such sacrifices to race, he replied, 'I don't know why ... Maybe for the same reason people climb mountains and parachute jump or fight bulls. I can't begin to explain.' Like Peter Ryan before him, he was also fatalistic about the risks: 'When the Great Man upstairs pushes the button, that's it.'[35] His funeral in Burnaby, BC was emotional:

> He was buried ... in a casket draped with a blanket of flowers on which his racing number ... was laid out in blue on a background of white, the same colours he painted his racing cars. His hearse was the van that carried the Lotus 23B to the track. And some of the fans who had cheered him at Westwood followed ... in a cavalcade two miles long.[36]

Perhaps because his fate paralleled Ryan's, McLean's death hit Chuck Rathgeb particularly hard. 'There is no doubt that Bob's death knocked some of the steam out of us.'[37] Craig Fisher feels Bob's death 'kinda really crushed him [Rathgeb]. He kept racing, but it really bothered him.'[38]

Eppie Wietzes continued to campaign the second GT40 for Comstock for the remainder of the 1966 season and took second place to Nat Adams in a McLaren in the over-two-litre national championship. The next year he was second in the overall national championship to Ross de St. Croix, who was also in a McLaren. This was a harbinger of change in North American racing. In the new Can-Am series, the McLarens and Lolas clearly outclassed the Comstock GT40, which was less powerful and much heavier. Having proved its point by winning Le Mans two years in a row, Ford US pulled out of international sports car racing after their 1967 victory. The company threw its weight behind the new Trans-Am sedan series, where it could showcase its production cars – Mustangs and Cougars – in competition against the other American 'muscle cars,' especially GM's Chevrolet Camaros. By that time, the team was costing Comstock about $100,000 per year and Revenue Canada was starting to question the relationship between the company's construction business and a car racing team. And so, at the end of 1967 the Comstock Racing Team folded.[39]

The Player's National Championship

While the Comstock team was grooming its select stable of top drivers in the first half of the 1960s, the national racing championship was being re-shaped to achieve the same result on a wider scale. In April 1962, at the behest of Player's, the CASC established a new national competition to succeed the CRDA driver's championship. Player's agreed to provide a trophy and to send the winner to compete in a major European race the following season. The CRDA, which was committed to professionalizing Canadian racing, readily agreed to the plan. The CASC's rapid approval of the idea may have been no coincidence. Its racing chairman in 1962 was Milt Wright, who was both a CRDA member and an Imperial Tobacco sales executive.[40]

Putting the championship together on short notice just before the start of the season, the CASC arbitrarily selected eight events that would qualify for the series. The Player's 200 and Canadian Grand Prix, both held at Mosport, were the 'headliners.' Ontario Region was given three other events, Quebec had one, while the Prairie Region could count two. Only the feature event at each of these, running for a minimum distance of fifty miles, counted for points, and the '200' and the Grand Prix were worth double. The races had to be open to non-production, sports-racing cars and the competitors had to be Canadian residents.[41]

Two things about the first series stand out. First, while it represented an attempt to be 'national', it was clearly weighted in favour of Ontario. By placing consistently high, the would-be champion could win it without leaving that province. Western drivers, by contrast, would have to compete frequently in the east if they hoped to have a chance at the championship. Second, the set-up favoured the specialized racing car, which dominated the grids at the '200' and the Grand Prix. Thus, the rules limited real contenders to a relatively small group who were sponsored well enough to drive high-end machinery and to travel and compete in most of the events. The final results bore this out. The first national champion was Francis Bradley, driving a Lotus 19. His only real competition was Ludwig Heimrath in a Porsche RS 60. Both were from Ontario, both were sponsored, and they were the only two who competed in all regions.[42]

The following year was virtually a carbon copy. This time the champion was Dennis Coad in a Lotus 19 (fifty-three points), with Heimrath in his Porsche RS 61 only one point back. Both had competed in the majority of races. The rest of the field was far behind; even third-place John Cannon in the Dailu had earned only sixteen points. Once again, Ontario races dominated the card, but there were differences. The series was extended to nine races, with the addition of the Player's Pacific at Westwood, where Heimrath placed second. The most significant change was in the cars permitted to compete. Whereas in 1962 the series had included production sports cars, the next year it was *limited* to specialized sports-racing cars. That reduced the field of contenders even further. In 1962 thirteen drivers had finished in the points; in 1963 only ten did.[43]

After two years as runner-up, Heimrath won the national championship in 1964, driving the Comstock Cooper-Ford 'King Cobra.' Prairie Region drivers Phil Smyth (Lotus 23) and George Chapman (in the ex-Comstock EXP), both from Winnipeg, took the next two places, in what was becoming a more balanced series. Of the eight races, only four (including the '200' and the GP) were in Ontario, one was in Quebec (at the new St-Jovite track), two on the Prairies (Davidson and Souris), and one was at Westwood. But Heimrath still locked up the series with wins in the Ontario races and a second place to Pedro Rodriguez's Ferrari 330P in the inaugural Player's Quebec. Instead of a trip to Europe for winning the championship, however, he took home a cash prize from Player's of $1000 – a substantial award at that time.[44]

The criteria of the championship continued to change. At the request of Player's, the National Competition Board (NCB) agreed to break the 1965 series into two contests: over and under two-litre engine capacity. Player's would award $1000 to the winner in each category, and the trophy and $500 to the overall winner. At the 1964 AGM 'Race Meeting' there was a lengthy and lively discussion about a proposal to double the number of eligible events. But Jim Gunn warned that Player's might not approve of the change, so a decision was deferred to the next AGM.[45] The ability of Player's to mould the championship rules to its liking demonstrated the influence of business sponsors on the sport; they were beginning to challenge the power of the national governing body.

For 1965, the Player's Challenge Trophy series consisted of nine races, four of which were in Ontario. Curiously, the Grand Prix was excluded. There were two races each in Quebec and the Prairies, and one at Westwood. Race officials interpreted the class rules liberally enough to permit a large and diverse field of entries in both categories.

The visionaries. The CASC's founders at their first meeting, Kingston, Ontario, 17 June 1951. Left to right: Tom Pearce, Norm Hain, Jack Fidler, Jim Gunn, Hugh Young, Jack Luck, Burt Punshon, and Jack Fee.

Airport racing. Primitive cars and primitive safety: no rollover protection for the drivers and no safety barriers protect the spectators standing close to the track. Here an MGTC is leading two TDs at Abbotsford, BC, c. 1955.

Generational change: A Morgan 4/4 is about to be overtaken by a more powerful MGA, driven by Ken Finnigan during the first race at Davidson, Saskatchewan, June 1957.

Westwood, BC, Canada's first built-to-purpose road-racing circuit. Built by the Sports Car Club of British Columbia and opened in 1959, it showed how costly building such tracks would be. Closed in 1990, it is now the site of a housing estate. This shot from 1972 shows Formula B cars on the dramatic rise to Deer's Leap.

The Carling 300 race, organized by the Canadian Racing Driver's Association at Harewood in May 1960, was the model for the future of Canadian pro racing: prize money, big crowds, international stars, and specialist sports-racing cars: #100 – Porsche RS60, Olivier Gendebien (Belgium); #132 – Lotus 15, Harry Entwhistle; #88 – Sadler-Corvette, Dave Greenblatt; beside him, Ray Carter, Jaguar XKSS; #140 – Porsche RSK, Bob Holbert (USA).

Genius and talent. Designer/builder Bill Sadler pushing his 'Formula Ferocious' with driver Peter Ryan at the wheel, Watkins Glen, 1960. Looking on are racers Bruce McLaren of New Zealand (left) and Joakim Bonnier of Sweden (right). Sadler was the first to put an American V-8 engine in the back of a European-style chassis, anticipating the future of racing car design. Ryan was the most naturally talented Canadian racer of that era and the first to be hired by an F1 team (Lotus in 1961), but was killed in a racing accident in 1962.

Auto sport journalists and competitors Heather Wilson (left) and Diana Carter (right) teamed up for the BCITF Trans-Canada Rally, April 1961. Carter became the premier Canadian woman racer and rallyist of the 1960s.

The home of Canadian racing; Mosport opened in June 1961, went bankrupt the following year, and was bought and turned into a business in 1966. Shown here in its heyday – the Can-Am race in June 1973 – it survived the loss of major events and remains the premier road course in Canada.

The cutting edge. With a powerful V-8 engine in the back the Sadler Mk. V sports-racing car was the prototype for the later Can-Am cars. Charles 'Chuck' Rathgeb (standing behind, hands on hips) used Sadler's cars to launch Canada's first commercially sponsored national racing team in 1961. In the drivers' seats are Bill Sadler (#50) and Grant Clark (#51).

The award-winning Renault team, Shell 4000 rally, 1962. Left to right: Ian Worth, Robin Edwardes, Bill Leathem, John Charters, Grant McLean, Sam Nordell. Their teamwork and service support raised the bar for professional rally teams. The Shell 4000 introduced speed sections that reshaped Canadian pro rallying.

David vs. Goliath. The season-long duels between Grant Clark (Mini-Cooper) and Craig Fisher (Pontiac Catalina), shown here at the Connor Circuit, Ontario, June 1962, were crowd-pleasers that showed the marketing potential of sedan racing.

The 'father' of formula car racing in Canada: Peter Broeker in his Stebro Formula Junior at Watkins Glen, where he placed seventh in the 1963 F1 US Grand Prix. He was instrumental in changing the national racing championship to open-wheel cars to better prepare Canadian racers for the top ranks of international racing.

Jacques Duval, racer and broadcaster, did much to popularize the very 'Anglo' pastime of sports car racing with French Canadians and was instrumental in creating Le Circuit in 1964 as the home track for Quebec racers.

Ice racing gave die-hard racers the opportunity to compete year round. Here Dave Greenblatt's 'Nassau Taxi' Mini demonstrates the audience appeal of the sport.

Prelude to tragedy. Bob Mclean's Comstock team Ford GT40 at the 1966 Sebring twelve-hour endurance race where a crash took his life.

Coming of age. The inaugural Canadian Grand Prix for Formula One, Mosport, August 1967. Here Al Pease, the only Canadian to finish the race, pushes his Eagle Climax past world champion Graham Hill, who spun his Lotus 49 in the wet. Hill recovered to finish third, while Pease was twelfth and last.

Taking it to the streets. The Trois-Rivières Grand Prix, launched in 1967, led the return to city-street racing in North America. This picture shows Formula Fords passing under the Duplessis Arch in 1974.

Muscle cars. Sedan racing matures with the Trans-Am series, which came to Canada at Le Circuit in 1968. Mark Donohue in the Penske team Camaro (#6) won the opener. Canadian Craig Fisher came fourth. The natural topography of Le Circuit made it a race-watcher's paradise without the need for grandstands.

John Cannon in his McLaren-Chev M1B winning at Laguna Seca, California, 13 October 1968. Choosing the right tires and driving skilfully on the rain-soaked track gave him Canada's only victory in the original Can-Am series.

George Eaton was the first Canadian to race full time in Formula One. He spent two seasons with the British BRM team, but without success. Here in a BRM P154 (#98) he placed third in the 1970 Can-Am race at Le Circuit.

The Eastern Zone Endurance Series gave Atlantic region racers a chance to prove their mettle against drivers from Quebec and Ontario. Here Halifax drivers John Risley and Dave Fram in their Shelby 427 Cobra claim the victory in the Moosehead 300 at Debert, Nova Scotia, en route to winning the 1971 series.

Winning formula. After a false start with Formula A cars, in 1971 the Canadian racing championship changed to Formula B, laying the groundwork for the highly competitive Formula Atlantic series, the training ground for many Canadian racing stars. Shown here is the Formula B of H.F. Johnson at Le Circuit, 1967.

Superstar in the making: Gilles Villeneuve, 1977. The following year he became the first Canadian to win in Formula One, taking the Canadian Grand Prix in Montreal. His undeniable talent was groomed through a professional racing school and the Formula Atlantic series – a fundamental break with past driver development in Canada. He was killed at Zolder, Belgium, in 1982.

From sport to spectacle: the last Molson Indy Vancouver, July 2004. With the city and mountains as backdrop, the huge crowds, televised hype, and rampant consumerism transform the MIV into a pop-culture event; the race is almost secondary. By contrast with the Abbotsford race fifty years earlier, spectators sit well away from the cars, which run between the concrete walls that line the track.

Seventeen drivers earned points in the over-two-litre series, won handily by Heimrath in a McLaren. The other drivers included both established names and new faces, including future champions Jacques Couture, Craig Hill, and Eppie Wietzes. About half were from Ontario, two from Montreal, and rest from the West (three from Vancouver). They competed in a variety of cars, including four Corvettes, two Shelby Mustang GT350s, two Sunbeam Tigers, two Austin-Healey 3000s, and a mixture of specials.

The under-two-litre series was even larger: twenty-two drivers, one-third from the Toronto area, two from Montreal, and the remainder from the Prairies and British Columbia. Western drivers dominated this series, with Bob McLean from Vancouver winning both the series and the overall championship. Like the large-bore series, it included many known racers and 'rising stars': future national champions George Chapman and Horst Kroll, as well as Nat Adams, Jacques Duval, Peter Keith, Wayne Kelly, Terry Nilsson, and Al Pease. While there were a few 'sports cars,' the field consisted mostly of sports-racing cars and specials. Lotus was the make of choice for nearly half the drivers, with Lotus 23Bs taking four of the top five positions. Yet, in many respects, the 1965 season looked like its predecessors. Heimrath faced no real competition in the large-bore series. He earned thirty-one points; the runners-up, John Hall from Vancouver in a Mustang and Wayne Jamieson from Winnipeg in a Sunbeam Tiger, earned only nine points each. Heimrath's car, not to mention his driving, was in a completely different league from his opponents'. He took third place at the Player's 200 behind Formula One champion John Surtees (driving a Lola T70) and Jim Hall's Chaparral. Likewise, in the under-two-litre category McLean finished with nearly twice as many points as George Chapman.[46] This did not reflect on the *quality* of the competition; rather, only Heimrath and McLean competed in a majority of events in various parts of the country, and thus accumulated many more points than their rivals.

At the 1965 AGM the CASC changed the championship rules yet again. Under the new scheme, the maximum number of eligible events was set at sixteen, with twelve counting for 1966. Drivers could earn points in any eight races, and would have to compete in two regions other than their own. All eligible races had to be at least 100 miles in length. Points were to be awarded from first to fifteenth place, but the scoring for the overall championship and within the two engine-capacity categories would be calculated separately. The new rules also limited the series to specialist cars: prototype sports cars and sports-racing cars as defined within appendix J of the FIA's International Sporting Code, the same as for the World Sports Car Championship.[47]

The result was a much more balanced and competitive series in 1966. George Chapman, driving his Lotus 23B, won the overall championship with a five-point margin over Harold Brown from Lethbridge, piloting an identical car. Eppie Wietzes was third in the Comstock Racing Team GT40. The over-two-litre category was an Ontario sweep, with Torontonians taking four of the top five positions. Nat Adams's McLaren was the winner, with Wietzes second, and George Eaton (scion of the department store family) third in a 427 Cobra.[48]

The Right Stuff?

Did the Comstock Racing Team and the national championship produce drivers with 'the right stuff' – the qualities of world champions?[49] Many Comstock alumni – Fisher, Heimrath, Wietzes, John Cannon, and George Eaton among them – had successful post-team careers. They were all talented drivers and might have achieved these results without Comstock's help. But the sheer number of them suggests that their shared experience with the team made a difference, however unmeasurable. It did not produce world-class 'superstars,' but, as Rathgeb intended, it had raised the standards and profile of Canadians within North American racing.[50] Unfortunately, the team folded just at the time when the cost of being competitive was escalating rapidly. That change threw these promising drivers back on their own resources and limited their opportunities.

Peter Ryan had shown that he could beat some of the best in the world. But his was a natural, untutored, *undisciplined* talent. At the top ranks of the racing world, that could take a driver only so far. Like a little knowledge, it was a dangerous thing. Colin Chapman regarded Peter as a very skilful driver, but felt that he 'was using his skill to get himself out of dangerous situations ... A year or two in Europe would give him experience he could not gain elsewhere. He will then be able to use his experience to keep him out of tight spots and his skill to win races.'[51] The season in FJ was supposed to prepare Peter for Formula One. But perhaps he had risen too rapidly through the amateur ranks at a time when the sport was changing dramatically. Or perhaps his death simply showed the limits of the sport in Canada at that time. Chapman felt Ryan had gone as far as he could in Canada. In Britain professional racing schools were already starting to train the next generation of F1 champions,[52] but another decade would pass before such training was available in Canada.

In the meantime, the national championship also did what it was designed to do: produce champions. Like the Comstock team it was a form of driver development, giving the best Canadian drivers from across the country an opportunity to compete against each other and against some of the best drivers in the world. As a result, Canadian drivers began edging their way into the big leagues and performing creditably, even if they rarely won outright. By the mid-1960s they had come a long way from 'run what ya brung' airport racing. But in the second half of the decade, when the Can-Am series and Formula One came to Canada, the stakes were raised dramatically in competitive, technological, and financial terms. Canadian racers received a humbling object lesson on how far they still had to go.

In fact, the championship demonstrated the 'Social-Darwinistic' character of major-league racing: 'survival of the fittest.' Winning was not just a matter of being a good driver. You had to have the right car, and the cost of a competitive car grew dramatically over the first half of the decade.[53] Furthermore, the series put a premium on car endurance and reliability over a whole season of long, hard races. Since they imposed a lot of 'wear and tear' on the car and its components, a racer had to be able to provide the parts and spares essential to get through the season. And on top of that the racers had to travel far. To win the 1965 series Bob McLean had 'criss-crossed' the country to enter every race, at a cost of $2600, over and above the cost of his car, spares, and maintenance. With his winnings, he earned barely enough to offset his operating costs, let alone to pay for the car.[54]

Thus, fortune favoured the sponsored driver with a competitive car. And by the mid-1960s it had become clear that 'competitive' meant a *foreign*, built-to-purpose, racing car; in fact, to be specific, a *British* sports-racing car. Ironically, as the following chapter explains, it was a *Canadian* 'special' that led the British sports-racing-car design revolution and launched a new international racing series.

10 The Cutting Edge: Bill Sadler and the Can-Am Series

They were the fastest, grandest cars in the world; that's what everyone remembers about the original, almost limitless Can-Am ... It was an automotive adventure, a noble experiment in virtually unrestricted technology which gave us the most powerful, fastest road course vehicles that had ever been seen.

Pete Lyons, *Can-Am*[1]

The Sadler Mk. V: The Can-Am Prototype

Chuck Rathgeb thought he knew a good thing when he saw it. And what he saw in the fall of 1960 was the Sadler Mk. V: a rear-engined sports racing car on the cutting edge of racing car design. In his hobby that had become a business, Bill Sadler – a self-taught race car designer – had been building fast, powerful cars by hand for years. Rathgeb believed the Mk. V could put Canadians into the winner's circle, so he paid for one and agreed to underwrite the costs of racing two of them for the 1961 season.[2]

The Mk. V never fully lived up to either man's expectations, and their partnership lasted less than a year. But in that short time it was notable for two achievements. First, it led Rathgeb to create the formidable Comstock Racing Team. Second, the Mk. V became the prototype for the most advanced sports cars of the mid-1960s to mid-1970s, and as such helped to launch the highly successful Can-Am series. At the same time, Sadler's story illustrated the limitations that prevented Canadian racing car builders from becoming major manufacturers. That factor, in turn, forced Canadian drivers to buy foreign racing cars, the cost of which made it harder for them to be competitive in leagues like the Can-Am.

Bill Sadler: Design Pioneer

Born in St Catharines, Ontario, in 1931, Bill Sadler grew up in an automotive-industry family. His British-born father George had a car parts business, and was the Canadian agent for Britain's Lucas Electric Company. Bill dropped out of high school, and working for his father demonstrated his talent early; he built a hot rod at age fourteen. While honeymooning in the UK in 1953 Bill saw his first car race and recalls: 'It was love at first sight.'[3]

Sadler bought an MG TD, shipped it home, and raced it at Edenvale. Finding the MG too slow, he sold it after the first race and decided to build his own racing car. The result was the V-8-powered Hillman Minx that drew Jim Gunn's caustic critique at Edenvale in June 1954. In the meantime, Sadler built the first of his numbered series of racing cars. There were no textbooks on how to do so, and Bill lacked any formal technical training. And so, he says, 'I started off with a clean sheet of paper and asked, how do I build a race car that will go as fast as possible? I learned how to engineer things by ... logic, if you will ... I would weld something and beat it till it broke, and weld it until I could beat it and it didn't break ... My cars were always strong and rigid, light, and [the chassis] never, ever broke.'[4] Over the next five years, he built and rebuilt several more specials, teaching himself while experimenting with materials, engines, and design. Bill spent 1957 racing in Britain while he worked for John Tojeiro, designer of the AC Ace-Bristol, the car that later became the basis for the Shelby Cobra. He capped a successful season by winning the FTD for a one-km 'drag' at the Brighton Speed Trials, beating 260 other cars. That caught the attention of the British motoring press, one writer observing that 'British enthusiasts were startled to find that the sports car in question was an abbreviated and rather shabby device driven by a virtually unknown Canadian whose name, it seems, is W.G. Sadler.'[5]

Sadler's cars had a mixed record of success in competition. His redesigned and rebuilt Mk. II won the 1958 unlimited race at Watkins Glen. That attracted the attention of American car importer Earl Nissonger, who commissioned Sadler to build a new car: the Mk. III. Seven weeks later, it was done. It proved to be very fast, but was plagued by minor technical 'gremlins.' In a race at Montgomery, New York, the Mk. III was much faster than the latest and most potent American specials – the Scarabs and the Lister Jaguars – but suffered a mechanical failure. At the 1958 Nassau races, his car was leading some of the world's best, but a crash cost Sadler and his driver the race.[6]

Back in St Catharines in the spring of 1959, Bill went into the racing car business. Using one of his father's old machine shops and the little money he had earned from racing, he founded the Sadler Car Company. Eventually he had more than a half dozen employees building cars.[7] They built the Mk. IV – a variant of the Mk. III – for Montreal racer Dave Greenblatt, who had won more than a dozen races driving a Corvette for Gorries, then Canada's largest Corvette dealership. That success caught the attention of a businessman and racing enthusiast, who offered him a job and time off to race, *and* bought the Sadler Mk. IV for him, renaming it the Gorries Sadler Corvette. According to Greenblatt, everybody thought he was frightened of the car; in fact, he says, it suffered from a number of inherent design problems:

> The braking power was just not sufficient for a car capable of speeds well in excess of 160 mph. The Mk. IV weighed 1600 lbs powered with a ... 290 bhp fuel injected engine ... We didn't have the tire technology or sufficient rubber-to-road surface for the power ... A major problem in ... Sadler's design ... was the offset of the engine ... from the differential ... which created extreme stress on the short driveshaft's universal joints, causing them to fracture very often.[8]

In spite of those problems, the Sadler Corvette gave Greenblatt the 1960 Quebec driver's championship. In the Formula Libre race at Watkins Glen that year, he recalls 'trying to keep the car in a straight line ... [The] mirrors [were] vibrating so badly they were useless and [I was] hanging on for dear life ... I had never gone that fast ... Stirling Moss gave me a glance and a casual wave ... And to top Moss was Olivier Gendebien, who passed me *standing* in his F1 car due to a broken hot oil or water hose.'[9]

Sadler also built and sold about two dozen Formula Juniors. With support from Austin-Healey, he used the engine and components from the Sprite, but designed his own body and frame. The result was a sleek, front-engined FJ, weighing just under 800 pounds. Bill believed that weight was the most important racing car design factor, so he concentrated on making his cars light. And, he added, 'It's what you choose to bolt onto it that makes the difference.'[10] He first tried to bolt a Chevrolet V-8 engine onto the front of his FJ, but when that didn't work it's what he did next that showed Sadler's genius. He designed a new FJ, put the V-8 in the back, and joined the cutting edge of the 'revolution' in racing car design.

> Just three weeks before October's [1960] Watkins Glen Formula Libre, Peter Ryan and Bill Sadler were discussing Peter's lack of a machine suitable for this race. Thoughts turned to the first Chevy single-seater – then to the idea of a rear-engined ... edition. With typically-Sadler speed such a car was designed and built in the three weeks ... The result ... was what Bill called 'without a doubt the best-handling car I've ever built.'[11]

It consisted of an extremely stiff eighty-pound tubular space frame, independent suspension, disc brakes, a 300-cid, 300-bhp Chevrolet engine, and a single high gear, all wrapped up in a sleek body that bore more than a passing resemblance to the new Cooper and Lotus rear-engine F1 cars. The whole car weighed only 1330 pounds, giving it a phenomenal power/weight ratio.[12]

Nicknamed the 'Formula Ferocious' for its incredible straight-line speed, the car showed its mettle in the US Grand Prix at the Glen. Ryan qualified sixth, behind the F1 Lotus of Stirling Moss and the F1 Coopers of Jack Brabham, Joakim Bonnier, Olivier Gendebien, and Roy Salvadori. In the race itself, Ryan ran as high as fifth before the engine blew. If the final result was disappointing, Bill had made his point. Moss, who had tried out the car before the race, went on to call Sadler 'one of the best innovators of the day.'[13] Coming from Moss, at a time when British constructors like Cooper and Lotus were leading the racing car design revolution, that was high praise indeed.

By this time, Bill was already working on his next (and last) design: the Mk. V. With backing from Rathgeb, he built two cars, identical except for the engines. Both had a tubular space frame that weighed only sixty-five pounds and was *extremely* stiff. They sported disc brakes, independent suspension, light-weight aluminum/magnesium alloy wheels, and the Chevrolet V-8 in the rear. One car had a slightly modified 283-cid engine bored and stroked to 327, while the second was rated at 364 cid and 370 bhp. Delivering all that power to the road was the tricky part, since there was no stock transmission for a Chevy engine mounted right over the rear wheels. Using a mix of Ford and Halibrand parts, Bill designed his own two-speed, synchromesh quick-change transmission. The car's overall dry weight was only 1475 pounds. Bill had married awesome power to a light, stiff chassis, thus creating, in his words, 'a dragster that handles.'[14]

But handling, in fact, was a problem. The Mk. V displayed noticeable understeer. It also displayed one of the unanticipated outcomes of the rear-engine revolution: when cars are light, fast, and aerodynamic, they want to *fly*. During practice for the 1961 Player's 200 at Mosport,

> at the end of the straight Grant (Clark) was about 200 yards ahead of Moss. But ... at the last crest of the hill before the end of the straight, Grant left the road in a vertical direction with all four wheels. When he came back down again the road was nowhere in sight ... so we've learned to back off just before the last hill ... We can't use the top speed we have, because it's theoretically impossible to hurl a projectile along that back straight as fast as our cars will go and still keep them on the ground.[15]

In the Player's 200 and in later events, it was not the handling but the transmission that frustrated the Mk. Vs. Pushing all that power through only two gears overtaxed the hybrid unit, causing it to break frequently. And so, from their first outing the two cars had a mixed performance record.[16]

One month after the Player's 200, in a move that stunned and puzzled the Canadian racing world, Sadler closed his shop and went back to Westinghouse, where he had been employed during his earlier racing years. At the time, his father said that the company had offered Bill 'a golden opportunity' and he decided to take it. But there was more to it than that. Hinting at discord with his sponsor, Bill said, 'I have decided that I am building too many frustrations by feeling too keenly about the treatment ... of my cars that ... I've decided to quit.'[17] And, as he told the *Sunday Sun* many years later,

> one day I looked up and my wife was gone, and that kind of made me reflect on what there was to life. Also, I was realizing that I'd put eight years into making my own cars, and yet the only way I could really do the job was with outside funding, which meant outside influence, which I couldn't take ... Back then I was pretty self-centered, pretty ego-centered, pretty hard to get along with ... Of course if I hadn't been that way, I'd not have made cars different from everybody else's.[18]

Sadler later moved to the United States and went back to school, earning an MSc in Electrical Engineering from MIT in 1966. Since then he has worked in the aviation electronics field. He later built one more racing car – a Formula Super Vee – but decided that he 'couldn't dabble in the sport – I have to give it my all.'[19] He walked away from the sport again and never returned.

Sadler's Legacy

Why was Sadler significant? After all, the rear-engine layout was as old as the car itself. The German rear-engine Auto Unions had dominated Grand Prix racing in the 1930s. After the war, Charles and John Cooper revived the trend with their 500-cc racers, and in 1958 Stirling Moss won the Argentine Grand Prix in Cooper's rear-engine F1 car. That signalled the way of the future, and major racing car builders such as Lotus and Ferrari adopted the concept at the beginning of the 1960s. What Bill Sadler did that was original – even 'revolutionary' – was to put a powerful American V-8 engine in the back of a European-style racing car. By the mid-1960s, almost all the major sports-racing, formula, and Indy car builders had adopted the rear-mounted V-8 layout. The 'proof of concept' was the Cosworth-Ford Dual Four Valve V-8, first introduced by Lotus in 1967, which eventually would claim 150 F1 victories. But until Sadler tried, *'nobody had ever done it before.'*[20] His idea changed racing forever.

Mounting a heavy V-8 block at the back put its weight directly on the driving wheels, delivering more power to the track. To exploit all that power builders adopted the new wide, low-profile, soft compound tires that provided greater adhesion at higher speeds. Placing the fuel tanks closer to the centre of the car distributed fuel weight change evenly, eliminating the tendency of cars to 'fishtail' as a rear-mounted fuel tank got lighter. Without an engine in the front a driver could sit lower and more securely inside a frame-less, stressed-skin 'moncocque' chassis. Thus, the whole car became lighter and more aerodynamic, allowing it to go faster. To reduce high-speed front-end lift, designers added front air dams, while rear spoilers kept the rear wheels glued to the road. American designer Jim Hall went further and mounted a movable 'wing' above his Chaparral sports-racing car to provide greater 'downforce.' Within a few years, every racing car had them. In short, by the mid-1960s a technological 'revolution' had swept the sport.[21] And it was led – in part – by a Canadian.

'It's ironic,' Allan Girdler writes, reflecting on Sadler's ingenuity, 'that the first person to use the Chevrolet engine in the proper place, and to experiment with gearboxes or the lack of same, was to get so little in return for his daring.'[22] Once he left the scene, Sadler's concept was all but forgotten among Canadian racing car builders. When his former Comstock teammates built their EXP, it was front-engined. Likewise, despite the Mk. IV's two seasons of mixed results, which ended with the car being stolen, it inspired Dave Greenblatt to design his own racing car. At a cost of $6000 and taking its curious name from it builders – Dave (Greenblatt) and Luigi (Cassiani) – the Dailu Mk. I made its debut in 1962. The car's striking resemblance to the Ferraris of the day was no accident. Luigi, who had worked at Alfa Romeo, learned from Ferrari's experience and constructed a space-frame chassis strong enough to endure rough-surface tracks, while Mike Saggars, who had trained on bodywork in Britain, built the sleek Ferrari-inspired aluminum body. They used some of Sadler's ideas for the front suspension, but designed and built their own independent rear suspension.[23]

Greenblatt himself may have lacked Sadler's intuitive eye for design – the Mk. I was front-engined – but Bill's influence was not lost on him completely. The Dailu's power came from a 364-cid, 365-bhp Chevrolet engine with an Iskendarian racing cam and three two-barrel carburetors (replacing an unreliable fuel injection system), married up to a Corvette four-speed transmission. The whole car weighed only 1640 pounds. To his credit, Greenblatt had stolen a page from Sadler's book, combining light weight with massive power. It was, in a word, *fast*.

But, stunned by the death of Peter Ryan, whom he had known well, David stopped racing for a while and convinced his new sponsor – Bardahl engine products – to let John Cannon drive the Dailu. Cannon won the feature event at the Indian Summer Trophy Races, bringing the first win for a Canadian-built car in a major Canadian race. He went on to qualify fourth for the 1962 Canadian Grand Prix behind the three reigning Americans: Dan Gurney, Roger Penske, and Jim Hall. Cannon led the first lap and stayed with the leaders until overheating forced a lengthy pit stop. Like the Sadler cars, that was typical of the Dailu story: great speed and great promise undone by mechanical gremlins. After their engine blew up at Riverside, Dave persuaded Bardahl to buy them the first Traco Engineering Chev road-racing engine. The six-carburetor, 377-cid, 437-bhp monster gave them a win in their first race at Laguna Seca, California. They finished the season at Nassau, where John and the Dailu won the sprint race, defeating Masten Gregory's Le Mans–winning Ferrari and Jim Hall's Chaparral.

But while running well in the feature event the Dailu caught fire and was destroyed. Cannon, fortunately, escape unhurt.[24]

That was the end of the Mk. I. Greenblatt built four more Dailus, including a rear-engine and coupe version. Girdler writes: 'They were able to stay with the smaller rear-engine racers on sheer power, but when the newer cars got bigger and better engines, the Dailus faded away.'[25] Even so, it had proved the awesome power of the big V-8.

Of the other Canadian builders, only George and Rudy Fejer designed a sports-racer with a V-8 in the back: the Chinook Mk. I. Thus, when the Can-Am series opened at Le Circuit in September 1966, theirs was the only Canadian-designed car on the grid. The Chinook Mk. I made two uninspiring appearances in the series; it was markedly slower than the McLarens and Lolas that dominated the Can-Am's first six years.[26] It was these British-built machines, rather than Canadian cars, that embodied Sadler's rear V-8-powered vision and his legacy. They also represented the larger process of technological change in the sport and a more professional and commercial approach to racing car construction, which in turn shed a critical light on the limitations of Canada's tiny racing car industry.

British racing car design was flourishing in the 1960s because of a unique combination of circumstances that favoured innovation. The decentralized network of parts suppliers that was the bane of the UK automobile industry's mass-production system was a boon to British racing car builders, who earned the sobriquet of 'kit car' constructors because they built their cars from 'off the shelf' components rather than producing everything themselves. They also benefited from the emergence of a 'sub-industry' of racing-specific firms (such as Cosworth Engineering) that grew up around circuits like Silverstone. There, the 'melting pot of drivers, technicians and businessmen, all of whom had their own ideas about how to improve the cars and expand the sport ... created a culture of invention and private entrepreneurship.'[27]

By contrast, the Canadian racing car industry never achieved the 'critical mass' needed to become self-sustaining, in part because the sport itself here was still too small; there were not enough racers in Canada to support it. Nor were Canadian builders tied into the 'mainstream' auto industry. There was no Canadian equivalent of Jaguar or Lotus, which built production *and* competition cars. It was the commercial success of the Lotus Elan and the Ford Lotus Cortina that put Chapman's company on a sound financial footing and underwrote Lotus's racing program.[28] Canadian racing car builders were always small and under-capitalized. As a result, they could build only a few cars, and lacked the resources to develop and 'prove' their cars to the point where they could be marketed outside Canada, in numbers large enough to keep a small company afloat. Owing to its corporate backing, the Comstock Racing Team was unique in having some resources to put into car development. But even they tried it only once after Sadler left, without success. Thereafter, they raced cars built by Ford. That was the face of the future of 'major league' racing in Canada.

The technological revolution in auto sport, which Bill Sadler had helped to shape, was changing racing car design at a rapid pace in the first half of the 1960s. It created a new cycle of competition for technical advantage and for dominant performance on the track, not unlike the Cold War arms race. As soon as one team fielded a more competitive car, the others had to follow suit just to keep pace. And if the object was to *win*, then no competitor could afford 'technological lag.' But because of the demands for constant design innovation, testing, and development, just staying in the technology race was increasingly expensive, and that left Canadian builders behind. Thus, as the Can-Am series was about to show, Canadians who aspired to be competitive in racing's major leagues would have to buy costly foreign-built cars, and few of them could afford to do so.

Undefended Border: The Can-Am Series

Nobody, it seems, was short of opinions about the Can-Am. John Ross, one of the 'movers and shakers' behind the series, felt it was 'the greatest thing that ever happened to motor racing in North America.'[29] Canadian race promoter Don Hunt believed that while 'the Can-Am as a spectator thing [was] superior to Formula One ... it doesn't have the charisma of the Grand Prix, or the name drivers.'[30] But Len Coates was less charitable: 'Some of the Canadian Can-Ams have been spectaculars, but more often they have been generally dull fare without about as much suspense as a Mary Poppins story.'[31]

There are many versions of the origins of the Can-Am series, all somewhat contradictory and none of them adequately documented. Pete Lyons, whose book offers the most complete account of the series, traces its lineage first to the maturing of the American 'home-built' specialist racing car technology in the early 1960s. He argues that while the cost of the series kept away some of the major builders, like Ferrari and Lotus, the Can-Am cars nonetheless represented the cutting edge of the 'revolution' in racing car technology in the mid-1960s. He credits the Sadler Mk. V with helping to lead that design revolution, but argues that it was Roger Penske's Zerex Special – a rebuilt F1 car thinly disguised as a sports-racer, first raced in 1962 – that forced the SCCA and the FIA to rewrite the rules governing modified sports-racing cars. The FIA defined this new class as Group 9 (later Group 7). The new class rules allowed builders a wide degree of latitude in design and power. Lyons then argues that the direct ancestor of the Can-Am was the SCCA's first professional racing series: the US Road Racing Championship (USRRC), established in 1963. The USRRC gave this new class a series of its own to 'show its stuff.' But what Lyons does not explain is how the USRRC became the Can-Am.[32]

Len Coates has a different version, which attributes the idea to a Canadian: Don Hunt of the public relations firm PRSL, which did promotion for the Player's 200. According to Coates, the very mixed character of the entrants in the early '200s' – a few 'stars' with good cars and a large number of 'local heroes' without – meant that the 'stars' invariably trounced the locals. The races were attracting an audience, but those crowds weren't seeing competitive racing. Hunt feared that this would eventually discourage the fans. But, as noted earlier, attendance at the Player's 200 climbed steadily because the race was drawing upon a new fan base that came to see the 'stars,' not the local heroes. Meanwhile, Hunt proceeded to develop his idea for a 'World Series' for Group 7 cars. He envisioned a six-race series: the Player's 200, races in the UK and Nassau, plus three in the United States: at Riverside, Daytona, and Sebring. There would be no appearance money, just a large purse at the end. The idea attracted early interest, but was put on hold when Mosport went into receivership. Hunt later discussed his idea with Ross de St. Croix (president of the CASC) and John Ross, race director of the MMRC. They were both involved in the development of Le Circuit and were interested in the 'world series' concept. The only obstacle was the SCCA, which Coates says was still wedded to amateurism. He asserts that the SCCA head, Jim (actually John) Bishop, was 'violently opposed' to the idea, and that the SCCA 'wanted no part of a series that would create an amateur-professional split in the U.S.'[33]

The flaw in Coates's account is the chronology. By the time de St. Croix was CASC president and Le Circuit was being developed – both in 1964 – the SCCA had already abandoned its opposition to 'pro racing.' In fact, it had launched its pro series, the USRRC, a year earlier. Thus, the prototype for the Can-Am was already in place. Coates writes that once people realized that the 'world' series could be limited to North America that eliminated one costly problem: transporting cars and crews across the ocean. Then it was simply a question of bringing together two good ideas: the USRRC and a North American series. Coates says the issue was settled at a race organizers' meeting in Chicago early in 1965. There, Jim Kaser, the SCCA's director of pro racing, enthusiastically endorsed the idea. George Moss and John Ross attended the meeting, representing Mosport and Le Circuit respectively. Ross later told Coates, 'That meeting was extremely important ... if only because everyone sat down and decided to agree-to-agree on the main principle of the Can-Am series.'[34]

In fact, while both Lyons and Coates probably are correct *up to a point*, a slightly different version emerges from the documents. In January 1963 the CASC reported that the SCCA had invited its Canadian counterpart 'to participate in 1964 in their new Road Racing Championship that they are starting this year ... They would like two CASC events, one at Mosport and one at Westwood.'[35] And so, the initiative to bring Canadian events into the USRRC seems to have *originated* with the SCCA, not with Canada. By April 1964 discussions had shifted to creating a *North American* Racing Championship in conjunction with the SCCA.[36] CASC president de St. Croix told the 1964 AGM that the US offered the greatest opportunities for growth of Canadian racing:

> With the return of big bore sports racing cars we find ourselves tied even closer to the American scene. To take advantage of this C.A.S.C. has approached the S.C.C.A. to help set up a N.A.R.R.C. This would be an effort to get big money into motorsport and put Sports car drivers on a par with American professional drivers who are rapidly becoming American Institutions in keeping with their abilities and earnings. This would give Canadian drivers and sponsors an excellent area to improve themselves.[37]

Thus, the CASC had taken the SCCA's original idea – an American series with Canadian events – and turned it into a joint championship. Still, the details were not settled until the meeting in Chicago (which actually took place in *August* 1965); de St. Croix attended along with Ross and Moss. There the promoters agreed that the series (initially referred to as the North American Road Racing Championship) would consist of six races, run through the fall season at six tracks: Mosport, Le Circuit, Kent (Washington), Laguna Seca and Riverside (California), and Las Vegas. A committee of one CASC and two SCCA officials would govern the series, contracting drivers to appear in every race. The race promoters would put up $10,000 for each race, split equally between prize money and expenses. There would be no appearance money, except for a few big stars. Describing the series as 'international in concept, continental in scope,' and using cars 'powered and ... built by American and Canadian components,' de St. Croix proclaimed to the 1965 CASC AGM, 'We have come of age.'[38]

The championship – now called the Can-Am Challenge Cup – was formally launched on 15 February 1966. But it still lacked the one thing that could make or break it: a major sponsor. The financial stakes for race promoters had been increased to $25,000 each ($20,000 in prize money for the event they ran, plus $5,000 towards the overall series prize). The pressure eased considerably on 14 April when Johnson's Wax announced that it would contribute $25,000 to the championship prize and would donate the trophy.[39] Even so, the Can-Am was not yet 'a done deal,' and money was still the problem.

First, the Kent track withdrew from the series because it could not provide the necessary financial guarantee; it was replaced by a race at Bridgehampton, New York. Then, late in the summer Le Circuit ran into financial difficulties that nearly cancelled what was to be the series opener. Player's stepped in and saved the event. The second problem, equally serious, was the issue of appearance money. Although the promoters originally had agreed to award it to a few big names, by 1966 they had dropped it in favour of prize money only. But European drivers preferred appearance money, particularly where their participation was going to involve considerable cost – such as bringing a team of cars, drivers, and crews to North America. Moreover, they felt that it was their 'star quality' that drew the crowds. As Teddy Mayer of the McLaren team told the Can-Am promoters: 'Let's face it, gentlemen, your attendance depends upon the fame of the entrants. You benefit from our appearance, not our performance.'[40]

There was more than a little truth in Mayer's claim. The audience was coming to see the big-name drivers and cars. That said, they didn't come to see them sit still; the big names drew the crowds because they were proven performers. According to Coates, two top drivers – John Surtees and Bruce McLaren – told John Ross they wouldn't come to the first race unless they received appearance money. Without these two stars, Coates says, 'the series would have been dead before it started.' So Ross took a gamble: 'I guaranteed that both of them would take away at least the equivalent of what they would have earned under the old starting money setup ... I had no idea where the money was going to come from, but it was the only way to get them here.'[41] In the event, Ross need not have worried. The Can-Am was launched with a total purse of $358,000, with the winnings sufficient to cover many participants.[42]

The Can-Am series opened in grand style on 11 September 1966 at Le Circuit. Against a backdrop of spectacular Laurentian autumn colours, some 53,000 to 58,000 fans – the largest crowd ever at a sporting event in Quebec – were treated to an impressive field of thirty-three cars and drivers: fourteen McLaren M1s, eight Lola T70s, and mixed array of other cars. Surtees, McLaren, and Chris Amon headed the field of drivers that included both established and up-and-coming American drivers such as Mark Donohue, George Follmer, Masten Gregory, Chuck Parsons, and Sam Posey. The Canadian entries included John Cannon, Ludwig Heimrath, and Peter Lerch in McLarens, Eppie Wietzes in the Comstock team GT40, and George Fejer driving the Chinook. Surtees and McLaren dominated the race, lapping the field, and Surtees won, beating McLaren by 6.5 seconds. But it was Amon who proved to be the driving sensation. Having dropped from third to last after a first-lap off-track excursion, he fought his way back up to third, putting on 'the greatest display of driving that Le Circuit fans had ever seen ... Tires screaming on the knife-edge of adhesion and running every lap below the previous record, Amon sliced his way through the field with ruthless precision.'[43] John Cannon finished a creditable fourth, while Heimrath and Wietzes came in twelfth and thirteenth. Two weeks later at Mosport Donohue won, and of the four Canadians (Cannon, Heimrath, Wietzes, and John Cordts) only Wietzes finished, driving the GT40 to sixth place.[44]

For some Canadian racing 'visionaries' the Can-Am wasn't an end in itself; it was a stepping stone to the ultimate prize: a Formula One Grand Prix race. Milt Wright asserted that the successful launch of the new series had 'put Canada in the International racing limelight.'[45] Art Moseley agrees: 'We had to prove our worth ... That's why we got involved with the Can-Am type cars, because we had to prove that we could organize an international-style race ... then we might get a Formula One race.'[46] Canada, they felt, had 'paid its dues' by the mid-1960s and was now ready for the next step. For aspiring Canadian Formula One racers, however, the results of those first Can-Am races were a harbinger of things to come.

PART THREE

From Sport to Spectacle, 1967–1991

11 Coming of Age? Canadians and International Racing

For the multitude of motor racing enthusiasts in Canada the best way to celebrate the country's Centennial Year was to stage a race for the prestigious international Formula One circus. It was the way to show the world the country had really come of age.

Gerald Donaldson, *The Grand Prix of Canada*[1]

The Canadian Grand Prix for Formula One, 27 August 1967

'It wasn't the most spectacular Grand Prix race in history, dripping more with rain than with drama.'[2] But like the rather dull race at the first Player's 200 six years earlier, that probably mattered little to the organizers or to the 58,000-plus fans who crowded the Mosport hillsides for a glimpse of history in the making. Although the rain slowed the pace for all but a brief dry spell, they were not to be disappointed. All the world's fastest cars and drivers were there. The grid included no fewer than six former and future world champions: Jack Brabham, Jim Clark, Graham Hill, Denis Hulme, Jochen Rindt, and Jackie Stewart. Other prominent international drivers included Dan Gurney, Chris Amon, and Bruce McLaren. The race marked the debut of the latter's V12-engined McLaren-BRM. Amon drove the lone Ferrari. The Lotus team fielded three of its new Cosworth-Ford-engined Lotus 49s, two in the hands of Hill and Clark, and one leased to Comstock Racing Team driver Eppie Wietzes. The only other Canadian in the race, Al Pease, drove Gurney's original Eagle, fitted with an under-powered four-cylinder Climax engine. The rain-soaked track and the usual mechanical 'gremlins' took their toll on the eighteen starters; one-third of them, including Clark, Rindt, Stewart, and Wietzes, failed to finish. Pease finished dead last, in twelfth, having completed barely half of the ninety-lap race.[3] It was an inauspicious, even prophetic, start to Canada's experience in Formula One.

Winning the Race

Nevertheless, Formula One then as now was considered the acme of auto sport. And so, for the Canadian sport this was an event of *monumental* significance. By sanctioning the Grand Prix, the FIA had affirmed that racing in Canada had 'matured' – that it now had the facilities, the organizational skills, and the sponsors worthy of the very best the world of racing had to offer. This fulfilled and validated in full the vision and determination of the CASC's founders and of those who had laboured to bring that vision to life. As CASC executive director Bob Hanna later told Len Coates:

> Right from the start, we had the dream of someday holding a Grand Prix race in Canada. That was always the general philosophy that guided us. There were maybe half-a-dozen guys, even back in the Edenvale days who were always working and planning toward that goal. We figured that Grand Prix racing was the ultimate, the best there is in this sport. And if we weren't working toward getting the best in Canada, then there really wasn't much point in the whole thing.[4]

As early as 1963, Canada had begun to seek the opportunity to run a Formula One race. A proposal for race on Île Ste-Hélène in Montreal never got past the talking stage, but in April 1964 the BEMC sought to change its annual sports car Grand Prix that year to an F1 event. The CASC board of directors authorized George Moss of BEMC to discuss the matter with the RAC's Dean Delamont. But Delamont told Jim Gunn, who had met him in Europe that summer, that 'motorsport in Canada was not progressing as fast as he thought it might. Canadian motorsport [is] not promoted on [a] proper businesslike basis.'[5] In short, Canada wasn't ready yet.

    The FIA *was* prepared to approve an F1 race that would not count for world championship points. CASC president Ross de St. Croix told the 1964 AGM that such an event could 'lay the groundwork' for a championship race in Canada within a few years. But, in spite of the efforts of George Moss, the race was cancelled, owing largely to lack of interest on the part of the F1 drivers. Jim Clark had swept the championship early in the 1965 season, and the drivers presumably had no incentive to risk their cars and their lives in a race that did not count. As Moss explained, 'We couldn't expect to run a Grand Prix Formula one race at this stage with no more than five or six first class drivers. The Canadian people deserve better than this.'[6] So the Canadian Grand Prix remained a sports car event for 1965 and 1966.

Canada finally was awarded a world championship F1 race for 1967. So what had changed in the interval? By that time Canada had run world-class sports car races for six years, culminating in the recently launched Can-Am series. The FIA was well aware of the Canadian role in establishing the Can-Am, through which the CASC had developed a good working relationship with the RAC and its American counterpart: the Automobile Competition Committee for the United States (ACCUS). But the biggest change probably was that Canadian auto sport had become more 'businesslike,' thereby addressing the concerns Delamont had raised in 1964. The Shell 4000 rally was a model of business and auto sport cooperation and quality competition. The attendance figures for the 1965 Player's 200, which set a record for sporting events in Canada, showed that the Canadian fan base for auto sport was by now large enough that a major race could attract a huge paying audience. Even so, the gate would not cover all the costs of an F1 event, estimated at $200–250,000. When the CRDA asked Imperial Tobacco if they would sponsor it, the company indicated that it was interested. In the meantime, a business consortium had purchased Mosport, putting the track on a more secure financial basis. CASC president Milt Wright told the AGM, 'We have learned some valuable lessons. Running major races, and rallies, is big business.'[7]

The CASC approached Delamont on behalf of the CRDA, who were prepared to run the race, with Player's as the principal sponsor. Delamont then took the request to the FIA meeting in August 1966. A month later the FIA sent a telegram awarding the race and setting a date. There immediately ensued a 'bun fight' among rival would-be race organizers. The CASC had tabled the CRDA's formal proposal, in order to allow the BEMC and the MMRC to submit bids. The directors of Le Circuit also submitted a brief and, according to Wright, Quebec premier Daniel Johnson requested that the race be held on top of Mont Royal in Montreal. On 22 September, on the advice of the NCB, competition chairman Dick Shelton awarded the race to the CRDA 'subject to their compliance with the Rules and Regulations and Requirements of CASC.'[8]

But the debate did not end there. At the CASC national committee meeting three days later Lloyd Brown and Charles Ryan, representing respectively the Quebec and Ontario Regions, criticized the CASC's decision, saying that other clubs had not been given sufficient opportunity to bid for the race. Ryan was annoyed that the NCB had taken this decision 'without the knowledge of the Directors or the Regions and had further negotiated with an Ontario Club [the CRDA] without informing Ontario Region.' Implying that the NCB had 'rigged' the outcome in favour of the CRDA, they tried to pass a motion to force the NCB to allow additional bids, but it was defeated after a lively debate. While some delegates recognized that it was too late to change the decision, '[m]any speakers felt that the matter had been handled badly.'[9]

In Art Moseley's view George Moss was the principal 'victim' of this process, and he largely blamed the CRDA for this. Moss had devoted his life, at the cost of his career, to Canadian auto sport, serving as the organizer for CRDA races. 'George's ultimate goal was to bring Formula One to Canada.' It was Moss who had taken the BEMC proposal to the RAC in 1964, even though he and others recognized that the CRDA was more likely to be awarded the race:

> It was pretty much admitted that Pepsi Cola could not be the sponsor, and that BEMC would probably lose out on it, not having a big enough sponsor. So it was decided that CRDA would have the Formula One. George would organize it for them ... We had a team of experts in every field. CRDA decided that what they wanted to do was to bring [one of] their own on stream who knew nothing about it ... As a result, George was never really asked to do it ... George was very slighted about it, he felt really hurt ... It was his baby. That's what he started up this whole exercise for ... to be the organizer of the first Formula One race in Canada ... and the CRDA kicked him in the you-know-what ... George quit ... He walked away from the sport as if it never existed.[10]

Moss was a casualty of the changing nature of the sport. With the prestige of a major international race came higher commercial and financial stakes and more intense rivalry between potential host tracks, organizers, and sponsors. And this was not the last time that the awarding of a major event would cause a crisis within the CASC. The Canadian race also caused a minor crisis inside the CSI, but the outcome ultimately redounded to the benefit of the CASC. In discussing the awarding of Formula One events for 1968 and after, some members of the CSI objected to giving an event to Canada because it meant, in effect, granting two races to the RAC (Canada's representative on the CSI), when every other CSI member country had only one. To resolve the crisis, Delamont advised the CASC to apply for direct FIA representation immediately. The CASC did so and was admitted to the FIA as a full member at its September 1967 meeting.[11] Thus, another one of the founders' original objectives – international recognition in auto sport – finally was achieved in full. No more would the CASC be a junior member, represented at the 'top table' by its 'parent,' the RAC. Together with the Formula One race and the Can-Am series, auto sport in Canada had 'come of age,' appropriately in the nation's centennial year.

Are We There Yet?

Thus, as he prepared to step down as CASC president, Milt Wright told the delegates to the 1967 AGM that those developments heralded 'an unlimited horizon for Canadian Motor Sport.'[12] From the perspective of being able to mount 'world class' events, Wright was quite correct. But for Canadian drivers, the horizons were anything but unlimited. And the Formula One and Can-Am races told the story. During the first decade of the Canadian F1 race, only six Canadians competed in the event: Bill Brack, John Cordts, George Eaton, Al Pease, Gilles Villeneuve, and Eppie Wietzes. Eaton was the top Canadian qualifier, being ninth on the grid for the 1970 event. Usually, Canadians started from the back of the grid. Canadian racers entered eight of the ten races from 1967 to 1977 (there was no Grand Prix in 1975), but finished only four: Al Pease (1967), Eaton (1970, 1971), and Gilles Villeneuve (1977). In each, they finished dead last.[13] Clearly, when F1 first came to Canada, Canadian racers were not quite ready.

In the original Can-Am series, however, which ran from 1966 through 1974, Canadians fared much better.[14] On 13 October 1968 at Laguna Seca, John Cannon 'rolled the dice,' prayed for rain, and made history. Driving a three-year-old McLaren M1 on borrowed F1 intermediate rain tires, he qualified sixteenth then charged through the field and the downpour to win. He became the only Canadian to win a race in the original Can-Am series. In all, fifteen Canadian racers competed in the championship. Cordts ran continuously from 1967 through 1974. Only Cannon and Regina racer Roger McCaig came close, putting in five seasons each. Eaton and Ottawa racer Gordon Dewar each raced three seasons, while BC driver David Saville-Peck ran regularly in the last two. The rest, including Nat Adams, Rudy Bartling, Rainer Brezinka, Harry Bytzek, Jacques Couture, George Fejer, Ludwig Heimrath, Peter Lerch, and Eppie Wietzes, ran only a few events. Between them all, they entered every race but one. Their largest single showing was at Mosport in 1967, when six Canadians competed.

Drawing upon their considerable experience in similar cars and races since the early 1960s, Canadians put on some impressive displays of driving in the Can-Am series. Starting twenty-seventh in the 1966 race at Mosport, Wietzes had pushed his over-weight, under-powered Comstock GT40 to a sixth-place finish. Almost overlooked in Cannon's upset victory at Laguna Seca in 1968 was Eaton's equally impressive run in the same event, qualifying seventeenth and finishing third. At Riverside in 1969, McCaig, in only his third season of racing, started twenty-sixth and finished third. The next year at Mosport and Road Atlanta he qualified seventeenth and eighteenth respectively, and finished fifth in both events. Two years later John Cordts did the same at Donnybrooke, Minnesota. In the final season, David Saville-Peck qualified sixteenth at Mosport and finished ninth. Canadian drivers were the quintessential 'come-back kids.'

But apart from Cannon's sole victory, Canadians had only five top-three finishes, with Eaton taking four of them between 1968 and 1970, and Cordts the last one in 1974. Both had one second place. In all, Canadian drivers placed among the top ten finishers fifty times in seventy-one events. The statistics show almost a Bell Curve of performance over time, starting with three top-ten finishes in 1966, increasing to seven in 1968, peaking at twelve in 1969, and declining steadily over the next four years, with a slight up-turn to five in the final season. In the final standings for each season, Eaton ranked highest, taking fifth overall in 1969; Cannon had placed sixth the previous year. He was tenth in 1966, a position also held by John Cordts twice and Roger McCaig once, in 1970. Canadians qualified in the top ten places forty-seven times (in about half of the races). Only two Canadians (Eaton and Cordts) qualified in the top five grid positions, but they did so thirteen times between them. Eaton's best was a third at Edmonton in 1969; Cordts qualified fourth in five events, including four of the five races in the final (1974) season.

In aggregate terms, Canadians' performance in the Can-Am looks even less impressive: only one victory in 177 starts, and thirty-five DNFs (about one out of every five starts). Canadian drivers qualified eleventh to twentieth or lower 130 times. But the point spread says it all. For the original series as a whole, the top Can-Am driver – New Zealander Denny Hulme – earned 551 points, while the second-place drivers, Americans Peter Revson and Mark Donohue, tied at 261 each. By contrast, the best Canadian driver – Eaton – wasn't even close. He ranked twenty-second with only sixty-six points. Cordts was one place back, with sixty-five, and McCaig was twenty-eighth with forty-nine. The rest ranged from forty-second to 110th place.

The raw statistics from F1 and the Can-Am suggest that Canadians were not ready for 'big league' racing in the late 1960s. How do we explain this? The answer is that they lacked the experience needed for Formula One and the cars needed for the Can-Am. Both problems were money-related; lack of funding hindered both driver training and access to competitive cars.

In Formula One, Canadian racers were competing against established teams and world champion drivers; in terms of experience, they were out of their league. Before 1967 only three Canadians had raced in F1: Ryan, Heimrath, and Broeker, and each had done so only once. Their successor was George Eaton. Coached through his novice season (1965) by Wietzes and Paul Cooke of the Comstock Racing Team, his first major victory was the Sundown Grand Prix in 1966, driving a 427 Cobra with Craig Fisher. In 1967, as the team was winding down, Eaton decided to go into racing full time and took Cooke with him as his manager. That launched his pro racing career and took him from the Can-Am series through the Formula A Canadian championship to Formula One. Eaton was the first Canadian fully contracted to an F1 team; he drove for BRM for two seasons, but – owing to car problems – without much success.[15]

That an F1 team hired Eaton at all speaks volumes for his ability. But his talent alone was not enough. F1 was (and still is) an exclusive 'club.' With a small number of teams, membership was by invitation only, and the normal selection process was through the multi-level European formula car series. Since Eaton had not come up through 'the system,' he and his agent Rod Campbell had to lobby hard to gain him a place on the BRM team.[16] So why was he the only Canadian racing regularly in Formula One at that time? Eaton felt that his fellow Canadian racers did not try hard enough:

> Canadian racing was good, but only up to a certain level. There were several very good Canadian drivers, but they stayed in Canada too long.

They were capable of winning the Canadian championship, but when they entered races against big league drivers, they drove the same way they did against Canadian racers. They reached a level of competence, didn't try to push themselves beyond it, and never improved.[17]

Bill Brack, who ran in three Canadian F1 GPs and later won three Canadian championships, agrees that there was a steep 'learning curve,' and that developing competence took time: 'I peaked very late ... In the late sixties, when I first got into formula cars, I didn't know how to drive them. I was miles off the pace, and I thought I knew how to drive. By the mid-seventies [racing in Formula Atlantic] ... I was pretty much unbeatable.'[18]

He had put his finger on the nub of the problem – and on its solution. Before 1967, Canadian racers lacked experience in powerful open-wheel racing cars. Their formula car racing was limited mainly to FJ and FV. The former was a small class and the latter were underpowered, and so neither provided the training and experience needed for competitiveness when they entered the Canadian F1 GP. And, as will be discussed in the next chapter, that situation did not change until the late-1970s, after the national racing championship had been transformed into the Formula Atlantic series and professional racing schools began to train drivers 'from the ground up.' The product of that change was Gilles Villeneuve.

Of Cars, and Costs

If lack of proper training was the main roadblock for success in Formula One, the lack of competitive cars was the main obstacle in Can-Am. While races like the Player's 200 had trained Canadian drivers well for the Can-Am series, nothing could have prepared them for the 'sticker shock' of the cars themselves. The Can-Am 'technology race' came at a hefty, constantly increasing price. The series became more lucrative, worth a million dollars by 1969, but the cost of competing in it escalated disproportionately. In 1967 Nat Adams was offering his Cooper Ford, raced the previous year in Can-Am, for $5000. Five years later, the 'list price' of a factory-prepared Porsche 917/10K was $124,000. Lyons estimates that in six years the cost of a competitive Can-Am car had increased eight times. And that did not include the costs of drivers and crews, spare engines and other parts, tires, testing, transportation, and travel. The engine alone for a 1972 McLaren could cost $21,000, and one engine was unlikely to last a season. While the series prize funds were distributed quite generously, they could not begin to cover the costs of any but the top finishers. Ultimately, the technology race became a self-defeating quest. By the end of 1974 the Can-Am series had simply priced itself out of existence.[19]

Thus, in order to have any hope of being a serious contender and finishing 'in the money,' a team had to be well funded. Lola and McLaren built and sold scores of racing cars, using the profits to support both car development and the teams themselves. And Porsche's was a lavish factory team effort. Critics argued that the cost of the series had produced a 'caste' system, with the McLaren team unbeatable at the top. Below them was a second tier of teams and drivers who could compete with the McLarens only at huge expense, and then a bottom rank who were not competitive unless the top drivers dropped out. British driver Jackie Oliver (1974 Can-Am champion) pointedly remarked that the escalating costs and the absence of appearance money meant that there never was a 'level playing field' in the series: 'It's a case of the rich – meaning the McLaren team – getting richer and the poor – everyone else – getting poorer. It's unreasonable to expect someone to invest $100,000 (the minimum to develop a new racer) in a car that can be destroyed at any time or can break down during a race, and then ask him to show up to put on the show for nothing.'[20]

Except for Eaton's term with BRM, the top Canadian racers lacked wealthy sponsors at a time when they had become essential. In fact, some critics said they were slow to take a professional approach to attracting them. Thus, they had to bear many of the costs themselves and hope to reap some prize money to offset their own expenditures and meagre sponsor funds. But, as they could not afford to buy the best, they typically drove cars that were one or two years old. George Eaton could afford to buy his own McLaren, but even his personal wealth did not guarantee him a first-rank car; his invariably were outdated. And when he drove for BRM, the firm was not fully behind the Can-Am effort, so its P154 was not a competitive car. Likewise, McCaig's business supported his racing, but his cars were always one step below the winners'. Cannon had to constantly 'shop around' for sponsors, who invariably found backing a racer too expensive. Dave Billes bought a McLaren for Cordts, but later withdrew from direct support of racing.[21] Thus, Canadians were limited to uncompetitive cars that could not bring them victory and the financial return on their investment. What is remarkable is not that the Canadians were financially outclassed in the Can-Am, but that they performed as well as they did in spite of it. That speaks volumes for their talent.

There never would be *enough* money in Canadian racing. As a result, some never got the opportunity to develop their talent when the time was right. Bill Brack feels that after the 1968 Grand Prix, 'I could have ... considered going to Europe, but I couldn't financially bring myself to do it.'[22] Running an automotive business at the time, he told *Track and Traffic*, 'I have too much to give up for a try at racing in Europe.'[23]

There were still alternatives to F1 and the Can-Am, especially in the United States. Ludwig Heimrath spent a couple of seasons on the USAC Indy Car circuit in the late 1960s.[24] John Cannon and Eppie Wietzes competed in the SCCA Continental Formula A championship. Maurice ('Mo') Carter, John Cordts, and Craig Fisher drove regularly in Trans-Am races. But as good as those series were, even when Canadian drivers did well these events were not the stuff that would generate front-page headlines at home. Nor would they capture the imagination of those fans who flocked to Mosport or Le Circuit hoping – as some surely did – for a Canadian to bring home a Formula One victory. They would have to wait more than a decade to see that dream realized.

12 Winning Formula: Formula Racing and the National Championship

To win a Grand Prix is something, but to win your first Grand Prix at home is completely unthinkable. This is the happiest day of my life.

Gilles Villeneuve[1]

Canada's First F1 Victory

Lionel Birnbom's photograph has immortalized the moment: under a steel grey October sky the fire-engine-red Ferrari streaks towards the finish line, Gilles Villeneuve's fists punch the air, the chequered flag is about to drop, and the hometown crowd is on its feet. You can almost hear the thousands of cheering voices obliterating the howl of the Ferrari engine.

There had never been a moment like it in Canadian racing. For the first time a Canadian driver had won the Canadian Grand Prix for Formula One. With Villeneuve's victory in Montreal on 8 October 1978, the vision of the CASC's founders had been fully realized and vindicated. Canada finally had produced a driver who could beat the best in the world at the pinnacle of the sport.

Clearly, Formula One racing in Canada had come a long way since that first race at Mosport eleven years earlier. What had changed in the interval? Without denying Gilles's obvious driving talent, it must be recognized that he was the product and beneficiary of a different, more professional approach to Canadian racing and to driver development than had existed earlier. In essence, to compete with Europeans on an equal level, Canadian racing had to become more 'European' itself. Gilles's driving career epitomized that different character. It was the very antithesis of the 'the seat of your pants' amateurism that had dominated the first two decades of Canadian racing.

Driving to a Different Drummer

In one respect, Gilles was no different from the hobby racers who had preceded him; he drove fast because he loved it. But in most other respects, he was different. He had not come up through club-based amateur sports car racing. There were no sports car clubs near his home in rural Berthierville, Quebec. That was an 'Anglo' pastime, centred in Montreal. And, when he started competing it was in drag races and stock car racing at local tracks and later at Napierville and Sanair. It was not until the late 1960s that he attended a race at Le Circuit, and saw Trans-Am sedans, Formula Vees, and Formula Fords in action for the first time. But as he told his biographer, 'It all looked completely inaccessible to me. The cars cost so much money.'[2]

Instead, Gilles turned to a new and more affordable sport: snowmobile racing. Starting with his father's machine, then gaining sponsorship first from a local dealer and later a manufacturer, he displayed immediate race-winning talent. Racing snowmobiles allowed him to develop the fast reflexes, the instinctive ability to push machinery to its limits and stay in control, and the distinctive power-slide cornering technique that became his hallmarks in car racing. In 1973 Gilles became the Canadian snowmobile racing champion. He was able to earn a modest living from the sport, but he had no other job to support his family. One of his snowmobiling friends who knew people involved in road racing suggested that he try the racing school at Le Circuit.[3]

This, obviously, was the turning point in his life and career. And the timing of his decision was just right, because it coincided with significant changes that had occurred quite recently in Canadian championship-level racing: the creation of professional racing schools and the conversion of the national racing championship to open-wheel formula cars. It was these two changes as much as his undeniable talent that set Gilles on the road to his victory in Montreal.

Schools for Speed

Canada's first racing drivers had been self-taught. The CASC eventually made attendance at a racing 'school' mandatory for attaining a racing licence, but as late as 1969 *Track and Traffic* described racing-driver training in Canada as 'a hit and miss affair at best ... The learning process is ... trial and error ... there are no real instructors ... Instruction is performed by experienced racers but ... there are instructors who are rank amateurs as drivers.'[4] This situation was underlined by the relatively poor showing of Canadian drivers in international racing in the late 1960s. In 1968 Alitalia – the Italian national airline – sponsored four Canadian regional champions to attend a racing school in Italy.[5] But this sort of opportunity was not accessible to the vast majority of racers.

In 1970 the Jim Russell International Driver's School stepped in to fill the vacuum. Russell was an experienced British racer who had established his first racing school in England in 1957 to teach enthusiasts the basics of car racing. It quickly gained a reputation for excellence, based on rigorous, disciplined, graduated training from the basics to actual competition. Using open-wheel formula cars, his instructors would teach, demonstrate for, observe, and critique each candidate as they practised every technique until the school's standard became second nature. After taking the course in 1969, Roger Peart suggested to Russell that he establish a school at Le Circuit. The CASC supported the plan, and it opened in 1970. Jacques Couture, Quebec Region chief driving instructor and future national racing champion, was appointed director and chief instructor.[6]

At about the same time, Gary Magwood, the 1970 Canadian Formula Ford champion, opened his own school in partnership with Mosport. Their training philosophies were different; the Russell school put drivers in the car almost immediately, while Magwood started with classroom work and reading before track time. But both were convinced of the value of professional training using open-wheel racing cars, as Couture explained: 'Formula Ford cars quickly show up any weaknesses a driver may have ... They are very sensitive machines, yet are fast and reliable. Even someone who is planning to race a sedan or a sports car can learn quite a lot from driving a Formula Ford.'[7] Couture's program graduated more than 150 students in its first year, drawing many from the United States, where SCCA rules prohibited racing driver training to anyone under age twenty-one. Magwood's output was more modest: forty students that first year. In 1975 former ice racing champion and national racing championship contender John Powell took over as chief instructor of the Mosport Racing School, which offered a three-day basic course sanctioned by the CASC.[8] These schools gave beginners the chance to get started in racing at a very low cost and low risk; the schools absorbed the cost of any damaged cars.

They also represented a 'paradigm shift' in Canadian professional racing. Magwood believes that the schools changed the 'career pattern' for aspiring Canadian racing champions. 'Regional racing no longer produces the upcoming drivers. Today, [most of] the top drivers ... come out of racing schools ... Any young driver who wants to make racing their living had better start at a racing school.'[9]

Gilles Villeneuve was the first Canadian to prove that point. He attended the Jim Russell School in 1973, and immediately impressed Couture. 'It rained during most of the classes and I was just a little bit nervous about how fast this kid Villeneuve was able to go in comparison to everyone else.'[10] But it was obvious that Gilles knew exactly what he was doing. Returning to Le Circuit the next weekend with his own Ford Capri sedan, Gilles was again the fastest in the class and passed the course with flying colours. He bought a used Formula Ford, and went on to win not only Rookie of the Year but the provincial Formula Ford championship as well, winning seven out of ten races.[11] The following year (1974) Gilles entered the Formula Atlantic series, where his career intersected with the second trend changing Canadian racing: the national championship.

Driving for Dollars: The National Championship

In 1969 the CASC switched the national racing championship to open-wheel formula cars. Once the mainstays of national racing, sports cars and sedans were assigned a separate series.[12] It was a change that altered dramatically the character of the national championship.

The switch was the brainchild of racer/builder Peter Broeker. He persuaded the 1967 CASC AGM that the series should be for Formula B and C cars, which were the successors to Formula Junior. But the following year a major dispute broke out over which cars would be eligible. The debate broke along provincial lines, with Quebec drivers supporting Formula B, since the cars were already in use there. But some Ontario racers, who also wanted to race in the SCCA Continental series, demanded that Formula A cars be included. The debate reflected two different racing philosophies, pitting cost against speed and spectacle. Formula A cars could use large (up to five-litre) American V-8s, while Bs were limited to the less powerful 1.6-litre Cosworth-Ford motors. Since the As were only slightly heavier than Bs, they were faster.[13]

Broeker felt that a Canadian championship car should be affordable. Roger Peart agreed; since using the more costly As would reduce the number of Canadian competitors, he felt the series should be restricted to the cheaper Bs. But the Ontario racers were unmoved by these arguments. Ted Kennedy said that Formula A 'would open the door to the rest of the world and since "speed is the name of the game" people would be able to see it with Formula A.'[14] Gordon Salisbury agreed that 'Canada must keep pace with the world,' so a national championship had to provide 'spectacular and fast races, and Formula A provided this.' Moreover, he asserted, 'there had to be sponsors for drivers and events and most sponsors were only interested in fast cars. The Championship would be a combination of a fast driver and a fast car and Formula A was the fastest in Canada.' Bob Attrell concurred, arguing that As offered 'greater potential for sponsors.'[15]

Bill Brack, also from Ontario, agreed that sponsors were more likely to support A cars. He dismissed the financial argument by pointing out that travel to events consumed half the costs of running any racing car, and since Bs were limited to one type of engine, the cost of the car was not a factor. Moreover, he pointed out that the CASC's rules mandated that a championship had to run for at least three years with one type of car. So racers who competed in a B car would not be able to move up. John Ross, a national director and also a Quebec racer, challenged the A advocates on the speed issue, saying that he 'did not believe spectacular racing was good racing. The name of the game is competition.' But Richard Rogers disagreed. The 'name of the game is money,' he said. 'The spectators would only come out in numbers if they were given the best and Formula A would help this.'[16] Ross had a point, but Rogers was right as well; in an expensive *spectator* sport, money mattered. After intense lobbying, the Ontario racers carried the day and Formula A was included with B for the 1969 season.

Ultimately, this proved to be a pyrrhic victory. Although Len Coates described it in 1970 as 'the coming thing in North American road racing,'[17] Formula A lasted only two seasons in the Canadian championship. Auto sport journalist F. David Stone opined that, while the races up to July 1969 had demonstrated 'that the time is right for a genuine Canadian Racing Championship ... there is still a long way to go before the new series will be a world beater.'[18] Gulf Canada sponsored the 1969 series to the tune of $44,000, but typically the grids were small; the fourth race that year, held at Westwood, had eleven entries, while the sixth, at Mosport, attracted only nine: five As and four Bs. There was no comparison in the performance of the two classes, and the races often degenerated into a 'parade.' Eppie Wietzes won the A championship handily both years, while Craig Hill did the same for B. At the 1969 AGM, Quebec Region proposed that 'the disastrous and ill considered decision taken last year to change the format of the national championship ... be revoked,'[19] and that the championship be limited to B and C cars. But, after considerable heated debate, Quebec was outvoted. CASC president Stanley Williams felt that the first year with Gulf sponsorship had been a good start. Over 50,000 people had watched the nine races, seeing 'more competitive cars than in the final year of our previous championship. This speaks well for the future of the series and should help to allay many of the misgivings voiced.'[20]

Williams could be forgiven for trying to put the best spin on the series, but both the entry and spectator numbers were disappointing. A race of fewer than a dozen mismatched cars, some of which would fail to start or finish, would hardly be a crowd-pleaser. Thus, the crowds usually were only a fraction of the size of those that had attended the big international events. In fact, they were closer in size to those at the club-run amateur races of the 1950s and early 1960s. In its favour, the championship was national in scope, with the nine races shared between five provinces from Quebec to BC.[21]

For 1970 Gulf Canada increased its funding to $50,000. Bob Hanna reported that the series saw better fields of cars and a more professional approach to racing. But still it struggled. Part of the problem was that the Canadian series was competing against the SCCA Continental championship, which ran three races in Canada and ten in the United States. Not only did that series draw larger and more competitive fields, it was also much more lucrative than its Canadian counterpart. The Continental race at Mosport in September 1970 had thirty-three entries for Formula A alone, and almost as many for B and C. The total cash prize package for that series in 1970 exceeded $400,000 (US), of which at least $150,000 was earmarked for Formula A cars. Where a Continental race winner would receive $5000, the winner of a Gulf Canada series race would take home a paltry $895. Given the rising costs of competing in formula cars, it is not surprising that the top Canadian drivers competed in the American as much as in the Canadian series. John Cannon, who won the 1970 Continental championship, did not even bother to pursue its Canadian counterpart. Wietzes came fourth in the SCCA series and earned $21,000 (over $2300 per race). He won five of the seven Gulf Canada events, but his victories brought him less than $5000.²²

Wietzes's near sweep of the Canadian series and his earnings in the SCCA championship highlighted the central and underlying problems of Formula A: competitiveness and cash. An editorial in *Track and Traffic* summed it up neatly: 'The fields in the Gulf series have been painfully short of competitive cars (Formula As) ... By competitive, we mean machines capable of running closely on the same lap and finishing an event ... machines that are maintained and operated in a professional manner. The only way to do this is with *money*, and this is badly lacking in Canada.'²³

As the editorial predicted, the fate of the championship was 'front and centre' at the 1970 CASC AGM. Tension was heightened by the announcement, just days before the meeting, that Gulf was withdrawing as the sponsor. This threw plans for the 1971 season into chaos, since the CASC national board had already decided to continue the Formula A championship for 1971. Consequently, the race workshop was more contentious than ever. Charges flew as to who was to blame for losing the sponsor, and the racers were angry that the national directors had decided the future of the championship – a decision that the drivers felt was theirs to make. Charlie Ryan said:

> I believe that we have burned our bridges in the past in connection with sponsors and we have repeated this with Gulf ... CASC did not see fit to exercise their authority and help to satsify the needs of the sponsors involved. Instead of that, we get people telling Gulf that they are a second rate company sponsoring a second rate team or sport. If we continue to operate in this way we might as well eliminate the entire championship.²⁴

Bob Surman announced that BC Region did not want to run any more Formula A races. Criticizing the board for its decision, he observed: 'What we have for this year [1971] is Formula ABC races with no sponsorship. I think we would be better off with nothing. No kind of championship races can be held without sponsorship.' Bob Harrington of Ontario Region reluctantly agreed that it was going to be very difficult to run an unsponsored championship because of the costs of competing. But he also pointed out that by its own rules CASC was locked into a three-year cycle for the championship. Roy Folland outlined a proposal from Quebec Region for an eight-race championship sponsored by a (then unnamed) tobacco company with a prize purse of $63,000. But the CASC could not accept it because this would have placed it in conflict with its major F1 sponsor, Imperial Tobacco. Broeker argued that a single tobacco company should not have a monopoly on race sponsorship and Jacques Couture agreed: 'For the first time we have had a large amount of money offered to us and the only reason it was turned down was because it was a competitive sponsor. Why should a major sponsor [be] dictating to C.A.S.C. what they can and can not have.'[25]

Roger Peart, by then a national vice-president, agreed: '[W]e could not have sponsors dictating to us ... but we can not tell sponsors how to run their business. They put money into a business venture to make money. If they do not ... they are allow[ed] to take their money and spend it somewhere else.'[26]

But it was Jim Muzzin of Ontario Region who recognized that what was at stake was not just money, but power. 'As much as we may think that we control racing in Canada we have to be realistic about it. No one group has 100% control.'[27] Muzzin had put his finger on the nub of the problem. Racing had changed, and it wasn't just that it was more expensive, making sponsorship essential for racers. It was because the need for sponsors meant that neither the competitors nor the CASC itself were free to make or change the rules whenever it suited them. From now on the sponsors, who provided the largest portion of the funding, would be able to influence – if not to dictate – the shape and the terms of the sport, in this case the national racing championship. As a result, within a few years that series would look very different.

In the meantime, changing the championship to formula cars had come at a steep price. First, since they competed abroad as well as at home, and aspired to move into the top ranks of international racing, the best Canadian drivers had to use cars that met international-class rules. Thus, in the virtual absence of domestic builders (the Fejer's Chinook Formula A car was a rare Canadian exception) the top Canadian racers bought the dominant British cars. In the 1971 Player's Challenge Series for Formula B, Brack, Brian Robertson, and others drove Brabhams, while Couture and David McConnell drove Lotuses. Ian Coristine was in a March, and John Powell drove a Chevron. Four years later, British makes still dominated Canadian formula racing.[28]

Second, to be and to remain competitive, even 'second tier' cars such as the Formula Bs had to have all the latest features. Class regulations forced owners and drivers to use the most current model, and in the early 1970s the base price of a B was about $12,000. But buying the car was just the start. To have a chance of winning the championship, racers had to compete across the country, which added substantial travel expenses. All of this pushed up the cost of the national series to the point where it became almost prohibitively expensive. Peter Bone observed that in the early 1960s he had run his Elva at a cost of about a hundred dollars for the season. 'I talked to somebody, less than ten years later, who was running a formula car, and it was costing him $20,000! That was $20,000 *after* he'd bought the car!'[29] Bill Brack recalled that in 1972 his team had spent $15,000 for the season. Two years later, Villeneuve's first season in Formula Atlantic was expected to cost $50,000–70,000. Brack pointed out that by the end of the 1970s, a two-car team was the norm. The cars were more expensive, and they required transporters, extra mechanics, and spare engines, pushing the total up to $300,000–400,000 per year.[30] Since the prize money in the championship was insufficient to offset such costs, they put competition completely out of reach of the hobby racer and limited it to only the well-sponsored teams.

At a minimum, sponsorship meant carrying advertising on the car itself. Indy 500 and NASCAR racers had been doing so for several decades, but FIA rules had prohibited on-car ads until 1968. As early as 1960, however, in defiance of the rules, commercial logos had begun to appear on some North American racing cars. In 1962 Dean Delamont of the RAC had advised the CASC that while FIA rules permitted 'no advertising whatsoever' on cars, national auto sport authorities could amend the rules. And so, for 1963 CASC adopted as national policy the Ontario Region practice that permitted advertising 'in good taste' on a car. In the end, the loss of a sponsor eventually forced the FIA to drop its ban on ads. Esso, which had been supplying fuel for F1 racing, announced in 1967 that it would no longer do so. With costs rising, this meant that the FIA had little choice but to permit direct sponsorship of cars and teams; it approved on-car advertising for 1968. Before long, racing cars became rolling billboards and drivers became spokesmen for their sponsors. The 'commodification of talent,' which had already begun to permeate other professional sports, soon spread to all forms of auto sport.[31]

The FIA's decision was a mixed blessing for Canadian championship competitors. On the one hand, racers could now actively solicit sponsorship money by selling the space on their cars. On the other, it was not easy to find Canadian companies that could provide sufficient funds to offset the costs of formula car racing. Consequently, racers had to devote more time to raising money. Eppie Wietzes and Gary Magwood were more successful than most. In 1971 Castrol Oils Canada signed contracts to sponsor Wietzes for the SCCA Continental Formula A series and Magwood for the Canadian championship. The funding from Castrol and a brake-pad manufacturer gave Magwood $20,000 for the season: 'That was more money than [almost] anybody else had. It was a huge amount of money' for that era, 'more than enough to run the entire series, travel expenses, car, maintenance, engines ... right across the country.'[32] But on-car advertising alone was just the start. To succeed at attracting sponsors, racers had to take a professional, business-like approach. They had to learn what businesses expected out of their investment, who their market was, and how to 'sell' themselves to it. Drivers themselves had to fulfil marketing obligations to their sponsors: photo sessions, personal appearances, product endorsements, and car shows. But marketability required name recognition, and most Canadian drivers were virtually unknown outside the racing fraternity. According to critics, what Canadian racing lacked in the early 1970s was a 'star system' that would produce racers known to the public.[33] That was soon to change.

In the meantime, however, for 1971 the national championship reverted to Formula B cars. Named for its new sponsor it became the Player's Challenge Series, consisting of six races from Quebec to BC, three of them paired with bigger events: the Grand Prix and two Trans-Am races. Although the purse remained small – just $27,000 for the 1971 season – in Bob Hanna's view, the series was an 'overwhelming success.' He was pleased to discover that 'there are a hell of a lot ... of Formula Bs in Canada. A lot of drivers had gone and ordered cars even before the series was announced.'[34] Bob MacGregor, editor of the CASC's *Canadian Motorsport Bulletin*, observed that 'nobody is bemoaning the loss of the Formula A's, not even the most zealous backers of the big machines. Everyone accepts it as a mistake; the series should have been Formula B cars right from the start.' The field in the Player's series averaged twenty-five cars per race; 'the racing was close and exciting and the level of car preparation would have done justice to any professional competition.'[35] Terry Jones, who covered the Edmonton race, wrote: 'Somewhere along the line somebody did something right. The new series ... that is the Player's Canadian series for Formula B cars provided the best single auto race that Edmonton has ever witnessed. That includes three Can-Am races, a Trans-Am and a Continental. And, er yes, two Gulf Series races.'[36] Race winner Jacques

Couture and runner-up (teammate) David McConnell traded the lead twenty-three times and finished only half a second apart. In the kind of close racing that characterized the whole series, only two seconds separated the first four cars. Couture emerged as the champion of the hotly contested series, which saw five different winners in six races.[37]

Offsetting the small prize package somewhat was the fact that the Formula B cars were cheaper to buy. Yet, drivers still needed their own sponsorship to cover the costs of competing, particularly travelling across the country. Moreover, the series did not draw big crowds, except when the races were paired with bigger events where there was, in effect, a captive audience.

Nevertheless, in what had to be seen as a vote of confidence, Player's increased the prize money to $75,000 for the 1972 season. The series was expanded to eight races, including for the first time the Debert, Nova Scotia, and Gimli, Manitoba, airport circuits. At the AGM Bob Hanna described the 1972 championship as 'the most exciting and competitive races ever seen in Canada.'[38] There were four different race winners and the top three places in the series were not decided until the last race, when Brian Robertson emerged as the champion. Still, the number of entries had dropped dramatically, to an average of nineteen per race. But that was many more than had entered Formula A, and so even at that level it was an improvement on the previous series. Moreover, while the audiences were small (only 2000 saw the Debert race), it should be noted that six of the races were run in the rain – a guarantee of poor spectator turnout.[39]

To its credit, Player's did not give up, and the next year the series rebounded. At the 1973 AGM, Hanna was ecstatic: 'The Player's Challenge Series has to be considered even by the most conservative standard, as a tremendous success.'[40] In what proved to be harbingers of change for the series, two factors drove this renaissance. First, the prize money drew an influx of American drivers, who pushed the entries up to an average of thirty-three per race, with the actual grids averaging twenty-eight. As this made the series more exciting and competitive, the number of spectators increased as well. A crowd of 11,000 watched the Westwood race, the largest audience ever for the series.[41]

During 1973 at least a dozen American drivers raced in the series. Much to the chagrin of Canadian drivers and spectators, Alan Lader of Oregon won it. Bill Brack, who finished second overall without winning a single race, was declared the Canadian champion. That decision caused some discontent among competitors and fans. While Brack insisted that winning the championship was 'a hell of a hard job,' even he conceded that he did not go 'all out' to win it: 'Some people ... have said the ... championship is a sham ... If the Canadian ... had had to win to get the title you definitely would have seen different racing. In our case, it was a matter of being first Canadian. That's all we had to do, and that's all we went out to do.'[42]

The second new factor was television coverage. CTV's 'Wide World of Sports' broadcast taped thirty-minute segments of each race a week after the event; TVA did the same in French for Quebec. TV coverage was just getting started in Formula One, and in the United States was limited to closed-circuit broadcasts of the Indy 500 and Daytona 500 on a 'pay per view' basis in a few theatres. And so, as Bob Harrington noted, regular coverage of the Canadian races represented a 'first for any Road-racing Series in North America.' The benefits were obvious. It helped many competitors attract new sponsors and raised the public profile of the sport. Said Hanna: 'The televising of these races on Wide World of Sport has given Canadian racing more exposure in one season than we have had in the last ten years.' He said that Player's was so pleased with the results that it had signed its 1974 sponsorship agreement three months early. Tom Lamont, Player's vice-president for marketing, lent credibility to Hanna's claim by describing the 1973 series as 'the most successful ever held in Canada' and by announcing that the company would increase the prize fund for the next season. He also announced that CTV and TVA had agreed to continue their coverage of the series. Johnny Esaw, CTV's sports director, said, 'The ratings have been good and the response excellent ... That's why CTV will be covering it again in 1974.'[43] This was a major step in the process that would transform auto sport into a media spectacle.

A Formula for Success

The Player's Challenge Series national championship was changing in other significant ways when Gilles Villeneuve joined it in 1974. First, it became Formula Atlantic, with new rules that allowed cars to use the more powerful 240-bhp Cosworth-Ford BDA engine. Since the minimum weight of the cars increased only slightly, cars with the new engine would be much faster. Second, the series was opened up to racers from any country. The Canadian championship would not be limited to Canadian drivers. Third, in addition to the seven points races in Canada, there would be three non-points races in the United States.

Finally, the series became more lucrative. Player's posted $13,000 for each of the points races, with the winner taking home at least $2500. Additional contingency awards pushed the total for the series to over $100,000.[44]

Thus, what had started as a purely national series was evolving into an international one, attracting some of the rising stars of European and North American racing. This clearly was taking the Canadian championship to a higher level, more in line with European racing. The corresponding rise in standards for all the drivers made the series much more demanding, and Villeneuve was the Canadian racer who benefited most from the change. It brought out the best of his natural ability. Developing talent among Canadian drivers had always been the intent of the championship, but finding the best way to do it had long been a matter of trial and error. The CASC and Player's were quite explicit about the intent of the changes:

> to increase competition so that one day Canadian drivers can compete along side drivers from many other countries of the world ... The Player's Championship has as its purpose the development of Canadian racing talent ... Formula Atlantic cars ... are a step up in rank. This was done to broaden the scope of the series, and make the transition into Formula 1 somewhat easier for our Canadian drivers.'[45]

Villeneuve apart, the changes received mixed reviews from drivers. Brack favoured them, saying, 'It's time Canada had an international series to attract drivers here and allow Canadian drivers to race in Europe. Otherwise we are never going to get anywhere as far as somebody ending up in Formula 1 is concerned.'[46] John Powell, runner-up for 1973, argued that the championship 'should go to the best driver, regardless of nationality.'[47] Others, however, were less convinced. David Ogilvy, who had competed in the 1972 series, suggested that perhaps the Canadian racing champion should be determined some other way. Another wondered what would happen to advertising potential if the champion was not a Canadian.[48]

The series continued to grow, with excellent competition and record crowds; attendance increased by 13 per cent. At least a dozen Canadian drivers competed that season, among them Gilles Villeneuve. Brack won his second championship convincingly, while Gilles's season was costly – in money, damaged cars, and injury (he broke his leg at the Mosport race) – and he finished sixteenth overall, ending the season deeply in debt.[49] But his talent clearly exceeded his position in the standings. Over the next four years, against increasingly tougher competition, he proved just how good he really was. In the meantime, as Brack recalls, his driving style enthralled the crowds:

> Gilles had incredible car control, absolutely unbelievable ... I've never seen anyone that could come out of the problems he used to get himself into by overdriving a car ... But he was able to drive a car beyond its limits ... and keep it on the track, somehow! I couldn't do it and I don't know anybody else who could. He'd get in incredible slides at extremely high speed ... but he'd come back on the track and drive away.[50]

At the end of the 1974 season Bob Harrington had predicted, 'If the Player's Challenge Series continues to grow in the manner it has, in a very few years it will be one of the premier racing Series in the world.'[51] The next few years seemed to prove him right. In 1975 the series drew seventy-seven drivers from ten countries, with an average entry of forty-two cars per race. The race at Le Circuit set an attendance record for the series – 21,000 – although overall season totals were down. Brack won his third consecutive and final Canadian championship, and Villeneuve came fifth overall, with a rain-sodden win on the Gimli track and a second at Le Circuit. Bob Hanna felt moved to claim that 'the Canadian Formula Atlantic Series has gained world wide recognition as tough competitive racing second only to Formula One.'[52]

Villeneuve was proof that Hanna's claim was no idle boast. In 1976 he dominated Formula Atlantic, winning ten times in eleven starts. He capped the season by winning the Grand Prix de Trois-Rivières, defeating several Formula One stars, including James Hunt (who won the F1 championship that year) and future champion Alan Jones. Hunt was so impressed by Gilles's ability that, on returning to the UK, he praised him to Teddy Mayer, the head of the McLaren F1 team. And he told John Hogan of Marlboro, McLaren's sponsor, 'I've just been beaten by this guy Villeneuve and he's really magic. You really ought to get hold of him.'[53] That was the break Gilles needed. In December 1976 McLaren signed him to a contract to drive in F1 for part of the next season. In the end, he raced only once for McLaren, placing eleventh at the British Grand Prix, but it was enough to convince Gilles that Formula One was where he was meant to be. It was also good enough for the influential British auto sport press to declare that Gilles was F1's 'brightest new star' and a 'future World Champion.' In 1977 he also won his second Atlantic championship, repeating his Trois-Rivières victory with a convincing win over future F1 champion Keke Rosberg, and future Indy Car champion Bobby Rahal. And so when McLaren dropped Villeneuve, it was only a matter of time before another team made him an offer. That moment came shortly after the Trois-Rivières race, and the offer came from Ferrari.[54] His victory in Montreal one year later confirmed that they had made the right choice.

Gilles Villeneuve was probably the most naturally talented racing driver to emerge in Canada since Peter Ryan. Like Ryan's, his was initially an untrained, undisciplined talent. What Canadian racing had lacked until the early 1970s was a means to refine that talent through proper training and to develop it further with experience in a competitive open-wheel racing series – in short, professionalism. Drivers like Eaton, Brack, Pease, and Wietzes had been forced to make the leap from sports-racing cars to F1 without adequate open-wheel preparation and experience. And it showed in their early performance in the Canadian F1 Grand Prix. The new professional racing schools, the Player's Challenge Series, and Formula Atlantic changed all that, giving Canadian drivers the opportunity to develop their talent and gain the experience and funding they required to reach the point where graduating to – and succeeding in – the major leagues of auto racing became a realistic, attainable objective. National pride aside, for Canadian racing that was the real significance of Gilles Villeneuve's victory in Montreal.

By the late 1970s these changes had altered yet again the face of Canadian sports car competition, professionalizing and commercializing it further. The end result was the ascendancy of Canadian drivers to world-class status. But the unintended consequence, in both racing and rallying, was that the gap between club-based amateur sport and commercial-professional competition widened further, gradually alienating the top levels of the sport from their original constituency.

13 Stage by Stage: Transforming the National Rally Championship

The marshal's hand drops ... the car surges forward ... leaving a plume of dirt and gravel as it hurls toward the first corner – 'sharp right – three – two – one' the driver flicks the steering ... to start a pendulum motion to bring the back end out to the left so he can power round the right hander in a smooth controlled powered drift ... The night is pierced by a million candlepower spotlighting the crest of the hill 400 yards away – what lies beyond? The co-driver ... yells 'flat' 2nd, 3rd, 4th gear, 100 miles an hour the car launches into the dark abyss over the crest – you're airborne, you land with a thud in a shower of sparks – downshift, swing the car sideways; there's barely time to set up for the next corner.

Robin Edwardes, 'Rallying in Canada'[1]

Robin Edwardes's account captures graphically the character of national championship rallying from the mid-1970s to the present. Like the national racing championship, it became professional, commercial, and highly specialized. Stage rallies replaced navex and endurance rallies, and turned the 'thinking man's auto sport' into a spectacle of speed that could entertain an audience. Little more than time-trials on bad roads, these high-speed European-style driver's events demanded a different kind of competitor: a racer at heart. They also pushed up the costs of car preparation – and repair. As it became more expensive to compete at that level, fewer did; for the aspiring champions sponsorship became essential. Consequently, the gap between the amateur and professional rallyist yawned ever wider and club-based rallying went into decline.

All the World's a Stage

With the experience of the Shell 4000 behind them, some Canadian enthusiasts wanted national rallying as a whole to emulate the European rally format, which stressed speed and car durability. In 1969 'selective' stages became a regular feature of national championship events. By limiting normal traffic as much as possible on sections of public roads, rally organizers allowed the competitors to drive through the stages much faster than normal. The Quebec Rally became the first North American rally to be scored entirely on its thirty-one selective stages. Robin Edwardes, who as rally master had introduced them into that event, explains that 'up to that point even the ones that were supposed to be "driver's rallies," like the 1000 Islands Rally and the Winter Rally, still required a great deal of navigation, and usually the navigators determined the winner. We tried to lean it a little more toward the driver, by introducing ... selectives.'[2]

Apparently, his goal was achieved. Quebec Region reported in 1969 that, 'with the introduction of the mini-stage, the events have taken on some of the European flavour of Rallying – where the driver really means something to the winning possibilities of the crew.'[3]

And, as intended, the change of emphasis had a noticeable impact on rallying as a whole in Canada. It sent crews in search of cars with a combination of power, handling, and reliability, and the manufacturers – determined to prove the worthiness of their cars – rose to the challenge. The success of factory teams in European and North American rallying in the 1960s and the marketing benefits associated with winning events like the Monte Carlo Rally had already drawn them into Canadian rallying. CASC executive director Bob Hanna told the 1970 AGM, that the manufacturers were finding the national rally championship a 'very attractive ... promotional vehicle.'[4]

His observation was borne out by car magazine ads highlighting rally victories, by the increase in manufacturers' contingency awards, which grew from $15,000 in 1968 to $40,000 in 1969, and by direct team sponsorship. But equally important from the rallyists' perspective, stage rallying prompted auto makers to produce built-to-purpose rally cars or to offer after-market performance options. For example, in 1971 Walter Boyce and Doug Woods of Ottawa initially competed in a special factory-prepared Datsun SSS that boasted a raised suspension (giving nearly ten inches of ground clearance), an engine modified to deliver 135-bhp instead of the stock ninety-six, powerful driving lights, a fibreglass driver's seat, and navigation equipment. While it was fast, it was not reliable, and part way through the season CMI offered the team a Toyota Corolla. With the two cars and their undoubted talent Boyce and Woods won seven rallies and their second championship. For Dwight Scott, who was national rally director in 1970, they represented 'the new breed ... that had the skill to drive a competitive car very well. And ... their track records were good enough to go to the sponsors.'[5] Over the next several years the Datsun, Toyota, and Fiat factory teams dominated rallying at the national championship level.

But there was a downside to these changes. Even with sponsorship, the cost of a competitive rally car was increasing. Consequently, the number of competitors declined; the five national rallies in Ontario in 1969 attracted an average of only thirty-four entries each. Of course, championship events were supposed to be tougher; not all rallyists were of national calibre, and inevitably the best would leave the others behind. But the change highlighted a growing gap between the amateur club event and the more expensive national championship rally. By 1970 it was clear: 'Somewhere between these two extremes we are losing a great many people who used to rally.'[6] 'And now, how much do you still rally?' *Track and Traffic* asked that year, pointing out that 'a surprising number of people no longer do ... Why ... don't rallyists stay involved like golfers or fishermen?' The article went on to answer its own question by arguing that

> rallying itself has been changing, ... and many people have left the sport because they don't like what it is becoming ... At the club level, the accent seems to be on longer, more rigorous events. However, more rigorous rallies necessarily involve higher average speeds ... Only very experienced competitors are capable of staying on time, all the time, while still retaining a reasonable safety margin.[7]

That was exactly the point John Charters had made in 1962. And just as the first wave of commercial professionalism had done in the early 1960s, this second wave ignited a debate over the purpose of rallying.

'Rallying should be fun,'[8] Werner Wenzel told the 1970 rally workshop. When the 1971 workshop discussed the question 'Can rallying be used as a means to bring people into the sport?' Wenzel repeated his point and Gordon McCallum supported him, saying, 'Clubs should think of their own members first instead of concentrating on Regional and National events.' Katherine (Kay) Edmond, who succeeded Scott as national rally director, argued that Canadian rallying needed both the amateur and the professional parts – that the two levels were linked, not mutually exclusive. Pierre Cayer agreed, saying he wanted 'to see the sport grow from a broad base of club participation to a pyramid resulting in a select group of professional rallyists.'[9] In effect, Edmond and Cayer saw the sport in terms of a natural progression from amateur to professional rallying. Yet, reflecting on the debate many years later, Dwight Scott was less convinced. 'I sensed then a bit of elitism from ... some groups within the rally community that they didn't want to be part of an amateur grass-roots level across the country. They wanted to be the "Rally Circus" just like the Formula One "Circus" ... I saw that tension there.'[10]

The gap between the two types of rallying was not just a matter of cost. The championship events required a higher degree of organization. To prepare for the BEMC Winter Rally in the 1970s, Art Moseley would spend several months driving the route, collecting signatures from residents, then meeting with district councils and the police, to get permission to close roads that were to be used as stages. In addition, organizers had to provide a qualified medical team and an ambulance, marshals with radios, and insurance. But there were never enough experienced organizers and officials, and some who served simply were not up to the task.[11] All of the work that stage rallies entailed raised the question: for whose good?

It was an important question, but not one that seems to have troubled Don Horne, Edmonds's successor as national rally director. An experienced rallyist out of the Atlantic Region, he was a man on a mission: to remake the national rally championship in the European image. His first step in this regard was to limit the number of national events; for 1973 it was reduced from twenty-three to twelve. Second, to ensure that the championship was truly national in scope, competitors could count only two rallies from any region.[12] This forced them to compete in at least two other regions to have a chance at winning the series.

But these decisions left important issues unresolved. Scott warned the 1972 rally workshop that while most new members came into auto sport as rallyists, there was a high turnover rate; they weren't staying in and the sport needed good events to keep them. It also required more people fully dedicated to running national rallies. Elio Rosati reminded the group that organizing the Tall Pines Rally had involved seven months of work: two on the route and five on sponsorship. This raised the question of cost and generated heated debate. Woods suggested that costs could be kept down by requiring rallyists to use stock motors, but Cayer replied that since the championship was a professional series, cost should not be a factor. Marcel Rainville then asked a fellow rallyist whether, if he were offered $20,000 by a manufacturer, he would still rally a stock vehicle and annoy the sponsor? He insisted that 'professional or amateur, we must please the sponsor.'[13] For Rainville, at least, the real beneficiaries – and indeed, the purpose – of rallying were obvious and indisputable.

Fast Times: The New Rally Championship

At first glance the 1973 championship season looked quite different from previous years. While it included many of the long-standing events, such as the Rallye Des Neiges, the 1000 Islands, the Lobster, and the Nova Scotia Highlands rallies, newer events – the Tall Pines and the Criterium du Québec Rally – filled out the series. However, the Canadian Winter Rally was dropped. At the 1973 AGM Horne, supported by Ontario Region rally director Iain Tugwell, insisted that the BEMC had been given 'every opportunity' over three years to upgrade the rally and it had not done so, but exactly what the club had been asked to do was not explained. In 1969 the rally had been criticized for failing to balance navigation and selectives. By the early 1970s, however, selective stages had been added.[14] As a result, it became more of a driver's rally, and navigation played a declining – and less satisfying – role. After the 1972 event, 'nearly every driver spoken to at the finish was ecstatic about their almost complete control of the rally. Navigators were not so enthusiastic. Many just went along for the ride, aware of their diminished role, while other, more competitive types, were bored with nothing very difficult to do.'[15]

The 1973 Winter Rally lived up to its well-earned tough reputation. The 1050-mile ice-covered route, with stages throughout, claimed almost half of the seventy entries. Top drivers Jean-Paul Perusse and Lee Bartholemew won, with Boyce and Woods taking second.[16] Thus, if being a 'driver's rally' was the major criterion for an event's inclusion in the championship, then the 1973 rally clearly met that test. But several of the other championship events that year did not, among them the Rallye des Neiges. *Driving* magazine described it as a 920-mile navex that disappointed most of the entries. They had expected a driver's challenge, but times on the selective stages were not factored into the final standings at all. By contrast, navigation was more important than had been expected. Bartholemew complained that 'The navigation may have been beyond the capabilities of many of the navigators. It was not illogical or inaccurate, but there was a lot of work. With the combination of high speeds and difficult navigation, the navigators were having a hard time keeping ahead of the drivers and figuring out what to do.'[17] Likewise, Lauri Paivarinta criticized the 1973 Highlands Rally for including what he regarded as 'Mickey Mouse navigation,' which he felt cost him a victory, and did 'not belong in a rally that is supposed to prove the capabilities of cars and drivers ... We were not prepared for the type of navigation we encountered, which we felt was more suitable for club rallies, not national championship events.'[18] Finally, the Golden Triangle Rally proved to be a navex of only 'regional quality.' In contrast to these, the tough, driver-oriented Winter Rally stood out. Whatever were Horne's and Tugwell's earlier concerns about it, the 1973 event must have put them to rest, since the rally was reinstated in the championship for 1974.[19]

And so 1973 proved to be a transitional season, and as such it forced the national rally committee to re-address a host of unresolved issues and to confront the purposes and future of the national rally championship. And there was debate, even among the relatively small clique of national-level competitors. Satch Carlson, who as an American was not eligible for the championship, nonetheless weighed in. He argued that if the rallies continued to get rougher,

> *nobody in his right mind would run them* ... The whole thing is beginning to resemble off-road racing, and I think the rank and file of Canadian rallyists will agree. Otherwise, how could a ... weekend of *two national rallies* draw a total entry field of fourteen teams ... Unless you insist that there just aren't many Canadians interested in rallying, you have to figure out why so many stayed home ... A destruction derby ... might even be fun to drive (in someone else's machinery), but it sure as hell isn't rallying.[20]

Gordon McCallum disputed Carlson's views, arguing that the number of entries simply showed preferences, and claimed (incorrectly) that the selective-based national rallies had the highest number of entries, while the lowest turnouts were for the navexes. In fact, the smallest entry field in 1973 was for the Trail of the Bison Rally, a tough selective-style event that drew only sixteen competitors. Nevertheless, McCallum went on to point out that 'the whole idea behind the championship is to determine the ... best rally driver in Canada ... who can compete with the champions from other countries ... We are trying to elevate National rallying in Canada to be in step with our counterparts in Europe. We can't do that if we retain navigational rallies at the national level.'[21] John Pearce, four-time Atlantic Region navigation champion and organizer of five Nova Scotia Highlands rallies, took issue with the notion that the object of the championship was solely to determine the best *driver* in Canada: 'Has he forgotten that rallying is a team sport? *Both* driver and navigator must be tested.' And he went on to remind rallyists that 'navigators are the backbone of rally organization and administration, simply by the nature of their role in the competitive side ... The lack of competent National organizers has ... become a problem due to the elimination of navigation in many National rallies.' After criticizing the rising speeds, rough selective stages, damage to cars, and high attrition rate, Pearce closed with a plea to 'keep Canada's National Rally series as a *team* effort, challenging the car, driver, *and* navigator!'[22]

Don Horne acknowledged that McCallum's views had generated 'a ton of mail,' and claimed – somewhat disingenuously – that he was more concerned with the concept of a national series than with the format of specific events. Still, he used his annual report to the 1973 AGM to press the case for a stages-only championship series. He cited Boyce and Woods's victory in the Press on Regardless Rally – a world championship event – as proof of great progress in Canadian rallying. But he conceded that the changes had not been well received, which made his first two years as national rally director 'a difficult time':

> The loss of many historic names – events, organizers, competitors – has accompanied the changing philosophy of Canadian rallying ... However, new events, new organizers, and exciting new competitors have come to the fore ... We are still far from our objective ... but ... we *are* moving forward. The winds of change have been blowing and, with them, have gone many of the traditions of Canadian rallying. Many of the new concepts ... have not been popular and, at the same time, many of the old concepts were not popular either. What we have been trying to do is to save the good parts of the old style while gradually introducing the new ... What has been at the heart of the issue during these past two years has been the extremely delicate restructuring of the Canadian rally ladder.[23]

Horne clearly had been feeling the heat and he lashed out at his critics. While praising most rallyists for 'rational discussion and serious concern' about the future of the sport, he faulted a few (unnamed) exceptions for engaging in 'irrational discussion' and for demonstrating a 'complete lack of concern for the serious nature of the subject.' He asserted that the latter represented the two extremes of the issue, not the wider interests of Canadian rallying:

> On the one extreme, those who prefer the driver-oriented style *at any cost* would lead us so quickly away from our past that an unacceptable void would be created between them and the large base of amateur rallyists. On the other extreme, *some of those* who champion the navigational style would have us believe that there is no place for the driver's rally in Canadian rallying. There is no place in our discussions for either.[24]

But Horne made it abundantly clear that *he* thought the future of the championship lay in eventually adopting the stage rally format as the standard for the entire national series. In fact, the national rally committee had already decided the future. Tugwell announced that the championship for 1974 would consist of twelve events, all of the selective format, and that for 1975 they would be full stage rallies. The discussion that followed did not challenge the decision in any fundamental way, but focused instead on how to make the new format work.[25] This shows just how much attitudes about rallying had changed among Canada's top rallyists, and suggests that Horne both understood his constituency and had timed his changes well.

There was much more debate about the growing gap between club and national rallies and the apparent decline in entries in the national events. Colleen Hughes (of SMCC) suggested that 'the drop-off in number of entrants might be because ... selective type rallies have come in ... To a Club member, entering ... a National is quite a step up and seems to be a bigger problem than it really is.' Ron Welgan (Saskatchewan Sports Car Club) echoed those concerns, asking how the novice was supposed to advance through the system to national-level rallying. When discussion turned to a North American rally series, Paul Manson (also of SMCC) pointed out, 'We are having enough problems trying to find people across Canada to enter rallies ... We ... must concentrate in getting Canadians entering Canadian nationals.' Gordon McCallum, supported by Roger Woloshyn of the WSCC, continued to insist that selective rallies drew the most entries, in spite of evidence to the contrary.[26] Some regional events and series fared better than the national, which had an average of fewer than thirty entries per event. Moreover, the national rallies drew far fewer entries than their counterparts a decade earlier. And the attrition rate was very high, exceeding 50 per cent in some events, mostly owing to road conditions and damage to the cars.[27] The championship had inherited the 'car breaker' tradition with a vengeance. For the amateur the implications were obvious. To win the national championship you needed three things: a superb racing driver, a fast, reliable car, and a generous sponsor. Without those there was no point in even entering a championship event; and so few did.

At the outset of the 1974 season, Doug Hardie wrote in *Canadian Motorsport Bulletin* that 'Canadian rallying is on the verge of breaking into the big time' and that this was going to be the 'make it or break it year.' He quoted Doug Woods, who enthusiastically endorsed the changes to the national championship: 'By going to an all-stage format people are going to say, "Hell this is fantastic, let's get out and compete." Competitors will enter the sport because they realise that by putting money into car preparation, it will only be their driving ability that will determine whether they win or lose ... I think positively; it's going to be just fantastic.'[28]

Boyce and Woods won the 1974 championship, their fifth in a row, and last as a team. Jean-Paul Perusse and John Bellefleur were runners-up only five points behind, while Chuck McLaren and Don Ford took third. Don Horne could take some satisfaction in a modest increase in the number of entries. Most of the rallies proved challenging for cars and crews, with the number of DNFs usually approaching or exceeding 50 per cent (two-thirds of the forty-four starters dropped out of the Tall Pines Rally). The Canadian Winter Rally made a successful return to the championship circuit. Rallymaster Bob Lindquist claimed that 'those who get a finisher's plaque will have earned it ... It was my job to put the event back on the map ... to make it a tough challenging drivex ... I feel we have accomplished that much.' Andrew Cowan from Scotland, who placed third, agreed, saying, 'It has improved 100 per cent over last year.'[29] This year, there were no complaints about 'Mickey Mouse' instructions in any of the rallies, only praise for the demanding road conditions on the stages. And so the transformation of national rallying that Horne had pursued for three years was now complete. Hardie and Woods, it seems, were right after all, and Horne himself – after three years at the centre of the storm – could feel that he had been vindicated.

In fact, one of the most significant highlights of the 1974 Canadian season was not a national but a *world* championship event. Two years in the making, the Rally of the Rideau Lakes was included in the World Rally Championship (WRC). Lancia sent a three-car team (including their world-beating built-to-purpose, Ferrari-engined Stratos), while Fiat deployed five cars, plus three truckloads of spare engines and parts. There were three other European entries, while Canadian and American entries filled out the rest of the eighteen-car field. Run in November in central Ontario, the all-stage rally claimed seven cars before the end. While the Lancia team took the top two places, with a Stratos winning, Walter Boyce (paired with Stuart Gray, as Woods was helping run the event) placed a highly creditable third in his underpowered Toyota Celica. All agreed it was a well-run event, fully worthy of world championship status, in striking contrast to the lacklustre Press On Regardless Rally held soon thereafter. In Horne's words, 'With the help of countless workers ... Marc Chappell and the rest of the organizing team turned Smiths Falls, Ontario ... into the Rally Capital of the World!'[30]

Boyce's third-place finish also seemed to validate Horne's policies, but the debate over the nature and purpose of rallying continued nonetheless throughout the season. Lindquist weighed in on the side of stage rallies, pointing out that such events were now the international standard and that the Canadian championship should reflect this fact. In his view, novice and regional rallies simply provided the opportunity for crews to hone their skills to the point where they could compete at the national level. Stages, he argued, should be introduced at the regional level to prepare crews properly for national competition. Canadian rallying, he concluded, had to change 'to meet the changed demands of the market place.'[31]

But Corley Leitch, an amateur rallyist from Ottawa, disputed Lindquist's underlying assumption that everyone involved in rallying in Canada was striving to reach national championship status. That would reduce all other rallying simply to 'training.' He cited the success of a number of amateur series as proof that he was not alone in these views. 'It seems to me that there are a number of recreational rallyists who are no more interested in competing in National Rallies than the average Sunday golfer is interested in competing in the PGA series.'[32]

What Leitch was asking for was simply sport for its own sake, for fun. A decade earlier his comments would have been unremarkable, even unnecessary. The fact that he had to make the argument at all demonstrates how much rallying – and attitudes about it – had changed in the interval. Professional rallying was dominant, and the amateurs had to plead for recognition. But they found little sympathy for their views among the advocates of pro rallying.

Nineteen seventy-four was the 'year Canada arrived. Boy did we arrive,' Don Horne told the AGM, referring with pride to the Rideau Lakes Rally. In his final report as rally director, he proclaimed with more than a touch of self-congratulation: 'We are on the threshold of a new era. Rallying has come of age ... Think of the changes that have taken place in three short years ... I had goals three years ago ... I believe that we've proven ... that my goals were your goals and my successes were your successes. Where we are today ... is light years ahead of where we were three years ago.'[33] Executive director Bob Hanna was more cautious, noting that the new format had experienced its share of problems. But he felt that the national rally championship had a bright future. Ontario Region had decided to create its own pro series of stage rallies, but elsewhere the changes at national-level rallying were greeted with mixed reviews. BC Region reported that their regional rallies had not been as successful as in the past, probably due to the wide gap between stage-type national rallies and the navigational-style novice events. Likewise, in Atlantic Region, 'Many regional rallyists suffered an identity problem this year – caught between the new National format and the traditional emphasis on navigation.'[34]

Nineteen seventy-five turned out to be a year of 'good news, bad news.' The good news was that Castrol Oil agreed to sponsor the 1975 national series, which became known as Castrol National Rally Championship. The series followed the twelve-event format of the previous year, but among several notable changes the Rally Perce Neige, run by the Club Auto Sport Laval, replaced the SMCC's Rallye des Neiges. The season turned into a rout for Perusse and Bellefleur, who won seven of the events in their Fiat 124. Their nearest rivals – Walter Boyce and Robin Edwardes in a Toyota – were not even close.[35]

The bad news was that the Rally of the Rideau Lakes was not able to attract a sponsor and was cancelled.[36] Once again the fortunes of pro rallying were hostage to the whims of corporate interests. As a result, having made it to the big time – the WRC – Canadian rallying had been unable to sustain its place there.

Several features of the 1975 championship stand out. First, confounding the predictions of stage-rally advocates there was no increase in the overall number of competitors. The Highlands Rally drew the smallest entry (thirteen) and the Tall Pines the largest (fifty-nine). Second, eastern Canadian events determined the outcome of the championship. The six Ontario and Quebec rallies tended to draw the most entries and crews from those provinces were dominant. They competed in the Maritimes, but few travelled west. Nor did they need to; owing to the schedule, Perusse and Bellefleur had won the championship before the Mountain Trials and Rocky Mountain rallies (in BC and Alberta) were run. And they had not even competed in the Pek K'lona rally earlier in the season.[37] This limited the western events mostly to regional competitors. Thus, the 'national' championship was still an eastern Canadian affair, just as it had been in the 1960s.

Third, the series illustrated the changes that were sweeping the automobile industry in the 1970s. Mirroring the decline in their industry, British cars – once the backbone of Canadian rallying – had vanished from the winner's circle. And, except for Fiat, European cars were notably absent from the top ten on any regular basis. American cars were equally rare at that level. Instead, from 1974 Japanese cars such as Datsun and Toyota began to dominate the Canadian championship, a surge that presaged the rapid growth of their share of the North American automobile market. And like the UK, European, and American manufacturers before them, the Japanese used their rally success to promote their cars.[38]

Finally, the 1975 championship reconfirmed the dominance of the factory-sponsored team. Privateers and dealer-sponsored teams usually filled out most of the top ten, especially in the western rallies, but they rarely could beat the factory teams and won only three events. This was the underlying, unifying theme of a series of articles in *Auto Sport Canada* in 1975. In the first – a feature on Perusse's Fiat 124 – racer John Powell observed that the rally championship was not exempt from the high costs associated with other auto sports. The base price of his car alone was $18,000–20,000. He concluded presciently that 'Jean-Paul Perusse is a strong bet to win the Castrol Canadian Rally Championship ... and this is the machine to make it happen.'[39]

An article on the Boyce and Woods decision to split up put the cost/sponsor relationship front and centre. Woods felt that they should be able to rally professionally, meaning that the manufacturer should cover all the costs of the car, preparation, and maintenance, so that the crew could simply 'arrive and drive.' Boyce estimated that would cost

$50,000 per year. But Woods explained that 'when the prize money is sufficient for the teams to do nothing but rally, that's when the series will have made it.'[40] In his five-part series on pro rallying, Brian Hillis drew attention to the high cost of certain essential components used by the pro teams, such as gas-filled shocks, magnesium wheels, special tires, and quartz iodine-vapour headlights. Unconsciously echoing the Renault experience, he also emphasized the importance of a well-trained service crew and a reliable and properly organized service vehicle. He concluded that 'a service crew will never win a rally for a driver, but they can most certainly lose it for him.'[41]

The May issue also featured 'The Great Debate' between Chuck McLaren and Paul Manson over the pros and cons of stage rallying. McLaren felt that the change to stage rallying was the right step for a variety of reasons: safety, by using closed roads; spectator appeal; and the marketing benefits of sponsorship. Drawing a comparison with the progress from shinny to professional hockey, McLaren argued that amateurs needed to proceed through the various levels of rallying if they wanted to compete internationally and professionally. Manson countered that the cost of stage rallying made it impossible for a privateer to compete against the likes of Perusse in his factory Fiat: 'After three months of preparation on the car and a minimum of $6,000 you are lucky ... if you end up between fourth and tenth in any national rally.'[42] Privateers simply couldn't win.

If there was still any doubt that Manson was right – that manufacturer sponsorship was the key to success – then Taisto Heinonen and Tom Burgess of BC soon put the question to rest. Driving for Toyota from 1977 through 1981, they won thirty-one of sixty national rallies and four championships, bringing their sponsor five straight manufacturer's titles.[43] This meant that factory-sponsored crews had held the top spot in Canadian national rallying for a full decade. The dominance of the small number of factory teams and the absence of other sponsors meant that there were few opportunities even for good amateurs to move up to the pro ranks.

That the Manson/McLaren debate occurred at all was an indication of lingering dissatisfaction with the changes to national rallying. The Atlantic Region gave voice to those feelings at the 1975 AGM:

> While being somewhat disenchanted by the type of National Rally Series currently being run, both N.S. and N.B. have determined to again run the Highlands and Lobster Rallies as part of the National Series in 76. Per-

haps the main reason for disenchantment is that it is increasingly hard for Atlantic competitors to enter even these two of the ... Series.[44]

Yet, in the end, the 'debate' was a pointless exercise. The future of the Canadian championship had been decided and it continued to evolve towards 'world class' status. At the AGM Tugwell announced that for the 1976 season five of the rallies would be FIA-listed in order to encourage foreign competitors to enter the Canadian series. They could win events, but would not earn series points. He explained this meant that 'the Championship is no longer a pure National Championship.'[45] Thus, rallying was following the example of the national racing championship; the Canadian champion would be decided in an *international* series, at least in theory. In reality, the championship never attracted many foreign entries and remained a predominantly Canadian series. In 1978 Molson Breweries replaced Castrol as the national championship sponsor; the total prize money in Canadian rallying had grown to $163,000.[46] Even so, the series still fell short of its goal: preparing Canadian rallyists for 'big league' international rallies.

Nothing demonstrated this shortcoming better than the Criterium du Québec Rally. From 1977 through 1979, the only North American rally in the WRC, it attracted some European crews and cars. Bob Hanna claimed that the 1977 event 'was so successful that it is virtually assured of a permanent place in the World Rally Championship.' Unfortunately, in spite of good publicity and Molson's sponsorship, it had organizational problems and was cancelled after 1979. Tugwell had told the 1978 AGM that the Criterium deserved and needed more Canadian entries and he encouraged Canadian rallyists to participate in 1979. But there was little incentive for them to do so. In 1977 and 1978 Europeans captured the top three places. The first year, Perusse and Bellefleur were the top Canadians, in fifth place, while Boyce and Edwardes were eighth. The next year Heinonen and Bellefleur finished fourth. That the Canadians managed to do so well is testament to their talent. But they could not match the resources that the European factory teams brought to bear. In 1977, for example, the Fiat team brought from Italy five cars, along with a contingent of forty-two people, their own DC-8 jet, 540 tires, and a budget of $300,000.[47] Against this juggernaut, Perusse and Bellefleur fielded a partly sponsored Saab, paying the balance themselves. Just as Canadian racers found when trying to break into Formula One in the 1960s, talent alone was not enough. Canadian pro rallyists of the 1970s were under-funded and under-prepared, and few had rallied abroad. And so, in Canadian rallies the Europeans handily defeated the best Canadian crews.

There was a curious irony in this since, in the second half of the 1970s, stage rallying had finally caught on and expanded at the regional level. Thus, at the 1978 AGM Iain Tugwell could claim with some validity that this had been the year 'when performance rallying was accepted across Canada by the lower levels of the Sport.' But, he also conceded, the year had marked 'the demise of the navigational rally as a National entity ... It is hoped that navigational competition at a Regional level will continue to generate future co-drivers and organizers ... It is this level of the sport that must be encouraged in order for the National and International levels to grow.'[48]

However, the growth of stage rallying had happened only at the expense of the other levels. Running novice, navex, *and* 'pro' rallies seriously taxed the limited human resources of the clubs and regions that, as the next chapter will show, had declined in the first half of the decade. Fewer people were available to run rallies. Thus, the number of events dropped dramatically during the shift to stage rallying. In 1972, when there had been over 1000 rallies in Canada, Horne could legitimately claim that 'the sport is enjoying unprecedented popularity.'[49] But by 1977 the number had fallen by *two-thirds* to 330. The following year it increased slightly and the number of entries grew. But participation remained well below the levels of the 1960s.[50] And in the final irony, in the 1980s Canadian rallying would experience a further serious decline, even though pro series stage rallies attracted two things that earlier events rarely had: live audiences and TV coverage.

14 Downshift: The Crisis in Amateur Auto Sport, 1969–1975

> Declining membership is ... a symptom of a far more serious illness which appears to be affecting many of our Clubs. No one will ever convince me that the problem is a lack of interest in motorsport.
>
> CASC, Report, 1972[1]

Bob Hanna's comments from his report to the 1972 AGM highlight the study in contrasts that was Canadian auto sport in the first half of the 1970s. On the face of it, the sport was flourishing. The Canadian Grand Prix for Formula One and the Can-Am series were bringing the world's best drivers and fastest cars to Canada and drawing huge crowds to watch them. The national championship was developing talented racers and evolving into the highly successful Formula Atlantic series. Rallying was at an all-time high and the rally championship was being completely reshaped into a demanding, professional European-style series. The Canadian Road Race of Champions, Atlantic Motorsport Park, and the national auto slalom championship were born during this period.

So what's wrong with this picture? It simply doesn't tell the whole story. These apparent successes obscured a sobering tale of decline. Clubs and members were fading away, Le Circuit closed, and after 1972 rallying went into a profound slump from which it never fully recovered. And so, even as the sport appeared to go from strength to strength, the amateur foundations upon which it had been built were eroding. The impact was as significant as the reasons were complex.

Amateurism's Apogee

Club and regional racing experienced noticeable growth in the early 1970s. Ontario Region held twenty-four races in 1970 with 2572 entries over the whole season. Most were regional and club events, one of which had a record entry of 217. In 1973 the region's twenty-two races had an average entry of 134. British Columbia was doing even better in 1970, with an average entry of 157 per race. Atlantic Region went from three races in 1969 to nine in 1972.[2]

The highly competitive Eastern Zone Endurance (EZE) series ran from 1971 to 1975 in Ontario, Quebec, Atlantic, and, later, Prairie regions. The series incorporated established events like the Sundown Grand Prix and newer races, such as the Atlantic Region's Moosehead 300. The races, lasting three to six hours, pitted veteran drivers like Duval and Heimrath against both 'rising stars,' such as Jacques Bienvenue, Marc Dancose, and brothers Klaus and Harry Bytzek, and the Atlantic Region's local heroes, including Murray Edwards, Dave Fram, Don Hogan, Ron Locke, and John Risley. Audiences were treated to a wide array of powerful and exotic cars – Camaros, Cobras, Corvettes, Ginettas, Landars, Lolas, Lotuses, and Porsches (which dominated the series) – as well venerable machines like Mini Coopers and MGBs.[3]

The Canadian Road Race of Champions (CRRC), which brought together the top amateur racers from all regions for a single run-off to determine 'the best of the best,' ran annually from 1971 into the 1980s. Borrowing the concept from the SCCA, the CRRC got under way with a promise of $35,000 from Player's to cover racers' expenses and prizes and another $3000 in contingency awards from several carmakers. Just as in the United States, each CASC region selected the top drivers in each class of cars from its own series of points-earning races. At the run-off there were ten classes of production sports cars, sedans, and open-wheel cars. After the first event at Westwood the CRRC moved to a different track each year (Le Circuit hosted it twice in the 1970s).[4]

The organizers of the first CRRC had hoped to attract some 200 racers, but only 100 entered. This proved typical of subsequent events; the largest entry was 130 at Le Circuit in 1975. Because of distance and cost, not every region was equally represented at each race. Some of the top eastern drivers did not attend the first one at Westwood; only two came from Atlantic Region. Thus, track familiarity gave the advantage to local drivers like Ed Clements, John Hall, and Don

Lamont. But easterners won about half of the races and dominated the formula classes.

Although rain kept the crowds away and slowed the pace, the CASC none the less felt the first national run-off was a success. Over the next few years, the CRRC helped to identify and promote those amateurs who had the ability to move up to pro racing. Gilles Villeneuve was one of them; later on, so were Scott Goodyear, who went on to success in Indy Car racing, and Ron Fellows, who was three-time runner-up in the Trans-Am series. It also showcased some who would make their names in various national series, such as Bienvenue, Dancose, Bill Adam, Harry Bytzek, Lewis Mackenzie, Dave Ogilvy, and Richard Spenard. It attracted as well veterans like Heimrath and Kroll.[5] Thus, the CRRC truly was a gathering of champions, and for the first few years at least, it was an amateur success story in a time of growing professionalism.

And there were plenty of options for hobby racers. Ice racing remained popular in Quebec, Ontario, and the Prairies. As one enthusiast explained, 'Since the ultimate in power and handling are not necessary in order to be competitive, the cost and convenience of ice racing are such that it has become the last vestige of "drive it to the track, tape the lights, and change the tires" possibility.'[6] As such, it featured mostly small sedans, and the top drivers, like Bob Barrell, Chris Cossette, Chris Cottenden, and Yvon Walsh, were almost unknown outside the sport. But it also continued to attract both established and up-and-coming 'stars,' like Gordon Dewar, Peter Ferguson, Perusse, Powell, and Wietzes. By the late 1960s it had become popular enough to attract sponsors. O'Keefe Breweries funded a multi-race series in Quebec, while the Esso Grand Prix ran during Quebec City's winter carnival until the mid-1970s. The only unpredictable element remained the weather, which could (and did) play havoc with schedules.[7]

During the same period, solo racing (auto slalom, in particular) grew rapidly, nearly overtaking rallies as the most popular form of 'grassroots' auto sport. Two trends stand out. First, solo became formally organized as a distinct auto sport discipline at the 1969 CASC AGM. There members agreed on definitions for solo events and adopted rules to govern them across the country. From 1970 solo had its own national director, the first being George Harker of Prairie Region. His successor, Allan Rae from BC, called 1972 'the year that Solo Events ... came of age.'[8] That year the solo committee organized the first national auto slalom championship. It was a unique event; all competitors competed on the same day in their own region, using exactly the same course layout. It was held in thirteen cities in every province but Prince Edward Island. Entries were divided into fourteen car classes based on SCCA rules, and ranged from Mini Coopers and MG Midgets to Shelby Mustangs, Corvettes, and big American sedans. The overall winner was David Long of London, Ontario, driving a Walker Formula 4. The first event, which drew 487 entries, was a complete success. The next year 583 competed. The event peaked in 1974 at 664 entries. After that, the national slalom day experienced a slump until the late 1970s.[9]

The second trend was that slalom events rapidly displaced driving skill tests. By 1972 slaloms had become the standard. Their appeal is not hard to understand; where driving skill tests were often slow, complex events, slaloms were more like racing on a short course (marked out by small pylons), albeit one car at a time. Anyone with a driver's licence could enter any slalom event (including the national championship), in any kind of road-worthy car, at almost no cost. Entrants did not have to belong to a car club and did not have to hold a solo licence, unless they were competing for points. In Ontario Region in 1969, when driving skills tests were the norm, entries averaged thirty per event, but once slaloms became the standard, they averaged one hundred. In many respects slaloms replaced rallying as the basic club-level competitive activity. Stuart Eagar, Atlantic Region president, told the 1974 AGM that, perhaps more than any other form of auto sport, slalom had brought new members into the clubs. 'Although this is the least professional aspect of motorsport in this region, it attracts more competitors than both circuit racing and rallying combined.'[10]

All regions experienced growth in solo racing in the early 1970s, but probably thanks to its climate, which favoured year-round competition, British Columbia was the 'solo capital' of Canada. In 1970 the region ran four hill climbs and six slaloms; three years later, it ran thirty solo events: twenty-six slaloms and four hill climbs. The number of competitors increased from 305 in 1970 to 990 in 1972. In 1973 BC drivers dominated the national championship, winning eight of fifteen classes; Stu Rulka of Victoria was first overall and later won his class at the SCCA championships. The next year BC racers took the top seven places in the Canadian championship, and virtually swept it in 1975.[11]

Not surprisingly, given its topography, BC also led the country in hill climbs. The Okanagan Hill Climb, held annually since 1958 at Kelowna, was famous nationally. Its two-point-two-mile Knox Mountain course, used from 1965, was called 'the most perfect paved track ... available for hillclimb in North America.'[12] The entire route, which rose 800 feet through seventeen turns, including three hairpins, was off-camber (sloping to the outside) and flanked by cliffs and rock outcroppings, making it very challenging; speeds on the straight could exceed 130 mph. The 1970 event attracted eighty racers and some 7000 spectators, the latter probably a record for a solo event. That turnout impressed Castrol Oil, which sponsored the 1971 event, providing overall and class winners with cash awards. In Quebec the ACAM club had taken over the Mont Gabriel hill climb from the JOA and their 1970 event, sponsored by Pennzoil, drew forty-six competitors. By contrast, the 1971 ASCC's Harbourville hill climb had only eighteen entries, although the Atlantic region was still running a hotly contested championship in 1975. In Ontario, however, where hill climbs once were notable and popular events, none was scheduled for 1969, and none was held in 1972.[13] While the reasons for the decline in Ontario are not clear, it may have become more difficult to close public roads or to gain access to private ones.

Navigational rallying also remained popular among club members in the early 1970s. Atlantic Region reported in 1969 that rallying involved most of its members. The eight regional rallies 'resulted in more active participation and keener competition than ever before.' The following year the region claimed that rallying 'continues to enjoy a resurgence of popularity.'[14] BC Region reported in 1970 that its 'strictly fun' Fraser Valley series was so popular that would-be entrants were being turned away at many events. Quebec Region called 1972 'a vintage year' for rallying, and in 1973 the sport was 'most outstanding' compared to racing and solo competition. Rallying's appeal to amateurs at this time was simple. Before the change to stage rallies, many national championship rallies were also club and regional events. The UNBSCC's Winter Carnival Rally was a case in point. It pitted regional stars like John Pearce against top national teams like Boyce and Woods in events that still offered a challenge for both drivers and navigators while risks and costs remained low.[15] Like solo, rallying appealed to the grass-roots enthusiast.

By far the most ambitious amateur undertaking in this period was the building of the Atlantic Motosport Park (AMP) race track in Nova Scotia. The sport in the Atlantic Region was constrained by lower incomes, relatively few competitors, and a poor highway network. The first sports car race was held at the Debert air base (near Truro, Nova

Scotia) in 1968. For the next five years the two-mile, ten-turn circuit hosted regional races. In 1971 it also held one of the first EZE series events, won by Fram and Risley in their 'Teem Atlantic' 427 Cobra. But in 1972 the Department of Transport decided to open Debert for civil aviation. For the next two years racers used the abandoned airport at Pennfield Ridge, near Saint John, New Brunswick.[16]

But Pennfield was a long way from Halifax, where most of the racers and fans lived. Thus, Atlantic Region race director Frank Jobborn announced at the 1972 CASC AGM that the region was going to build a track. 'If the members of one Club on the west coast can build a race track like Westwood, then the members of this Region can do it here.'[17] It was a bold comparison. The BC track had been built by a large and comparatively wealthy car club in a large city; still, by 1968 Westwood was deeply in debt and facing closure. The Atlantic Region plan depended on a collective effort by six small car clubs in the poorest part of the country, with no more than a hundred car racers among them, in addition to the bike racers. But, undeterred by these numbers or by the financial problems experienced by other tracks, the region forged ahead. Frank McCarthy, who had managed 'Teem Atlantic' and was well known for his promotional skills, was put in charge of fundraising. The clubs founded a non-profit company, Atlantic Motorsport Park Inc., in 1973 and bought the land: a 428-acre farm near Shubenacadie, between Halifax and Truro. Each of the clubs had to purchase shares in the company. Bike racer Jack Canfield used his connections in the construction industry to persuade local firms to help build the track at the lowest possible cost. Several other businessmen-racers like Edwards, Fram, Hogan, and Locke pitched in to ensure the bills were paid.[18]

Robert Guthrie, then an architecture student and Formula Vee racer, came up with the track design. Spending his final term in Europe, he had taken a racing school course in the United Kingdom and attended races on the Continent. On his return to Canada he had to do a project to complete his degree. 'I wanted to do something that I was really interested in ... so I designed the track for AMP ... in Europe I had visited a lot of tracks: Spa, Zandvoort, Monza, Nurburgring, and Silverstone. I had learned a lot, and I applied that to the design of the track.'[19] His design was a tight, twisty course, with eleven turns and seven changes of elevation in 1.6 miles. It was, and is, in his words, 'a real driver's track.' 'I just followed the natural contours of the ground. We ... couldn't afford to do a lot of digging, cutting, and filling, just a bit of banking and grading. Turn two [the hairpin] is where it is because of a big oak tree. It would have cost too much to take it out, so we left it there and built the track around it. Couldn't do that today ... for safety reasons.'[20]

The total cost of the track was about $300,000. Fund-raising generated about $130,000. The province provided a long-term loan to cover the first mortgage on the land, which cost about $100,000. Not surprisingly, it took longer than expected to raise the funds. In January 1974, with the project at risk of falling behind schedule, Jobborn chided the enthusiasts for not pulling their financial weight: 'I owe many thanks to the few faithful racing supporters who have purchased shares in the operation and enabled us to get this far. I now plead with the remainder, by far the majority, to get off their duffs and send us some money.'[21]

To anyone who knew the Westwood and Mosport stories, this would have been a familiar refrain. The opening of AMP had to be postponed by three months, when funding promised by the Nova Scotia government was frozen owing to a provincial election. The opening race – the Player's Maritime Formula Atlantic – was delayed another week to complete construction. The asphalt, laid only two days before the opening, did not have time to 'cure' before practice and the qualifying round. With the sun beating down, oil sweated onto the surface, making the track extremely slick, and the asphalt broke up under the pounding of the tires. Many of the drivers spun off the track and damaged their cars, some totally. Then, on race day the rain poured down, turning the infield into a quagmire of red mud. But some 15,000 fans still turned out to watch Bill Brack lead from start to finish and win the 1974 Canadian championship. Over the next three years the F/Atlantic race featured some of the rising stars of international racing: future F1 champion Keke Rosberg, future Indy Car champ Bobby Rahal, and Gilles Villeneuve, whose lap record (fifty-nine seconds) stands unbroken to this day.[22] AMP beat the odds; unlike Westwood, Mosport, and Le Circuit, it survived as a club-owned and -run track – perhaps the last amateur success story in what became an era of decline.

A Shrinking Subculture

Ironically, even as both pro and amateur events were helping more Canadians discover sports car competition, a 'downshift' of major proportions was undermining the sport at its roots – among the clubs and their members. Membership in CASC-affiliated clubs declined about 20 per cent from a high of 6636 in 1968 to a low of 5264 in 1973, then remained stagnant for the next two years. Likewise, the number of clubs also shrank. On paper, in 1968 the CASC consisted of 112 clubs, with ninety-seven in 1976. In reality, some clubs were inactive due to a shortage of members, and so the actual number of *dues-paying* clubs was ninety-one in 1968, rising to 96 in 1972, then declining steadily to seventy-nine in 1975.

The steepest drop in club members (about 42 per cent) occurred in Ontario Region, which had peaked at 3005 in 1970 and had fallen to 1714 in 1975. It had forty-six active clubs in 1968; by 1975 that number had shrunk to twenty-five. The BEMC, which had boasted nearly six hundred members in 1957, was down to thirty-four by 1975. Nine other clubs were inactive because they were too small. The Hamilton Sports Car Club had shrunk to seven members, the Lynn Valley Sports Car Club to five, and the Quinte Auto Sport Club to three. The Sports Car Club – one of the three founding CASC clubs – had folded, along with many others. Quebec Region experienced a 25 per cent drop between 1968 and 1973. Only the Atlantic Region bucked the trend; it grew steadily to 443 members in 1972, before staying flat for the next few years.[23]

This decline was a source of great concern to the CASC, since it was supposed to operate as a confederation of clubs. If they and their members disappeared, the CASC would be an empty shell, with no internal sources of authority or funds. In his address to the 1971 AGM, marking the CASC's twentieth anniversary, president Stanley Williams said, 'We are particularly concerned with the question of membership.'[24] Executive Director Hanna was much more blunt:

> The total membership ... disturbs me greatly. It has been virtually stagnant for a number of years, yet general interest in motorsport during that time has increased tremendously ... The Confederation of Australian Motorsport, has a membership of 20,000 which makes our 5,800 look rather ridiculous especially when we have almost twice the population to draw from. We must attract new members if we are to have a vigorous and healthy Club and at the same time we must hold our older members in order that we may maintain a degree of stability and continuity.[25]

But two years later he reported that the CASC had been unable to stimulate growth. His appeal for each member to recruit one more yielded only 143 in 1974, and the following year the erosion continued.[26] There was no expansion until after the mid-point of the decade.

From a competition perspective, the impact on the sport was uneven. Rallying was affected most dramatically. As discussed in the previous chapter, by 1977 the number of rallies had fallen by *two-thirds*. In racing, the CRRC continued to fall short of original expectations. The number of entries peaked in 1975 and declined substantially after that. Only sixty-five cars competed at the 1977 event at AMP. Participation in the national auto slalom day dropped by one-third in 1975 and it had a disappointing turnout the following year.[27] Clearly, Canadian amateur auto sport was in crisis, but with all of the positive changes that had occurred during the first half of the decade, the big question was, 'Why?'

Cataloguing the decline is easy; explaining its causes is much harder. While it would be easy to blame the dwindling numbers solely on the commercial professionalism trend, that would be misleading. During this period, the sport and the CASC were being buffeted by a complex array of problems. Some of these were self-inflicted, while others originated outside the sport, which could not be insulated from the influences of the wider world. There is no single definitive explanation.

No Pay, No Play

On the face of it, the problem was a lack of money, and here the Canadian economy, which went into recession in the 1970s, was to blame. Inflation grew by nearly 40 per cent from 1971 to 1975. The middle class – the social base of the sports car subculture – found their disposable income declining, and their purchasing power reduced, while the costs of consumer products (such as cars) increased. The 1972 unemployment rate of over 11 per cent among young men hit the most important source of competitors. By every measure, the subculture's base was in financial distress.[28] If that weren't enough, the 1973–4 energy crisis caused a decline in sponsor funding, which made racing less affordable. CASC executive director Bob Hanna told the 1974 AGM: 'Some companies used it to rationalize a negative decision made for some other reason and some people genuinely thought there was a problem and therefore chose to divorce themselves from activities that were visible users of fuel. The competitor and the promoter both found the search for sponsorship very difficult.'[29] At the same meeting national racing director Robert Harrington observed, 'Our base, the amateur side has stagnated. We have no more cars or drivers, and fewer events and tracks than we did at the start of the decade.'[30] The next year Hanna identified the economy as the CASC's main problem, and said that it was evident that the CASC had to be financially self-sufficient in lean years when it was difficult to find outside (i.e., sponsor) funding. BC Region president Blake McGuffie also blamed the economy for a serious drop in race entries in that province.[31]

The CRRC was one of the victims of the funding shortfall. Player's sponsored the first two races and British Leyland did promotion for the third, but after that the money dried up. Without it, many drivers could not afford to enter, raising concerns about the future of the series. Harrington told the 1974 AGM that, while CASC firmly supported the CRRC, some changes were needed: 'Competitors are facing ever increasing costs and feel the travel fund is no longer adequate. We have yet to attract a major crowd to the event. Perhaps the date should be changed. Perhaps it should be fixed at one venue. Perhaps we can't afford it at all.'[32]

In the absence of a regular sponsor, it made sense to move the CRRC to a different track annually. Different regions would share the costs and the burden of running the event, and the competitors' travel costs would not be high every year. Few BC racers went to the 1975 race at Le Circuit, because there were not enough funds to make the trip affordable. Asked why the CRRC lacked a sponsor, Harrington replied that 'the event has to be held in a major marketing area before any sponsors will consider it.'[33] He clearly meant Ontario and Quebec, much to the annoyance of western competitors. But there was more to the difficulties than that. Held late in the year because regional racing seasons had to be completed first, the CRRC invariably suffered from poor weather. Moreover, the lack of sponsor money to promote the event meant that few people heard about it. Thus, the CRRC drew only small audiences. Yet it is not clear that better marketing would have drawn larger crowds. Even the Player's Challenge Series, which was promoted professionally and televised, struggled to draw an audience of more than a few thousand at any time during the season. The problem, it seems, was not the weather or even the promotion, but the fans; they simply were not interested in watching amateurs anymore.

The problem became a vicious circle. If people wouldn't come to watch the amateurs, then the sponsors, who were needed to promote the races and who counted on drawing a crowd to market their products, wouldn't come either. Instead, they spent their money elsewhere.

As Bob Hanna noted in 1973, 'competition with other forms of entertainment for the leisure dollar is becoming increasingly tougher.'[34] That applied to both spectators and sponsors, and nowhere was this more obvious than in Quebec after the closure of Le Circuit.

Crisis in Quebec

In the late 1960s Le Circuit was flirting with disaster. CASC Quebec Region president Peter Roberts, a businessman and amateur racer, had concluded that without drastic action sports car racing in the region might collapse. He proposed that the region take over all aspects of race organization and negotiate with Le Circuit on behalf of the Quebec clubs. Unafraid to step on a few toes, he confronted the region's clubs with a blunt dose of realism:

> For good or ill ... the days of purely amateur, internally supported racing are gone. The day Le Circuit was built, the sport became committed to ... dealings with financially motivated groups outside the sport. To make this possible, the sport has to act as one body, with one aim, able to muster its full resources under one leadership and to act with the full authority of all its members at a level above the rivalries of club or language.[35]

Roberts got both the clubs and the track on side, and forged ahead, appointing John Ross as race director. Ross later became Le Circuit's track manager. In September 1968 it had hosted the second Canadian Formula One Grand Prix. The entries consisted of twenty of the world's best drivers, including four world champions: Jack Brabham, Graham Hill, Denny Hulme, and John Surtees. Forty thousand fans clogged the roads for forty miles from the track. Pierre Trudeau, Canada's new youthful, flamboyant prime minister, waved the cars off to start the race. Against all of this, with brilliant sunshine and a spectacular Laurentian autumn setting, the race itself was almost secondary. In fact, the track and the pace took its toll. By the time Denny Hulme took the chequered flag only six cars were still running. Bob Hanna later told the 1968 AGM: 'Quebec Region ... jumped into a racing season that would have frightened many more experienced groups ... The season was a tremendous success and they can now go forth with confidence.'[36]

But three years later, after a string of successful F1, Can-Am, Indy Car, and Trans-Am events, Le Circuit closed. It had been plunged into crisis in July 1970. After months of dispute Jacqueline Paradis, who had bought the track in 1969, fired Ross. His successor, Phillipe Alary, explained: 'It was a conflict of personalities ... Both Ross and Miss Paradis have strong personalities.'[37] Paradis, an experienced accountant, had been given *carte blanche* by the track's board of directors to make any changes she deemed necessary. But when she fired Ross, the result was chaos. He sued the track, there were acrimonious exchanges in the press, anglo-franco tension surfaced, and the F1 Grand Prix seemed to be in jeopardy.[38] In fact, this was just the opening salvo in a showdown between Paradis and the CASC.

Money was part of the problem; the track was refusing to pay the region $11,000 that it owed from the 1970 F1 Grand Prix. It also needed to make safety improvements in order to host the race again in 1972. Fundamentally, however, this was a dispute over power. At issue was nothing less than the CASC's authority to govern the sport – authority that Mlle Paradis was reluctant to accept. She wanted to bypass the CASC and deal directly with the FIA. That was unacceptable to the CASC, and the FIA would have refused anyway. In April 1971 the CASC and Le Circuit's management met and reached a one-year agreement, giving the track the right to host three major FIA-sanctioned events in 1971. In return, they agreed to accept the CASC's authority over those events. The deal covered the duties and responsibilities of each party and the fees to be paid to CASC for its race services. Imperial Tobacco offered to settle the funding dispute by paying the track's debt to the region.[39] It looked like a solution was at hand.

But in June, barely ten days before the Can-Am event, the SCCA announced that the race had been cancelled. The CASC, still concerned about the track's finances, had insisted that it come up with a third party to guarantee the prize money and other funds for the race. Naturally, the owners resented being made subject to special rules that applied to them alone. The result was a standoff, and the CASC notified the FIA, which withdrew its sanction for the event. If Le Circuit went ahead with the race, it would not count for series points, and teams and drivers could be penalized for participating in it. Since few, if any, would take that risk, the track was facing disaster. Two days later, after behind-the-scenes negotiations and a lot of media attention, the race was reinstated. It went off without a hitch, Jackie Stewart driving his Lola Chev to victory in 'one of the best Can-Ams ever held.' But only 21,000 fans attended, 'probably because they weren't sure if there even was a race scheduled for that ... weekend.'[40]

The Trans-Am race on 31 July – a runaway victory for Mark Donohue in his AMX Javelin – was also run without problems. Then, abruptly, Paradis cancelled the Formula A race, scheduled for September. This prompted Jim Gunn, who was acting as consultant to Le Circuit, to issue a stern warning to Paradis that her actions would 'adversely affect' the future of the track and undermine the gains already made. He 'strongly advised' her to reinstate the Formula A race, which was to be sponsored by Molson, to accept the authority of CASC, to immediately hire a track manager, and to settle the outstanding debt to Quebec Region on a negotiated basis rather than through the courts. 'Unless this debt is settled soon,' he warned, 'no-one, I emphasize *no-one* will organize races at Le Circuit. I have talked with Clubs in the Montreal area and none of them would take on the task of organizing "International" races because they would not get paid. Ask them yourself.'[41] Gunn went on to say that adopting his proposals would end the controversy among racers, sponsors, advertisers, and the public. 'If you cannot accept these recommendations then I advise you ... to sell Le Circuit, before your personal investment is lost. Le Circuit is a source of pride to Quebec and Canada ... It is up to you to strengthen and expand this pride, not destroy it.'[42]

The Formula A race went ahead, then the track closed and did not reopen for another four years. Any hope that it might do so any sooner was dashed by the final round of sparring between Paradis and the CASC. She ignored the end of December deadline to sign contracts for the 1972 FIA events, including the Grand Prix. The deadline was extended into January, but Le Circuit rejected the CASC's 'unreasonable requirements' and issued a press release saying that the track was severing all ties with the national body. Quebec Region race director John Sambrook told the 1972 AGM that le Circuit's closure

> had a double impact on the Region. First, we lost any revenue that we might have derived from any International event ... held there ... Second, it had a very strong psychological effect on the racing fraternity in Quebec. From the point of view of the driver, Mont Tremblant cannot be compared with the other race tracks in Quebec, as it is a much more challenging track. Consequently, we suffered a morale loss with its closing.[43]

The loss was in more than just a good track and morale. Molson had sponsored amateur sports car racing in Quebec from 1969 through

1971, but for 1972 it limited that funding to the Trans-Am race (held at the new Sanair track) and the Trois-Rivières street race. The rest of its auto sport money went into stock car racing, with good reason. While Le Circuit closed, four new road courses opened: Deux Montagnes, Sanair, St-Croix, and St-Félicien. But they were mere appendages of stock car oval tracks and drag strips, and only Sanair attracted major events. By contrast, the province had gained *forty-eight new* stock car tracks in the 1960s, and added another dozen in the 1970s. Thus, stock car racing had a presence in every part of the province, on every weekend. Sponsors naturally gravitated to spectators, so Molson's decision made sense. In addition, Sambrook told the AGM, '[t]he strong rise in stock car racing has resulted in a great number of people who have been road racing to decide that the way to go is stock car racing.'[44]

The only bright spot on the Quebec scene was the success of the street races at Trois-Rivières. In 1967 Guy Poirier, the local agent for Labatt Breweries, persuaded racer Jean Ryan to organize a race within the city as a centennial project. The Club Autosport Mauricien ran the first one at the exhibition grounds, then moved it to the city streets the next year. The course, redesigned several times, was one and a half miles long, roughly wedge-shaped with two long straights connected to several shorter ones by seven sharp turns (five of them being ninety degrees and one a hairpin). Spectators crammed into bleachers or watched the races from the windows and rooftops of buildings along the route. Promoters touted the 'Grand Prix de Trois-Rivières' as 'Le Petit Monaco Québécois' and it became famous as one big party for fans, racers, and their sponsors. But pointing to the trees, telephone poles, lamp-posts, and fire hydrants along the course, Dave Shaw called it 'potentially the most dangerous sports car track in Canada, if not North America.' The *Canadian Motorsport Bulletin* wrote: 'It's ... not a circuit for the weak at heart. A false move and you can end up in the trees, the curbs, buildings or sidewalks which line many parts of the track. Drivers ... have to go through the Duplessis Memorial Arch, which sits threateningly at the bottom of a steep hill right on the apex of a sharp right hand turn'[45]

Nevertheless, Trois-Rivières hosted an annual Player's Challenge race, its Formula Atlantic successors, and their supporting races. It was there in 1976 that Gilles Villeneuve defeated a grid-full of F1 drivers, gaining the profile that would propel him into racing's top ranks. Three years later the track became a permanent fixture on the Trans-Am series schedule.[46] At the time it was created, no one regarded the street course as a substitute for or as a threat to circuit racing. But it offered race organizers, sponsors, and promoters something that no track out in the country could match: a captive audience and market. As discussed in the next chapter, that fact was not lost on race enthusiasts in other cities.

Self-Inflicted Wounds

The CASC and the clubs themselves contributed to the decline. Perhaps as a legacy of Milt Wright's 'top-down' leadership style, the CASC had become plagued by communication problems, friction, and discontent between the executive and the members. At the 1970 AGM Ontario Region expressed its 'serious and growing concern over the single most important problem facing C.A.S.C. and that is the growing rift between us.' The region complained that this had developed over several years into a situation 'of animosity, bitterness, and distrust.'[47] The next year, president Stanley Williams conceded that it was 'all too easy for the administration to get out of touch with the "grass roots."' He added that the CASC had to ensure that it did not 'assume an independent character that is alien to the basic membership.'[48] Discussing the 1972 report on CASC administration, vice-president George Chapman said: 'Clubs didn't want to be pushed into a subservient position – the Clubs liked to feel they could do something and offer something to their membership.'[49] He had asked them: 'What is wrong with C.A.S.C.?' and they had responded unanimously: 'One major complaint was that of communication and the ... feeling of being out of touch with national ... It was suggested that perhaps we are getting an illusion of grandeur and professionalism.' Communications, the report said, 'has left a lot to be desired' and, equally important given the membership problem, it conceded that the CASC had 'not yet undertaken a significant public relations program.'[50]

The communication problem was two-fold: getting essential information from the national level to the clubs and publicizing club activities to the wider audience of existing and potential members. Until the late 1960s CASC national had mailed to clubs and regions printed bulletins that dealt with administrative matters, rules, results, and other information. By that time, however, the bulletins had increased in size and number (to as many as 100 per year) and had to be sent to more clubs at greater cost. In addition, *Canada Track and Traffic* magazine originally had carried a regular column on CASC news and monthly reports on club and regional events. But by the late 1960s the column and news of smaller club events (especially outside Ontario) had all but disappeared. Moreover, the magazine gave priority to racing over rallying and to international and national racing over regional. The CASC tried placing its news in another publication, but that was unsuccessful.[51]

At this point Bob MacGregor, a veteran competitor and CBC auto sport journalist, offered to publish a monthly CASC news magazine. His proposal was accepted, and *Canadian Motorsport Bulletin* was launched in 1971. It featured international and national events, but included regional reports in almost every issue. Bob Hanna told the 1971 AGM that *CMB* was 'possibly one of the biggest happenings in CASC's history ... Now that it is going, it is up to each and every one of us to keep it going.'[52] He urged the members to send in news, to use the magazine as a recruiting tool, and to patronize its advertisers. But with a small and shrinking subscription base limited to CASC members, *CMB* could not attract enough advertising to be financially viable. By the end of 1972 it was feared that *CMB* might be about to collapse. Consequently, CASC felt compelled to subsidize it, a move that kept it going for two more years. But *CMB* died shortly after the 1974 AGM, and the CASC returned to distributing bulletins.[53]

CMB's decline and fall paralleled the erosion of the CASC's membership, which the magazine had been unable to reverse. And so, it wasn't just a matter of communication. The clubs and the national body were undergoing a 'generational change.' In 1966, fifteen years after the CASC was founded, the national executive included many who had been active since the earliest years of the sport. But by 1972, only three 'veterans' – Chapman, Hanna, and Peart – remained on the executive. Likewise, regional representatives included very few who had been active a decade earlier. Since the national executive drew upon the clubs for its members, the changes at the top mirrored the same process at club level.[54]

Yet those who retired were not being replaced on a one-for-one basis. Thus, there was more going on than a mere 'passing of the torch.' Peter Bone, who got out in the late 1960s, found – like many others – that getting married changed one's personal priorities. Jim Maddin joined the RCMP in the early 1970s and they simply would not let him continue racing. WOSCA's leadership was 'decimated' in 1975 when some key members moved away. For others, it was club or CASC politics. Wright found being CASC president quite stressful, and when his term was done he just walked away from the organizational side of the sport. Iain Tugwell quit the St Catharines Motor Club in 1969, when he concluded that it was not sufficiently committed to competition. Art Moseley pointed out that most clubs were small and did not have enough people to run events.[55] Veteran SMCC and UNBSCC rallyist Dorothy Scott agreed that clubs became overstretched: 'It was *always* the same people that would organize ... that would be stewards ... that would be scoring ... check-pointing ... your friends started dropping out and nobody was coming in, and so the clubs were getting smaller so your responsibility got bigger ... It became not fun anymore ... You just wore the organizers out.'[56] She added that even in club-run rallies, 'if people were very competitive, there were always *protests!* ... You were scared to organize a rally in case you made a mistake ... and when prize money was offered that made it even worse.'[57]

Money, especially fees and cost sharing with CASC national, was also a long-standing source of dispute within clubs and regions. At the 1970 AGM BC Region delegate Dudley Wingfield asked: 'What use is our money being put to for us?'[58] The problem, Don Horne explained in 1973, was that funding from the clubs was insufficient for CASC to fulfil its mandate: 'We're too big for our finances and we're too small for our ambitions. CASC must [have] ... a sound financial structure *before* it can ever hope to provide all of the things that ... CASC Clubs now expect of it. We must change, either our finances or our expectations.'[59]

The problem was the same at the regional level. Both Ontario and BC Regions reported financial difficulty as early as 1969, and by the early 1970s were curtailing activities and losing members.[60] As Art Moseley explains, it became yet another vicious circle: 'A lot of clubs went broke because the cost ... got out of hand ... When a club gets into financial stress it also has membership problems, because people have those [financial] problems in their everyday business, and they don't want to go to their "fun" things and hear ... the same thing.'[61] As members left, competitive events declined. Some clubs simply never broke out of the spiral.

Finally, the sport may have been a victim of shifting patterns of leisure activity. The 1970s were notable for increased participation in personal fitness activities, such as jogging. Many more Canadians bought boats, rode bikes, and went camping. They also spent much more money on vacation homes and on hotels. But during the recession they spent less on attending sports events, and that apparently included auto sport. Moseley points out that car clubs had to compete not only with other sports, but also for the time of families who travelled and owned cottages.[62] With a weak economy, changing personal priorities, and competing recreational opportunities, there simply was not enough time and money to do everything. By the 1970s, auto sport – racing and rallying in particular – had become both time- and money-intensive and even club-level politics could be quite stressful. In retrospect, with all of the negative forces at work on the sport, the downturn in membership and participation hardly seems surprising. In fact, what is remarkable is not that auto sport declined, but that it survived, and even rebounded in the second half of the decade.

15 Final Laps: The Decline and Fall of the CASC

Canadian Motorsport is going through another of its periodic political squabbles. But, for once, the sport ... may emerge the winner.

David Hatter, 'Dateline'[1]

From Death to Dissolution

Even by the standards of auto racing it was a horrific crash. 'In the final minutes of qualifying for the Belgian Grand Prix at the Zolder circuit, Gilles Villeneuve's Ferrari touched the right-side tires of Jochen Mass's March at about 140 mph on the approach to the difficult Terlamenbocht corner. Gilles's car was catapulted into the air for over 100 metres, crashing nose down into the ground, then continuing a series of cartwheels. The chassis disintegrated, the front end of the car was sheered off, and Gilles himself was hurled another fifty metres through the catch fencing. A helicopter whisked him to a nearby hospital, but his injuries were too severe and he never recovered.'[2]

The ultimate prize – the Formula One world championship – had eluded Villeneuve. Following team orders, he had finished second to his teammate Jody Scheckter in 1979. In 1980–1, he struggled with cars that handled poorly, but he never gave up. His flamboyant driving style and his personal charm made Gilles immensely popular with fans and fellow drivers alike. Enzo Ferrari treated him as one of his family. Scheckter's euology said it all: 'He was the fastest driver in the history of motor racing ... [and] the most genuine man I have ever known.'[3]

Gilles Villeneuve had taken Canadian auto racing to a level it never had achieved before, and his death touched the nation in a manner not seen in the sport since the loss of Peter Ryan. His coffin, draped in a Canadian flag, was flown to Montreal on a Canadian Forces jet. Thousands came to pay their last respects as he lay in state at the Berthierville cultural centre. Prime Minister Pierre Trudeau and Premier René Lévesque of Quebec were among the nine hundred invited guests who attended his funeral. Thousands more lined the highway overpasses as Gilles's funeral cortege drove to Montreal.[4] It was a quite remarkable outpouring for a country that had only recently discovered its auto sport identity.

The decade that opened with the death of Villeneuve closed with the death of the CASC. In 1991 it ceased to be the national governing body of Canadian sports car competition, its power usurped by forces partly of its own making, yet beyond its control. Like a creature from ancient mythology, having achieved its vision the CASC ultimately was consumed by its own creation.

Turning the Corner

In the years between Villeneuve's victory in Montreal in 1978 and his death at Zolder, Canadian auto sport rebounded from its recession. Within a year, the number of clubs had increased to 106 and membership to 6615. The next year it topped 7000 – higher than ever before. Although the number of events scarcely increased from 1977 to 1978 (742 to 747), participation grew from 20,473 to 23,086 entries and on-site audiences expanded dramatically, from 336,000 to 570,000. Prize money increased to $2 million in 1978, up by 20 per cent over the previous year. President George Chapman told the 1977 AGM that he was gratified by the 'turn around of the lethargy that has been with us for quite a few years.'[5]

How do we explain this rapid recovery? As with the decline, there was no single factor. To its credit, the CASC tried to improve communication with its members. *Autosport Canada* (*ASC*), the new CASC news magazine, first appeared in March 1975. But it soon faced the same problems that had killed *Canadian Motorsport Bulletin*; it could not make money from the CASC membership alone, and there simply weren't enough members to generate sufficient advertising revenue. And so *ASC* redefined itself as a general auto sport magazine to increase its readership among the general public. It focused mainly on major international and national races and rallies, people, and technical issues; it carried no club news. By 1980 it had dropped any reference to the CASC; regional reports and bulletins appeared rarely.[6] Thus, it is not clear that the magazine contributed to the sport's revival.

In the meantime, BC Region president Blake McGuffie had taken the CASC to task and proposed a more effective solution to the membership issue:

> CASC must ... recognize that we are not ... representative of motorsport in Canada. We have no stock racers, no four-wheel drive enthusiasts, no drag runners ... no motorcycles. We represent perhaps 25% of the ... bodies involved in Canadian motorspor ... The major emphasis in CASC ... MUST be to do everything possible to broaden our base of membership to include these ... enthusiasts. Put very simply and bluntly: They have numbers, they have money, and more importantly, they have enthusiasm. There is a great deal of work involved in ... motorsport. Surely it makes sense to spread that workload. There is a great deal more money needed ... [I]t makes sense to acquire more dues ... Surely it makes sense to tap that enthusiasm. If these objectives are not put PARAMOUNT ... I see motorsport ... becoming far more expensive than it is already. *This cost is the major factor to the tapering off and attrition of competition.*[7]

The CASC apparently took his advice to heart. While the stock car and drag racers never joined, the CASC expanded its base largely by affiliation with four-wheel-drive and go-kart clubs. The former were very popular in BC and Quebec, and the latter had grown rapidly in Ontario. The four-wheelers accounted for the largest increase in members, but karts were more significant for the sport as a whole.[8]

Karts, or go-karts as they were called originally, had first appeared in Canada in the early 1960s. At that time, auto sport enthusiasts contemptuously dismissed the tiny underpowered contraptions as 'make-believe' racers. Thus, karts were ignored by CASC until 1977, when it held its first joint convention with the Canadian Karting Federation (CKF). One year later the CASC created a National Karting Committee (NKC) to help bring professional standards to the sport.[9]

Both the CASC and the sport itself benefited from the new relationship. The CASC gained new members from the affiliation of karting clubs. And the integration of karting into auto sport at the grass-roots level gave Canadian racing something it had lacked previously: a junior league. Now, just as in hockey, kids could enter the sport and begin to hone their skills at an early age. CASC president Chapman stressed – presciently, as it turned out – the importance of karting in racing driver development. 'If you look at the successful people in motor racing today, ... a lot of them started in Karting and we have probably got more Gilles Villeneuves in our Karting activities today.'[10] Calling kart racing the 'Training Ground of Champions,' NKC director John Magill empowered his committee to establish a racing program to give 'the most promising Canadian karters special training and upward mobility ... Such programs are already in place in Europe as a quick glance at the racing background of many of the current Formula 1 drivers will show.'[11] As will be discussed later, for Canadian racers the CASC investment in karting would pay off handsomely in Indy Car racing in the 1990s.

Notwithstanding the successful efforts to broaden the base of the CASC, the statistics cited above suggest that it was competition itself, and racing in particular, that was bringing people back into the sport. A whole new range of racing opportunities at all levels opened up in the second half of the 1970s.

At the pro level the Can-Am series was revived, albeit in a curious form. With a push from Mosport owner Harvey Hudes, who had revived the Player's 200 in 1976, the SCCA converted its less popular Formula A championship in 1977 into a series for closed-wheel sports-racing cars similar to those of the first Can-Am. This was achieved by draping a full-coverage body (provided by Lola at a cost of about $6000 each) over the Formula A chassis. Some teams later modified the kit body when the front end showed a tendency to lift at speed. The new cars retained the five-litre engines, and so they were light, powerful, and fast.[12]

Just like the original series, Can-Am's successor opened at Le Circuit. But the field was small by comparison – little more than a dozen cars in all. The futuristic Schkee (on a Lola chassis) piloted by American Tom Klausler took the pole. Can-Am veteran Chris Amon qualified second in Canadian Walter Wolf's Dallara. Unlike the 1966 event, the race began in steady rain. Klausler won, while Amon dropped out with engine trouble. In spite of drying conditions later in the race, Horst Kroll stayed on rain tires and did not pit for fuel. He led for seven laps, but his tires deteriorated, allowing Klausler and John Gunn to pass. Two laps down at the end, Kroll came in third, his best finish in international racing.[13]

Two races later at Watkins Glen, Gilles Villeneuve made an inauspicious debut in the series, taking the Dallara driver's seat vacated by

Amon, who lacked confidence in the car and had graduated to being team manager. Villeneuve qualified fourth, but went out of the race after six laps with gearbox problems. The team redeemed themselves in the next race at Road America (Elkhart Lake), where Gilles brought the car home in third place – his only finish in four starts. His brother Jacques fared better, winning the championship in a Frissbee in 1983.[14]

This Can-Am series (officially called the SCCA Citicorp Challenge) lasted ten seasons. Whether it offered crowd-pleasing competition or not is open to question; as in the original series, one team (in this case, the Carl Haas Lolas) swept the title in the first four years.[15] Nevertheless, the revival of big-bore racing with Canadian venues and drivers could hardly be a bad thing for the sport.

Amateurs had three new series to choose from. The Molyslip Endurance Series began in 1977 with five races, two in the Atlantic region, and one each in Quebec, Ontario, and Manitoba, almost a carbon copy of the EZE championship. Races were to be a minimum of two hours and a maximum of six, with two drivers sharing each car. The sponsor put up $14,000 in prize money. The first season opened with nineteen cars competing at Le Circuit and ended with a near sweep by the Porsche RSR of Klaus Bytzek and Rudy Bartling of Toronto, who won four of the events. Arnold Hoar's Datsun 710 from Moncton, New Brunswick, was second overall and Ontario's Bob Esseltine third in a Datsun 240Z.[16]

All new series experience growing pains and the Molyslip was no exception. In its first year it suffered from a lack of continuity in organization, which was remedied by the appointment of a series coordinator for the next season. That year the series expanded to include a final seven-hour race at Westwood. Hoar clinched the championship there, but except for his co-driver Paul Lambke the mostly eastern competitors skipped the event. By 1979 the Molyslip had grown to seven races in five provinces from Newfoundland to British Columbia. Yet in spite of the enthusiasm of its sponsor, especially company president Les Joyce, the grids remained small (the Westwood race attracted only ten starters) and were shared among as many as nine classes of cars. Quebec driver Jacques Bienvenue took the championship that year in his Porsche RSR. It was not until 1980 that the series really took off, thanks perhaps to the increased prize money ($4000 per race), plus a tow fund that helped to offset the travel costs. The Gimli, Manitoba, race drew a record thirty-seven entries. Despite being injured in a heavy crash at AMP, Porsche pilot David Deacon went on to share the series win with his co-driver Peter Moennick.[17] The Molyslip series confirmed what critics said nearly two decades earlier; endurance racing appeals to a limited group of truly die-hard competitors and does not always make for great spectator sport.

Much more popular was the Honda / BF Goodrich Challenge Series. Capitalizing on the market success of the sub-compact Honda Civic, it offered the very thing that had been lost in the surge towards professionalism: *low-cost* competitive racing. For $2875 racers could buy the basic car, to which they had to add safety equipment, an approved exhaust, and the series sponsor's radial tires. The engine was sealed to prevent changes. Launched in 1976, the Challenge was an immediate success, attracting more than four hundred racers over the next seventeen years. Its stars included Frank Allers, Marc Dancose, and Gilles Villeneuve's brother Jacques. By 1978 the series had five closely contested regional divisions with over fifty competitors. National race director Jim Weber asserted in 1978 that small sedan racing along the lines of the Honda/BFG series represented the future of affordable amateur racing; it would appeal to racers, spectators, and car manufacturers alike. Peter Christianson, who was dominant in Ontario that year, described the series as 'the best thing to happen to racing since nonflammable underwear.' But two years later *Auto Sport Canada* editor Pete Chapman was complaining that the Honda / BFG was merely 'a pale shadow of its former self.'[18] The series waxed and waned over the next dozen seasons.

For enthusiasts who yearned for a return to 'the good old days' of cheap, fun competition, 'vintage racing' was by far and away the most popular amateur program at that time. Following a growing trend in the United States and Europe, it offered real racing in older sports cars like MGs and Sprites, without the high cost of professional competition. In the fall of 1976 a small group held an informal race between older racing cars at Le Circuit. Then some forty owners met in Kingston in November and founded the Vintage Automobile Racing Association of Canada (VARAC). The following year they held six races at three tracks, and by 1981 vintage racing had grown enough to attract eighty-five cars to a single event.[19]

Solo racing also rebounded in the second half of the decade. In 1978 clubs ran 245 solo events, attracting 6364 entrants and 23,810 spectators. That prompted national Solo director Robert Garnett to claim, 'There are now more people competing in solo events than ... in any other single facet of motorsport ... As the costs of going racing and stage rallying have increased astronomically over the past few years ... more people are turning to solo events where they can get the same level of competition for far less cost.'[20] By contrast, hill climbs were all but extinct. Access to roads on hills became difficult, and the CASC's increasingly stringent safety standards made organizing and competing too onerous. In addition, since stage rallying had become the norm across the country, navex rallying never recovered to earlier participation levels.[21]

An important, albeit intangible, influence on the post-recession recovery of auto sport may have been Canadian racing's own 'superstar.' While it is hard to measure exactly the impact that Gilles Villeneuve had on the sport in Canada, his victories gave sports car racing the high, national, public profile it had previously lacked and probably attracted more enthusiasts to the sport. By 1980 amateur racing had expanded greatly in his home province thanks largely to well-promoted ACAM events that drew large entries and big crowds.[22] Even so, in the decade that followed Villeneuve's death, professional racing flourished, while the amateur side of the sport floundered yet again. Ultimately, this proved fatal for the CASC.

Hot Wheels: The Pro Series

Canadian professional sports car competition experienced both 'bust and boom' in the 1980s. The national rally championship was divided into eastern and western series in order to keep costs down by eliminating the need for rallyists to compete across the country. But by mid-decade it was down to seven events and had lost its major sponsor, and the big factory teams had withdrawn. Moreover, the ongoing decline of club and regional navex rallies diminished the training of performance rally competitors and created a shortage of experienced co-drivers. None the less, by the end of the decade the championship rebounded. In 1988 it regained a full-season series sponsor (General Tire) and TV coverage of two events on The Sports Network (TSN).[23]

Pro racing gathered momentum. By 1989, in addition to Formula Atlantic, which was now an American-run series with four Canadian events, the Grand Prix, and two Indy Car races, there were five sponsored national 'pro' series: the Honda/Michelin Challenge; the Rothmans Porsche Turbo Cup; the Export 'A' F-2000; the Player's/GM Motorsport; and the Firestone Firehawk Endurance Challenge. Between them they constituted some sixty races, nearly three hundred racers, and a lot of money. In 1992 the Player's/GM series alone offered $750,000 in prize money, as well as TV coverage.[24] Martin Chenhall, an experienced racer and rallyist who served as General Motors' Director of Motorsport (1986–91), explained that the idea of sponsoring a racing series was a tough sell to upper management: 'Racing is not very firmly entrenched in any [American] automotive corporation, certainly not in GM ... It is much more so today than twenty-five or thirty years ago. But it's still not part of the mainstream ... But we needed to do something to enhance our image, so getting involved in motorsport made sense.'[25]

GM launched its series in 1986, at a time when Canadian racing needed a boost from something new and GM needed the exposure. 'So it looked like we had the opportunity to ... further motorsport by sponsoring a series that was reasonable [in] cost, and highly competitive. We moved motorsport up a big step along with the perception of General Motors.'[26] The Corvette might have seemed the natural choice for the series. It had a long and impressive racing pedigree, and in 1981 Eppie Wietzes had driven one to victory in the Trans-Am championship. But for marketing reasons the series was limited to Camaros and Firebirds. They had a bigger market share than Corvettes and had dominated the Trans-Am series in 1983. The initial response of racers seemed to validate GM's decision; seventy-four cars competed in the first year of the series.[27]

Over the next seven years, the series's ranks included many of the rising stars of Canadian racing in the 1980s: David Empringham, Ron Fellows, Scott Maxwell, and Kenny Wilden. Indeed, the GM series benefited greatly from previous ones; drivers like Marc Dancose and Richard Spenard had 'cut their teeth' on the Honda and Molyslip championships before moving up to the big cars. From a business perspective, however, the series had mixed results for GM. In its second year, sales of both Camaros and Firebirds in Canada fell by 50 per cent, because they appealed to younger drivers whose insurance rates were highest. Nevertheless, to its credit GM did not lose heart and continued to support the series. Apparently, it paid off; as Chenhall claims: 'Relative to what we got out of it, I think it was the best investment anybody's ever spent in motorsport.'[28]

The growth and success of the pro series imposed structural change on the CASC. In 1978 it established a professional competition division to guide all pro events 'effectively and more efficiently.' The division was incorporated separately from CASC, but was wholly owned by it, with an interlocking board of directors. The pro board included some 'friends of the sport' whose experience and business connections could guide and assist the CASC in managing professional auto sport. By 1980 the division was being asked to assume 'a strong supporting role' in the pro rally program, the Formula Atlantic series, and the Grand Prix.[29] From a purely operational standpoint, this undoubtedly made sense. Events like the GP were 'big business' and required more attention, simply because they involved so much money, organizational effort, and even prestige. Yet with a full-time executive director and office staff, the CASC was still a largely amateur, volunteer-based organization. It was hard pressed to meet all the expectations and demands of diverse amateur and professional programs. Still, the creation of a separate pro division raised questions about the CASC's priorities and whose interests it served.[30]

Those questions were answered unequivocally at a national directors' meeting in December 1984. Pursuing a new image of 'dedication through professionalism,' the CASC made it clear that the amateur side of the sport had to meet the standards set by the professional side:

> The reality facing the amateur division of this organization is, that we cannot underestimate either the value or the responsibilities of CASC Amateur through viewing it as a pastime to be enjoyed at leisure. It cannot be overemphasised that this is a *business* that should be perceived, by any observer, as being run in an orderly and professional manner, as is any *successful* business venture.[31]

The CASC's new image notwithstanding, it had apparently allowed its pro racing division to wane, for in November 1988 it had to create a 'Pro Race Board' yet again to control its professional series. The new board included officials from each series and an advisory group representing the promoters, manufacturers, and sponsors. It reported to the national board through the CASC's executive committee. Paul Cooke was chairman and Len Welin served as series director.[32] With the exception of the Rothmans Porsche series, pro racing continued to flourish, although it is not clear whether the new board had anything to do with that. Furthermore, as will be discussed later, the board became one focus of the disputes that ultimately brought down the CASC. In the meantime, the faces and places of Canadian racing continued to change and to gain 'world class' stature and recognition.

From Karts to CART

It was the closest finish in Indy Car racing history: 0.043 of a second. In less time than the blink of an eye, American 'Little Al' Unser Jr nosed out Canadian Scott Goodyear to win the 1992 Indianapolis 500. No Canadian had ever come so close. Goodyear, from Toronto, who had started at the back of the thirty-three-car pack, said afterwards, 'It's overwhelming, but it's second place and you want to finish first. Getting up on Monday morning it still hurts.'[33]

If Goodyear was disappointed, Canadian racing fans were ecstatic. Although Jacques Villeneuve (Gilles's brother) had been the first Canadian to win an Indy Car race (at Road America, 1985),[34] it was Scott's performance in the '500' that said Canadian racers were back in the big leagues in a big way. Goodyear himself won his first Indy Car race at the Michigan 500 later that year, and Paul Tracy soon eclipsed him, winning five Indy Car races and finishing third overall in the 1993 season. Two years later, another Jacques Villeneuve – son of Gilles – outshone them both by winning both the Indy 500 *and* the championship. Jacques then jumped to Formula One and in only his second season won the world championship that had eluded his father. And more Canadians followed.

Where did they all come from, and why were there so many all of a sudden? In auto sport, as in so many other things, timing is everything. As it happened, two trends converged in the late 1980s. Canadian racing driver development was maturing just as the Championship Auto Racing Teams (CART) Indy Car championship had grown into a highly competitive, popular, and lucrative series that included races in Canada.[35] The Canadian investment in professional racing schools and pro racing series was paying off just as it had for Gilles Villeneuve. But this new generation of drivers had an added advantage; like budding hockey stars, they had started racing at a much younger age. George Chapman's predictions proved to be correct. For Canadian racers, success in CART was all about karts.

The numbers suggest that this was no coincidence. Scott Goodyear, whose father owned a go-kart shop, won his first kart race in 1969 at age six. Four years later he was Canadian junior champion and North American Grand National champion. He won the Canadian national kart championship two years running (1975–6), before moving up to Formula Ford and a pro racing school. Paul Tracy got started in karts around age ten, but by the time he was sixteen he had won seventy-four kart races in eighty-two starts and placed sixth in the 1984 World Karting Championship. The next year he moved up to and won the national Formula Ford series. Future CART stars Patrick Carpentier, Greg Moore, and Alex Tagliani pursued the karting route before graduating to 'real' race cars.[36]

Thus, karting followed the same path as the other forms of Canadian auto sport and other sports; it began as a hobby then was professionalized. In the process, however, it completed the driver development circle that now included the pro racing schools, the pro racing series, and the Formula Atlantic championship. And it paid off most obviously in the CART series.

Powerslide: Amateurism in Decline

In contrast to the growth of pro racing, amateur auto sport suffered another decline in the first half of the 1980s, followed by only a modest revival in the second. The reasons were familiar. An economic recession in the early 1980s cost the CASC clubs and their members. From the peak of 7000 in the late 1970s, membership fell back to about 6000 and stagnated. Relations between CASC national and its regions and clubs continued to be plagued by communication problems. Club and regional rallying waxed and waned over time and between regions. Stage rallies proliferated, while navexes continued to decline. The national auto-slalom championship hit an all-time low of 217 entries in 1982, and in 1987 was held in only nine locations. Regional slalom series were hurt by the rise of Sunday shopping, which cut off access to parking lots.

By 1988 CASC national was increasingly focused on the pro series, which received the lion's share of sponsor funding. It had no national program for amateur racing, leaving that in the hands of the regions. The consequences were noticeable. The endurance championship was cancelled mid-decade for lack of racers and organizers. The national class run-offs were dropped in favour of a single 'winner-take-all' event, which drew two hundred entries at the new Shannonville, Ontario, track (with Petro-Canada as sponsor) in 1984. But the usual problems – distance, cost, and regionalism – continued to hamper the event; in 1987 there were only three entries from outside Quebec and Ontario.[37]

Major-General Lewis MacKenzie, then an amateur Formula Ford racer, observed later that the exposure the pro series offered to sponsors siphoned off 'all of the support from the entry level ... The money dried up there.' Thus, amateurs had to work even harder to fund their hobby, spending more time 'looking for sponsors than ... working on the car.'[38] The pro series were important; they developed promising drivers and gave the sport visibility. But by simultaneously raising the bar for amateur performance and safety standards while cornering the lion's share of sponsor funding, they forced hobby racers into the dollar wall. The amateur disciplines of the sport were just recovering some of their lost ground when the CASC self-destructed in 1991.

Tracks in Trouble

As the amateur side of the sport struggled, so did the race tracks, and the two problems reinforced each other. The closure of Edmonton International Speedway in 1982 hit Prairie region racing hard. EIS had suffered the same financial problems as Mosport and Le Circuit. Neither the city nor the region could generate enough spectators for major events to cover the track's operating and capital costs. Moreover, being close to the downtown eventually became a liability instead of an asset. The city closed in around the track, and its land had greater value for housing than for racing. Today the site is a mix of residential and retail.[39]

Most of its racers headed to Westwood or to the United States, as the only alternative on the Prairies was Gimli Motorpsort Park, north of Winnipeg. Built in the early 1970s by the Winnipeg Sports Car Club, Gimli hosted regional and national events and Formula Atlantic races. However, it was little more than a 'jumped up' airport circuit. Never a favourite with racers, it nonetheless survived. But by the end of the decade, Westwood was gone. The SCCBC's lease on the land expired in 1989 and was not renewed. The next year the track closed to make way for a housing development. Offsetting these losses, Race City Speedway (now Race City Motorsport Park) on the outskirts of Calgary opened in 1987 for sports car racing. Another oval / drag strip / road course combo, it hosted Player's/GM and Formula Atlantic races and eventually attracted many regional racers.[40]

In the east, Le Circuit enjoyed a brief respite. The CRRC ran there in 1975 and 1976, and the course hosted the Formula Atlantic series the same years, with large crowds watching Gilles Villeneuve win the second race in convincing style. Then, as quickly as it had appeared, that series left Le Circuit. Federal legislation regarding cigarette advertising forced out Player's and the new sponsor – Labatt – took the races to the city streets. Although the Trans-Am and the revised Can-Am series returned to Le Circuit for a few years, the big races and big crowds never did. In the years that followed, the track hosted races only for the Canadian pro series: Formula Ford/1600, Rothmans Porsche, and Player's/GM. In the meantime, several of the other Quebec road courses (St-Croix and St-Félicien) also shut down.[41]

By the time the Formula Atlantic cars raced there for the last time in 1977, it was clear that the Atlantic Motorsport Park was too rough and too narrow, and the run-off areas too short, for the rapidly evolving 'fast movers.' Repaving plans fell through when the series promoters could not fund the 1978 F/Atlantic race.[42] That shortfall highlighted the real problem; AMP was simply too remote from the central Canadian auto sport market to draw the big crowds and big money that big events required. But the news wasn't all bad. Its lower debt load and minimalist approach allowed AMP to sustain regional racing. Likewise, Shannonville Motorsport Park (originally Nelson International Raceway), which opened near Belleville, Ontario, in 1977, bucked the trend. It came on the scene too late and too small to land a major race, so it was limited to regional amateur events and the smaller-scale Canadian pro series, such as the Honda/BFG and Molyslip Endurance. But track owner Jack Boxtrom, who has run it since 1978, later expanded the circuit to offer a variety of lap lengths and added a drag strip and kart track to ensure a wider client base.[43]

Mosport's condition was only slightly less precarious than that of Le Circuit, but ultimately its fate was similar. After its heyday in the early 1970s, Mosport's world was turned upside down. The original Can-Am series ended in 1974. Then, four years later, the Grand Prix moved to Montreal.

This was the result of converging developments at Mosport in the mid-1970s. According to Roger Peart, who at the time was the CASC track inspector, track owner Harvey Hudes had become disenchanted with the Grand Prix. Bad weather had plagued the race, keeping audiences smaller than expected and revenues down. It took only a hint of poor weather to discourage people from attending a race. Then Mosport lost the 1975 Grand Prix in a dispute with the Formula One Constructors Association (F1CA, later FOCA), which negotiated appearance fees on behalf of the teams. The 'official' CASC version of events, as related by Bob Hanna, traces the dispute to 1973, when Mosport and Watkins Glen reached an agreement with F1CA about the price for their 1975 events. But in late July 1975 F1CA boosted its fees per event from $500,000 to $565,000, plus the cost of transporting cars to North America ($200,000). F1CA director Bernie Ecclestone gave the tracks little more than a week to meet the new terms. Watkins Glen agreed, but Hudes refused and the F1CA teams withdrew from the Mosport race. Hudes replied with a lawsuit and a court injunction against F1CA, which was later settled out of court. As F1 historian Ivan Rendall explains, at this time Ecclestone was testing F1CA's bargaining power. In Hanna's view, he had decided to make an example of Mosport to extract a better deal from European race organizers. Thus, Mosport was just a victim of F1 business power politics.[44]

Hudes also had a falling out with Labatt, which in 1972 had signed a five-year agreement with Mosport and the CRDA to serve as principal sponsor of the Grand Prix. By the mid-1970s Labatt was diversifying its sporting interests and wanted to put money into sports in Quebec. Finally, as will be discussed below, in 1977 the FIA decided that Mosport would not host the next Canadian Grand Prix.

The loss of those major races should have killed the track. Yet it survived, hosting a mix of professional and amateur, regional, national, and international events, such as the Trans-Am, the second-generation Can-Am, IMSA, and Formula Atlantic. Hudes boasted that he had 'resisted change for the sake of change or on the whim of whatever prima donna driver happened to be making the biggest noise.'[45] That attitude earned him his share of critics, who argued that the track had not kept pace with the changes in racing. In truth and in spite of Hude's claims to the contrary, during his tenure Mosport was modernized substantially. To keep the events he still had, he made the numerous safety upgrades – such as tire walls, gravel traps, and longer run-off areas – demanded by the CASC and other sanctioning bodies.[46]

That said, Hudes was also a canny businessman. He had no incentive to sink millions into a track that would never again host the Grand Prix. But he believed that racing was 'more entertainment than sport,' and invested in the things – grandstands, a restaurant, and a stock car oval – and the kinds of events that would bring enough people to the track to keep it afloat. And he succeeded; the track survived the demise of the second Can-Am series and later weathered another financial crisis.[47] In one sense, by the 1980s both Mosport and Le Circuit had come almost full circle. Started by clubs, they had become businesses in order to attract 'world class' pro races; Mosport still does. But they have ended up mostly as tracks for the very groups who had created them: the club-based amateurs. In the meantime, the pros and the promoters had gone downtown.

The Circus Comes to Town

If business was changing the face of auto sport, it was also changing its location. The idea of racing downtown was hardly new. City locales had been used in the early days of racing in Europe. Over time, safety concerns and objections to the noise and inconvenience had pushed racing out to airports or to road courses like Mosport built out in the country. But promoters recognized the marketing advantages in taking the races to the people instead of bringing people to the races. A local audience of thousands or millions on the doorstep of the circuit itself is a race promoter's and sponsor's dream come true. And so, in 1967, seventeen years before Indy Cars took to the streets of North American cities, and bucking the trend in Europe where the Monaco Grand Prix remained the only F1 street race, city racing had been reborn in Trois-Rivières. While city-street tracks proved commercially successful and popular with TV and spectators, eventually they would change the character of Canadian racing yet again.

The success of the Trois-Rivières event had not gone unnoticed elsewhere. In September 1968 a promotional group calling itself Lakeshore Auto Raceway Holdings Limited, led by John Bassett, Jr (owner of the *Toronto Telegram*), Don Hunt of PRSL, and his client Imperial Tobacco, announced a proposal to run the 1969 Telegram Trophy Indy Car race *and* the Canadian F1 Grand Prix on a street circuit laid out on and around the grounds of the Canadian National Exhibition (CNE) in Toronto. While they agreed that such an event could create 'thousands' of new fans, Len Coates and others worried that it would kill the established tracks. Rod Campbell, then *Track and Traffic* publisher, criticized Canadian racers such as Ludwig Heimrath who supported the plan. Campbell felt they 'should know better ... What astounds me is that Canadian drivers don't seem to realize or care that they'll never drive at the CNE unless they move into the Indianapolis or Grand prix strata. There will be no supporting races.'[48]

Campbell pointed out that Indy car racing had a limited following in Canada. Moreover, he reminded readers, the F1 Grand Prix was supposed to rotate between Ontario and Quebec, and so the Toronto track could jeopardize the future of both Mosport *and* Le Circuit. Finally, Lakeshore Racing had agreed to relinquish its rights to the site if the city decided to develop it for other purposes. Thus, it had no long-term commitment to the track. At the 1968 AGM, national president Richard Drouin made it clear that while the CASC could hardly oppose a venture that would introduce more Canadians to auto sport, 'we will not permit major races to be held on a non-permanent circuit at the price of ... closing down a track which is the fundamental instrument to the breeding of Canadian Drivers.'[49]

In the event, just as the bill was going to third reading before Toronto city council early in 1969, Bassett dropped the idea. The residents of a nearby neighbourhood had threatened to use pickets and injunctions to stop the project, and that was enough to persuade him to pull out.[50]

Even so, the scheme should have been a wake-up call to the CASC. It showed that, its race sanctioning power notwithstanding, the CASC – indeed, the sport itself – was vulnerable to being outmanoeuvred by powerful business interests. Mosport clearly was the better track, but racing was increasingly about spectacle and money and less about sport. And when the street-race idea was revived eighteen years later for Indy Car racing, spectacle carried the day. By that time, however, Mosport and Le Circuit were no longer factors in the equation.

The apparent success of the Trois-Rivières events had proved that a city street race was a viable proposition. Furthermore, in 1974 a Formula Atlantic race run through the streets of St John's, Newfoundland, drew a crowd of 18,000. If that many would turn out in a small city for a 'second tier' event, it was realistic to expect a much larger crowd for an F1 race in a major city like Montreal or Toronto.[51] Spectator access to racing was a major issue for race organizers and sponsors. They were involved in racing to make money, and they needed to get those spectators and potential consumers to and from the tracks easily. While Mosport is not far from Toronto, the secondary roads leading to the track could not readily absorb and disperse thousands of spectators' cars within a short time. The traffic jams were legendary; it could take many hours to reach or leave the track, and that problem had become a source of discontent among fans and local residents alike. Thus, Peart says, 'the move to hold events in cities really got its start that way. People find it kind of neat just to go on the subway and be right there.'[52]

Even so, the FIA's November 1977 announcement that the Grand Prix would not return to Mosport shook the Canadian racing community. And Labatt Breweries, which owned the promotional rights to the race, had to find a new venue quickly. The CNE site was considered, but on 7 December Toronto city council rejected that idea. What happened over the next twenty-four hours showed the real power of sponsors. According to Roger Peart (then race director of FAQ, CASC's Quebec region), Labatt president Donald McDougall called FAQ president Benoit Mailloux to ask if Montreal could host the GP. Mailloux immediately called Peart, and asked, 'Hey, where can we run the Grand Prix in Montreal?' Roger assured him that a site could be found. On the strength of that remark, Mailloux called McDougall and told him, 'Okay, we'll do it.' And on 8 December Labatt held a press conference to announce that the Grand Prix would be held in Montreal.[53]

Peart says there followed 'a mad scramble' to find a location for the race. The promoters soon chose Île Notre-Dame, site of the former Expo 67 world fair. They also had to secure the city's permission for the event and the site, and that was not a foregone conclusion. Montreal was still reeling from the huge cost of the 1976 Olympics, and some city officials were a little annoyed that they had not been consulted before Labatt announced its intentions. But at this point fate intervened in the form of a burly, charming, energetic, Austrian-born Canadian self-made oil millionaire and racing team owner by the name of Walter Wolf. In 1977 his Wolf WR1, piloted by Jody Schechter, won the Canadian Grand Prix. Wolf was an ardent Canadian nationalist, and his cars displayed the maple leaf flag prominently. He was the first Canadian team owner since Chuck Rathgeb to win a major international event, and the first to win in Formula One.[54]

The element of fate was a chance meeting between Wolf and Montreal mayor Jean Drapeau; early in 1978 they were taking the same flight from Dorval airport. Wolf seized the opportunity to sell the idea of the Grand Prix to Drapeau by appealing to the mayor's love of spectacle, his nationalism, and perhaps his vanity. He predicted that a Grand Prix event in Montreal 'would be an automatic success in the eyes of the world, because internationally, everyone knows our mayor, everyone remembers Expo 67 and the Olympics ... It is ... a great spectacle ... When you hold your race in Trois-Rivières it gets play in newspapers around the world. Think what projection a race in Montreal would get.'[55]

While the environmentalists and city councillors sceptical about yet another costly 'show' opposed the idea, Wolf's vision set the tone for the debate, which was all about the millions of dollars it would generate for the city. The promoters, Grand Prix du Canada Inc. (a subsidiary of Labatt) – agreed to absorb all the costs of building the track and its associated facilities (estimated at $2 million). In a bid to ward off criticism they guaranteed that, unlike the Olympics, the city would not be saddled with any debt after the race, and agreed to post a $500,000 bond to that effect. After months of discussion and ten hours of formal debate, on 9 June city council approved a five-year contract for the race.[56]

In the meantime, if there was going to be a GP in 1978 then planning the track had to proceed before the city approved it. Unfortunately for Roger Peart, who had been given the job of designing the new track, the December press conference had coincided with the first major snowfall of the winter. 'So, I never got a chance to ... do any detailed planning on the actual site, when it wasn't covered by ... snow which [made] it ... very hard to visualize the terrain ... plus the pavilions were still there ... Luckily, I knew which ones were coming down. So I designed the track right through the pavilions on the assumption that [the demolition] would be done by the time we laid the roadbed. And it was.'[57]

Roger went to London in April to meet with CSI's Circuit and Safety sub-commission, which would have to approve the plan. They identified some problems, so he adjusted his design in ten days, and at a meeting in Monte Carlo they approved a nineteen-turn 4.5-km circuit. A firm of highway engineers then produced the detailed design. Sub-commission chairman Alberto Rogano visited Montreal that month and was very impressed with the plan and the site. But he asked Roger, 'You're not really thinking of running the Grand Prix here in 1978?' When Peart said, 'Yes,' Rogano replied,'Well, that would take a miracle.'[58]

But, for the promoters there was no turning back. On 15 June Labatt announced that the Grand Prix would take place in Montreal in October. Track construction began on 28 June. The contractors faced a huge task and a short deadline. The existing road had to be torn up and completely resurfaced. Pit buildings, a control tower, grandstands, communications systems, and safety fencing were constructed from scratch. Nevertheless, work finished on 22 September. The circuit opened with a Formula Atlantic race two days later. That day, Peart sent Rogano a telegram saying, 'Miracle accomplished.'[59]

Taking It to the Streets

The success of in-town racing at Trois-Rivières and Montreal revived the long-standing dreams of race promoters in Toronto. In 1984 Molson had negotiated an agreement with CART, acquiring the rights to stage Indy Car races in Canada. It organized the first one at Sanair, the only Canadian venue on the schedule that year. But the tight Sanair tri-oval, where Rick Mears was seriously injured in the first event, was unpopular with the CART teams. Thus, the following year Molson's revived the proposal for a race in downtown Toronto. This time it was able to ease the concerns of local residents, and that paved the way for approval by city council and the province by November 1985. The track, laid out through the CNE grounds and along the adjacent Lakeshore Boulevard, followed closely the original design. The result was a fast, smooth, eleven-turn course that impressed CART racers mostly disenchanted with street tracks. On 20 July 1986, Indy 500 winner Bobby Rahal won Toronto's first Molson Indy race, before an on site-audience of 60,000 and a TV audience in the multi-millions. Frank Orr of the *Toronto Star* called the event 'an idea that took a very long time to get here.'[60]

With the success of the Toronto Molson Indy, as well as that of the Grand Prix in Montreal, it was not long before other Canadian cities tried to follow suit. As Mark Douglas Lowes points out, this was consistent with the behaviour of sports promoters and their political allies in many major North American cities. Sports spectacles like the Indy Car races are seen as revenue generators, but even more important, as a vehicle to promote a 'world class' image for the host city. In an era of economic transformation and intense global 'inter-urban competition,' 'for civic boosters, it seems that ... more than ever before, *image is everything*.'[61]

Both Vancouver and Halifax launched downtown races in 1990, and they were a study in contrasts. The former hosted the Molson Indy Vancouver (MIV), Canada's second prestigious CART race, which ran until 2004, while the latter had the Moosehead Grand Prix for the American Indy Car Series (AIS), then one level below CART, and subsequently for several other series. It lasted only six seasons.

The MIV was a race promoters' and advertisers' dream. It would draw at least 100,000 fans to the race site and could claim a TV audience in excess of 100 million. Local race boosters touted Vancouver as a rival to the glamour of Monte Carlo, home of the Monaco Grand Prix. Moreover, as organizer, Molson brought four years of experience from running the Toronto race. It had 200 full-time employees in its dedicated sports division working year-round on both races, in addition to the 1200 volunteers (mostly from CASC clubs) working the events themselves. The circuit was designed to challenge high-performance machinery, and the MIV had the cars and particularly the stars to match it: Mario and Michael Andretti, Emerson Fittipaldi, A.J. Foyt, Bobby Rahal, Danny Sullivan, Al Unser Jr, and the rising Canadian racer Scott Goodyear. Some team owners, like Paul Newman and Roger Penske, were household names in their own right. In 1996 *Performance Racing News* (*PRN*) proclaimed, 'It's become the largest, most important single sporting event in Western Canada.' Until the Grand Prix that year, it held the Canadian single-day sporting event attendance record. The MIV, said *PRN*, 'is all about entertainment and that it will have in spades.'[62]

By contrast, the Moosehead Grand Prix lacked everything that the MIV had. While not short on charm, Halifax did not have the same cosmopolitan image and had a much smaller local population and fan base to draw upon. Nor was its race the product of years of planning by a major series and promoter. Rather, the first Moosehead GP was organized hastily, the result of the converging interests of two minor-league players. As then company president Derek Oland later explained, the Moosehead brewery, which had sponsored racing in the region since the 1970s, 'wanted a high profile event to show current ... and potential customers ... that the company is a market leader and it's growing more valuable each year.'[63]

According to Harold MacKay, at the time general manager of Moosehead, a Rothmans Porsche Turbo Cup series race was supposed to run in St John's, Newfoundland, but the funding for it did not materialize. And so, early in 1990 John Graham, who was racing in that series and promoting it, contacted his friend MacKay. They persuaded Oland – an auto sport enthusiast himself – that Moosehead should organize a street race in Halifax. But nothing happened until early September, after MacKay and his promotions manager returned with enthusiastic reports from the inaugural MIV. A seat-of-the-pants affair from the outset, the Grand Prix was put together in the space of a month: 'the shortest organization-to-construction time in history. We had nothing. No city approval, no barriers, nothing.' The organizers brought in the AIS as the feature race, acquired 1400 concrete safety barriers (once used for a Rothmans Porsche race) from Niagara Falls, New York, and laid out a course on the streets around Citadel Hill. 'Despite the inevitable logistical problems [and] upset residents,' the mayor and city council supported the event vigorously.[64] The first race attracted 30,000 spectators. From 1993 on the race was run in the spring to improve the chances of better weather and a larger crowd.

However, racers complained that the two-kilometre, bow-tie shaped circuit of short straights and sharp turns was too tight and slow for the high-performance cars to perform at their best. Of the fifteen cars entered in the 1992 AIS race, only twelve made it to the grid, and only four finished; the rest broke down. For 1993 the Formula Atlantic series and the British Formula Two replaced the AIS cars; good weather and huge crowds made for a very successful event. But that was the final race on the streets of Halifax. For the Moosehead's last two years the cars raced on the runways of nearby CFB Shearwater. The British F2 cars returned for 1994, and in 1995 the IMSA Exxon World Sports Car series was the feature event. Supporting races included local stock cars, the Esso Protec Formula Ford and Player's/GM series, and the regional amateur sedan racers.[65] Thus, even if the race did not attract the big-name stars, for six years spectators got to see some exotic cars – Lolas, Marchs, Ferraris, and Porsches – and some good racing, although not always in the headliner events. The Grand Prix also revived Atlantic region racing, which had languished in the 1980s; the grids at AMP swelled with new racers and cars. But the audiences never came back to watch them.

By regional standards the race was big business. It brought in some $8 million to the Halifax area in the first two years. Moosehead initially established a subsidiary – Atlantic Grand Prix – with MacKay as its head to run the event, but in 1994 John Graham's company Motorsport Management took over, leaving Moosehead as just the sponsor. The first race had cost Atlantic Grand Prix $1.3 million. Associate sponsors, such as Player's, invested up to $500,000 each. The TNN, TSN, and CBC networks covered the feature and some of the supporting races.[66] But all this wasn't enough to keep the event going. Unlike the MIV, the Moosehead Grand Prix did not attract the major American TV networks, whose huge audiences and big advertisers could make or break a race financially. In short, it was not quite a 'world class' spectacle. Spectator fees were not sufficient to offset the advertising shortfall, and so the Grand Prix died after the 1995 race.

What the races in Montreal, Toronto, Vancouver, and Halifax all had in common was that they were commercial spectacles as much as – if not more than – sports events. Their dominant feature was not the cars or even the racers but the larger-than-life billboards, banners, and TV ads promoting the sponsors' products. The racing cars themselves, including those of the amateurs, were plastered with sponsor logos. CASC president George Chapman had been only half right when he said in 1980 that '[p]rofessional racing is a commodity ... a saleable product.'[67] In fact, marketing had displaced racing as the *purpose* of these events. In the end, those same market forces had the power to displace the CASC itself.

Beer and Power: The Death of the CASC

Indeed, by the mid-1980s the CASC no longer controlled Canadian auto sport; the promoters, teams, and sponsors did. The CASC could write rules, but found that it lacked the power to enforce them, at least in the case of major events. The organizers simply bypassed CASC and dealt directly with teams, sponsors, and media networks. As far as they were concerned, the CASC had ceased to be relevant or even necessary. It was a simple application of the 'golden rule': 'He who owns the gold makes the rules.' That rule proved fatal for the CASC.

The essential backdrop to this is the power struggles among Formula One racing, CART, their sponsors, and the FIA/FISA. The key figure in this was Bernie Ecclestone, then head of FOCA, the powerful F1 team cartel. Well financed by tobacco and TV money, the teams were the real owners of F1, and Ecclestone was their hard-nosed, influential front man. He not only embodied the power that business wielded at this level of racing; he *was* the power.[68]

Early in 1984 a dispute arose among CART, Molson, and the CASC over the key issues of the sponsorship and control of racing. The CASC refused to sanction Molson's first CART race at Sanair, but it went ahead anyway and thirty-seven Canadians competed in one of the supporting races. The CASC could do no more than fine them.[69] The dispute was an object lesson in the shifting locus of power in racing. The CASC had been outmanoeuvred by the combined influence of CART and its corporate sponsors. It was a harbinger of worse things to come.

In fact, the CASC faced a bigger dispute with Labatt over control of the Canadian Grand Prix. In December 1984, Bob Hanna went to the FISA meetings in Paris and briefed Yvon Leon (the FISA general secretary) on the problem with the brewery. Leon told Labatt 'quite firmly' that it had to reach an agreement with CASC, otherwise the Grand Prix could not happen; FISA would not intervene in what it saw as a domestic dispute. Within a week, the CASC and Labatt had signed a contract for the 1985 and 1986 Grand Prix, with an option for 1987. CASC general manager Bryan Sangster told the national board: 'It is my opinion that we have created the beginnings of an excellent relationship with Labatt. This ... cannot but benefit motor sport in Canada.'[70]

But the harmony was short-lived. By spring 1985 it was clear that CART racing would continue to grow in Canada, to include races at Sanair and in Toronto with or without the CASC's approval. This time FISA refused to get involved, telling CASC to solve the problem by itself. Thus, the Toronto race joined the CART calendar in 1986 with sponsorship from Molson. In December that year the CASC awarded Labatt a five-year contract for the rights to the Grand Prix. But Molson challenged the decision, and the ensuing battle proved costly for the CASC. For reasons that were not clear but probably related to the sponsor/sanctioning dispute, Ecclestone refused to deal with Labatt. Without his support, there would be no FOCA teams and, therefore, no 1987 Canadian Grand Prix. He held firm and the race was cancelled.[71]

The consequences for the CASC were disastrous. Arguing that it had exceeded its authority by extending the Labatt contract, FISA stripped CASC of its national sanctioning power in October 1987, twenty years after admitting it to the fold. CASC appealed, but FISA apparently did not give it serious consideration. In December, Labatt relinquished its rights to the Grand Prix, handing control of the Montreal track to FAQ. Shortly thereafter the Grand Prix was reinstated for 1988. Molson won the sponsorship rights to the event, but the CASC was shut out. Pierre Compagna, president of FAQ, remarked that 'the actions of FOCA, FISA and FIA showed a dictatorial disdain for the grass roots of the sport.'[72]

Through 1988 the CASC struggled to get reinstated as the national sporting authority (ASN) to no avail. In January 1989 FIA appointed Benoit Mailloux, former FAQ president and one of the developers of the Montreal Grand Prix circuit, as 'trustee' of the Canadian ASN. Then CASC president Roger Peart told the CASC board: 'It will be good to have the situation clarified and the uncertainty removed, although the outcome is not what we had expected – or hoped for.'[73] By the time the board met with Mailloux in February, Peart had learned that it was Ecclestone who had asked Mailloux to suggest a solution to the problem, and who had taken his proposal to the FISA meeting in December. FISA had accepted it and appointed Mailloux.

He told the board that FISA had seen the awarding of the contract to Labatt as 'an unauthorized subcontracting of the sporting authority.'[74] In light of FISA's hands-off attitude towards the earlier CART dispute, the charge seems curious at best.

Mailloux stated that although he was the ASN trustee, he felt he had 'no alternative but to delegate to CASC which has full authority to deal with all national matters.' He and the board agreed that it would continue to act as 'the governing body for motorsport within Canada' on behalf of the ASN, which would retain jurisdiction over all international affairs, such as the Grand Prix. For the time being at least, CASC would function almost as if nothing had happened.[75]

But further trouble was brewing over professional racing *within* Canada. At issue was the CASC's authority to govern the pro series. The pro racing board's autonomy clearly irked the national competition committee, which felt *it* ought to have the power to make decisions on *all* competition matters. The upshot was that in February 1990 Paul Cooke, who apparently objected to 'interference' from the national board, resigned from the pro race board, leaving it leaderless. At this point, it appears that ASN and the pro series sponsors, disillusioned with the CASC's internal problems, stepped in to save their investment in those series. According to Len Welin, who took part in a meeting in March between the sponsors, Mailloux, and Peart, 'The sponsors were quite adamant about removing the pro series from the amateur decision-makers ... They wanted their own entity, with its own identity, to deal with the commercial side of the sport.'[76] And they got it: a full-time, pro racing division directly under ASN control, completely separate from the CASC. Henceforth, the CASC would be the governing body for amateur auto sport only.[77]

The 'divorce' initially was greeted with relief by amateur and pro racers alike. 'I think it's a step in the right direction,' said Richard Spenard, at that time the top pro series driver. Former national race director Tommy Meecham said the pro series had been 'a pain in the neck ... Pro racing never did anything for the amateurs ... It's no great loss.'[78] But Peart and others who had sided with the ASN in order to preserve their control of pro racing were forced to resign their CASC positions. Then, the ASN insisted on issuing licences for *all* Canadian racers. But the CASC rejected this demand and continued to issue amateur racers' licences. Likewise, the CASC stewards and some volunteer track marshals were upset by the ASN's actions. As a result, many of them boycotted the Grand Prix in June 1990, forcing the ASN to appeal through the media for volunteers to serve as marshals. Optimistic assurances could barely disguise a mood of genuine personal bitterness.[79]

The CASC met in May 1990 to restructure itself for an amateur-only future. But soon the SCCA was refusing to honour CASC licences, sponsors were uncertain about its authority, and the regions were affiliating to the ASN. The pro rallyists created the Canadian Association of Rallysport (CARS) to run their series.[80] And so, by the end of 1991, fifty years after its founding, CASC national simply vanished. Canadian sports car competition had outgrown its amateur origins, and in the eyes of those who now controlled the sport – the commercial/professional teams, promoters, and sponsors – the CASC had fulfilled, indeed outlived, its intended purpose and was no longer needed.

Epilogue

Pennfield 1994

Forty minutes west of Saint John, New Brunswick, along the often fog-shrouded Bay of Fundy shore, the highway rises sharply up a short escarpment to cross the wind-swept plateau that is Pennfield Ridge. There, barely visible amid the scrub brush and spindly trees, you will find an abandoned wartime airfield. Fifty years later, the runways hum to a different tune: the thunder and whine of racing car engines. For a few weekends in the 1990s, the Atlantic Region racers left the relative comforts of AMP and returned their sport to its roots.[1]

Turn off the highway down the rutted track through the trees and you find the paddock – a few clearings of pitted broken asphalt and weeds among the remnants of the old hangars. Parked wherever space will allow, the racing cars present a crazy quilt of colours, designs, ages, shapes, and sizes. At the far end we see Eugene Pettipas's massive red 69 'Vette. Next to him, the Tim Horton's / Baxter Dairies Racing Team's trailer looms over Steve Breed's impeccably prepared red and white Mazda RX-7. Dale Mackay's hulking black Camaro lurks in the underbrush nearby. The ungainly white VW Scirocco of Derek Lugar and Diane Standing is getting a last-minute brake repair from their skilled and enthusiastic Vantage Motors crew. The matching red, yellow, and blue VWs of John Rankin and Bob Guthrie wait impatiently to do battle. Arnold Hoar's aged but fast Datsun 510 sits on its trailer. Though you'd never know it now, Darrell Whitehead's wrinkled yellow and white car was once a 510 too. Oblivious to the early autumn cool, Walter Tennant tinkers with his balky Mercury Bobcat wearing his trade-mark outfit: shorts, sandals, and the biggest grin in the Maritimes. The rest of the paddock is a collage of gaudily painted VWs, Hondas, Suzukis, Nissans, Toyotas, and a smattering of American cars. Off in a far corner, as if to distinguish themselves from the 'hoi polloi' sedans, lie a classy cluster of Formula Fords belonging to Tim Chesnutt, Tim Clowater, and Mark Cruickshank.

The atmosphere of the paddock is friendly and informal. Wives wander and kids frolic among the cars. Tools, toil, and tall tales are traded without a second thought. They may be fierce competitors on the track, but in the paddock the drivers and crews of all the teams help each other to make sure everyone gets out to race. Finally, the word filters through the paddock. Drivers don their suits and helmets, buckle themselves in, and the engines cough to life, filling the air with a miasma of noise and exhaust fumes. Stacy Chapman and his marshals from the NBSCC wave the eager column of chugging cars out onto the runways. With solid pavement under their feet, the racing cars stretch their legs and wind their engines up to full song. And overseeing it all like an impressario is Ralph Brooks, the tall, bald, bearded, and barrell-chested race director. With one eye on the track and the other on the rule book, he skilfully conducts this cacophonous concert of unruly talent and tempermental technology.

A painted white line and bright orange cones mark the course around the mile and a half triangle of wide, but crumbling, bone-jarring asphalt. The straights are long and fast and the turns are tight, piling the g-forces onto car and driver. No gravel traps, tire walls, or catch fences here. Not even Armco barriers or hay bales. Go off the track, and it's a skidding, bouncing trip into the trees, with the flinty rock tearing at your tires. But that's no deterrent to racers. They may be pals in the paddock, but once the green flag drops on the rolling start, the gloves come off. It's 'pedal to the metal and take no prisoners!' Fuelled by adrenaline, hearts pounding at 180-plus, out-dragging each other on the straights, trading paint and rubber in the corners, no quarter is asked or given. This isn't Mosport or the Molson Indy, no fortune or career is at stake, but the will to win is no less intense. The bumper sticker on Blu Vandaalen's Toyota GTS says it all: 'Second Sucks.'

If you allow your eyes to stray from the action on the track, they are drawn to a jarring vision: not what you see, but what you don't see. There are no bleachers full of thousands of race fans. In fact, there is no crowd at all. The spectators number no more than a few dozen, mostly family and friends of the racers, and a few curious enthusiasts drawn by word of mouth. Amid the trees and weeds, they lounge in deck chairs or sprawl on blankets under beach umbrellas. There are no TV cameras, not even the community news channel. At best, the local papers might give the race a couple of column inches, buried below bowling. As you survey the scene, your eyes are not bombarded by acres of corporate logos on billboards and buildings. The cars carry the names of their local sponsors: mostly car dealers, body shops, and garages. A lone Moosehead Beer banner decorates the concrete retaining wall at the start/finish. The brewery pays for some trophies and has provided a few cases for the awards ceremony. You can get hot dogs and pop from a rudimentary concession stand, but most people picnic. And forget the autographs and souvenirs. There's nobody famous here and nothing to buy.

When the racing is done, the drivers, crews, marshals, and hangers-on gather with beer in hand for the awards ceremony, a kind of racers' tailgate party. For the lucky few, there's a trophy or plaque, accompanied by some raucous cheering; most go home empty-handed, and poorer than when they arrived. More than a few drivers can look forward to body work and engine repairs before the next race. Except for the Formula Fords, whose sponsors have deeper pockets, there is no prize money. But even with the aid of a sponsor or two, most will have to dig into the family finances one more time. And so, at sundown, with the cars loaded on makeshift trailers and tow dollies, the racers, crews, and officials begin the long drive home. If Francis Bradley, Ross de St. Croix, or Ludwig Heimrath had been here, they probably would have experienced a lingering sense of déjà vu.

Montreal 1997

Jump ahead three years to the Canadian Grand Prix in Montreal,[2] and you are struck by the dramatic contrast with the Pennfield race. Few racetracks in the world – Monaco or Vancouver perhaps – can boast a more spectacular setting. Laid out on an island in the St Lawrence River with the city's skyscrapers and Mount Royal as its backdrop, the circuit threads its way around a pond among the futuristic ruins of the Expo 67 World's Fair. F1 star Jackie Stewart once described it as 'a little paradise in the middle of a great river.'[3] Today it is the most enduring monument to Canadian racing's favourite son: Gilles Villeneuve.

The Grand Prix is the culmination of a year of preparation and about a week of festivities. The drivers are fêted at parties and mobbed at press conferences. Cars and crews are on display downtown in a city now awash with racing fans from across the country and around the world. The atmosphere of spectacle is enlarged by the presence of celebrities like late show host David Letterman, himself the co-owner of Bobby Rahal's CART 'champ car' team. The *Montreal Gazette* devotes whole sections to the event, which – for a few days at least – is the 'talk of the town,' even among instant race fans who give the sport scarcely a thought during the rest of the year.

On a brilliant Sunday in June, over 100,000 spectators pour off the buses, out of the subway, and across the bridges to claim their cramped places in the grandstands that dot the perimeter of the track. The bleachers, which become a multicoloured sea of hats, t-shirts, and flags proclaiming allegiances to this team or that driver, are set well back from the track, safe from cars that might go astray at speeds that exceed 200 mph. Where you sit and what you see depends on how much you pay. But even gold ticket holders and the select few with sponsor passes, who roam the paddock or mingle with the drivers and team owners in the hospitality tents, can see only a small portion of the track. The cars themselves are 'rolling billboards' bedecked with sponsor logos that blur the identities of the racers; only the tops of their helmets are visible. Giant TV screens project larger-than-life images from parts of the track. Many fans also carry small radios and TVs to hear and see the same play-by-play commentary, in-car video, and the ads being broadcast live around the world to an audience numbering in the hundreds of millions. This is sport become spectacle, a subculture transformed into pop culture, in a globalized and televised 'theater of speed.'[4]

The crowds have come to watch the superstars and the super-cars and they will be rewarded in full. This day, as so many have in the past and will again in the future, belongs to Ferrari and Michael Schumacher. Much to the dismay of his loyal local fans, Jacques Villeneuve's race ends with a spin into the wall on the second lap. But he will have the last laugh later that year, beating Schumacher in the final race of the season to become the first – and so far only – Canadian to win the Formula One World Championship.[5] With the racing done, the fans swarm home the way they came, and the site will lie dormant for a year.

Rear-View Mirror

The demise of the CASC closed a significant chapter in the development of Canadian sports car racing and rallying, but as the vignettes above clearly show, it was not the end of the sport itself. Yet it was not quite the future that the CASC's founders had set out to create either. They had believed that they could raise Canadian auto sport from its amateur roots to world-class status without commercial exploitation. They had not imagined that business eventually would *own* the sport and would turn it into a commodity, sidelining – and ultimately killing – the CASC in the process. They also had envisioned the future of the sport as a continuum from amateur to professional competition; what they got was 'two solitudes': the sport and the spectacle. They coexist, but follow different trajectories that rarely intersect.

The irony is that this was not imposed from outside by greedy promoters or huge, faceless multi-national corporations. Indeed, the latter had to be coaxed into supporting the sport, and only a few, such as the tobacco companies and the breweries, have sustained a long-term commitment. Rather, it was the recreational enthusiasts themselves who professionalized and commercialized Canadian sports car competition. This transformation was driven by the dialectic of individual and technological competitiveness inherent to the sport. Those racers who wanted to be the best had to have the best: good tracks, professional training, and better cars. The latter, in particular, required a greater and on-going investment, since racing technology was changing constantly. Few racers could afford to keep pace out of their own pockets. Of course, many of the 'movers and shakers' driving this trend were business-men themselves – the auto sport entrepreneurs who founded the CRDA. But their original intent was to raise the standards of competition and to keep it affordable. Cost recovery, not profit, drove them to seek corporate sponsors, thereby opening the door to a significant change in the nature of the sport.

To achieve their goals, the entrepreneur-enthusiasts envisioned a different purpose for sports car racing. If it was to pay for itself, the sport could not survive on self-gratification alone. It would have to entertain an audience and promote the sponsors' products. Neither one could be satisfied through recreational club-based racing, which never would provide 'world class' entertainment and draw an audience large enough to make major sponsor support worthwhile. Thus, the goals of the aspiring pros and the potential sponsors converged. From that point on, racing developed along parallel but separate paths: recreational and career.

The career path today looks dramatically different from its counterpart fifty years ago. In the late 1970s, William Boddy and Brian Laban blamed the creation of the World Driver's Championship for the 'circus' atmosphere of Formula One, which drew attention away from the technical quality of the cars and onto the drivers. But F1 has been transformed further by television, which has made celebrities out of its top drivers. Just as in NASCAR and Indy Car racing, it has evolved into a culture of hero worship that lionizes the 'one vital, essential man.'[6]

Of course, this culture is not peculiar to auto sport; the cult of the male hero has long been central to sport. But what Garry Whannel calls the 'tabloidization' of televised sport allowed TV to take this phenomenon to another level. It turns sports stars into 'larger than life' characters – even *caricatures* – in events and stories that take on a kind of 'soap opera'-quality life of their own. The triumphs, flaws, and failures of sports superstars are now mythologized and scrutinized with the thoroughness and carelessness once reserved only for movie stars. TV is also central to their commodification. It is the principal vehicle by which the commercial forces that drive professional sports – and the players themselves – can franchise their fame. And just as in other pro sports, top-rank auto racing shamelessly promotes itself through iconography as well as 'fame by association' with the rich and famous. Actors and rock stars may know little about auto racing, but they understand the mutual promotional benefits of 'being seen' at such events, because it is celebrity more than competition that draws the crowds to the spectacle that is top professional racing. Indeed, the racing is almost secondary.[7]

Yet TV is not entirely to blame, since it cannot be separated from the market imperatives that drive and shape the sport. It only makes good business sense to take the event *to* the consumers in the cities and via TV, using a street track once a year. And so, many 'real' race tracks became irrelevant white elephants, while others were built or modified not just for safety and bigger crowds, but with an eye to making them better suited to TV's broadcast requirements.[8]

Technological change within the cars and the sport itself also imposed a degree of uniformity on top-rank competition. Light carbon-fibre bodies allow the cars to go faster and are safer for the drivers because they diffuse impact energy by breaking up during high-speed crashes. However, the price of performance and safety has been a more delicate racing car that cannot survive more than the slightest contact with another car or an off-track spin. Since both the rules and the technical complexity of the cars preclude most repairs, the effect on races has been to rapidly deplete the ranks of competitors, often on the first lap. Computers integral to the F1 and Indy cars' engines and other on-board systems are linked by radio telemetry to the crew in the pits. This allows them to monitor performance and fuel consumption and thus to plan pit stops with a high degree of precision.[9] The racer still makes tactical decisions on the track, but communications and computers allow the team bosses to manage races *strategically*. The downside to this is that the cars are vulnerable to a whole new array of computer-related 'gremlins' and failures.

The result has been a certain 'homogenization' of F1 racing. The races now may be more suitable for TV, but they are less exciting for the drivers and spectators. The limited passing opportunities on many tracks and strategic management of races (including for a time 'team orders' that favoured 'star' drivers over their teammates) has introduced an element of predictability to Formula One that risks audience boredom. Some races degenerate into being little more than a high-speed 'parade.'[10]

To compensate for this potentially dull *macro* spectacle, television has given the viewer a more exciting *micro* view of the race. At the track, the cars and drivers may be little more than a colourful blur beyond fencing and concrete. But in-car video cameras, some even mounted on the driver's helmet, transcend those barriers and take chair-bound viewers into the car, allowing them vicariously to share the visceral thrill of racing. This has reconnected the enthusiast with an activity that technology and cost have otherwise made inaccessible.[11]

Whether or not this TV coverage actually boosts the sales of beer, tobacco, or any other product, or re-casts the image of a city, one thing is abundantly clear. From the promoters' and sponsors' perspectives, if a major network covers a race, then the TV ad revenues mean that, except for their visual impact and marketing potential, the presence of an on-site paying audience is almost unnecessary.

But step out of the limelight, away from the hustle and the 'circus' that is F1 and Indy Car racing, and what do you find? The Pennfield race seems to suggest that the amateur level of sports car competition has come full circle in fifty years. Today, just as in the 1950s, it is club- and region-based; there are only a small number of clubs and at most a few thousand active members, concentrated mainly in Ontario and Quebec. The sport is volunteer-run, and is organized and regulated to ensure fairness and safety. It remains predominantly, but not exclusively, a male subculture, and only a few women continue to challenge that hegemony. And, for the most part, fun is still the primary purpose of competition at this level.

The CASC's successor – ASN Canada FIA – performs most of the same functions of its predecessor: it sanctions all auto sport events in Canada except for stock car and drag racing; it regulates and insures the sport for safety; licenses officials, competitors, pro racing schools, and tracks; resolves disputes; and represents Canadian auto sport on the various FIA commissions. The regions are represented at the AGM, and ASN supports them with revenue from the big international races. And its leadership includes some familiar names: Roger Peart, Paul Cooke, and Barry Morton.[12]

Just as in its early years, the amateur level of the sport is concentrated in Quebec and Ontario. The single 'national' racing championship – a revived series now called the Honda Civic Championship series – runs only in those provinces. Likewise, the national rally championship is mostly an eastern series; in 2005 three of its six events were held in Quebec, one in Ontario, and two in the West.[13] Except in the West, competitors or series rarely cross regional/provincial boundaries. The 2004 national auto slalom championship event at Sanair drew 101 entries from eastern Canada and New England and only one from the West.[14] Club rallies are mostly of the navex format. Forty years on, Mosport remains Canada's premier 'real' race track. But airport racing has not disappeared entirely. In fact, Gimli is still used regularly for club and regional racing, and the North Alberta Sports Car Club has raced at the former RCAF Namao base (Edmonton) since the mid-1990s.[15] And so, while history may not repeat itself, familiar themes endure.

The echoes of the past, however, dissipate upon closer scrutiny. The amateur level is fragmented into five self-governing regions, wholly independent of each other.[16] ASN Canada FIA is a non-profit business, not a federation of clubs and regions. While the region presidents sit on its advisory committee and can provide input, they have no voting privileges as they once had within the always fractious but roughly democratic CASC. Nor is there any guarantee that the ASN will act on their suggestions; it *dictates* the rules, from the top down. Concerned primarily with the major professional events – the Grand Prix and the CART races – and the national championship series, it leaves amateur auto sport largely to run itself. Moreover, pro rallying is run by a separate body – CARS – that sits on the ASN governing board. Thus, today there is no single national body that binds auto sport together as the CASC, however imperfectly, once did.

While they remain in the minority, many more women participate in auto sport today and some non-Canadians have excelled in the international pro ranks. In 2005 Danica Patrick became the first woman to lead the Indy 500, where she finished fourth overall.[17] Canadian women have not reached that level quite yet. Tiina Larsen and Elaine Willis won Formula 2000 championships in the 1990s, while Kathryn Teasdale of Toronto was the first Canadian woman to hold an international racing licence. She moved up rapidly from Formula 2000 to the Player's/GM and the Firestone Indy Lights series (the Indy Car 'junior league,' where she was the only woman). By the end of the 1990s, however, her racing career was 'on hold.'[18]

At that time, Marybeth Harrison from British Columbia had come up through go-karts, racing schools, and the ProFormance Toyota racing series to capture the 1998 Canadian Formula Racing Drivers Association championship. Two years later she moved up to the SCCA Trans-Am series, driving a Camaro. In 2003 she won the GT1 class in the Canadian GT championships. Despite being a skilled racer and a savvy businesswoman, she found it difficult to raise sufficient sponsor funding to compete full-time, and thus did not rise as high in racing as Teasdale did.[19]

But for a serious traffic accident that ended her career prematurely, Ashley Taws of Toronto might have surpassed both Harrison and Teasdale. Starting in go-karts in 1993 at age nine, she won several championships, then graduated to a Formula 1200 race car at sixteen. She came third in the CASC Ontario Region F1200 championship in her first season (2000) and was second overall the next year, before jumping to the national Formula Ford championship, where in 2002 at age eighteen she tied for third overall. Taws raced a few times after her accident, but lost her sponsor.[20]

All of these women benefited from the professionalization of Canadian racing driver training. But the experiences of Teasdale and Harrison suggest that one thing has not changed; it is still hard for women to attract racing sponsors. Consequently, it is that much harder for them to prove their skills and worth and thus to move up to the pro levels. The sports car subculture still lags behind the wider Canadian society in terms of gender balance; inclusiveness is not yet equality.

The sports car subculture has outgrown its British roots and become thoroughly Canadian in character, that is to say multicultural.

Nowhere is this more apparent than in the cars used for competition. The familiar British makes of the 1950s – Austin-Healey, Jaguar, MG, and Triumph – now appear only at vintage meets. Amateur auto sport features mostly German and Japanese cars; VW is the only hold-over from the earlier era.

Of course, the mere fact that the Grand Prix and CART Champ Car races take place in Canada at all – and that Canadian drivers are among their stars – represents the most obvious, fundamental difference between the past and the present. It is ironic, however, that while most of the world-class races (such as the Champ Car events) run on temporary street courses, it is the amateurs who have largely inherited the very tracks that they built to attract the top-rank races. That top-rank racing turned its back on these fine circuits is stark testimony to the 'power of the purse.'

In any case, not all of those tracks succumbed to auto-sport market pressures. Westwood – Canada's first purpose-built track – has been swallowed up by the BC lower mainland's vast suburban sprawl. Where MGs, Minis, Porsches, and Ferraris did battle for three decades, children now ride their bikes through a subdivision, while their parents play golf at the nearby country club. Only a handful of local street names – Lotus, Lancia, Firestone, Paddock, Carousel, and Deer's Leap – evoke a different era that the current residents can scarcely imagine.[21]

Many of the purpose-built circuits still currently in use, such as Mission Raceway in British Columbia and Race City Motorsport Park in Calgary, are extensions of drag strips and stock car ovals. This reflects the new reality; these are the growth sectors of Canadian auto sport, and a natural extension of their success and popularity south of the border.[22] Stock car and drag racing draw the crowds and sponsor dollars that keep these tracks afloat. If it weren't for those events, many sports/sedan, formula, and vintage car hobby racers probably would have no place to race at all.

The same processes that professionalized and commercialized racing also occurred in rallying. It was the rallyists themselves – or at least some of them – who set out to change their sport from TSD to stage rallies. Their intent was to make rallying more like racing, by emphasizing speed, power, and driving skill over navigation, in a sense more 'brawn over brain.' As with racing, as rallying became more rigorous and specialized, it became more expensive, requiring corporate sponsorship of teams, events, and series. And so, pro rally cars are ablaze with sponsor logos, and the national rally championship, which consists solely of stage rallies, is sponsored and televised, and the events draw an on-site audience. The newest of these is the (non-championship) Targa Newfoundland, a week-long 2200-km stage rally that attracts entries from around the world and large crowds of local spectators. Launched in 2002, it is probably the most innovative and successful addition to Canadian rallying since the Shell 4000. Once 'the thinking man's auto sport,' exciting only to its participants, rallying has become an *entertainment spectacle*.[23]

But the comparison with racing is not exact. Stage rallying cannot be divorced completely from its club-based navex roots, which provide pro rallying with its recruiting base and its training ground. Moreover, for Canadian rallyists, it has not provided a self-supporting professional career path similar to racing's. While stage rallies have attracted the sponsors, audiences, and TV coverage that TSD rallies never could, it is not clear that entertainment and promotion could ever be their primary purpose. Compared to pro racing, rallying is a lesser spectacle.

The Grand Prix and the CART Champ Car series still come to Canada, but their futures are uncertain. The decade-long conflict with the Indy Racing League has taken its toll on CART's team ranks and sponsors. Paul Tracy finally won the championship in 2003, but until the very start of the 2004 season it was unclear whether there *would* be another season. The Molson Indy Vancouver ran for the last time in 2004, replaced by a new race in Edmonton. Furthermore, in 1997 the Canadian government had passed legislation banning tobacco advertising at sporting events; for auto racing the law came into force in 2003. And so, after more than forty years as the major sponsor of Canadian racing, Player's withdrew from the sport. Tracy had to claim his victory without his sponsor's logo on his car.[24]

Even worse, as a consequence of the law, in 2003 the FIA cancelled the 2004 Canadian Grand Prix. Unlike NASCAR, which has made a successful transition to a new sponsor, F1 remains addicted to its tobacco advertising revenue like a smoker unable to quit. The Grand Prix was reinstated for 2004 only after the Quebec government agreed to make up the difference in funding to offset the absence of tobacco ad revenue for the race.[25] Thus, Canadian race fans got a reprieve and the opportunity to see Schumacher win yet again. But the long-term future of the Grand Prix remained precarious until May 2006, when Formula One renewed the Canadian event for five more years.[26]

258   The Chequered Past

After several disastrous seasons, Jacques Villeneuve was let go by British American Racing, the team he had created. Sidelined for most of 2004, he was picked up by the Sauber team, but his performance in the 2005 season prompted F1 chief Bernie Ecclestone to assert that Villeneuve had 'lost his motivation.'[27] He finished 14th overall in 2005, but in the opening stages of the 2006 season he appeared to be faring better. Canadians still had a 'local hero' to cheer in Formula One, but not for long.

What, then – if anything – does this history of sports car competition in Canada tells us about Canadian values or culture? On the one hand, the sport seems representative of many changes in and features of post-1945 Canadian society. It was a by-product of the expanding post-war middle class, the growth of suburbia, and the 'car culture.' Blessed with discretionary income and leisure time, its participants embodied Canada's rising prosperity in the era of 'conspicuous consumption.' And when economic growth declined in the 1970s, the sport's fortunes sagged as well. The car culture itself symbolized the emergence of a society increasingly dominated by modern technology, a domain that initially belonged largely to men. Women joined the car and technological cultures in large numbers, but without the profile and power of men. In those respects, auto sport accurately reflected its wider setting. Likewise, it highlights the encroaching professionalization and the bureaucratization of social functions that Max Weber proclaimed as features of modern consumption-oriented societies.[28] The same process is visible in many other aspects of Canadian life, including other sports. Finally, in Canada's highly commodified lifestyle, TV – and now the Internet – has transformed sport into a 'pop culture' entertainment consumption spectacle. Ultimately, auto sport is now about power, promotion, and fame.

On the other hand, the overall participatory depth of sports car competition in Canada is minuscule in aggregate terms on a national scale, and only on a few occasions does it attract a large audience. This may reflect the sport's perceived risks or perhaps the fact that, unlike hockey, it was not 'invented' here. And until karting became a phenomenon in its own right in the 1970s, it lacked a 'little league' that could launch children on the path to the sport's top ranks. But what is likely more important, racing requires a significant financial commitment. In these respects, it probably has more in common with yacht racing and golf, both of which tend to be expensive and exclusive. And so, comparisons of auto racing with most stick-and-ball sports are probably inappropriate. The most accessible entry-level activity is autoslalom; any driver can enter with an ordinary car. But even that form requires organization and a sizeable space to be run safely. Thus, apart from illegal and dangerous 'street racing,' auto sport has no equivalent of a pickup game of ball hockey. And as Muriel Knap observed, professionalism so permeates even the amateur level that 'it's hard to have fun in motorsport anymore. It is so bloody serious.'[29]

Therefore, notwithstanding the best efforts of its founders, the amateur enthusiasts, their successors, and the superstars, auto sport has yet to generate a passion among Canadians to rival that displayed for hockey. For all of the reasons discussed in this book it may never do so. And so, across the competition spectrum from the hobby racer and navex rallyist to the career-pro elite drivers, it remains a small, self-contained subculture.

Nevertheless, the struggles over the ownership of sports car competition in Canada suggest that the differences between auto sport and other forms of sport may not be as great as sports historians have generally assumed. Most, if not all, competitive activities have been subject to and changed by the same influences that shaped auto sport: commercialism, media hype, and commodification. Whether in baseball, golf, soccer, or tennis, in salaried sports or the Olympics, events have been transformed into spectacles and competitors into celebrities. The battles over power and rewards between players, owners, teams, organizers, and promoters in auto sport are little different from those in baseball or hockey, where they emerged gradually. What the Canadian experience shows is that the very nature of auto sport – with its high speeds, high risks, and high costs – brought in commercialism and imposed a certain level of professionalism on *all* of its participants at a much earlier stage. This is merely one dimension of auto sport that begs for comparison with other sports. It opens the door to the opportunity to integrate the history of auto sport into sport history generally.

This brings us back to the Canadian Motorsport Hall of Fame. Launched with such style in 1993, it is now more than a decade old, but still struggling to define its role and its place. It has a temporary home at a specialty car dealership outside Toronto, but unlike its hockey counterpart, where names like Rocket Richard and Wayne Gretzky confer upon it the status of a national shrine, the Motorsport Hall of Fame remains largely unknown to most Canadians. Whether it ever will find a special place in their hearts remains to be seen. In the meantime, for those who gave something of themselves to Canadian auto sport and who found it rewarding in whatever fashion, this book stands as a testament to what they achieved in the sport's first half-century. It shows that sports car competition in Canada has a fascinating past fully deserving of a place in Canadian sports history. Whether it has a future or not must be left to another book.

Notes

References that are listed in the select bibliography are given here in their short form only. All other references are given in full the first time they are used in each chapter.

Introduction

1 The author attended the event on 19 August 1993. See also Jim Kenzie, 'Canadian Auto Racing Greats Honoured,' *Toronto Star*, 20 August 1993. The list of nominees is printed in the program: 'The First Annual Gala Dinner in Support of Canada's Motorsport Hall of Fame.'
2 Robin Miller, 'Players Ban to Hit before Season Ends,' 11 July 2003, at www.espn.com; 'Tracy Wins First CART Driver's Crown,' *Globe and Mail*, 26 October 2003, at www.theglobeandmail.com.
3 Donaldson, *Gilles Villeneuve*, 160, 210, 230–1, 263, 303–5, 324.
4 Fred Hyde, 'Arleigh Pilkey: Old Man, Young Ideas,' *Canada Track and Traffic* [hereafter *CTT*], July 1962, 24–6.
5 Jeremy Shaw, 'Rain Can't Stop Montoya: Weather Provides Excitement for the 10th Annual Molson Indy Vancouver,' *Performance Racing News*, November 1999, 24–5; Lowes, *Indy Dreams and Urban Nightmares*, 14–16; and CBC TV coverage of the race.
6 Rendall, *Chequered Flag*, 344, 352; Assael, *Wide Open*, 10–11; Pillsbury, 'Stock Car Racing,' in Raitz, ed., *The Theater of Sport*, 283–6, 293.
7 Roberts and Olson, *Winning Is the Only Thing*, 70–3, 126, 145–50, 153–60, 201, 207, 209; John J. MacAloon, 'Are Olympic Athletes Professionals? Cultural Categories and Social Control in U.S. Sports,' in Staudohar and Mangan, eds., *The Business of Professional Sports*, 268.
8 Roberts and Olson, *Winning Is the Only Thing*, 113, 118–22, 128–9, 140–60,

262   Notes to pages 9–18

209. See also Joan M. Chandler, 'Sports as TV Product: A Case Study of Monday Night Football,' in Staudohar and Mangan, eds., *The Business of Professional Sports*; Susan Tyler Eastman and Timothy P. Meyer, 'Sports Programming: Scheduling, Costs, and Competition,' and Richard Gruneau, 'Making Spectacle: A Study of Television Sports Production,' in Wenner, ed., *Media, Sports, and Society*, 97–119, 134–54.
9   Post, *High Performance*, 255.
10 Assael, *Wide Open*, 11–12; Huff, *Insider's Guide to Stock Car Racing*, 54–7, 71; Tremayne and Hughes, *Concise Encyclopedia of Formula One*, 245; Rendall, *Chequered Flag*, 326–7, 352–3; Grange, 'Refuelling F1,' *EnRoute*, 2000, 46–8.
11 Colin Howell, 'Two Outs: Writing about Sport and Maritime History,' The W.S. MacNutt Lecture, University of New Brunswick, 27 October 1998. In his book *Blood, Sweat, and Cheers*, 7, 145, Howell goes further, asserting that sport history is 'contested territory' and thus essentially a work constantly in progress.
12 M. Adelman, 'Neglected Sports in American History: The Rise of Billiards in New York City,' *Canadian Journal of the History of Sport* 12 (1981), 28.
13 Dominick Graham, 'Stress Lines and Gray Areas: The Utility of the Historical Method to the Military Profession,' in David A. Charters, Marc Milner, and J. Brent Wilson, eds., *Military History and the Military Profession* (Westport, CT: Praeger, 1992), 148.

1. The Visionaries and Their Vision

1   Canadian Automobile Sport Committee [hereafter CASC], 'Minutes of Meeting held at the Frontenac Hotel, Kingston, Ontario, Canada,' 17 June 1951, bulletins file (CASC archive).
2   Interview with Jim Gunn by telephone, 16 June 1995; 'T & T Guest of the Month – Jim Gunn,' *CTT*, May 1966, 19.
3   Gunn interview; CASC, *1967 Yearbook*, 8, 10; CASC minutes, 8 March 1952, Annual General Meeting (AGM), 9 December 1961, minute books (CASC archive); 'Crest Designer Passes,' *CTT*, March 1964, 46.
4   'Guest of the Month – Jim Gunn'; CASC minutes, 27 February, 22 October, 3 December 1960; CASC, *Yearbook 1959*, 27–8, *Yearbook and Calendar 1964*, 17–19.
5   Rendall, *Chequered Flag*, 12–14, 28, 46–7; Garrett, *The Rally Go-Round*, 1–6.
6   Rendall, *Chequered Flag*, 16, 36, 44, 62–4; Lynch, Edgar, and Parravano, *American Sports Car Racing*, 10; Phillips, *American Motorsports*, 8.
7   Huff, *Insider's Guide to Stock Car Racing*, 5; Moorhouse, *Driving Ambitions*,

26–8; Rendall, *Chequered Flag*, 36; Lynch, Edgar, and Parravano, *American Sports Car Racing*, 9–14.
8 West, 'Automobile Racing,' *The Canadian Encyclopedia*, 1: 150. The first race is described in email, Tugwell to Brockington, 12 June 2000, author's copy. See McNamee, 'Memoirs,' unpublished typescript, March 1962, 9, CAA national office library, Ottawa; Durnford and Baechler, *Cars of Canada*, 20, 64, 213, 215; and Howell and Howell, *Sports and Games in Canadian Life*, 298–9. See also photographs PA-56260-64, 56354, and 57710, in Sports and Amusements, Racing, Automobiles, Photographic Section, National Archives, Ottawa.
9 John Charters, 'Montreal's Oldest Car Club Observes 25th Anniversary,' *Montreal Gazette*, 27 July 1962, 21, in John Charters's auto sport scrapbook, in author's possession.
10 Johnny Edmonson, 'History: Observations and a Few Memories: Part 1: Genesis,' *Small Torque* [BEMC club magazine], March 1966, typescript copy, 13, in private papers, Roy McLaughlin, Toronto.
11 Edmonson, 'Observations and a Few More Memories: Part 2,' *Small Torque*, April 1966, typescript copy, n.p.; Carol Phillips, 'The Heroes among Us,' *Canadian Biker Magazine*, July/August 1992, 23; and BEMC, 'Constitution,' August 1932, McLaughlin papers. See also 'British Empire Motor Club Has Long History,' *London Free Press*, 30 August 1966, 9.
12 'Statement to the Joint Executives of the British Empire Motor Club by a Group of Interested Members,' 14 May 1951, and Roy McLaughlin, 'Draft BEMC History,' n.d., unpublished handwritten ms, McLaughlin papers; Doug Ort, *The Western Ontario Sports Car Association History* (typescript, 1980), 1, club files (CASC archive).
13 Gunn interview; 'Statement to the Joint Executives.'
14 Noble, ed., *Jubilee Book of the Royal Automobile Club*, 21–2. See also Phillips, *American Motorsports*, 8, 10–12; Fleischman and Pearce, *Inside Sports NASCAR Racing*, 6; Moorhouse, *Driving Ambitions*, 39–42, 46–7; and Post, *High Performance*, 54–8.
15 Lynch, Edgar, and Parravano, *American Sports Car Racing*, 14.
16 Ibid, 14–17, 123; 'Proposed By-laws, Article 1,' *Sports Car Newsletter* [SCCA's official magazine], issue 35, 31 March 1958, 1, correspondence files (CASC archive). See also CASC minutes, 17 June 1951, 8 March 1952, November 1955, 26 May 1956, 3 May 1958.
17 CASC minutes, 17 June 1951.
18 CASC AGM minutes, 4 December 1971, appendix A.
19 Rendall, *Chequered Flag*, 168.
20 Pope, 'Amateurism and American Sports Culture,' 292–6; Metcalfe, 'The

Meaning of Amateurism,' 33, 36–7, 39–40, 44; Wayne Simpson, 'Hockey,' in Morrow, Keyes et al., eds., *A Concise History of Sport in Canada*, 180–1.

2. Canadian Club

1 Ort, *Western Ontario Sports Car Association History*, 1–2.
2 Sample minutes, 6 September 1956, LASC affiliation file (CASC archive).
3 Interview with Les Stanley, 20 August 1992.
4 Coffman, 'Canadian Racing Drivers' Association,' *Mosport Competition Magazine*, 1970, 44; CRDA, *Constitution*, as revised 11 November 1958, club files; entry for 11 February 1960, minute book 1, University of New Brunswick Sports Car Club, private papers, Alvin Ashfield, Fredericton, NB.
5 Coates, *Challenge*, 9.
6 CASC minutes, AGM, 3 December 1960.
7 Granatstein et al., *Twentieth Century Canada*, 302–5; Bothwell, Drummond, and English, *Canada Since 1945*, 15, 19–24, 30, 83; Owram, *Born at the Right Time*, 7–8, 17, 55–7; Collins, *You Had to Be There*, 132, 134; Watson, *National Pastimes*, 10. See also: Kelly and Godbey, *The Sociology of Leisure*, 89, 328–34, 418.
8 Occupational data on the people mentioned came from interviews, data in club files, and biographical notes in the enthusiast literature.
9 Owram, *Born at the Right Time*, 70.
10 Bothwell et al., *Canada Since 1945*, 54
11 Ibid., 142. See also *Facts and Figures of the Automotive Industry*, table 28; Collins, *You Had to Be There*, 112; Owram, *Born at the Right Time*, 71; John N. Jackson, *The Canadian City: Space, Form, Quality* (Toronto: McGraw-Hill Ryerson, 1973), 143; and Paul-André Linteau, 'Canadian Suburbanization in a North American Context: Does the Border Make a Difference?' *Journal of Urban History* 13 (May 1987), 259–60. Automobile historian James Flink coined the phrase 'car culture' in his book by that name.
12 Martha Radice, *Feeling Comfortable? The Urban Experience of Anglo-Montrealers* (Quebec: Les Presses de l'Université Laval, 2000), 52–5; James Lemon, *Toronto since 1918: An Illustrated History* (Toronto: James Lorimer, 1985), 134; and Robert R. Bonis, *The History of Scarborough* (Scarborough, ON: Scarborough Public Library, 1965), 241. See membership lists for the Lower Canada Motor Club and the British Automobile Racing Club–Ontario Centre (BARC-OC), club files.
13 Desmond Morton, *A Military History of Canada*, 3rd ed. (Toronto: McClelland and Stewart, 1992), 226; Bothwell et al., *Canada since 1945*, 23–4, 30; Collins, *You Had to Be There*, 105–6, 125; Post, *High Performance*, ix–xiii, xx, 4; Kelly

and Godbey, *The Sociology of Leisure*, 67; Larrabee and Meyerson, eds., *Mass Leisure*, 14, 163, 270, and 274–5; Brown, *Freewheeling*, 20–1, 71, 82, 107–9; Moorhouse, *Driving Ambitions*, 144, 152–8; Kraus, *Recreation and Leisure in Modern Society*, 5th ed., 63, 70, 72; and Barendse, 'Individualism, Technology, and Sport,' 18. On the character types attracted to sports car racing, see Johnsgard, 'Personality and Performance.'
14 Photo in Coates, *Challenge*, 8–9; quote from Taylor, *Modern Classics*, 141.
15 BEMC, 'Edenvale Sports Car Races – Results,' with steward's report and letter, 24 July 1954, club files; movie by John Charters, in author's possession. The author also attended this event.
16 BEMC, Canadian Winter Rally, results, 1956–8; SCCBC, 'Results of the Ladies Division Centennial Year Rally Held Sunday, January 26 1958,' club files.
17 *Facts and Figures of the Automotive Industry*, table 23; Rhys, *The Motor Industry*, 135.
18 Coates, *Challenge*, 7–8; Girdler, *American Road Race Specials*, 14; Lynch, Edgar, and Parravano, *American Sports Car Racing*, 13–14, 19.
19 Church, *Rise and Decline of the British Motor Industry*, 37–8, 378–82. Statistics Canada data on British car exports for 1960 provided to the author by historian Stephen T. Koerner.
20 Sobel, *Car Wars*, 26. See also Whisler, *At the End of the Road*, 195; and Lawrence, *A to Z of Sports Cars*. For the purposes of this study a limited-production sports car is one built in numbers of less than 10,000.
21 Whisler, *At the End of the Road*, 191, 193. Statistics on MG sales in Canada from: Society of Motor Manufacturers and Traders (UK), 'Canada – Registrations Total,' MSS 226/ST/3/0/CA/ 20, Modern Records Centre (MRC), University of Warwick, provided to the author by S.T. Koerner.
22 Smith, *Consumer Demand for Cars in the USA*, 9–10; Rae, *American Automobile Industry*, 99, 109–10, 119–21; Yates, *Decline and Fall of the American Automobile Industry*, 35–7, 89–90, 116, 124, and *passim*; and Sobel, *Car Wars*, 4–8, 10–13.
23 Gartman, *Auto Opium*, 180–1, 193; Auto Editors of Consumer Guide, *Corvette*, 38–9, 47–8, 51–2, 55–7, 59; Batchelor, Poole, and Robson, eds., *Great Book of Sports Cars*, 114–20; Von Dare, *Corvette Racers*, 18–19, 21–2, 28–30, 33–7; Whisler, *At the End of the Road*, 177, 194, 199; and 'List Prices of Imported and Compact Cars Sold in Canada,' *CTT*, August 1960, 51.
24 Noad, *VW Beetle in Motorsport*. See also BEMC, 'Fourth Annual Canadian Winter Rally Official Results,' and St Lawrence Automobile Club (St LAC), 'Results Thousand Islands Rally – October 9, 10, 11, 1959,' club files. No Alfas were among the 92 entries for the BEMC fifth annual races, June 1955, and only one was among the 122 entries for the 1956 SCC Trophy Races.

25 Canada's first Ferrari dealer operated out of his home in the author's then home town of Baie-d'Urfé, in the Montreal suburbs. See ad in *CTT*, January 1962, 11.
26 Whisler, *At the End of the Road*, 61. See also Stein, *British Sports Cars in America*, 54; Batchelor, Poole, and Robson, eds., *Great Book of Sports Cars*, 80; and, 'List Prices,' *CTT*, August 1960, 51.
27 Donald Baird, 'A Sprite for Competition,' unpublished typescript, 1959, author's copy.
28 Lionel Birnbom, 'Opening Meet at St. Eugene,' *CTT*, September 1959, 33.
29 Morrison, *Motor Racing: The Records*, 95–6, 117. See also Stein, *British Sports Cars in America*, 63; and Taylor, *Modern Classics*, 227–9. Canadian race results are from *CTT*, 1959–60.
30 Granatstein et al., *Twentieth Century Canada*, 308–9; Freda Hawkins, *Canada and Immigration: Public Policy and Public Concern*, 2nd ed. (Kingston and Montreal: McGill-Queen's University Press, 1988), table 6, p. 54; Alan C. Green, *Immigration and the Postwar Canadian Economy* (Toronto: Macmillan Canada, 1976), 50, 69, 73, 98, 101, 107–9, 113, 149, 163, 165, 167–8, 190–1, 197–8, 203–7, 220; and Locke interview, 20 August 1992.
31 Neale Johnson, written response to author's questionnaire, 6 April 1992; interviews with Peter Bone and Roger Peart, 6 November 1991 and 21 June 1990, respectively.
32 Interview with Francis Bradley, 23 October 1992, and his written answers to questionnaire. See also 'Francis Bradley,' *CTT*, December 1962, 19–20.
33 Interview with John Gallop, 2 May 1991. See also Coates, *Challenge*, 7; BARC-OC, affiliation form, 15 September 1960, club files. Biographical data from interviews, articles, questionnaires, and club records showed that 47 of 110 enthusiasts (43%) were from Britain and Europe.
34 Interview with Don Baird, 21 January 1990.
35 Stanley interview.
36 Interview with Art Moseley, 6 November 1991.
37 CASC minutes, 22 February 1958; 'Constitution of the Deutscher Automobile Club Incorporated,' affiliation file.
38 Moorhouse, *Driving Ambitions*, 22; Daniel R. Wolf, *The Rebels: A Brotherhood of Outlaw Bikers* (Toronto: University of Toronto Press, 1991), 342–8.
39 Locke interview.
40 Interview with Bill Brack, 21 June 1991. See also: Aurora Motor Sport Club, 'Constitution,' 1960, club files; and CRDA, *Beginners' Guide to Canadian Motor Racing*, 8, author's copy.
41 Interview with Alvin Ashfield, 7 May 2001.
42 Interview with Roy McLaughlin, 23 October 1992. See also Coates, *Chal-*

lenge, 9, 10; Moorhouse, *Driving Ambitions*, 26–42, 47, 57–8; Barendse, 'Individualism, Technology, and Sport,' 19; Corran, *History of the St. Catharines Motor Club*, 3; BARC-OC, 'Constitution,' 1958; Sudbury Sports and Light Car Club, 'Constitution,' ca. 1957; SCC, 'By-Laws 1959.'
43 Interview with Ross de St. Croix, 22 October 1992.
44 Bone interview.
45 Kraus, *Recreation and Leisure*, 63; Coates, *Challenge*, 8; Sobel, *Car Wars*, 45. Club badges are plainly visible in virtually any auto sport photograph from the 1950s.
46 De St. Croix interview; interview with Fred Motton, 2 May 1991. See also Haskell, 'Lexicon of the Sports and Racing Car Enthusiast'; Rodney Walkerly, 'A Glossary for Race Goers,' *CTT*, July 1962, 45–7, and August 1962, 46–8; Alexander and Block, *The Racer's Dictionary*, passim; Rueter, *The Sports Car Club*, 10, 12, 79–88. The social events are described in club newsletters: the *Exhaust* (SMCC), copies in private papers, John Gallop, Montreal; the *Broken Spoke* (Calgary Sports Car Club); *Small Torque* (BEMC); and *Wheel Chatter* (Northern Ontario Motorsport Association) in club files.
47 Hamilton Motor Sport Club and BARC-OC, CASC affiliation applications, 21 January 1956 and 15 September 1960, respectively, in affiliation files.
48 BEMC, *Spring Trophy Races 1950–2000*, commemorative program (2000), n.p., author's copy; BEMC, 'B.E.M.C. Sports Car Races Official Results,' *Fifth Annual Edenvale Sports Car Races*, 17–18 June 1955, club files. See also 'Reflections,' *CTT*, September 1959, 35; and 'Westwood Ho!' *CTT*, December 1960, 34.
49 BEMC, Canadian Winter Rally results, 1956; SCCBC, Centennial Year Rally results, 1958, and Ladies Rally results, 1959; St LAC, Thousand Islands Rally results, 1959; all in club files. SMCC, First Evening Rally, 7 June 1960, results in the *Exhaust*, vol. 17, no. 3 (June 1960), n.p.
50 Veronica Strong-Boag, 'Home Dreams: Women and the Suburban Experiment in Canada, 1945–60,' *Canadian Historical Review* 72 (1991), 473, 475–6, 479–81, 491. See also Collins, *You Had to Be There*, 158–61, 165, 167–9; Granatstein et al., *Twentieth Century Canada*, 280–1, 315, 359–60, 394; and Owram, *Born at the Right Time*, 12, 19, 22–4, 27–9, 130–1, 251–4.
51 Kleif and Faulkner, 'I'm No Athlete [but] I Can Make This Thing Dance!' 296–7, 310. See also Smith, *Consumer Demand for Cars*, 6; Wernick, *Promotional Culture*, 71–2, 74, 76–7; and Post, *High Performance*, 259, 278–83.
52 Interview with Jane Jenkins, 7 May 2001.
53 Patricia Malcolmson, 'Bobby Socks and de Beauvoir: Growing Up Female in the 1950s,' *Queen's Quarterly* 102 (1995), 557–61; Helen Lenskyj, 'Whose Sport? Whose Traditions? Canadian Women and Sport in the Twentieth

Century,' *International Journal of the History of Sport* 9 (1992), 141–50; Mary Keyes, 'Women and Sport,' in Morrow, Keyes, et al., eds., *Concise History of Sport in Canada*, 230–55; Don Morrow, 'Sweetheart Sport: Barbara Ann Scott and the Post World War II Image of the Female Athlete in Canada,' *Canadian Journal of the History of Sport* 18 (May 1989), 36–50; Howell, *Blood, Sweat, and Cheers*, 4, 112–21.

54 CASC minutes, 14 June 1952; *CASC Yearbook and Calendar 1961*, 7.

3. Run What Ya Brung

1 McLaughlin interview.
2 CASC, '1954 Calendar of Events,' in minutes, 27–28 February 1954; CASC, *1959 Yearbook*, 23–6.
3 'Steward's Report, Circuit Races – Sports and Production Cars, Edenvale Airport,' 26 June 1954, letter from Jim Gunn, 24 July 1954, and 'Edenvale Sports Car Races Results,' club files.
4 Locke interview.
5 McLaughlin interview.
6 *1954 Calendar of Events*; William N. Sullivan, 'Winnipeg's Dice-on-Ice,' *CTT*, May 1960, 23–4; Art Johnson, 'Muskoka Dice-on-Ice,' *CTT*, June 1960, 19–21.
7 Le Mans, Monza, and Nurburgring pre-dated the war and reopened thereafter: Saward, *World Atlas of Motor Racing*, 39, 63–4, 74–5. On the American circuits see: Valent, *Road Racing at Watkins Glen*, 14–16, 19–26; Lynch, Edgar, and Parravano, *American Sports Car Racing*, 30, 52–3.
8 CRDA, *Beginner's Guide to Canadian Motor Racing*, 5; Coates, *Challenge*, 11.
9 Coates, *Challenge*, 10; see also Bob Brockington, 'Where Have All the Race Tracks Gone?' typescript, 7 April 1995, in Race Tracks – Canada and USA binder (CASC archive); and William N. Sullivan, 'Manitoba Racing Scene' and 'Racing in Manitoba,' *CTT*, December 1959, 30–1, and November 1960, 48–9, respectively.
10 Coates, *Challenge*, 12–13.
11 'Is Professional Motor Sport Here to Stay?' *CTT*, September 1959, 31.
12 Quotes from Ralph Zbarsky, 'Memories of a Great Adventure: Westwood Motorsport Park,' *Sporting Classics*, May/June 1991, 28–9; and SCCBC, '*Special Notice – Important*,' 31 December 1957, SCCBC file, club files. Emphasis in original.
13 'Track Building Western Style,' *CTT*, September 1959, 28; Zbarsky, 'Memories of a Great Adventure,' 28–9; SCCBC, '*Special Notice*,' and 'The Sports Car Club of British Columbia, 6% 10-year Mortgage Debentures, 1st Issue, Dated February 15, 1958,' SCCBC file.

14 Track map [1974] attached to memorandum re 'Closing of Westwood Motorsport Park' (1990), SCCBC file; Zbarsky, 'Memories of a Great Adventure,' 29; quote from interview with Jim Maddin, 20 March 1993.
15 SCCBC notice, 23 March 1959, '*A Special and Urgent Message to All Club Members,*' 15 July 1959.
16 SCCBC, 'Westwood Grand Opening,' and 'Results of Westwood Opening July 26, 1959,' in notice to members, 12 August 1959, SCCBC file; Bill Barford, 'Westwood Opens with a Bang,' *CTT*, October 1959, 32–4. The number of entries is an estimate based on the official results and event report.
17 CASC, '1954 Calendar of Events,' and *Yearbook 1959*, 23–6.
18 Interview with John Gallop, 2 May 1991.
19 Rueter, *The Sports Car Club*, 21–5. See also Thomas Barker, 'Rally Roots,' *Autosport Canada*, March 1981, 16–19; 'Amendments and Additions to RAC General Competition Rules – Rallies and Trials,' in CASC minutes, 27–28 February 1954, minute books.
20 Radosta, *Complete Guide to Auto Racing*, 155.
21 Morell, 'Rallying,' *New Brunswick* 1 (1976), 16, quoting Jack McIrvine, ed., *The Sports Motor Car Club Rally School Manual 'How to Rally'* (Montreal: SMCC, 1969), 8, in Ashfield papers.
22 Frank W. King, 'The Social Rally,' in 'Amendments and Additions'; Ort, *Western Ontario Sports Car Association History*, 12, 23; CSCC, *Broken Spoke* 2, January 1960, 3, Prairie Region files, 1960–1 box; and Rueter, *The Sports Car Club*, 82–3.
23 McIrvine, *'How to Rally,'* 6, 12, 16–26, 32–6, 39–44, 46–7; Bud Mackley, 'Navigation Rallies' in 'Amendments and Additions.'
24 Lower Canada Motor Club, *Triskaidekaphobia 1959*, *Instructions* and *Results*, 13 November 1959, private papers, John Gallop, Montreal.
25 Interview with John Charters, 4 May 1991.
26 Stanley interview; and letter, Stanley to author, 21 February 2006.
27 Letter, Stanley to author, 4 December 1991.
28 Ross Brander, 'Endurance Rally,' in 'Amendments and Additions.'
29 Bone interview.
30 Garrett, *The Rally Go-Round*, 2–3, 6, 10, 21–3, 26, 35–6; Rendall, *The Power and the Glory*, 162–4; Radosta, *Complete Guide to Auto Racing*, 155; Barker, 'Rally Roots,' 17–18.
31 CASC minutes, 4 August 1951, 29 November 1952, 21 February and 14–15 November 1953, 27–28 February and 6–7 November 1954, 26–27 February 1955.
32 CASC minutes, 10–11 September 1955, 26 May and 24 November 1956, 23 February, 25 May, 7 September, and 17 November 1957.

270   Notes to pages 48–54

33 CASC minutes, 22 February, 6 December 1958; 'Results – Thousand Islands Rally, 9–11 October 1959,' Gallop papers.
34 Brander, 'Endurance Rally.'
35 CASC, *1957 Calendar of Events*, 10; P.E. Goodall, 'Calgary Loop Rally,' *CTT*, February 1960, 30; Geoff Howe and Al Trenear, 'Loop Rally IV 1960,' *Broken Spoke*, November 1960, 16–17.
36 Canadair Automobile Club, *1956 Quebec Rally Route Books, Official Rules and Regulations, Supplementary Regulations*, in private papers, Les Stanley, Montreal; letter, Stanley to author, 21 February 2006.
37 Eve White, 'The Canadian Winter Rally,' *CTT*, February 1966, 34; Barker, 'Rally Roots,' 19; BEMC, *International Canadian Winter Rally Rules and Regulations 1961*.
38 White, 'Canadian Winter Rally,' 34, 36; Brent Davies, 'Canadian Winter Rally: Twenty One Years of High Adventure,' *Driving*, January/February 1974, 10; BEMC, *Rules and Regulations, 1962*, 2, Gallop papers.
39 'Drifting Closes Roads; Auto Rally Disrupted, 50 Vehicles Fail to Finish Sport Event,' *Globe and Mail*, 15 February 1960, in scrapbook, private papers, John Charters. See also Roger Proulx, 'Canadian Winter Rally,' *Road and Track*, June 1960, 73, 75; Bill Wordham, '1960 Winter Rally – Tough, Tougher, Toughest,' *CTT*, April 1960, 18–20; White, 'Canadian Winter Rally,' 34; BEMC, *Rules and Regulations 1961*, 9, 13, 16 and *Rules and Regulations 1962*, 3, 4, 8–10.
40 BEMC, *Fourth Annual Canadian Winter Rally Official Results* (1956) and *Rules and Regulations 1958*, club files; Barker, 'Rally Roots,' 19.
41 SMCC, *Fourth Annual Rallye Des Neiges Rules and Regulations March 2–3 1962*, 1, and, Tony Wilson, '1961 Rallye Des Neiges,' *Exhaust*, March 1961, 7, both in Gallop papers.
42 SMCC, *Rallye Des Neiges, Supplementary Rules and Regulations, 1960*, 1, and *Rallye Des Neiges 1961 Rules and Regulations*, 1, in Gallop papers.
43 Robin Edwardes, 'Rallying in Canada,' unpublished typescript, ca. 1990, 1, author's copy. See also CASC minutes, 10–11 September 1955, 23 February 1957, 22 February 1958; CASC, *Calendar and Yearbook 1958*, 26.
44 CASC minutes, 17 November 1957, 6 December 1958, 23 January 1960 [1959 AGM]; 'Bulletin no. 11 – Rallies, 25 July 1960,' bulletins file; CASC, *National Yearbook 1972*, 170.
45 Radosta, *Complete Guide to Auto Racing*, 160–3. See also, Ort, *History*, 7–8; Corran, *History*, 20; Ottawa Light Car Club memorandum, 'Terminology,' submitted to CASC, 27 May 1954, CASC Regulations file; CASC, *1958 Yearbook*, 31.
46 *Jubilee Book of the Royal Automobile Club*, 83–4.
47 CASC, *1954 Calendar*; *1958 Yearbook*, 24, 31; Ort, *Western Ontario Sports Car*

Association History, 7; Hockley Valley hill climbs, results 1955–6, club files; Tony Swain, 'Behind the Scenes of "The Groeneveld,"' and 'Groeneveld 1960,' *Broken Spoke,* November 1960, 4–5, 22–4; Roger Proulx, 'Slithering Up Rattlesnake,' *CTT,* September 1959, 41–2; Bruce Young, 'Up and at 'Em,' *CTT,* July 1960, 32–3; J.E. Langton-Adams, 'Westbank Hill Climb,' *CTT,* 1960, 24.

48 CASC, *1954 Calendar of Events*; 'Coming Events,' 'Club News,' and event reports in *CTT*, 1960.

4. Rules and Regs

1 Callwood, 'The Fatal Fascination of Car Racing,' 26.
2 'The 13th of August' and 'Reflections by Allison,' *CTT*, October 1960, 20, 31, 50.
3 Callwood, 'Fatal Fascination,' 26–7, 63–8.
4 Lionel Birnbom, 'Opening Meet at St. Eugene,' *CTT*, September 1959, 33.
5 Chimits and Granet, *Williams Renault Formula One Motor Racing Book*, 43.
6 CASC, *1961 Yearbook*, 3; CASC minutes, 14 June 1952.
7 CASC, *1961 Yearbook*, 11–12. Howell, *Blood, Sweat, and Cheers*, 144, cites Bruce Kidd's work, which stresses Ontario's role as builder of a sporting nation.
8 Interview with Art Moseley, 6 November 1991.
9 McLaughlin interview. See also 'British Empire Motor Club has Long History,' *London Free Press*, 30 August 1966, copy in McLaughlin papers.
10 Moseley interview; Coates, *Challenge*, 85, 87–8; CASC minutes, 1959 and 1960 AGMs, 23 January and AGM 3 December 1960, respectively.
11 CASC minutes, 1951–61.
12 CASC minutes, 26–7 November 1955.
13 'Draft by-laws,' 19 December 1955, affiliation files.
14 CASC minutes, 8 September 1956; 'Basic Plan for a National-regional Organization of C.A.S.C.,' 25 May 1957, region files.
15 CASC minutes, 25 May 1957, 22 February, 3 May, and 6 December 1958, including 'Rules of Procedure' annex to February 1958 minutes.
16 Interview with Bob Randall, 2 March 1992.
17 CASC minutes, 26–27 November 1955, 8 September 1956; Letter, H.W. Punshon, General Secretary, CASC, to Dave Brown, Honorary Secretary, SCCBC, 13 January 1957, club files.
18 Letter, Punshon to Robert G. Sayle, Secretary, SCCBC, 2 March 1958.
19 Letter, Sayle to Punshon, 13 March 1958; CASC, minutes, 3 May 1958.
20 International Conference of Northwest Sports Car Clubs, 'Charter' [1957],

272 Notes to pages 62–9

with letter, Michael Balfe, President SCCBC, to Punshon, 16 July 1958; Sayle to Punshon, 13 May 1958.
21 Punshon to Sayle, 24 May 1958.
22 CASC minutes, 8 March 1952, 21 February 1953, 23 February and 25 May 1957.
23 CASC minutes, 22 February and 6 December 1958, 13 June 1959, 23 January and 6 May 1960.
24 CASC, *1958 Yearbook*, 9, and *1961 Yearbook*, 29–31; Alan B. Sands, *CASC Bulletin no. 6 Proposed Race Classifications*, 18 July 1960, bulletins file. There was no class A until 1962.
25 CASC minutes, 26–27 February 1955; CASC, *1959 Yearbook*, 14; interview with Bill Brack, 21 June 1991.
26 'B.E.M.C. 8th Annual Sports Car Races July 19, 1958 Provisional Results,' *Small Torque*, August 1958, 10–12; Sports Car Club of Saskatchewan, *Davidson Race Results*, 22 May 1960, 1960–1 Prairie Region file, 1960–1 file box. ICNSCC, *Competition Regulations 1958*, 4–5, 19–20, with letter, Balfe to Punshon, 16 July 1958; 'Results of O'Keefe Grand Prix, May 8 1960,' in SCCBC newsletter, 31 May 1960, club files.
27 *CASC Bulletin no. 6*.
28 Coates, *Challenge*, 11.
29 CASC minutes, 6–7 November 1954, 26–27 February 1955, 8 September 1956, 3 May 1958, 23 January 1960 (1959 AGM); CASC *Bulletin* 2–60, 15 May 1960; CASC, *1961 Yearbook and Calendar*, 34–5, 37–8. See also 'Race Driver Safety,' display in Transportation Exhibit, National Museum of American History, Washington, DC (author's notes, December 1997); SCCA, *Sports Car Newsletter*, no. 35 (31 March 1958), n.p., correspondence files.
30 'The 13th of August' and 'Reflections by Allison,' 20, 31, 50. Five days after Pope's crash the CASC banned tonneau covers.
31 *Ottawa Citizen*, 29 August 1955.
32 RAC, 'Organization of Race Meetings and Speed Events' [1954], regulations file; CASC minutes, 8 March 1952, 'Rules Governing Control of Race Events,' Appendix 1 to minutes, 10–11 September 1955, Competition Briefs file (1950s), and minutes, 25 February 1956. See also photos in Valent, *Road Racing at Watkins Glen*, 22–3, 32, 34–5; and Lynch, Edgar, and Parravano, *American Sports Car Racing*, 52, 53, 60.
33 CASC minutes, 3 May 1958; CRCA, 'Constitution' [1960], affiliation file; CRCA, *Twenty Years to Sport* [ca. 1979], n.p.
34 CASC minutes, 8 September 1956, 17 November 1957; CASC, *1958 Yearbook*, 12.
35 CASC, minutes, 13 June 1959.

36 CASC minutes, 8 March 1952, 21 February and 14–15 November 1953, 27–28 February 1954; Competition Chairman, 'A Revised System for Issuing Competition Licences,' October 1956. See also Competition Chairman, memo to all CASC member clubs, 8 August 1956.
37 CASC minutes, 22 February, 3 May, and 6 December 1958, 6 May and 3 December 1960.
38 CASC minutes, 3 May and 6 December 1958 (AGM); *1961 Yearbook*, 53–4; Tom Gilmour, 'CRDA Report,' *CTT*, February 1960, 29; Bill Wordham, 'CRDA Spring Driving School,' *CTT*, July 1960, 37–8; interview with John Charters, 4 May 1991.

5. Powershift

1 Quoted in 'Is Professional Motorsport Here to Stay?' *CTT*, September 1959, 31.
2 The description of the starting grid scene is derived from the cover photo of the *CTT*, issue cited above. See also Coates, *Challenge*, 17; Bill Wordham, 'Carling 300,' *CTT*, July 1960, 26–9; CRDA, *The Carling 300 Official Race Programme, Harewood Acres, May 27–28, 1960*, 1960–1 box; Tom Gilmour, 'CRDA News,' *CTT*, August 1961, 53, explained the race costs.
3 Lynch, Edgar, and Parravano, *American Sports Car Racing*, 125–9; Friedman, *Pro Sports Car Racing*, 7–11; Radosta, *Complete Guide to Auto Racing*, 169, 171; Moss, *A Turn at the Wheel*, 25, 91, 135.
4 Lynch, Edgar, and Parravano, *American Sports Car Racing*, 129, 155; Friedman, *Pro Sports Car Racing*, 57–8; Radosta, *Complete Guide to Auto Racing*, 121–2; SCCA, 'News from Club Office,' 31 July 1961, with letter of Hugo P. Rush (executive director, SCCA) to James H. Gunn (president, CASC), 2 August 1961, US correspondence file, 1960–1 box.
5 Bill Coffman, 'Canadian Racing Drivers Association,' *Mosport Competition Magazine* 2 (13–14 June 1970), 44.
6 Ibid.; Bradley interview.
7 Moorhouse, *Driving Ambitions*, 22–3.
8 Coates, *Challenge*, 47, 48. See also 'One Man's Point of View,' *CTT*, 1959–60; CASC, *1961 Yearbook*, 10. Fergusson Motors–sponsored teams are listed in BEMC, *Indian Summer Trophy Races Official Program, Edenvale, Oct. 1, 1955*, and '1957 International Canadian Winter Rally Provisional Results.'
9 The information on these individuals and companies is based on race and rally programs and records from the mid–1950s to early 1960s and on ads in *Canada Track and Traffic*. See also CASC, *1968 Yearbook*, 10; and 'Guest of the Month – Peter Broeker,' *CTT*, October 1966, 17.

10 'Guest of the Month – Bob Hanna,' *CTT*, February 1968, 26; 'Interview: CASC Executive Director Bob Hanna Replies to His Critics,' *CTT*, February 1971, 19–21; Coates, *Challenge*, 11; CASC, AGM minutes, 4 November 1968.
11 Rendall, *Chequered Flag*, 12–20; Huff, *The Insider's Guide to Stock Car Racing*, 8; Assael, *Wide Open*, 16; Radosta, *Complete Guide to Auto Racing*, 194–5. The original slogan has been slightly altered in Grange, 'Win on Sunday ... Sell on Monday,' *Report on Business Magazine*, August 2001, 36–40, but the meaning is the same.
12 Callwood, 'The Fatal Fascination of Car Racing,' 65. Leavens's victory was probably a class win – not overall. An Austin A–40 did not win the 1958 Canadian Winter Rally, but might have taken a class win the next year.
13 Interview with Martin Chenhall, 24 October 1992. On the many car-market variables see Smith, *Consumer Demand for Cars in the USA*, 15, 17, 21–5, 27–8, 78. On the uncertain links between advertising, sponsorship, sales, and profits, see Gratton and Taylor, *Sport and Recreation*, 222–3.
14 Quote attributed to Gilles Villeneuve.
15 CRDA, *Constitution of the Canadian Racing Drivers Club*, Toronto, Ontario, Canada, as revised 11 November 1958, folio 321, affiliations file. This version did not differ in any significant way from the original, drafted 15 February 1958.
16 Tom Gilmour, 'CRDA Report,' *CTT*, September 1959, 46.
17 'Is Professional Motorsport Here to Stay?' *CTT*, September 1959, 30.
18 Ibid., 31.
19 Ibid.
20 Ibid.
21 'Professional Motorsport,' 34.
22 Ibid.
23 Ibid.
24 Staff article, 'CT&T Interviews Stirling Moss,' *CTT*, September 1959, 27.
25 R.C. Evis, 'CASC News,' *CTT*, October 1959, 41.
26 Ibid.
27 Ibid.
28 BEMC, *Indian Summer Trophy Races Official Programme Edenvale Oct. 1 1955*, and *Rules and Regulations Indian Summer Trophy Races, 1958*; CRDA, *Carling 300 Official Race Programme*; Roger Proulx, 'Sundown Grand Prix Report,' *CTT*, October 1959, 12–16.
29 Bill Wordham, 'Carling 300' and 'O'Keefe Sundown Grand Prix,' *CTT*, July 1960, 26–9, and November 1960, 7, 9, 11, 54; 'CT&T Interviews Stirling Moss,' *CTT*, September 1959, 37.
30 'Letters to the Editor,' *CTT*, October 1959, 7.

31 'Letters to the Editor,' *CTT*, December 1959, 7.
32 CASC minutes, 29–30 May 1954, 17 November 1957. See also ads in CASC, *Calendar of Events* (1956–8 issues) for car dealers, distributors, and parts suppliers.
33 'President's Address A.G.M. Dec. 9/61,' *Bulletin (Special)*, 12 January 1962, bulletins file.
34 Gratton and Taylor, *Sport and Recreation*, 223, 227, 229.
35 CASC minutes, 17 June 1961.

6. Behind the Wheel

1 Wright, 'The History of Motor Sport [in Canada],' reminiscences dictated to tape, May 1992; sent to author.
2 Ibid. See also 'Guest of the Month – Milton Wright,' *CTT*, November 1966, 19.
3 CASC, *1959 Yearbook*, 27–8; *1964 Yearbook*, 17–19.
4 CASC minutes, 3 December 1960 (AGM), 11 November 1961, 9 December 1961 (AGM), 27 January 1962, 19 January, 23 March 1963; and D.P. Stewart, 'General Manager's Western Trip,' 5 March 1962. See also Bill Wordham, 'Sports Car Black Sheep May Enter CASC Fold,' *Toronto Telegram*, 12 December 1961, club files; and *CASC 1963 Yearbook and Calendar*, 18.
5 CASC, 'General Manager's Report,' minutes, 23 March 1963.
6 J.H. Gunn and D.P. Stewart, 'Report on Visit to Proposed Atlantic Region, C.A.S.C., July 5–7, 1963'; CASC minutes, 24 August 1963; *1964 Yearbook*, 19; *1967 Yearbook*, 19.
7 CASC, *Yearbooks*, 1961–7. See also Luc, *L'histoire du Sport Automobile au Québec*, 16, 18, 41, 47, 51; interview with Roger Peart, 21 June 1990.
8 Paul-André Linteau et al., *Quebec since 1930*, trans. Robert Chodos and Ellen Garmaise (Toronto: James Lorimer, 1991), 307–9, 337–40, 354–5; Anne Griffin, *Quebec: The Challenge of Independence* (London and Toronto: Fairleigh Dickinson University Press, 1984), 40–1; Kenneth McRoberts and Dale Posgate, *Quebec: Social Change and Political Crisis*, 2nd ed. (Toronto: McClelland and Stewart, 1980), 33–53, 70–7, 97, 101–3.
9 L.G. Rice, 'Quebec Region Report,' CASC, AGM minutes, 6 November 1965.
10 CASC minutes, 17 June 1951, 8 September 1956, 13 June 1959, 22 October and 3 December 1960; CASC, *Bulletin 64-28 C.A.S.C., R.A.C., and F.I.A.*, 4 May 1964, bulletins file; Royal Automobile Club (UK), minutes, Competition Committee, 11 November 1953, 11 May 1960, author's copies, courtesy of RAC Library, London.

11 CASC, 'Objects of a Canadian Charter of Incorporation,' 29 May 1954, minute file books; R. Lafleur, 'Letters Patent Incorporating Canadian Automobile Sport Clubs,' 9 January 1964, CASC-FIA affiliation file.
12 CASC, *By-laws Canadian Automobile Sport Clubs* (Toronto: CASC, 1964), CASC-FIA affiliation file.
13 CASC minutes, 6 May 1960; CASC *Yearbooks* (1962–4).
14 CASC, *1961 Yearbook*, 15. The creation of the NCB did not change these powers.
15 CASC minutes, 13 June 1959, 23 January 1960 (1959 AGM), 9 December 1961 (AGM), 27 January 1962, 19 October 1963.
16 CASC minutes, National Competition Board, 14 January 1965, and National Committee, 7–8 May 1965; CASC, *Bulletin 65-13*, 25 May 1965.
17 Memo, D.P. Stewart to Members of the National Committee, 'Definition of Authority – Competitions,' 1 April 1965; *CASC Bulletins 65-14*, and *65-15*, both issued 25 May 1965; 'Motorsport Enthusiasts – Track and Traffic Talk,' *CTT*, November 1965, 3.
18 Memo, Stewart to National Board of Directors, 'Organizational Education Bulletin,' 18 August 1966.
19 CASC, 'Draft for Bulletin.' Meeting minutes later indicate that the CASC did circulate it.
20 CASC, 'President's Message 1966,' appendix to AGM minutes, 5 November 1966.
21 Rod Campbell, 'Last Lap at St. Eugene,' *CTT*, November 1963, 40.
22 This list is based on race reports from the various regions in *CTT*, 1960–6.
23 'Paul Cooke Clicks in 221–mile Endurance Test,' *CTT*, September 1964, 28. See also *CTT*, August 1966, 37, and July 1967, 46; LASC, *Great Lakes Trophy Races Official Program*, 1966; Kerr, 'Comstock Racing Team,' 8; and Luc, *L'histoire du Sport Automobile au Québec*, 18, 151, 156, 162–3.
24 Sports Car Club of Saskatchewan, 'Davidson Race Results, May 22, 1960,' Prairie Region file, 1960–1 file box, CASC; Dieter Rahn, 'Big Day at Bon Accord,' *CTT*, March 1962, 38; Paul Melin, 'Pike Lake Ice Races,' *CTT*, April 1962, 39. Johnston, *Sports Car Road Racing in Western Canada* does not mention any women racers.
25 See race results in SCCBC, 'Newsletter,' 31 May 1960 and 12 July 1961, club files, CASC. See also J.E. Langton-Adams, 'Westwood Lidlifter,' *CTT*, June 1962, 29. In October 1960, McColl was second in the H production championship standings.
26 Interview with Hilda Randall, 2 March 1992. See also 'Guest of the Month – John Randall, A Family Effort,' *CTT*, September 1967, 15.
27 Karen Hall was shown leading the B Sedan class in the BC Region Champi-

onship: *CTT*, July 1968, 55. Hall and McColl had both competed in a 'powder puff' race in 1961.
28 Diana Carter, 'Motorsport History – Personal Background,' unpublished typescript, September 2004, 2, copy sent by email, Carter to author, 14 September 2004.
29 Ibid., 3.
30 'Miss Diana Carter,' in CASC, *Press Information Fact Sheet # 2 Personality Profiles*, 2, 1965 CASC minutes file.
31 'Canadian Touring Trophy Race,' *CTT*, September 1965, 30.
32 Rod Campbell, 'St. Eugene: The Flying Dutchman Scuttles the Fleet,' *CTT*, August 1962, 26–7; 'G.V.C.C. Grand National Races,' *CTT*, August 1963, 56.
33 Batchelor, Poole, and Robson, *Great Book of Sports Cars*, 310, 370–1, 386, 388–9; Whisler, *At the End of the Road*, 62–4, 68–9, 232–40, 244.
34 Of the thirty-four entries in the 1967 Le Circuit four-hour endurance race, twenty-one were American sports sedans, and they took the first three places at the finish: 'Le Circuit/4 Hours,' *CTT*, July 1967, 46.
35 Hall, *Fearsome Fords*, 9, 50–1; and Huntington, *American Supercar*, 28–9.
36 'Ford Returns to Competition,' *CTT*, March 1963, 29.
37 Huntington, *American Supercar*, 101–2; Smith, *Consumer Demand for Cars*, 24. A selection of Ford's 'Total Performance' and Mustang ads can be seen in Frumkin, *Muscle Car Mania*, 61–3, 65, 67.
38 Hall, *Fearsome Fords*, 137–8. Iacocca and Novak, *Iacocca*, 64–75, and Lacey, *Ford*, 536–8, offer different versions of the Mustang's marketing. See also: Pritchard, *Ford vs. Ferrari*, 45–6; and White, *The Automobile Industry*, 17.
39 Wyss, *Shelby's Wildlife*, 17–31, 142–61; Huntington, *American Supercar*, 116.
40 Bochroch, *Trans-Am Racing*, 12–14, 46–9, 199; Friedman, *Trans-Am*, 7, 9, 23.
41 'T & T Guest of the Month: Peter Broeker,' *CTT*, October 1966, 17.
42 Hodges, *A–Z of Formula Racing Cars*, 64–6, 136–7, 143–5, 273; CASC, *1963 Yearbook*, 40–1. In 1961 Norm Namerow was asking $4000 for his used Elva FJ, a high price at the time. See ad in *CTT*, November 1961, 61.
43 Rod Campbell, 'Stebro Formula Junior,' *CTT*, November 1961, 40–1; Pete Chapman, 'Focus – Peter Broeker ... Not an Ordinary Man,' *Autosport Canada*, January 1981, 2. See also Hodges, *A–Z of Formula Racing Cars*, 236.
44 Interview with Tony Short, 15 April 1997.
45 Radosta, *Complete Guide to Auto Racing*, 145–6; *All About Formula Vee*; 'T & T Formula Vee Track Test,' *CTT*, January 1965, 39; 'The Vee Phenomenon,' *CTT*, February 1969, 15; *CASC Yearbook 1964*, 42–3; entry list, 'Race No. 1 – Formula Cars,' in *Programme 5th Canadian Grand Prix (1965)*; entry list, 'Thanksgiving Speed Weekend,' 'Formula Cars – Races 1, 2 & 8,' 'Novices – Race No. 7,' *Mosport Competition Magazine*, 1969, 13.

46 Interview with Horst Kroll, 21 August 1993; Dan Proudfoot, 'Personality: Horst Kroll,' *Canadian Motorsport Bulletin* [hereafter *CMB*] (February 1972), 33.
47 CASC, *Yearbook 1970*, 142; Frank Orr, 'Kelly's Cars,' *CTT*, December 1968, 40; Ken Schindler, 'Kelly: From Marville to Mosport,' *CMB*, September 1971, 26, 28.
48 Orr, 'Kelly's Cars,' 40.
49 Ibid., 41.
50 Ibid., 40; 'Aftermath,' *CMB*, October 1971, 35.

7. Trans-Canada

1 Interview, 13 August 1990.
2 Interview with John Charters, 3 May 1991. His recollections are supported by the accounts in 'Shell 4000,' *CTT* June 1962, 21–2; Bruce McCall, 'Shell 4000,' *Road and Track*, July 1962, 78; Bill Ivens, 'It Was No Paper Chase,' *Shell News*, April–May 1962, 28, 30; and 'Tense Moment for Local Team,' *Montreal Gazette*, 16 April 1962. Trant Jarman, 'Shell 4000 Rally,' *Car and Driver*, July 1962, 58, at http://Shell-4000-rally.org/1962 (site maintained by Marcel Chichak), names the mechanic, but identifies the wrong team car.
3 CASC minutes, 25 February 1956, 23 January 1960; Jim Gunn, 'The Book,' unpublished manuscript (no date), 7, at http://Shell-4000-rally.org/Book.pdf (original is in Canadian Motorsport Hall of Fame archives).
4 CASC minutes, 27 February 1960; Letter, Doug Wilson to Jim Gunn, 26 May 1960, general correspondence file, 1960.
5 CASC: minutes, 22 October 1960, 3 December 1960 (AGM), 15 April 1961; letter, BCITF to Lawrence Bateman and attached brief, 8 September 1960, Trans-Canada Rally file 1961, 1960–1 box; *1961 British Columbia International Trade Fair Car Rally April 30–May 6, 1961 Rules and Regulations*, 5 (author's copy); and Gunn interview.
6 'BCITF Cross-Canada Rally,' *CTT*, 1961, 17–22; *British Columbia International Trade Fair Car Rally Route Book* (author's copy); 'B.C.I.T.F. Car Rally, Steward's Report' and 'BCITF Car Rally Official Results,' 12 May 1961, both in CASC Trans-Canada Rally file; *Montreal Gazette*, 3 May 1961, in Charters scrapbook; Gunn, 'The Book,' 11–13.
7 'B.C.I.T.F. Car Rally, Steward's Report.'
8 'Second Trans-Canada Car Rally,' *CTT*, November 1961, 30. Interview with Peter Bone, 6 November 1991.
9 Bone interview.
10 Ibid.; 'T&T Guest of the Month – Jim Gunn,' *CTT*, May 1966, 19.

11 Bone interview.
12 BCITF, *1961 Rules and Regulations*, 7, 12, 16, 20–2; Staff report, 'BCITF Cross-Canada Rally,' *CTT*, June 1961, 18; BCITF, *Newsletter* 1, no. 6 (October 1960), Trans-Canada Rally file. The Shell logos are plainly visible in photographs of the cars.
13 'T&T Guest of the Month – Jim Gunn.'
14 Media coverage described in letter, Gunn (rally organizer for Shell 4000) to CASC Competition Committee, 11 February 1963. See also 'BCITF Car Rally Official Results'; rally reports in *Montreal Gazette*, 3, 4, 6, and 8 May 1961, *Montreal Star*, 27 April 1962, and the full-page Shell rally ad published just before the 1961 event. CBC Radio Montreal provided daily reports, and features on its auto sport program RPM twice during the rally: items and notes from 'Racing and Rallying' scrapbook, Charters papers. See also the ads in *CTT*, June and July 1961 issues, and in issues from later years.
15 'Second Trans-Canada Car Rally,' *CTT*, November 1961, 30; costs of 1962 event are in Gunn to CASC Competition Committee, 11 February 1963. See also Memo, Stewart to National Directors, 25 September 1966.
16 CASC, *Bulletin 65-23 C.A.C. 'Quebec Rally' – September 24–26, 1965* (5 August 1965).
17 Rendall, *Chequered Flag*, 12–13; Garrett, *The Rally Go-Round*, 21–3.
18 Robson, *A–Z of Works Rally Cars*, 5.
19 Ibid., 152–4; Garrett, *The Rally Go-Round*, 51–3.
20 Eve White, 'The Canadian Winter Rally,' *CTT*, February 1966, p. 34. See also BEMC, *1957 International Canadian Winter Rally Provisional Results*, BEMC file; and interviews with Stanley and Chelminski, 20 August 1992.
21 BEMC, *Provisional Results Ninth International Canadian Winter Rally*, BEMC file; 'Ninth Winter Rally,' *CTT*, April 1961, 20–3; 'B.C.I.T.F. Cross Canada Rally,' *CTT*, June 1961, 17, 22; 'Shell 4000,' *CTT*, June 1962, 16, 22.
22 See the list of entrants published in the newspapers, and the Studebaker Lark ads in *CTT*, July 1961, 6, and July 1962, 31. O'Neill quoted in Rod Campbell, 'Montreal Dateline,' *CTT*, March 1962, 44.
23 Robson, *A–Z of Works Rally Cars*, 133; O'Neill quoted in Jim VanVliet, 'Round the Bend,' *Montreal Gazette* (n.d. 1962).
24 Charters interview.
25 Van Vliet, 'Round the Bend.'
26 Ibid. The description of the team members is based on personal knowledge and photographs. It originally included Dave Pengally, but for reasons unknown he was replaced by Edwardes.
27 The team's event results are recorded in articles from the *Montreal Gazette*,

1962, in Charters scrapbook; and '10th Annual Canadian Winter Rally,' *CTT*, April 1962, 24. Edwardes quoted in interview.

28 CASC, *Bulletin #100 'Fidler Championship'* (1962 national rally championship results), 14 February 1963, bulletin files.

29 'Club News: SMCC Rallye Des Neiges,' *CTT*, May 1963, 57, 59; 'Shell 4000 Car Rally Official Results, 6 May 1963' (author's copy); CASC, *Bulletin 64-4 National Rally Championship for Automobile Manufacturers*, 14 January 1964, bulletin files. A photo of the Nordell/Maclean R-8 is included in Arthur Thompson, 'Monte Carlo Rally,' *CTT*, March 1963, 22–4. Bone quoted in interview.

30 Charters interview.

31 Edwardes interview.

32 Team changes and quotes from Charters and Edwardes interviews; National Rally Championship results from CASC bulletins.

33 Thompson, 'Monte Carlo Rally,' 24; 'Ford Returns to Competition,' *CTT*, March 1963, 29; Robson, *A–Z of Works Rally Cars*, 75–6; Hall, *Fearsome Fords, 1959–73*, 25–8; 'Shell 4000 Official Results 1963,' Charters papers.

34 Diana Carter, 'Shell 4000,' *CTT*, June 1966, 24–7.

35 '1964 Shell 4000 Rally Guide,' *CTT*, April 1964, 16; 'East-West Route for 4000,' *CTT*, December 1964, 5.

36 CASC, *1961 Yearbook*, 21–2. Johnny Campbell, 'WOSCA Auto-Mapic Marathon Scheduled for June 19,' *CTT*, July 1960, 44; Ted Langton-Adams, 'Columbian Canyon Rally,' *CTT*, August 1960, 23, 52; 'Club News East and West,' *CTT*, August 1961, 55, 58; Ort, *Western Ontario Sports Car Association History*, 49.

37 CASC minutes, 27 January 1962; CASC, *Bulletin #71 Proposed Rally Rule Changes*, 7 June 1962, *Bulletin #97 National Rally Championship for Automobile Manufacturers*, 10 January 1963; CASC, *1962 Yearbook*, 16–17, 92, and *1963 Yearbook*, 81, 87.

38 'Canadian Winter Rally,' *CTT*, April 1965, 23–4.

39 BEMC, *Canadian Winter Rally Rules and Regulations February 10, 11, 12, 1961*, 1, 1960–1 records box; '10th Annual Canadian Winter Rally,' *CTT*, April 1962, 24; 'Canadian Winter Rally', *CTT*, April 1965, 22.

40 'Editorial,' *Exhaust*, September 1961, 1.

41 Ibid. See also 'Quebec Rally,' *CTT*, November 1961, 59. Canadair Auto Club, *6th National Quebec Rally Instructions*, in Gallop papers.

42 'The President's Page,' *Exhaust*, September 1962, 5–6. See also letters, columns, and editorials in the May/June, July, and August 1962 issues.

43 'Editorial,' *Exhaust*, February 1962, 1; and Letter to the Editor, 21 April 1962, *Exhaust*, May/June 1962, 5.

44 BCITF, *Car Rally Route Book*; 'Shell "4000",' *CTT*, June 1962, 15, 18.

45 Gunn, 'The Book,' 27–8; McCall, 'Shell 400,' 77.
46 *1963 Shell 4000 Car Rally Route Book*, Charters papers; 'Shell 4000,' *CTT*, June 1963, 23. The first five cars accumulated fewer than 40 penalty points. Shell Oil Company of Canada, Ltd., *Press Release, Shell '4000' Latest News*, May 1963 (author's copy). See also 'Supplementary rules and regulations' in [Shell 4000] *Regulations* booklets for 1961–3 (author's copies).
47 Bone interview.
48 P.E. Goodhall, 'Loop Rally VI,' *CTT*, November 1962, 46–7.
49 '1964 Shell 4000 Rally Guide,' *CTT*, April 1964, 15–17; Diana Carter, '1964 Shell 4000 – A Shell-Shocked Survivor Recalls Some Highlights of the 1964 Shell Rally,' *CTT*, July 1964, 42.
50 Carter, 'A Shell-Shocked Survivor,' 42; Hall, *Fearsome Fords, 1959–73*, 27–8.
51 'Volvo Sweeps Shell 4000,' *CTT*, June 1964, 19.
52 Ibid., 18.
53 Bone interview.
54 Ibid.
55 '1965 Shell 4000 Rally,' *CTT*, April 1965, 33, 35; Phil Murray, 'Shell 4000 Rally,' *CTT*, June 1965, 24.
56 Diana Carter, 'Shell 4000,' *CTT*, June 1966, 24–7; CASC, 'Steward's Report Shell 4000 Car Rally, April 30th to May 6th 1966,' Shell 4000 file.
57 CASC, *Bulletin #66-9 National Rally Championship* (undated).
58 CASC, *Bulletin #66-34 National Rally Championship*, 26 July 1966.
59 Chris Allan, 'Shell 4000,' *CTT*, July 1968, 17–20.
60 *British Columbia Centennial Car Rally '71 Preliminary Information*; John Kerr, 'B.C. Centennial Rally,' *CTT*, August 1971, 32–4, 46.

8. Making Tracks

1 Staff Report, 'Player's 200,' *CTT*, August 1961, 20.
2 Ibid., 20–2; Coates, *Challenge*, 35.
3 McLaren, 'Mosport Park: 25 Years!' *Mosport Competition Magazine*, 1985, 10–11; Brockington, *Mosport International Raceway*, 23; 'Canadian Grand Prix,' *CTT*, November 1961, 14–18; Coates, *Challenge*, 85–8. The author attended both events.
4 'Player's 200,' *CTT*, July 1965, 19; *CTT*, reports on the Grand Prix, 1962–5.
5 McLaren, 'Mosport Park: 25 Years!' 9.
6 Coates, *Challenge*, 37, 40–1.
7 Ibid., 34; McLaren, 'Mosport Park: 25 Years!' 9; Wright, 'The History of Motor Sport.'
8 Moseley interview.

9 All three quotes are in Coates, *Challenge*, 36.
10 McLaren, Mosport Park: 25 Years!' 11.
11 McLaughlin interview; Dick Byatt, 'Now Is the Time,' *Small Torque*, November 1958, 5, McLaughlin papers.
12 Brockington, *Mosport International Raceway*, 18; *Mosport Park* (advertising prospectus) (Toronto: Mosport Limited, 1960) (author's copy); Mosport Limited, press release, 9 April 1960, McLaughlin papers; CASC minutes, 6 May 1960; McLaughlin interview.
13 C.A. Bunting, Secretary (BEMC) (circular letter), 29 April 1959, *Mosport Shareholders Newsletter* [1959], Bill Wordham, *Report on Mosport* (reprinted from the *Globe and Mail*), 11 April 1960, *Mosport Park* (advertising prospectus), Mosport Limited, *Annual Accounts*, 31 January 1961, all in McLaughlin papers; Staff report, 'Quo Vadis Mosport?' *CTT*, October 1960, 33; Brockington, *Mosport International Raceway*, 18.
14 Brockington, *Mosport International Raceway*, 18; Coates, *Challenge*, 37.
15 McLaren, 'Mosport Park: 25 Years!' 14.
16 'Controversy: Racing's Strange Paradox – Can Mosport be Saved?' *CTT*, January 1964, 23–4, 39; Brockington, *Mosport International Raceway*, 27, 32.
17 McLaughlin interview.
18 Frank Orr, 'The Fall and Rise of Mosport,' *CTT*, April 1971, 26.
19 Interview with Muriel Knap, 2 March 1990.
20 'Track and Traffic Talk: Mosport and CT&T,' *CTT*, February 1966, 3; Brockington, *Mosport International Raceway*, 32; McLaren, 'Mosport Park: 25 Years,' 22; McLaughlin interview.
21 Coates, *Challenge*, 12; Pierre Luc, *L'histoire du Sport Automobile au Québec*, 14, 16–18; Rod Campbell, 'Montreal Dateline,' *CTT*, August 1962, 26–7, 60.
22 Campbell, 'Montreal Dateline,' *CTT*, August 1962, 60, November 1962, 55, and February 1963, 40, and 'Races and Places – Last Lap at St. Eugene,' *CTT*, November 1963, 40; Coates, *Challenge*, 67; Luc, *L'histoire du Sport Automobile au Québec*, 51.
23 Interview with Lionel Birnbom, 22 April 2001; de St. Croix interview; Campbell, 'Montreal Dateline,' *CTT*, June 1962, 60; Luc, *L'histoire du Sport Automobile au Québec*, 51, 136–7; Coates, *Challenge*, 68.
24 Coates, *Challenge*, 68–70; Luc, *L'histoire du Sport Automobile au Québec*, 138–9; Sid Priddle, 'Major Track near Montreal,' *CTT*, July 1964, 41, and 'Le Circuit Mont Tremblant – St. Jovite,' *CTT*, August 1964, 25–6. Luc says that 172 investors pledged $1000 each.
25 Priddle, 'Le Circuit'; 'Laurentian Track Success Story,' *CTT*, November 1964, 31; Brockington, 'Le Circuit Mont Tremblant,' 32; 'Player's Quebec,'*CTT*,

November 1964, 32–3; Coates, *Challenge*, 71–2; Luc, *L'histoire du Sport Automobile au Québec*, 249.
26 'A Track is Born,' *CTT*, September 1964, 18–19. See also Brockington, 'Le Circuit,' 33; Saward, *The World Atlas of Motor Racing*, 167; 'Track and Traffic Talk – Business Brainpower,' *CTT*, September 1964.
27 De St. Croix interview.
28 Coates, *Challenge*, 81; CASC minutes, 4 December 1966, 14–15, 20 January, 18–19 February, and 27–8 May 1967, and memo, Milton J. Wright to National Board of Directors, May 1967.
29 'Pinetree Races,' and Paul Melin, 'Prairie Dateline,' *CTT*, December 1961, 49–50, 55.
30 Coates, *Challenge*, 64–5; '$1.3 Million Motor Sport Park for Edmonton,' *CTT*, March 1965; Johnston, *Sports Car Racing in Western Canada*, 130.
31 Bob Brockington, *Where Have All the Race Tracks Gone?* (typescript, 7 April 1995), in 'Race Tracks – Canada and USA' binder, CASC; 'Harewood Acres, Jarvis Ontario – Evolution of a Race Track,' in LASC, *Great Lake Trophy Race May 6–7, 1966 Official Souvenir* [*Programme*], in private papers, Lewis Mackenzie; 'Harewood Paving Fund,' *CTT*, May 1964, 39; 'Races & Places – Progress at Harewood,' *CTT*, July 1965, 47.
32 Coates, *Challenge*, 33–4, 36; Moseley interview.

9. Reach for the Top

1 Staff report, 'Charles Rathgeb: The Man Behind Sadler Cars,' *CTT*, September 1961, 17.
2 Clark Wallace, 'Peter Ryan: Young Man in a Hurry,' *Montreal Star Weekend Magazine*, November 1960, 5, and Jim Van Vliet, 'Ryan Dies in Hospital in France,' *Montreal Gazette*, 3 July 1962, in Peter Ryan papers, Canadian Motorsport Hall of Fame (CMHF), Toronto; Kerr, 'Peter Ryan,' 25; Callwood, 'The Fatal Fascination of Car Racing,' 68.
3 Callwood, 'The Fatal Fascination of Car Racing,' 27
4 Van Vliet, 'Ryan Dies in Hospital' and 'CRDA Championship Races – St. Eugene,' *CTT*, September 1960, 34; Kerr, 'Peter Ryan,' 25.
5 Wallace, 'Young Man in a Hurry,' 5.
6 Ibid.; Bill Wordham, 'O'Keefe Sundown Grand Prix,' *CTT*, November 1960, 7, 54.
7 Kerr, 'Peter Ryan,' 25–6; Frank M. Blunk, 'Ryan Takes Vanderbilt Cup Race at Bridgehampton,' *New York Times*, 7 August 1961, in Ryan papers.
8 Interview with Charles Rathgeb, 21 June 1990. See also Kerr, 'Comstock Racing Team,' *Sporting Classics*, 1991, 9.

9 'Curriculum Vitae for Charles Irwin Rathgeb,' author's copy, compliments of Mr Rathgeb. See also 'The Man behind Sadler Cars,' 17.
10 Rathgeb interview; 'The Man Behind Sadler Cars,' 16–17.
11 'The Man Behind Sadler Cars,' 17–18; Kerr, 'Comstock Racing Team,' 9, and 'Peter Ryan,' 26; Donald Grey, 'Ryan Wins Canadian Grand Prix,' *Globe and Mail*, 2 October 1961; Staff report, 'Canadian Grand Prix,' *CTT*, November 1961, 14–18. See also Allan, 'The Sports Car Spectacle of the Year,' *Canadian Sport* (1961), 8–10, and Eve White, 'First Canadian Grand Prix,' *Motor News Week*, 13 October 1961, 4–5, both in Ryan papers.
12 Kerr, 'Peter Ryan,' 26.
13 S.C. Kaback (Weathermatic Corporation) to Peter Ryan, 9 August 1961, Ryan papers; 'Ryan to Join Team Lotus,' *Sports Car Graphic*, February 1962, 7.
14 Kerr, 'Peter Ryan,' 26–7.
15 Canadian Press, 'Canada's Peter Ryan Building His Own Race Car,' 3 May 1962; 'Ryan Ready,' undated May 1962; and 'Ex-Ski Star Peter Ryan Dies after Reims Crash,' *Montreal Star*, 3 July 1962, all in Ryan papers.
16 Grossman and Whitmore quoted in Associated Press, 'Canadian Driver – Ryan Finishes Race Digging in Sand,' *Montreal Star*, 25 June 1962, Ryan papers.
17 Callwood, 'The Fatal Fascination of Car Racing,' 68.
18 Kerr, 'Peter Ryan,' 27; Jim Van Vliet, 'Round the Bend,' *Montreal Gazette*, n.d.; Eddie MacCabe, 'Sportspiel,' *Ottawa Journal*, 3 July 1962; *Montreal Gazette*, 3 July 1962, all in Ryan papers.
19 Mike Twite, 'Heimrath Has a Hard Time but Proves a Point,' *CTT*, June 1962, 38–9.
20 Pete Chapman, 'Focus – Peter Broeker ... Not an Ordinary Man,' *Auto Sport Canada*, January 1981, 2.
21 Interview with Bill Sadler, 20 October 1990.
22 'The Man and the Car – Chuck Rathgeb,' *CTT*, March 1963, 19.
23 Ibid.
24 Rathgeb interview.
25 CNE auto show photos, and 'Chuck Rathgeb,' Ford of Canada News Services (press release), 8 May 1964, in 'Comstock Racing' scrapbook, Charles Rathgeb, private papers, Toronto; 'Canadian Grand Prix,' *CTT*, November 1963, 15–18. Kerr, 'Comstock Racing Team,' 10, incorrectly identifies the race as the Player's 200. Wietzes placed sixth and Miles seventh overall.
26 Rathgeb interview.
27 Photos of the Cooper Ford are in the 'Comstock Racing' scrapbook. Interview with Eppie Wietzes, 20 August 1993.

Notes to pages 139–44 285

28 'Ridenour Races to Westwood Win,' *CTT*, July 1964, 22–3; CASC, *Bulletin 64-59 1964 National Racing Championship*, 7 October 1964, bulletins binder.
29 Kerr, 'Comstock Racing Team,' 10; 'Paul Cooke Clicks in 221-mile Endurance Test,' *CTT*, September 1964, 28.
30 Interview with Craig Fisher, 22 October 1992.
31 'Sundown Grand Prix,' *CTT*, October 1965, 63–5; Rathgeb interview.
32 Pritchard, *Ford vs. Ferrari*, 45.
33 Ibid., 47–57, 60–7, 73–4, 87–93. See also Spain, *GT40*, 199, 236. Fisher quoted in Kerr, 'Comstock Racing Team,' 10–11.
34 Eve White, 'Comstock Hopes Die with McLean,' *Toronto Star*, 27 March 1966, in 'Comstock Racing' scrapbook; Wietzes quoted in Kerr, 'Comstock Racing Team,' 11; Rathgeb interview.
35 Both quotes from Coates, *Challenge*, 56–7. See also Philip Murray, 'Profile of a New Canadian Champion,' *CTT*, January 1966, 34–5; 'Track and Traffic Talk,' *CTT*, May 1966, 3; 'A Token of Respect,' in LASC, *Great Lakes Trophy Race Official Souvenir [Program] May 6–7 1966*, club files.
36 Coates, *Challenge*, 57.
37 Kerr, 'Comstock Racing Team,' 11.
38 Fisher interview.
39 CASC, *1968 Yearbook*, 89, *Bulletin 66-50 Final Standings National Racing Championship 'Over 2 Litre Award – First 10,'* and *Bulletin 67-35 1967 National Racing Championship*, 17 August 1967; Lyons, *Can-Am*, 245–9; Bochroch, *Trans-Am Racing 1966–85*, 14, 20, 29–30, 44; Spain, *GT40*, 148–50, 156–7; Pritchard, *Ford vs. Ferrari*, 161; Rathgeb interview.
40 CASC, *Bulletin #66 from Milt J. Wright Racing Competition Chairman Re: National Racing Championship*, 23 April 1962, bulletins file.
41 CASC, *Rules and Regulations for the 1962 Season National Racing Championship Player's Challenge Trophy* (n.d. 1962).
42 CASC, *Bulletin # 84 from P. R. Lighthall, National Scorer re: 1962 National Racing Championship*, 24 September 1962, bulletins file. Bradley's sponsor was the R.M. Hollingshead Corporation. Heimrath's sponsor was Eglinton-Caledonia Motors, a Porsche dealership.
43 CASC, *1963 Yearbook*, 95, and *Bulletin #126 from Peter R. Lighthall, Secretary re: 1963 National Racing Championship*, 21 October 1963, bulletins file; 'Player's Pacific, Westwood/1963,' *CTT*, June 1963, 55.
44 CASC, *1964 Yearbook*, 92, and *Bulletin 64-59 from G. R. Shelton, Chairman, National Competition Board, re: 1964 National Racing Championship Final Standings*, 7 October 1964, bulletins file; 'Player's Quebec – Mexican Ace Wins in Laurentians,' *CTT*, November 1964, 32–3.

45 CASC, NCB meeting minutes, 14 October 1964; CASC, AGM minutes, 20 November 1964.
46 CASC, *Bulletin #65-29 from Peter W. Bone, Race Chairman, National Competition Board, re: 1965 National Racing Championship – Final Results*, 21 September 1965; 'Player's 200,' *CTT*, July 1965, 19–22.
47 G.H. Grant, 'Suggested Plan Re: National Championship Races,' presented to NCB meeting, 13 January 1965; 'Committee Reports: Report of the Racing Rules and Regulations Committee,' AGM minutes, 6 November 1965; CASC, *1966 Yearbook*, 114–15.
48 CASC, *Bulletin #66-50 from Peter W. Bone, Race Chairman, NCB Re: Final Standings National Racing Championship* (n.d.); 'Races and Places,' *CTT*, November 1966, 47. Brown actually beat Chapman in the under-two-litre category, but had placed high only in races that his rival did not finish, allowing Chapman to take the overall victory.
49 The ideal – keeping one's cool and staying focused under extreme stress – is explored in the case of American astronauts in Tom Wolfe, *The Right Stuff* (New York: Bantam, 1980), 16–34.
50 Luc, *L'histoire du Sport Automobile au Québec*, 18.
51 Chapman quoted in 'U.S. Grand Prix,' *CTT*, November 1961, 44–5.
52 Peter Bone, 'Racing School Report,' *CTT*, March 1962, 32–5, 46.
53 In 1961 Al Pease offered his race-proven MGA Twin-cam – a competitive car at that time – for sale with eight spare wheels *and* a trailer for $2000. Four years later, Peter Lerch was asking *$18,000* for his moderately competitive Lotus 19–based McKee Ford special, albeit with a truck to haul and service the car. See 'Classified,' *CTT*, January 1961, 57, 59, and August 1965, 51.
54 Murray, 'Profile of a New Canadian Champion.'

10. The Cutting Edge

1 Lyons, *Can-Am*, 7.
2 Girdler, *American Road Race Specials*, 5–17.
3 Corran, 'History of the St. Catharines Motor Club,' appendix, 'The Sadlers,' 1, author's copy courtesy of Mr Corran. See also Tim Lucas, 'Canada's Home-Made Racers Are Burning up the Tracks,' *Toronto Daily Star*, 30 June 1960, in private papers, Bill Sadler, Scottsdale, Arizona.
4 Interview with Bill Sadler, 20 October 1990; Corran, 'History of the St. Catharines Motor Club,' appendix, 2. See also Rich Clee, 'The Sport in Canada,' *Road and Track*, December 1961, 82.
5 Clee, 'The Sport in Canada'; Lucas, 'Canada's Home-Made Racers'; Edward

Monroe, 'Buzz Bomb,' *Hot Rod Magazine*, April 1956, 30–1; Edward Monroe, 'The Sadler Chevrolet Special,' *Sports Car Illustrated*, February 1958, 32–4, 37, 50, 52, 54, 56; Larry Perks, 'Canadian Auto Maker Invading U.S. Market,' *Financial Post*, 13 February 1960, Sadler papers.
6 Sadler interview; Clee, 'The Sport in Canada,' 83; and John Christy, 'Crises Dices,' *Sports Car Illustrated*, March 1959, 25, in Sadler papers.
7 Lucas, 'Canada's Home-Made Racers.'
8 Interview with Dave Greenblatt, 7 June 1993; and letter, Greenblatt to author, 17 March 2006.
9 Letter, Greenblatt to author.
10 Perks, 'Canadian Auto Maker'; *The Sadler Canada Formula Junior Single Seat Racing Car* (sales prospectus and specifications) (The Sadler Car Company, ca. 1959), and 'Chevy Single-Seaters,' *Car and Driver*, April 1961, 46, both in Sadler papers.
11 'Chevy Single-Seaters.'
12 Ibid.
13 'Watkins Glen,' *CTT*, December 1960, 24; Walter St. John, 'Technical Report: Canadian Challenger Sadler Mk.V,' *Sports Car Graphic*, November 1961, 22; and Des Corran, 'Clutch Chatter,' *St. Catharines Standard*, February 1978, all in Sadler papers.
14 St. John, 'Technical Report,' 22–5, 80–1; Roger Proulx, 'Comstock-Sadler Mk V,' *Road and Track*, November 1961, 89. See also Girdler, *American Road Race Specials*, 120–1.
15 Proulx, 'Comstock-Sadler Mk V,' 88.
16 'Track Testing the Sadler,' *CTT*, June 1961, 24. See also Coates, *Challenge*, 27–8, 30.
17 Corran, 'Clutch Chatter.'
18 Dan Proudfoot, 'Homage to a Dream Car,' *Toronto Sunday Sun*, 1 August 1982, in Sadler papers.
19 Corran, 'History of the St. Catharines Motor Club,' appendix 'The Sadlers,' 5; William George Sadler, 'Curriculum Vitae,' enclosed in letter, Sadler to author, 1 November 1989.
20 Rendall, *The Power Game*, 27, 39–41, 69–70, 74–5; Grant, *500-c.c. Racing*, 68–75; Nye, *History of the Grand Prix Car, 1966–91*, 11, 15; and Proudfoot, 'Homage' (emphasis added).
21 Boddy and Laban, *History of Motor Racing*, 142–3, 152 (photos); Sakkis, *Anatomy and Development of the Indy Car*, 21; Girdler, *American Road Race Specials*, 189–90.
22 Girdler, *American Road Race Specials*, 122.
23 Greenblatt interview; letter, Greenblatt to author.

24 Ibid. See also 'Indian Summer Trophy Races,' *CTT*, October 1962, 50–1; and 'Canadian Grand Prix,' *CTT*, November 1962, 21–3.
25 Girdler, *American Road Race Specials*, 128.
26 'The Fejer Brothers,' *CTT*, March 1972, 25–6; Lyons, *Can-Am*, 245, 247–8.
27 Rendall, *Chequered Flag*, 212; Rhys, *The Motor Industry*, 25, 60–2, 216, 389; Whisler, *At the End of the Road*, 123–5; Couldwell, *Formula One: Made in Britain*, 3–4, 32, 98.
28 Rendall, *The Power Game*, 90–1; Lawrence, *A to Z of Sports Cars*, 192.
29 Coates, *Challenge*, 111.
30 Ibid.
31 Ibid., 109.
32 Lyons, *Can-Am*, 18–25, 29.
33 Coates, *Challenge*, 97–8.
34 Ibid., 99.
35 CASC, Directors' meeting minutes, 19 January 1963.
36 CASC, 'Competition Chairman's Report,' National Committee meeting minutes, 11 April 1964.
37 'President's Report,' in AGM minutes, 20 November 1964.
38 CASC, National Committee meeting minutes, 7–8 May, 2 October 1965, and 'President's Report,' AGM minutes, 6 November 1965.
39 CASC, 'Competition Chairman's Report,' in National Committee meeting minutes, 15 January 1966; *Press Information: Johnson Wax to Sponsor Championship Race Series*, [original dated 14 April] 1966, bulletins file.
40 Lyons, *Can-Am*, 30, 32.
41 Both quotes from Coates, *Challenge*, 99.
42 Lyons, *Can-Am*, 32.
43 Ibid., 34, 245.
44 Ibid., 245; 'Can-Am Trophy Races: Canadian Grand Prix, Mosport Sept. 24,' *CTT*, November 1966, 24–6.
45 'President's Message 1966,' AGM minutes, 5 November 1966. See also 1964 and 1965 president's reports.
46 Mosley interview.

11. Coming of Age

1 Donaldson, *Grand Prix of Canada*, 8.
2 Coates, *Challenge*, 118.
3 Donaldson, *Grand Prix of Canada*, 9–14; Brockington, *Mosport International Raceway*, 35.

4 Coates, *Challenge*, 113.
5 CASC minutes, 19 January and 25 May 1963; 11 April, 8 August, and 14 October 1964.
6 CASC, 'President's Report,' AGM minutes, 20 November 1964; 'Track and Traffic Talk – Formula One Racing in Canada,' *CTT*, September 1965, 3.
7 Donaldson, *Grand Prix of Canada*, 9; Coates, *Challenge*, 112–13.
8 CASC minutes, 25 September 1966; Coates, *Challenge*, 113; Wright, 'The History of Motor Sport' (audio).
9 CASC minutes, 25 September 1966.
10 Moseley interview.
11 Memo, Stewart to National Board of Directors, 'Direct Affiliation with F.I.A.,' 19 May 1967, and letter, Stewart to Delamont, 30 May 1967, with Delamont's marginal replies, FIA affiliation file; CASC minutes, 27–8 May, 30 June–1 July and 13–15 October 1967.
12 CASC, 'President's Report – 1967 Convention, 100 Years for Canada – 16 for C.A.S.C.,' AGM minutes, 4 November 1967.
13 Statistics collated from Donaldson, *Grand Prix of Canada*, passim.
14 All of the following Can-Am statistics are from Lyons, *Can-Am*, 70–1, 245–66. See also David B. Lamb, 'Roger McCaig Racing,' *CTT*, May 1972, 29–32, 40; and Connie Goudinoff, 'About People,' *Auto Sport Canada* [*ASC*], March 1977, 12, 36 (article on Saville-Peck).
15 Orr, *George Eaton*, 9–14, 118–24, 143–9.
16 Ibid., 118, 143–9; 'Interview: George Eaton Talks about his 1971 Racing Plans,' *CTT*, April 197), 42–3.
17 Orr, *George Eaton*, 13.
18 Interview with Bill Brack, 21 June 1991.
19 Lyons, *Can-Am*, 60, 80, 207, 240; Lamb, 'Roger McCaig Racing,' 32. See also Adams's ad in 'Classified,' *CTT*, April 1967, 60.
20 Coates, *Challenge*, 110.
21 Lyons, *Can-Am*, 245–64, and car descriptions throughout; Orr, *George Eaton*, 1, 4, 12, 14, 33; Coates, *Challenge*, 143–5, 149; 'Comment,' *CTT*, January 1971; Dave Shaw, 'Quebec News,' *CTT*, February 1971, 38; Craig Hill, 'As I See It,' *CTT*, May 1972, 45; David B. Lamb, 'Sponsorship & Racing,' *Driving* [successor to *CTT*], April 1973, 31–3.
22 Brack interview.
23 Frank Orr, 'Brack,' *CTT*, October 1968, 31.
24 'Ludwig Heimrath,' CMHF inductee, at http://www.cmhf.ca/execs/inductees.htm.

12. Winning Formula

1 Donaldson, *Grand Prix of Canada*, 91.
2 Donaldson, *Gilles Villeneuve*, 24–5, 27.
3 Ibid., 29–30, 31–3.
4 'Canadians at the Jim Russell Driving School – Six of Canada's Best Start All Over Again,' *CTT*, June 1969, 11.
5 Rod Campbell, 'Back to the Basics,' *CTT*, August 1968, 18–19.
6 Peter Bone, 'Racing School Report,' *CTT*, March 1962, 32–5, 46; 'Canadians at the Jim Russell Driving School,' 11, 21, 49; 'Jim Russell – School's Out,' *CTT*, June 1970, 23.
7 Gary Magwood, 'Teaching Them to Race, at Mosport Park,' *CTT*, January 1972, 21; Couture quoted in 'Racing Schools,' *CMB*, May 1971, 11.
8 *Go Racing! Mosport Racing School Limited* (Toronto: Mosport Park Ltd, 1976) (official course brochure); interview with Gary Magwood, 13 March 1996.
9 Magwood interview.
10 Donaldson, *Gilles Villeneuve*, 34.
11 Ibid.
12 CASC, 1967 AGM minutes; 'Minutes of the speed committee meeting,' 1968 AGM minutes; CASC *1969 Yearbook*, 130–3.
13 CASC, 'Minutes of the speed committee meeting,' 1968; CASC, *1969 Yearbook*, 57–9; Hodges, *A–Z of Formula Racing Cars*, 273–4; F. David Stone, 'Grand Prix Racing – North American Style,' *Mosport Competition Magazine*, 1970, 10, 12; Rod Campbell, 'Comment,' *CTT*, November 1968, 4; 'The Canadian Road Racing Championship 1969–1970: The Formula "A" Years,' *Canadian Racer*, at http://www.motorsportscentral.com/formula-a.asp (accessed 26 May 2005).
14 CASC, 'Minutes of the speed committee meeting,' 1968.
15 Salisbury and Attrell quoted ibid.
16 Ross and Rogers quoted ibid.
17 Coates, *Challenge*, 137.
18 F. David Stone, 'Canadian Championship Rounds One, Two – Gulf Canada Series,' *CTT*, July 1969, 19.
19 F. David Stone, 'Two on the Trot for Wietzes,' *CTT*, August 1969, 2, 27; 'List of Entrants – Thanksgiving Speed Weekend – Wm. Cleland Memorial Trophy Race for the Gulf Canada Series Race No. 6,' *Mosport Competition Magazine*, 13 October 1969, 11 (author's copy); CASC, 'Minutes of the race workshop meeting,' AGM, 1 November 1969; CASC, *Yearbook 1971*, 115.
20 CASC, 'President's Report,' 1969 AGM.
21 'The Formula "A" Years.'

22 'More Money in '70 Gulf Series,' *CTT*, April 1970, 2; 'L & M Ups Continental Championship to $400,000,' and provisional entry list, in 'Mac's Continental Formula "A" Race,' *Mosport Competition Magazine*, 1970, 18, 38, 40, 51; CASC, 'Executive Director's Report,' AGM minutes, 7 November 1970; 'Frank Orr' (editor's page), *CTT*, January 1971, 10; and Radosta, *Complete Guide to Auto Racing*, 123.
23 'Comment,' *CTT*, November 1970, 2;
24 CASC, 'Minutes of race workshop meeting,' 1970 AGM.
25 Surman, Couture, and others quoted ibid. The rival company was MacDonald Tobacco: Dave Shaw, 'Quebec News,' *CTT*, February 1971, 38.
26 Peart quoted in CASC, 'Minutes of race workshop meeting,' 1970 AGM.
27 Muzzin quoted ibid.
28 Zimmerman, *The Atlantic Championship*, 21; Chris Allan, 'National Racing: Players Challenge Series – Formula B,' *CMB*, October 1971, 32–4; entry list, 'Official Results: Players Challenge Series, July 18, 19 and 20 1975,' *Mosport Competition Magazine*, August 1975; Hodges, *A–Z of Formula Racing Cars*, passim; 'Comment,' *CTT*, April 1969, 3.
29 'What Is a Formula B,' in *Player's Challenge Series*, Player's Atlantic, Debert, N.S. Sept. 10th [1972] (official program), copy in private papers, Bruce Buntain. See also Bone interview.
30 Donaldson, *Gilles Villeneuve*, 38; Brack interview.
31 CASC minutes, 24 March, 2 June, and 23 June 1962; CASC, *1962 Yearbook*, 25, and *1963 Yearbook*, 29; CASC, *1966 Yearbook*, 34; Rendall, *The Chequered Flag*, 250, and *The Power Game*, 103, 123. See also photographs in Friedman, *Pro Sports Car Racing in America 1958–1974*, 17, 18, 32, 44, 46, 51, 59, 60.
32 CASC, *Yearbook 1970*, 34–5, 55; 'Eppie Wietzes & Gary Magwood Sign Up with Castrol,' *CTT*, April 1971, 46; Magwood interview.
33 David B. Lamb, 'Sponsorship and Racing,' *Driving*, April 1973, 31–3.
34 CASC, *Yearbook 1971*, 113, 115; CASC, 'Executive Director's Report,' AGM minutes, 4 December 1971; 'National Racing,' *CMB*, May 1971, 9.
35 'National Racing,' 9.
36 Terry Jones, 'National Racing Edmonton,' *CMB*, August 1971, 22.
37 See race reports in *CMB*, August–November 1971.
38 'National Racing: The 1972 Player's Challenge Series – Here Come the B's,' *CMB*, May 1972, 18; CASC, 'Report from the Executive Director,' AGM minutes, 25 November 1972.
39 See race reports in *CMB*, July–December 1972.
40 CASC, 'Report from the Executive Director,' AGM minutes, 24 November 1973.
41 CASC, 'Report from the National Race Director,' 1973 AGM minutes;

see also race reports and standings bulletins in *CMB*, July–September 1973.
42 Bob English, 'Brack's "Brain Power,"' *CMB*, October 1973, 30–1.
43 'The Player's Challenge,' *CMB*, June 1973, 30–1; Radosta, *Complete Guide to Auto Racing*, 30, 185–6; Zimmerman, *The Atlantic Championship*, 21; CASC, 1973 AGM minutes; Lamont and Esaw quoted in '1974 Player's Encore,' *CMB*, October 1973, 28; Rendall, *The Power Game*, 135, 141.
44 Zimmerman, *The Atlantic Championship*, 22; Kevin Brazendale, 'Looking Back: The Evolution of the North American Championship,' *ASC*, June 1982, 42; CASC, 'Report of workshop on race matters,' 1973 AGM; CASC, *Player's Challenge Series 1974 Supplementary Regulations* (author's copy); *Player's Challenge Series – Player's Maritime*, August 1974 (official program), Buntain papers.
45 Quote from *Player's Maritime* (1974) official program.
46 English, 'Brack's "Brain Power,"' 31.
47 Powell quoted in CASC, 'Report of workshop on race matters,' 1973 AGM minutes.
48 '1974 Player's Challenge Series,' *CMB*, June 1974, 14; CASC, 'Report from the Executive Director' and 'Report from the National Race Director,' AGM minutes, 30 November–1 December 1974.
49 CASC, 'Report from the Executive Director' and 'Report from the National Race Director,' 1974 AGM. See also Donaldson, *Gilles Villeneuve*, 39–41.
50 Brack interview.
51 CASC, 'Report from the National Race Director,' 1974 AGM.
52 CASC, 'Report from the Executive Director' and "Report from the National Race Director,' AGM, 29–30 November 1975; CASC, *Press Release Player's Challenge Series – 1975 Final Standings*, 20 August 1975; Donaldson, *Gilles Villeneuve*, 46.
53 Donaldson, *Gilles Villeneuve*, 55–69.
54 Ibid., 72–9, 84–6, 89–110.

13. Stage by Stage

1 Edwardes, 'Rallying in Canada,' 2.
2 Edwardes interview; Thomas Barker, 'Profile: Robin Edwardes – The Consummate Right-Hand Man,' *ASC*, March 1984, 29.
3 CASC, 'Quebec Region report,' 1969 AGM.
4 CASC, 'Executive Director's report,' 1970 AGM; Garrett, *The Rally Go-Round*, 36, 40–1, 45–6, 49–52, 56–7, 63, 65, 72; Robson, *A–Z of Works Rally Cars*, 5.

5 Ken Schindler, 'Canadian Champion Walter Boyce Tells: How to Prepare a Rally Car,' *CMB*, May 1971, 14–16, and Schindler, 'Boyce and Woods Are Champions,' *CMB*, December 1971, 26–7; 'Executive Director's report' (1970); interview with Dwight Scott, 17 April 2001.
6 CASC, 'Ontario Region report,' 1969 AGM; minutes of the rally workshop, 1970 AGM.
7 R. Cossar, 'Rallying – Quo Vadis?' *CTT*, June 1970, 34–5.
8 CASC, minutes of 1970 rally workshop.
9 McCallum, Edmond, and Cayer quoted in minutes of 1971 rally workshop.
10 Dwight Scott interview.
11 See CASC AGM minutes, 1968–70. See also Moseley interview.
12 CASC, 'Report from the National Rally Director' and 'Report of workshop on rally matters,' 1972 AGM.
13 CASC, 'Report of workshop on rally matters,' 1972 AGM.
14 CASC, 'Official Bulletin 73-41 Final Standings 1973 National Rally Championship Results,' *CMB*, February 1974, 43–4; 'Report of workshop on rally matters,' 1973 AGM; *Yearbook*, 1970–2; 'Phil Murray' [editor's column], *CTT*, February 1969, 6.
15 Val Gulde, 'A Private Fiat Wins,' *CMB*, March 1972, 29.
16 Bob English, 'Fiat Wins Canadian Winter Rally,' *CMB*, March 1973, 21–4.
17 Brian Hillis, 'Rallying/Rallye des Neiges,' *Driving*, March 1973, 45; quote from Bartholemew in 'Fiat Breaks Toyota's Hold,' *CMB*, February 1973, 18.
18 'Sour Notes,' *CMB*, August 1973, 30.
19 'Toyota Wins the Golden Triangle,' *CMB*, April 1973, 32–3; CASC, 'Official Bulletin no. 74-7 National Rally Championship – Calendar 1974,' *CMB*, April 1974, 50.
20 'Letters to the Editor,' *CMB*, February 1973, 4.
21 'Opinion,' *CMB*, April 1973, 34; Ann Lloyd, 'Datsun Wins the Trail,' *CMB*, August 1973, 33.
22 'Letters to the Editor,' *CMB*, June 1973, 6–7.
23 Donald Horne, 'Rally – Rallying: Pro or Amateur?' *CMB*, June 1973, 18; 'Report from the National Rally Director,' 1973 AGM.
24 'Report from the National Rally Director,' 1973.
25 'Report of workshop on rally matters,' 1973.
26 Hughes, Welgan, Manson, and McCallum quoted ibid.
27 Event report statistics in *CMB*.
28 Doug Hardie, 'Rally "74,"' *CMB*, February 1974, 13.
29 Event report and final standings statistics from CASC official bulletins in *CMB*; CASC, 'Ontario Region report,' 1974 AGM; Linquist and Cowan

294 Notes to pages 197–204

  quotes from Carole McLaughlin, 'The Canadian Winter Rally – Four Years for Fiat,' *CMB*, April 1974, 27–8.
30 CASC, 'Report from the National Rally Director,' 1974; Hugh Bishop, 'Big Time Rallying in North America,' *CMB*, November–December 1974, 34–6.
31 Bob Lindquist, 'Opinion,' *CMB*, February 1974, 23, 26–7.
32 'Letters,' *CMB*, June 1974, 4.
33 CASC, 'Report from the National Rally Director,' 1974.
34 CASC, 'Executive Director's report,' and region reports, 1974 AGM.
35 CASC, *Bulletin 75-6 1975 Castrol Rally Championship*, 27 January 1975, *ASC*, March 1975, 38; 'Final Standings: The Castrol Rally Championship of Canada,' *ASC*, December 1975, 19.
36 CASC, 'Report from the Executive Director,' 1975 AGM.
37 Statistics in event reports and CASC bulletins, *ASC*, March–December 1975.
38 CASC, 'Bulletin No. 74-41 Standings National Rally Championship Provisional,' *CMB*, November–December 1974, 52, shows the dominance of Datsun and Toyota. See also Toyota ads in *CMB*, February 1974, inside front cover, and September 1974, 29.
39 John Powell, 'Factory Fiat!' *ASC*, March 1975, 23–6, 32.
40 Doug Mepham, 'Marital Breakdown,' *ASC*, May 1975, 9.
41 Brian D. Hillis, 'Rally Right,' *ASC*, June 1975, 16–17, 27, and 'Service Right,' *ASC*, September 1975, 14–15.
42 'The Great Debate,' *ASC*, May 1975, 14–15.
43 Robin Edwardes, 'Toyota's Success in Automobile Rallying in Canada,' 3.
44 CASC, 'Atlantic Region report,' 1975 AGM.
45 CASC, 'Report of workshop on rally matters,' 1975 AGM.
46 CASC, 'Report of the Executive Director,' 1978 AGM.
47 Barker, 'Rally Roots,' 19; Edwardes, 'Rallying in Canada,' 4; Paul Chater, 'Fiat Sweeps the Criterium,' *ASC*, December 1977, 16–18, 20.
48 CASC, Report from the National Rally Director,' 1978 AGM.
49 CASC, 'National Rally Director's report,' 1972.
50 CASC, 'Report of the Executive Director,' 1977, 1978. The average entry list was fifteen cars per event.

14. Downshift

1 CASC, 'Report from the Executive Director,' 1972 AGM.
2 CASC, 'President's report,' 1969 AGM; region reports, 1969–73. See also CASC Ontario Region, *Motorsport in Ontario Competition Calendar and Directory 1970*, 15–18, 20, 22.

3 CASC, 'Minutes of race workshop meeting,' 1970 AGM; 'National Race Director's report,' 1975. See also *1974 Eastern Canadian Endurance Series Rules, Regulations*, private papers, Bruce Buntain; and race reports and series results in *CMB*, 1971–3.
4 CASC, 'minutes of race workshop meeting,' 1970; 'Player's Run-off,' *CMB*, May 1971, 11; Carole McLaughlin, 'Player's Race of Champions,' *CMB*, December 1972, 30.
5 CASC, 'Executive Director's report,' 1971, 1975 AGMs; 'Player's Centennial Race of Champions,' *CMB*, November 1971, 17–24; annual race reports in *CMB*, 1972–4. Fellows and Goodyear are shown in *1981 Canadian Road Race of Champions, Entry List, Schedule*, original in private papers, Lewis Mackenzie. See also chapter 15.
6 Jack W. Ondrack, letter to the editor in 'Miscellany,' *CMB*, April 1974, 13.
7 CASC/FCSA, *Région du Québec Region Competitions and/et Regulations 1968*; CASC, Ontario, Quebec, and Prairie Region reports, 1972–5; 'Barrell Wins O'Keefe St. Eustache Ice Bash,' *CTT*, March 1968, 37; 'Icy Dices,' *CTT*, April 1968, 19, 40; John Windsor, 'IIIIce Races,' *CTT*, April 1970, 25–7; Dave Shaw, 'Quebec News,' *CTT*, March 1971, 37; Tony Hampshire, 'The Labatt's Two Hour,' *CMB*, May 1973, 43–4.
8 CASC, 'Minutes of the solo event workshop,' 1969 AGM; *1970 Yearbook*, 19; 'Report of Solo Events Director' and 'Report of the solo events workshop,' 1971 AGM; 'Executive Director's report,' 1972; and 'Report from the National Solo Events Director,' 1972–4.
9 CASC, 'National Solo Events Director report,' 1975; 'Executive Director's report,' 1973, 1974; 'Solo workshop report,' 1976; Allan Rae, 'Solo Events,' *CMB*, May 1973, 20.
10 CASC, 'National Solo Events Director's report,' 1972, 1973; 'Atlantic Region report,' 1974; CASC Ontario Region, *Motorsport Ontario 1973 Ontario Region Regulations Solo Events*, 36, 38, 44, 46; CASC, *National Auto Slalom Championship Regulations and Vehicle Classification July 7, 1974*, 3–4, 8, in competition files; 'Solo Events,' *CMB*, July 1974, 46–7.
11 CASC, 'BC Region report,' 1970, 1974, 1975; 'BC Region Solo report,' 1972, 1973; 'National Solo Events Director's report,' 1973.
12 Ron Allerton, 'Knox Mountain Hillclimb,' *CTT*, July 1969, 38.
13 Ibid.; CASC, *Yearbook 1969*, 105; 'BC Region report,' 1970; 'Ontario Region Solo report,' 1972; 'Atlantic Region report,' 1975; 'Revving Up with Phil Murray,' *CTT*, July 1968, 5; 'The Regions – B.C. Region,' *CMB*, May 1971, 29 and July 1971, 32; 'Atlantic Weekend,' *CMB*, July 1971, 42; 'Solo Events,' *CMB*, November 1971, 26–7.
14 Quotes from CASC, 'Atlantic Region reports,' 1969, 1970.

15 CASC, 'BC Region report,' 1970; quotes from 'Quebec Region reports,' 1972, 1973; 'National Rally Director's report,' 1972; Orest Ulan, 'Down East,' *CTT*, April 1970, 37.
16 CASC, 'Atlantic Region report,' 1968; Atlantic Region race reports,' 1971, 1972; 'CASC Atlantic Region Debert Circuit,' undated track plan, ca. 1970, in race tracks binder; F. Schagen, untitled typescript, 1, attached to 'A.M.P. Background & History' (Atlantic Motorsport Park, Inc., February 1980), in track files. See also George H. Condon, 'Racing – Down East,' *CTT*, February 1969; and race reports in *CMB*: September 1971, 30, 32, November 1971, 41, April 1973, 41, July 1973, 46–7, and September 1973, 48.
17 Richard Russell, 'Atlantic Region,' *CMB*, January 1973, 39–40; quote in CASC, 'Atlantic Region race report,' 1972; Richard Russell, 'On Target at AMP,' *ASC*, March 1975, 12.
18 CASC, 'Atlantic Region race report,' 1972; 'Report from National Race Director'; Schagen, typescript, 1–3; 'A.M.P. Background & History'; Russell, 'Atlantic Region,' *CMB*, January 1973, 40, March 1973, 46, 'Atlantic,' June 1974, 31–2; on Westwood: interview with Bob Randall, 2 March 1992.
19 Interview with Robert Guthrie, 22 September 2001.
20 Ibid.
21 Quoted in Russell, 'Atlantic,' *CMB*, January 1974, 43.
22 Russell, 'Atlantic,' *CMB*, June 1974, 31; 'A True Champion – Brack Brilliant,' *CMB*, September 1974, 23–5; Chris Waddell, 'Brack Takes Lead in Canadian Championship,' *ASC*, October 1977, 8, 10.
23 CASC, *Yearbooks*, 1968, 1972; 'Annual Summary: Clubs and Members Voting Strength,' AGM minutes, 1968–76.
24 CASC, 'President's Address,' 1971 AGM.
25 CASC, 'Executive Director's report,' 1971 AGM.
26 Ibid., 1972–5.
27 W.E. Chapman, 'CRRC – 1977,' *ASC*, December 1977, 28, 30; CASC, 'Report from National Solo Director,' 1975 AGM; 1976 AGM minutes.
28 Granatstein et al., *Twentieth Century Canada*, 393, 400–5; Alvin Finkel, *Our Lives: Canada after 1945* (Toronto: James Lorimer, 1997), 141–6; Bothwell, et al., *Canada since 1945*, 18–19, figures 2–4; Owram, *Born at the Right Time*, 306.
29 CASC, 'Executive Director's report,' 1974.
30 CASC, 'Report from the National Race Director,' 1974.
31 CASC, 'Report of workshop on race matters,' 1975.
32 CASC, 'Report from the National Race Director,' 1974, 1975.
33 CASC, 'Report of workshop on race matters,' 1975.
34 CASC, 'Executive Director's report,' 1973.

35 Coates, *Challenge*, 83–4.
36 Donaldson, *Grand Prix of Canada*, 16–22; CASC, 'Executive Director's report,' 1968.
37 'Le Circuit Director Loses Post to Employee after Internal Dispute,' *Globe and Mail*, 15 July 1970, in track files.
38 Luc, *L'Histoire du Sport Automobile au Québec*, 144; 'Comment – Le Circuit Merry Go-Round,' *CTT*, September 1970, 2.
39 Letter, Hanna to Paradis, 3 December 1970; 'Draft Agreement,' 14 April 1971; Letter, Peter Roberts, CASC Quebec Region, to Paradis, 20 May 1971; Dave Shaw, 'Quebec News – Le Circuit Closes,' *CTT*, March 1972, 44.
40 Lyons, *Can-Am*, 144; Dave Lamb, 'Jackie Does It!' *CTT*, August 1971, 16.
41 Bochroch, *Trans-Am Racing 1966–85*, 126; James H. Gunn, *Report to Mlle J. Paradis Re: Le Circuit Mt. Tremblant August 1971*, in track file.
42 *Report to Mlle J. Paradis*.
43 'Par Real Desrosiers,' *CMB*, October 1971, 41; F. David Stone, 'News and Views,' *CTT*, March 1972, 22; CASC 1971 AGM, appendices C and K; 'Quebec Region race report,' 1972.
44 CASC, 'Executive Director's report,' 1973; 'Quebec Region race report,' 1972; Allen E. Brown, *History of America's Speedways*, 574–83.
45 Quotes from Dave Shaw, 'Canadian Championship Round 4 (Wet),' *CTT*, October 1971, 45, and 'Unique in North America: Grand Prix Molson Trois Rivieres,' *CMB*, May 1973, 33–4. See also track plan from 1976 promotional brochure in CASC track files; Zimmerman, *The Atlantic Championship*, 29, 38, 88–9 (photos); Luc, *L'histoire du Sport Automobile au Québec*, 170; Brown, *History of America's Speedways*, 580; and Saward, *World Atlas of Motor Racing*, 171.
46 Bochroch, *Trans-Am Racing, 1966–85*, 170, 174, 201–3; Donaldson, *Gilles Villeneuve*, 65–72.
47 CASC, 'Annual Report of the Ontario Region,' 1970 AGM.
48 CASC, 'President's Address,' 1971.
49 CASC, 'Report of workshop on administrative matters,' 1972 AGM.
50 Quotes from CASC, 'Committee on Administrative Organization report,' 1972 AGM.
51 CASC, 'President's report,' 1968; 'Report of administrative workshop,' 1970. The changes in CASC national and club/regional coverage are apparent from a survey of *CTT*, issues, 1959–69.
52 CASC, 'Report of administrative workshop,' 1970; 'Executive Director's report,' 1971.
53 CASC, 'Report of workshop on administration matters,' 1972, 1974.
54 CASC, *Yearbooks*, 1966, 1972; AGM minutes, 1972, 1978. See also data from

newsletters, affiliation sheets, and executive lists of the SCCBC, Calgary Sports Car Club, and BARC-OC.
55 Bone interview; Maddin interview; Moseley interview; CASC, 'Prairie Region report,' 1970; Ort, *Western Ontario Sports Car Association History*, 6; Wright, 'The History of Motor Sport'; Corran, 'History of the St. Catharine's Motor Club,' 44–6, 49.
56 Interview with Dorothy Scott, 18 March 2003.
57 Ibid.
58 CASC, 'Report of administrative workshop,' 1970.
59 CASC, 'National Rally Director's report,' 1973.
60 CASC, Ontario and BC Region reports, 1969, 1973; Ort, *Western Ontario Sports Car Association History*, 26.
61 Moseley interview.
62 Jarmilia L.A. Horna, 'Trends in Sports in Canada,' in Ramphorts and Roberts, eds., *Trends in Sports: A Multinational Perspective*, 40–5; Watson, *National Pastimes: The Economics of Canadian Leisure*, 78–9, 81; Granatstein et al., *Twentieth Century Canada*, 392; and Moseley interview. Auto sport participation did not figure in any of the data.

15. Final Laps

1 Hatter, 'Dateline – Divorce, Canadian Style.'
2 Donaldson, *Gilles Villeneuve*, 9–11, 313–16.
3 Ibid., 316–18, 321–2, 324–5, 327; Jones, *Ultimate Encyclopedia of Formula One*, 177.
4 Donaldson, *Gilles Villeneuve*, 320–2.
5 CASC, 'Opening address and report – the president, George E. Chapman,' 1977 AGM; 'Executive Director's reports,' 1977, 1978; 'Summary: Clubs and Members Voting Strength,' 1978 AGM.
6 Doug Mepham, editorial director, 'Report on *Autosport Canada*,' 1975 CASC AGM. The author also did a content survey of issues from 1976 to 1980.
7 CASC, 'BC Region report,' 1975 (emphasis added).
8 CASC, 'Executive Director's report,'1977.
9 Peter Murdoch, 'Are Go-Karts Part of Motor Racing?' *CTT*, February 1962, 37–8; CASC, 'Workshop on karting,' 1977 AGM; 'National Karting Director's report,'1978.
10 CASC, 'President's report,' 1978.
11 CASC, 'National Karting Director's report,' 1978.
12 Lyons, *Can-Am*, 240; Hodges, *A–Z of Formula Racing Cars*, 274; Harold Pace, 'Can-Am Racing Part 2: Cultivating Up-and-Coming Champions, 1977–

1986,' at http://www.advanceautoparts.com/english/youcan/html; Connie Goudinoff, 'Can-Am Returns,' *ASC*, August 1977, 8, 10; McLaren, *Mosport 25 Years*, 57.
13 Goudinoff, 'Can-Am Returns,' 8–10, 35.
14 Connie Goudinoff, 'Tambay Wins First Time Out,' *ASC*, September 1977, 6; 'Gethin Victorious at Road America,' *ASC*, October 1977, 23; Donaldson, *Gilles Villeneuve*, 81–2, 331; Pace, 'Can-Am Racing Part 2.'
15 Jim Matthews, 'Hot Shoes and the Big Honkers,' *Canadian Motorsport Annual, 1981–82* (Toronto: Wheelspin News, 1981), 51.
16 'Molyslip Enduro Underway Soon,' *ASC*, June 1977, 30; Pete Chapman, 'Molyslip Endurance Series Opener,' *ASC*, August 1977, 25; 'Klaus Bytzek Continues to Win,' *ASC*, September 1977, 31; Pete Chapman, 'Molyslip Endurance Series Wrap-up,' *ASC*, October 1977, 32–3.
17 'Report of the workshop on race matters,' 1977 CASC AGM; CASC, *Molyslip Endurance Series Supplementary Regulations 1979* (author's copy); Pete Chapman, 'Focus,' *ASC*, August 1979, 2, December 1979, 2; Pete Chapman, 'Not a Pale Shadow,' *ASC*, October 1980, 29–32; Pete Chapman, 'Loaded for Bear,' *ASC*, September 1981, 52; and series race reports in *ASC*, December 1978, 36, August 1980, 42, September 1980, 45–7.
18 Canadian Honda Motor Limited, *An Introduction: The Honda/Goodrich Challenge Series* (Agincourt, ON, May 1977) (author's copy); comments by Klaus Bartels in 'Report of workshop on race matters,' 1977 AGM; 'National Race Director's report,' 1978; Christianson comment in series ad, *ASC*, May 1978, inside front cover; 'Current Regional Standings' in series ad, *ASC*, December 1978, 26; comment on Honda/BFG series in Chapman, 'Not a Pale Shadow,' 29; Honda Canada, 'Honda/Michelin Series Returns to Historic Grand Prix of Trois-Rivières after a 12-Year Hiatus,' 29 July 2004, at http://www.honda.ca/AutoRacingEng/PressReleases/2004-07-29-01.htm.
19 R.J. (Bob) Hanna, 'Director's Chair – "Moving Forward into the Past,"' original draft of column written for *ASC*, 16 February 1976, affiliation files; 'Vintage Racing Underway,' *ASC*, January 1977, 39; 'Vintage Car Racing,' *ASC*, February 1978; John Winter, 'A Brief History,' in *First Annual Vintage Festival: Vintage and Historic Automobile and Motorcycle Races Shannonville Motorsport Park August 18 & 19 1979* (program), copy in Mackenzie papers; Michael Kingston, 'Vintage Racing: Auld Lang Syne Revisited,' *Canadian Motorsport Annual*, 1981–2, 58–9.
20 CASC, 'National Solo Director's report,' 1978.
21 There were 368 rallies in Canada in 1978, but no hill climbs in Ontario in 1979 and only one in 1980. Many former competitors mentioned the loss of access to roads on hills. CASC, 'Executive Director's report,' 1978; Ontario

Region, *Motorsport in Ontario Competition Calendar and Directory*, 1979, 1980; Ort, *Western Ontario Sports Car Association History*, 7.
22 See comments on Villeneuve in CASC, 'Report of the President,' 1978 AGM; Michael A. Turner, 'Draft report on FAQ activities,' 26 November 1980, 5, 6, 8, appendix A to board of directors meeting minutes, 5–7 December 1980; Pete Chapman, 'The Thiffault Formula for Success,' *ASC*, March 1981, 2.
23 CASC, 'Rallying committee report,' 1985; '1988 Report on rallying in Canada,' 1989.
24 Len Welin, Director of National Series, *CASC Professional Racing Division Year End Report*, October 1989, 3–4. See also Player's Ltd., *1992 Media Guide* (author's copy).
25 Interview with Martin Chenhall, 24 October 1992.
26 Ibid.
27 Ibid.; Bochroch, *Trans-Am Racing 1966–85*, 168–70, 197.
28 Chenhall interview; Player's Racing, *1992 Media Guide*.
29 'Report of the President,' 1978 AGM; 'Report to the Clubs,' 1 June 1980.
30 The 1978 report of the national racing director, for example, was limited to the amateur side of the sport. It said nothing about pro series.
31 'The New Image of CASC,' brief to national board of directors meeting, 8 December 1984.
32 CASC, *Bulletin 88-49 CASC Establishes Pro Race Board*, 8 November 1988; *Professional Racing Division ... Report* (1989); Peart memo to all members of CASC, 15 December 1989.
33 Brunt, 'Fantastic Indy 500 Finish Rates a City Hall Visit'; Shaffer, *CART*, 137.
34 Shaffer, *CART*, 211.
35 Ibid., 19–20, 23, 25, 27–30, 218–24.
36 Scott Goodyear biography (c.v. 1989), in CASC driver files; Hough, 'Driving Ambition,' *EnRoute*, May 1991, 70; Ferriss, *Never Too Fast*, 6–8. See also driver biographies of Patrick Carpentier and Alex Tagliani, at http://sportsrpm.espn.go.com/rpm/drivers?seriesid=5; and Neal Jones, 'A Champion in Every Sense of the Word,' *Performance Racing News* [*PRN*], January 2000, 4 (tribute to Greg Moore).
37 The assessment in these two paragraphs is based on the regional, discipline, and executive reports presented to the CASC AGMs, 1983–91.
38 Interview with Lewis Mackenzie, 28 June 1990.
39 Johnston, *Sports Car Road Racing*, 132; Bob Brockington (CASC office) email to author, 15 April 2002, says the last races were held in 1981.
40 CASC, 'Prairie Region race report,' 1971, 1972; 'Gimli Motorsport Park track plan,' 1973, in race tracks binder; 'Race Track Capsule no. 1 Gimli,'

ASC, July 1975, 28; Pete Chapman, 'Focus: Save the Tracks,' *ASC*, April 1981, 2; Zbarsky, 'Westwood Motorsport Park,' 28; 'BC Region reports,' 1989, 1990.

41 'Race Track Capsule no. 2 – And the Siege of Jovite,' *ASC*, July 1975, 29; Chris Waddell, 'Villeneuve Again, This Time at St. Jovite,' *ASC*, September 1976, 8–9; Brockington, 'Le Circuit Mont Tremblant,' 33.

42 Schagen, typescript, 3; drivers' complaints about the track are found in 'CRRC–1977,' *ASC*, December 1977, 28. See also CASC, 'Atlantic Region annual report,' 1979 AGM.

43 Brown, *History of America's Speedways*, 572; entry for Shannonville Motorsport Park on the *Canadian Racer* website, at http://www.motorsportscentral.com/track-display.asp.

44 Peart interview; Rendall, *The Power Game*, 135–6, 150; 'War, and Background: It Had to Come,' *ASC*, September 1975, 8–9, 32, 34; 'Closed File,' 'Reflections over an Open Grave,' and Hanna's 'official' account in 'Director's Chair,' all in *ASC*, October 1975, 4–5, 19–20

45 Brockington, *Mosport International Raceway*, 61–113; Hudes quoted in McLaren, *Mosport Park*, 80.

46 Brockington, *Mosport International Raceway*, 19–20; Ian MacRae, 'A Track in Need of a Tune-up' (letter to the editor), *Globe and Mail*, 23 December 1987.

47 Brockington, *Mosport International Raceway*, 19–20, 98–9, 101, 104, 106, 116; quote from 'In Tribute to Harvey Hudes,' *Mosport 1996 Media Guide*, 10.

48 'Comment' and 'CT&T Newsletter,' *CTT*, October 1968, 3, 53; 'Comment,' *CTT*, November 1968, 4.

49 'Comment,' November 1968; CASC, 'President's report,' 1968 AGM.

50 'Comment,' *CTT*, March 1969, 3.

51 CASC, 'Executive Director's report' and 'Atlantic Region report,' 1974; McLaren, *Mosport Park*, 62; 'Interview – What's a Nice Ale Like You Doing in a Race Like This?' *CTT*, May 1972, 28; 'Focus,' *ASC*, October 1978, 2, 49; and Peart interview.

52 'Clearing the Air,' *CTT*, November 1962, 3; 'Controversy – Racing's Strange Paradox'; Frank Orr, 'Mosport: Where Grime Does Pay,' *Toronto Star*, 5 June 1965, copy in Mosport scrapbook (1965), Mosport Collection, CMHF; Frank Orr column, *CTT*, November 1968, 9; Coates, *Challenge*, 61, 133, 156; McLaren, *Mosport Park*, 13; and Peart interview.

53 Clairoux, *Montréal: 25 ans de Formule 1*, 14.

54 Peart interview; Clairoux, *Montréal: 25 ans de Formule 1*, 14; Alan Brinton, 'Walter Wolf Racing,' ASC, August 1977) 22–3.

55 George Hanson, 'Wolf Pushes Grand Prix,' *Montreal Star*, 27 March 1978, CMHF media clippings file.

56 Julia Elwell, 'The Montreal Grand Prix: Pros and Cons,' *Montreal Gazette*, 10 June 1978; Tim Humphreys, 'Grand Prix Secrecy Hit' and 'City Okays Grand Prix,' *Montreal Star*, 8, 9 June 1978, CMHF media clippings file; Clairoux, *Montréal: 25 ans de Formule 1*, 16.
57 Peart interview.
58 Ibid.; McLaren, 'About People,' 14; Donaldson, *Grand Prix of Canada*, 87.
59 Clairoux, *Montréal: 25 ans de Formule 1*, 16. Donaldson, *Grand Prix of Canada* 86–7; McLaren, 'About People,' 49.
60 'Molson Indy History: Getting the Green Flag to Go Racing in Toronto,' on-line at http://www.molsonindy.com/toronto/race/history.html; Shaffer, *CART*, 210; Saward, *World Atlas of Motor Racing*, 170–1.
61 Lowes, *Indy Dreams and Urban Nightmares*, x, xiii–xiv, 9–11, 14–15, 17–21.
62 Ibid., 67, and Lowes, 'Indy Dreams in the World Class City,' in Donnelly, ed., *Taking Sport Seriously*, 147–9; Shaffer, *CART*, 37, 124, 126; Gerry Frechette, 'Best in the West,' *PRN Souvenir Edition*, 1996, 3.
63 Partridge, 'The Moosehead Grand Prix,' *Atlantic Lifestyle Business*, 1992, 44.
64 Quotes from Partridge, 'The Moosehead Grand Prix,' 43, and 'The Moosehead Grand Prix: Five Years of Racing Success in Eastern Canada,' *Moosehead Grand Prix May 19, 20, 21 1995. Official Souvenir Program* (author's copy). See also: Jeff Wright, 'Moose Loose on Halifax Streets,' *GT Magazine*, November/December 1990, copy in album no. 1, John Rankin, private papers, Fredericton.
65 Wright, 'Moose Loose.' See also official programs for 1994 and 1995. The author served as a crew member in the 1992 event, and raced in the regional sedan events at the GP in 1994 and 1995.
66 Partridge, 'The Moosehead Grand Prix,' 42–4. 'Moosehead and Motorsport,' *Moosehead Grand Prix Official Commemorative Program September 11, 12, 13 1992* (author's copy).
67 Quoted in 'Interview: George E. Chapman,' *ASC*, May 1980, 8.
68 Rendall, *The Power Game*, 150, 155, 157, 161–4, 166–8, 176, 182.
69 CASC, national board meeting minutes and 'Administrative workshop notes,' 1983 AGM; 'Executive committee meeting minutes,' 26 May, 25 July 1984; 'Executive and Board meeting minutes,' 1984 AGM.
70 R.J. Hanna, 'Report to: CASC Executive Committee, Subject: FISA Meetings, December 1984,' 4 January 1985; Bryan Sangster, CASC general manager, 'Memo to: National Board of Directors, Subject: Grand Prix of Canada,' 21 December 1984.
71 CASC, 'Executive and Board minutes,' 1984 AGM; 'President's report,' 1987 AGM; Executive meeting minutes, 15 February 1987.
72 CASC, *Bulletin 87-34 CASC to Challenge Decision of World Motorsport Author-*

ity, 26 October 1987; 'Note for file information,' 19 November 1987 (updated to 19 February 1988), FIA affiliation file; quote from 1987 report from Pierre Compagna, president, FAQ.
73 Roger Peart, 'Memo to: all members of the national board of directors, subject: our next meeting and other matters,' 18 January 1989.
74 CASC, 'Board of director's meeting minutes,' 4–5 February 1989.
75 Ibid.; the delineation of authority was confirmed in an exchange of letters: Mailloux to Peart, 4 February, and Peart to Mailloux, 8 February 1989. See also Peart, 'Memo to: all members of CASC,' 15 December 1989.
76 CASC, 'National competition committee meeting minutes,' 21 January 1990; AGM minutes, 9–11 February 1990; Professional Racing Division Series meeting, 3 March 1990; Welin quoted in Hatter, 'Divorce, Canadian Style.'
77 CASC, 'Press release,' 11 April 1990.
78 Both quotes from Hatter, 'Divorce: Canadian Style.'
79 George Webster, 'Commentary: Can Road-Racing's ASN Make Peace with Its Volunteers?' *PRN*, September 1990, 5.
80 CASC, 'Special meeting of members,' 5 May 1990; 'Board meeting minutes,' 26–27 January 1991; National rally committee, 'Text of conference call,' 20 October 1991. See also Motorsport Sanctioning Agreements negotiated between ASN Canada FIA and Western Canada Motorsport Association, FAQ, and CASC Ontario Region, 1991.

Epilogue

1 This account is based on the author's experience racing at Pennfield one day in September 1994.
2 This description is based on the author's attendance at the 1997 Grand Prix. See also 'Grand Prix 97,' *The Gazette*, 16 June 1997, sections D and E.
3 Quoted in Donaldson, *Grand Prix of Canada*, 86.
4 On the concept of a race track as a 'theater of speed,' see Pillsbury, 'Stock Car Racing,' in Raitz, ed., *The Theater of Sport*, 282, 292.
5 Tremayne and Hughes, *Concise Encyclopedia of Formula One*, 55.
6 Boddy and Laban, *History of Motor Racing*, 152. On the cult of the male sport hero and its place in auto sport, see: Kennedy 'Bad Boys and Gentlemen,' 59–60, 64–7.
7 Whannel, *Media Sports Stars*, 36–7, 40–5, 129–30, 145, 190; Howell, *Blood, Sweat, and Cheers*, 54–5; in auto sport, see Rendall, *The Power Game*, 7–8, 243; Huff, *Insider's Guide to Stock Car Racing*, 9, 11, 48–9, 109; Pillsbury, 'Stock Car Racing,' 280–2, 294; and Post, *High Performance*, 235–7.

8 Roberts and Olson, *Winning Is the Only Thing*, 95; Wenner, 'Media, Sports and Society: The Research Agenda,' in Wenner, ed., *Media, Sports and Society*, 15; Rendall, *The Power Game*, 135, 141, 146, 150, 182, 228, 234, 243.
9 Nye, *History of the Grand Prix Car*, 158–9, 171; Sakkis, *Anatomy and Development of the Indy Car*, 82–90.
10 Grange, 'Refuelling F1,' *EnRoute* (2000), 48, 50, 60, 62–3, 65.
11 Davis, 'How TV Goes Along for the Ride.'
12 See the official ASN Canada FIA website: http://www.asncanada.com.
13 Information accessed at http://www.honda.ca/AutoRacingEng/RaceSchedule (2005, no longer active); see also http://www.civicchampionship.com.
14 The 2004 Canadian Autoslalom Championship Official Results, accessed 22 July 2004, at http://cadl.qc.ca/cac/results/cac2004resultsweb.pdf.
15 Gimli Motorsport Park and Capital City Raceway (Edmonton) are the last remaining airport-based race tracks in Canada: Johnston, *Sports Car Road Racing in Western Canada*, 211, 215.
16 The five regions are Atlantic Region Motor Sports; FAQ; CASC Ontario Region; Western Canada Motorsport Association; and Confederation Auto Sport Clubs (BC).
17 'Danica Proves Her Mettle at Indy,' *Sports Illustrated*, 29 May 2005.
18 Douglas, 'Kat Teasdale,' *TG Magazine*, 1992, and 'Kathryn "Kat" Teasdale and Katko Racing.'
19 Harris-Adler, 'Speed Diva'; Noel Simpson, 'Bridgestone F2000 Series Takes Off,' *Performance Racing News*, August 1999, 22; 'Marybeth Harrison's Mach 1 Racing Offical Website,' at http://www.marybethharrison.com.
20 See http://www.girl-racers.com/drivers/taws/index.html; http://www.racerchicks.com/news/M_TawsUPD.html; and http://www.aimautosport.com/Content/drivers/Current/Taws/tawsbio.htm.
21 Johnston, *Sports Car Road Racing in Western Canada*, 119; 'Vancouver City Map,' 1997.
22 Johnston, *Sports Car Road Racing in Western Canada*, 208–9, 212. During the 1990s stock car and drag racing occupied a growing share of the pages of *PRN*.
23 See event details at http://www.targanewfoundland.com. See also Jenkins, 'Rallying Thrills as a Spectator Sport (Once You Adjust).'
24 Feschuk, 'Champ Cars Still Have Some Gas Left in the Tank'; 'Tracy Cashes in on the Gold Coast,' *Champ Car News*, Monday 27 October 2003, at http://champcarworldseries.com/News/Article.asp?id=7337.
25 Rendall, *The Power Game*, 9, 12–17, 217, 231–5, 247; Todd, 'Formula One Bosses Kill '04 Grand Prix'; LeBlanc and Pappone, 'Canadian Grand Prix

Saved.' Dewhurst and Sparks, 'Intertextuality, Tobacco Sponsorship of Sports, and Adolescent Male Smoking Culture,' 373, 384–5, 388–92, argue that tobacco's association with F1 and Indy Car racing supports a marketing narrative designed to create a desirable image of the self-reliant, risk-taking young male, embodied by Jacques Villeneuve.
26 'Five More Years for Canadian Grand Prix,' 7 May 2006, at http://www.tsn.ca/auto_racing/news_story.asp?id=165130.
27 Beacon, 'Villeneuve Intrigued by NASCAR'; Pappone, 'Villeneuve Seeking Job with Former F1 Employer'; 'Ecclestone Adds to Villeneuve Woes.'
28 H.H. Gerth and C. Wright Mills, *From Max Weber: Essays in Sociology* (New York: Oxford University Press, 1958), 196, 212.
29 Knap interview.

Select Bibliography

Primary Sources

Archival Material

Canadian Automobile Association National Office, Ottawa
  McNamee, George A. 'Memoirs.' Unpublished typescript. March 1962
Canadian Automobile Sport Clubs, Ontario Region (formerly National)
  Office, Archive, Toronto
  Affiliation files, bulletins, club files, correspondence, memoranda, minutes, region files, track files, yearbooks, 1951–1991 (The archive has been reorganized several times since the start of research on this book. Document citations in the notes reflect their location at the time the research was done.)
Canadian Motorsport Hall of Fame, Toronto
  Media clippings file
  Mosport Collection
  Peter Ryan Papers
  Gunn, Jim. 'The Book.' Unpublished manuscript (no date), accessed at http://Shell-4000-rally.org/Book.pdf (original is in CMHF archives).
National Archives of Canada, Photographic Section, Ottawa
  Photographs PA-56260-64, 56354, 57710, Sports and Amusements, Racing, Automobiles
National Museum of American History, Washington, DC
  'Race Driver Safety,' display in Transportation Exhibit, December 1997
Royal Automobile Club Library, London, UK
  General Competition Rules, 1955 edition
  Minutes, Competition Committee, 11 November 1953, 11 May 1960

308   Select Bibliography

Private Papers

Ashfield, Alvin, consulted in Fredericton
Baird, Donald, Montreal
Bradley, Francis, Toronto
Buntain, Bruce, Halifax
Charters, David, Fredericton
Charters, John, Montreal
Chelminski, Les, Montreal
Gallop, John, Montreal
MacKenzie, Lewis, Oromocto, NB
McLaughlin, Roy, Toronto
Rankin, John, Fredericton
Rathgeb, Charles, Toronto
Sadler, William, Scottsdale, AZ
Stanley, Lester, Montreal
Wietzes, Eppie, Toronto

Interviews

Ashfield, Alvin, 7 May 2001
Baird, Donald, 21 January 1990
Birnbom, Lionel, 22 April 2001
Bone, Peter, 6 November 1991
Brack, Bill, 21 June 1991
Bradley, Francis, 23 October 1992
Charters, John, 3 May 1991
Chelminski, Les, 20 August 1992
Chenhall, Martin, 24 October 1992
De St. Croix, Ross, 22 October 1992
Edwardes, Robin, 13 August 1990
Fisher, Craig, 22 October 1992
Gallop, John, 2 May 1991
Greenblatt, David, 7 June 1993
Gunn, James, 16 June 1995
Guthrie, Robert, 22 September 2001
Jenkins, Jane, 7 May 2001
Knap, Muriel, 2 March 1990
Kroll, Horst, 21 August 1993
Locke, Graham, 20 August 1992

MacKenzie, Lewis, 28 June 1990
McLaughlin, Roy, 23 October 1992
Maddin, Jim, 20 March 1993
Magwood, Gary, 13 March 1996
Moseley, Arthur, 6 November 1991
Motton, Fred, 2 May 1991
Peart, Roger, 21 June 1990
Randall, Hilda, 2 March 1992
Randall, Robert, 2 March 1992
Rankin, John, 11 September 1992
Rathgeb, Charles, 21 June 1990
Sadler, William, 20 October 1990
Scott, Dorothy, 18 March 2003
Scott, Dwight, 17 April 2001
Short, Tony, 15 April 1997
Stanley, Lester, 20 August 1992
Wietzes, Eppie, 20 August 1993

Audio Recording

Wright, Milton J. 'The History of Motor Sport' (self-taped personal reminiscences), May 1992

Film Recordings

Charters, John. 'Racing at St. Eugene.' 8-mm home movie, June 1960
Chichak, Marcel. 'Shell 4000' (1962–8). Video compilation
National Film Board. *Rallye Des Neiges.* 1961

Correspondence

Brockington, Bob, (email) to author, 28 January 2003
Carter, Diana, (email) to author, 15 September 2004
Corran, Des, to author, January 1992
Edwardes, Robin, to author, 7 June 1990
Greenblatt, David, to author, 17 March 2006
Johnson, Neale, to author, 6 April 1992
Koerner, Stephen T., to author, 27 September 2001
Locke, Graham, 19 November 1992
Magwood, Gary, (email) to author, 21 April 2006

Monahan, David, (email) to author, 15 March 1999
Purdy, Alec, to author, 9 February 1992
Stanley, Lester, to author, 4 December 1991, 21 February 2006
Steventon, David, Manager, Technical and Travel Services, Canadian Automobile Association, Ottawa, to author, 14 February 1995
Tugwell, Iain, (email) to Robert Brockington, 12 June 2000
Wright, Milton J., to author, 15 January 1992

Speech

Howell, Colin D. 'Two Outs: Writing about Sport and Maritime History,' The W.S. MacNutt Lecture, University of New Brunswick, 27 October 1998

Secondary Sources

Books and Articles

Alexander, Don, and John Block. *The Racer's Dictionary.* Santa Ana, CA: Steve Smith Autosports, 1980.
Allan, Chris. 'The Sports Car Spectacle of the Year.' *Canadian Sport* 46, no. 10 (October 1961), 8–10.
Assael, Shaun. *Wide Open: Days and Nights on the NASCAR Tour.* New York: Ballantine, 1998.
Associated Press. 'Study Blasts Brewers Sponsorship.' *Globe and Mail*, 12 May 1990.
Auto Editors of Consumer Guide. *Corvette: America's Sports Car.* Lincolnwood, IL: Publications International, 1989.
Barendse, Michael A. 'Individualism, Technology, and Sport: The Speedway Nexus.' *Journal of Sport and Social Issues* 7, no. 1 (1983), 15–23.
Batchelor, Dean, Chris Poole, and Graham Robson, eds. *The Great Book of Sports Cars.* New York: Portland House, 1988.
Beacon, Bill. 'Villeneuve Intrigued by NASCAR, Hasn't Written Off Formula One.' Canadian Press, 12 December 2003, at http://www.canada.com.
Berrett, Tim, and Trevor Slack. 'An Analysis of the Influence of Competitive and Institutional Pressures on Corporate Sponsorship Decisions.' *Journal of Sport Management* 13 (1999), 114–38.
Best, Dave, ed. *Canada: Our Century in Sport: 1900–2000.* Markham, ON: Fitzhenry and Whiteside, 2002.
Bishop, George. *The Concise Dictionary of Motorsport.* New York: Mayflower Books, 1979.

Bochroch, Albert R. *Trans-Am Racing, 1966–85: Detroit's Battle for Pony Car Supremacy.* Osceola, WI: Motorbooks International, 1986.
Boddy, Bill. *Brooklands Giants: Brave Men and Their Great Cars.* Sparkford, UK: G.T. Foulis / Haynes Publishing, 1995.
Boddy, William, and Brian Laban. *The History of Motor Racing.* London: W.H. Smith, 1988.
Bothwell, Robert, Ian Drummond, and John English. *Canada since 1945: Power, Politicians, and Provincialism.* Toronto: University of Toronto Press, 1989.
Brockington, Bob (Robert J.). 'Le Circuit Mont Tremblant: Quebec's Answer to Mosport.' *Inside Track*, 4, issue 9 (19 June 2000), 32–3.
– *Mosport International Raceway: Four Decades of Racing.* Mosport International Raceway, 2001.
Brown, Allan E. *The History of America's Speedways Past and Present.* 2nd ed. Comstock Park, MI: America's Speedways, 1994.
Brown, Ian. *Freewheeling: The Feuds, Broods, and Outrageous Fortunes of the Billes Family and Canada's Favourite Company.* Toronto: Harper and Collins, 1989.
Brunt, Stephen. 'Fantastic Indy Finish Rates a City Hall Visit,' *Globe and Mail*, 27 May 1992.
– 'The Indy Comes of Age.' *Globe and Mail*, 15 July 1995.
Callwood, June. 'The Fatal Fascination of Car Racing.' *Maclean's Magazine*, 19 November 1960, 26–7, 63–8.
Cameron, Stevie. 'High-Powered Vancouverites Try to Fuel Car Race with Beer Money.' *Globe and Mail*, 27 April 1989.
Campbell, Colin. *The Sports Car: Its Design and Performance.* 4th ed. Cambridge, MA: Robert Bentley, 1978.
Canadian Honda Motor Limited. *An Introduction: The Honda / Goodrich Challenge Series.* Agincourt, ON: May 1977.
Canadian Racing Drivers Association. *Beginner's Guide to Canadian Motor Racing.* Toronto: Canada Track and Traffic Magazine, ca. 1963.
Chimits, Xavier, and François Franet. *Williams Renault Formula One Motor Racing Book.* London, New York: Dorling Kindersley, 1994.
Church, Roy. *The Rise and Decline of the British Motor Industry.* London: Macmillan, 1994.
Clairoux, Benoit. *Montréal: 25 ans de Formule 1 / 25 Years of Formula One.* Montreal: Éditions Hurtubise HMH Ltée, 2003.
Coates, Len. *Challenge: The Story of Canadian Road Racing.* Sherbrooke, PQ: Progressive Publications, 1970.
Coffey, Frank, and Joseph Layden. *America on Wheels: The First 100 Years, 1896–1996. The Companion to the PBS Special.* Los Angeles: General Publishing Group, 1996.

Coffman, Bill. 'Canadian Racing Driver's Association,' *Mosport Competition Magazine*, 2, no. 5 (13–14 June 1970), 44.
Collins, Robert. *You Had to Be There: An Intimate Portrait of the Generation That Survived the Depression, Won the War, and Re-Invented Canada*. Toronto: McClelland and Stewart, 1997.
Corran, Des. 'History of the St. Catharines Motor Club 1953–1975.' Unpublished typescript, n.d.
Cosgrove, Michael. 'Race Driver Must Be as Fit as Fast Car.' *Globe and Mail*, 24 March 1989.
Couldwell, Clive. *Formula One: Made in Britain. The British Influence in Formula One*. London: Virgin Books, 2003.
Crompton, John L. 'Sponsorship of Sport by Tobacco and Alcohol Companies: A Review of the Issues.' *Journal of Sport and Social Issues* 17, no. 3 (December 1993), 148–67.
'Danica Proves Her Mettle at Indy.' *Sports Illustrated*, 29 May 2005, online at http://sportsillustrated.cnn.com.
Davis, Ted. 'How TV Goes Along for the Ride.' *Globe and Mail*, 6 August 1993.
Dewhirst, Timothy, and Robert Sparks. 'Intertextuality, Tobacco Sponsorship of Sports, and Adolescent Male Smoking Culture: A Selective Review of Tobacco Industry Documents.' *Journal of Sport and Social Issues* 24, no. 4 (November 2003), 372–98.
Donaldson, Gerald. *Gilles Villeneuve: The Life of the Legendary Racing Driver*. Croydon, UK: Motor Racing Publications, 1989.
– *The Grand Prix of Canada*. Scarborough, ON: Avon Books, 1984.
'Don't Knock This Woman Driver – She's a Champion Behind the Wheel.' *Oshawa Times*, 27 April 1972.
Douglas, Donna. 'Kat Teasdale,' *TG Magazine*, 1992; reissued 1999 at http://collections.gc.ca/generation/90cptext/90cp3.htm.
Durnford, Hugh, and Glenn Baechler. *Cars of Canada*. Toronto: McClelland and Stewart, 1973.
Ebershoff-Coles, Susan, and Charla Ann Leibenguth. *Motorsports: A Guide to Information Sources*. Detroit: Gale, 1979.
'Ecclestone Adds to Villeneuve Woes.' BBC Sport, 10 June 2005, at http://newsvote.bbc.co.uk.
Edwardes, Robin. 'Rallying in Canada.' Unpublished typescript, 1990.
– 'Toyota's Success in Automobile Rallying in Canada.' Handwritten manuscript, n.d.
Edwards, John. *Auto Dictionary*. Los Angeles: HP Books, 1993.
Facts and Figures of the Automobile Industry 1968. Toronto: Motor Vehicle Manufacturer's Association, 1968.

Ferriss, Paul. *Never Too Fast: The Paul Tracy Story.* Toronto: ECW Press, 2001.
Feschuk, Dave. 'Champ Cars Still Have Some Gas Left in the Tank.' *National Post*, 21 February 2003.
Fleischman, Bill, and Al Pearce. *Inside Sports NASCAR Racing.* Detroit: Visible Ink Press, 1998.
Flink, James J. *The Automobile Age.* Cambridge, MA: MIT Press, 1988.
– *The Car Culture.* Cambridge, MA: MIT Press, 1978.
Friedman, Dave. *Pro Sports Car Racing in America, 1958–1974.* Osceola, WI: Motorbooks International, 1999.
– *Trans-Am: The Pony Car Wars 1966–1972.* Osceola, WI: MBI Publishing, 2001.
Frumkin, Mitch. *Muscle Car Mania: An Advertising Collection, 1964–1974.* Osceola, WI: Motorbooks International, 1981.
'Full Probe Ordered into Deaths of Spectators at Carp.' *Ottawa Citizen*, 29 August 1955.
Garrett, Richard. *The Rally Go-Round: The Story of International Rallying.* London: Stanley Paul, 1970.
Gartman, David. *Auto Opium: A Social History of American Automobile Design.* London: Routledge, 1994.
Georgano, Nick. *The American Automobile: A Centenary, 1893–1993.* New York: Smithmark Publishers, 1992.
Girdler, Allan. *American Road Race Specials, 1934–70: Glory Days of Homebuilt Racers.* Osceola, WI: Motorbooks International, 1990.
Granatstein, J.L., Irving Abella, David J. Bercuson, R. Craig Brown, and H. Blair Neatby. *Twentieth Century Canada.* 2nd ed. Toronto: McGraw Hill, 1986.
'Grand Prix Notebook: Villeneuve Packs 'em In' and 'Grand Prix 97.' *Montreal Gazette*, 16 June 1997, sections D and E.
Grange, Michael. 'Refuelling F1.' *EnRoute*, 2000, 46–63.
– 'Win on Sunday ... Sell on Monday.' *Report on Business Magazine*, August 2001, 36–40.
Grant, Gregor. *500-c.c. Racing.* London: G.T. Foulis, 1950.
Gratton, Chris, and Peter Taylor. *Sport and Recreation: An Economic Analysis.* London: E. & F.N. Spon, 1985.
Hall, Phil. *Fearsome Fords 1959–73.* Osceola, WI: Motorbooks International, 1982.
Harris-Adler, Rose. 'Speed Diva.' *Canadian*, October 1998, 43–50.
Haskell, Ann Sullivan. 'The Lexicon of the Sports and Racing Car Enthusiast.' *Publication of the American Dialect Society*, no. 42 (November 1964), 1–10.
Hatter, David. 'Dateline: Canada – Divorce, Canadian Style.' *On Track*, Spring 1990, 51.

Hilton, Christopher. *Inside the Mind of the Grand Prix Driver*. 2nd ed. Sparkford, UK: Haynes Publishing, 2003.
– *Jacques Villeneuve: Champion of Two Worlds*. Sparkford, UK: Haynes Publishing, 1997.
Hodges, David. *A–Z of Formula Racing Cars*. Bideford, UK: Bay View Books, 1990.
– *The Hamlyn Encyclopedia of Grands Prix*. London: Hamlyn, 1988.
Horna, Jarmilia L.A. 'Trends in Sports in Canada.' In Teus J. Ramphorts and Kenneth Roberts, eds., *Trends in Sports: A Multinational Perspective*, 40–5. Voorthuizen, Netherlands: Giordano Bruno Culemborg, 1989.
Hough, Robert. 'Driving Ambition,' *EnRoute*, May 1991, 40–3, 74.
Howell, Colin D. *Blood, Sweat, and Cheers: Sport and the Making of Modern Canada*. Toronto: University of Toronto Press, 2001.
Howell, Nancy, and Maxwell Howell. *Sports and Games in Canadian Life*. Toronto: Macmillan, 1969.
Huff, Richard. *The Insider's Guide to Stock Car Racing. NASCAR Racing: America's Fastest Growing Sport*. Chicago: Bonus Books, 1997.
Huntington, Roger. *American Supercar: Development of the Detroit High-Performance Car*. Tucson, AZ: HP Books, 1983.
Iacocca, Lee, with William Novak. *Iacocca: A Biography*. New York: Bantam, 1984.
Ibrahim, Hilmi. *Leisure and Society: A Comparative Approach*. Dubuque, IA: Wm. C. Brown Publishers, 1991.
Incandela, Sal. *The Anatomy & Development of the Formula One Racing Car from 1975*. 3rd. ed. Sparkford, UK: Haynes Publishing Group, 1990.
Ivens, Bill. 'It Was No Paper Chase.' *Shell News*, April–May 1962, 27–32.
Jenkins, Anthony. 'Rallying Thrills as a Spectator Sport (Once You Adjust).' *Globe and Mail*, 15 January 1996.
Johnsgard, Keith. 'Personality and Performance: A Psychological Study of Amateur Sports Car Race Drivers,' *Journal of Sports Medicine and Physical Fitness* 17 (1977), 97–104.
Johnston, Tom. *Sports Car Road Racing in Western Canada, 1949–2003*. Vancouver: Granville Island Press, 2004.
Jones, Bruce. *The Ultimate Encyclopedia of Formula One: The Definitive Illustrated Guide to Grand Prix Motor Racing*. London: Carlton Books, 1998.
Kelly, John R., and Geoffrey Godbey. *The Sociology of Leisure*. State College, PA: Venture Publishing, 1992.
Kennedy, Eileen. 'Bad Boys and Gentlemen: Gendered Narratives in Televised Sport.' *International Review for the Sociology of Sport* 35, no. 1, 2003, 59–73.
Kenzie, Jim. 'Canada's Auto Racing Greats Honoured.' *Toronto Star*, 20 August 1993.

Kerr, Greg. 'Comstock Racing Team.' *Sporting Classics*, May–June 1991, 8–11.
– 'Peter Ryan: Canada's First Superstar Race Driver.' *Sporting Classics*, March–April 1992, 24–7.
Kingston, Michael. 'Vintage Racing: Auld Lang Syne Revisited.' *Canadian Motorsport Annual*, 1981–2, 58–9.
Kleif, Tine, and Wendy Faulkner. '"I'm No Athlete [But] I Can Make This Thing Dance": Men's Pleasures in Technology.' *Science, Technology and Human Values* 28, no. 2 (Spring 2003), 296–325.
Kraus, Richard. *Recreation and Leisure in Modern Society.* 5th ed. Toronto: Jones and Bartlett, 1998.
Lacey, Robert. *Ford: The Men and the Machine*. Toronto: Seal Books, 1986.
Lamb, David. 'Sponsorship and Racing.' *Driving*, April 1973, 31–3.
Larrabee, Eric, and Rolf Meyerson, eds. *Mass Leisure*. Glencoe, IL: Free Press, 1958.
Lawrence, Mike. *A to Z of Sports Cars, 1945–1990*. Bideford, UK: Bay View Books, 1991.
– *Directory of Classic Sports-Racing Cars*. Bourne End, UK: Aston Publications, 1987.
LeBlanc, Daniel and Jeff Pappone, 'Canadian Grand Prix Saved.' *Globe and Mail*, 19 November 2003, at http://www.globeandmail.com.
Levine, Joshua. 'Ringmeister.' *Forbes* 168, no. 1 (9 July 2001), 90–4.
Lewis, David L., and Laurence Goldstein. *The Automobile and American Culture*. Ann Arbor: University of Michigan Press, 1983.
Lowes, Mark Douglas. *Indy Dreams and Urban Nightmares: Speed Merchants, Spectacle and the Struggle over Public Space in the World-Class City.* Toronto: University of Toronto Press, 2002.
– 'Indy Dreams in the World Class City.' In Peter Donnelly, ed., *Taking Sport Seriously: Social Issues in Canadian Sport*, 147–9. 2nd ed. Toronto: Thompson Educational Publishing, 2001.
Luc, Pierre. *L'Histoire du Sport Automobile au Québec / The History of Auto Racing in Quebec*. Montreal: Les Éditions de la Table Ronde, 1971.
Lynch, Michael T., William Edgar, and Ron Parravano. *American Sports Car Racing in the 1950s*. Osceola, WI: MBI Publishing, 1998.
Lyons, Pete. *Can-Am*. Osceola, WI: Motorbooks International, 1995.
– *Ferrari: The Man and His Machines*. Lincolnwood, IL: Publications International, 1989.
McCluggage, Denise. *By Brooks Too Broad for Leaping: Selections from Auto Week*. Santa Fe, NM: Fulcorte Press, 1994.
MacDonald, Ian. 'St. Laurent's Dr. Dancose Makes It 3-for-3 in Honda Series.' *Montreal Gazette*, 11 June 1990.
McDonald, Norris. 'Yesterday's Heroes.' *Formula*, July 1994, 30–1.

McLaren, Chuck. *Mosport Park: 25 Years! Mosport Competition Magazine*, special issue, vol. 11, no. 3 (1985).
MacRae, Ian. 'A Track in Need of a Tune-up.' *Globe and Mail*, 23 December 1987 (letter).
Mandell, Richard D. *Sport: A Cultural History*. New York: Columbia University Press, 1984.
Matsumoto, Rick. 'The New Auto Racer: A Finely Tuned Machine. Only Real Athletes Can Take Indy Cars.' *Toronto Star*, 17 July 1999.
Metcalfe, Alan. 'The Meaning of Amateurism: A Case Study of Canadian Sport, 1884–1970.' *Canadian Journal of the History of Sport* 26, no. 2 (December 1995), 33–48.
Miller, Robin. 'Player's Ban to Hit Before Season Ends.' ESPN, 11 July 2003, at http://www.espn.com.
Milton, Brian Gerard. *Social Status and Leisure Time Activities: National Survey Findings for Adult Canadians*. Sociology no. 3, in Canadian Sociology and Anthropology Association Monograph Series. Montreal: Canadian Sociology and Anthropology Association, 1975.
Moorhouse, H.F. *Driving Ambitions: A Social Analysis of the American Hot Rod Enthusiasm*. Manchester, UK: Manchester University Press, 1991.
Morell, Dave. 'Rallying: The Safe Sport That's Catching On.' *New Brunswick* 1, no. 3 (September 1976), 15–17.
Morrison, Ian. *Motor Racing: The Records*. Enfield, UK: Guinness Superlatives, 1987.
Morrow, Don, Mary Keyes, Wayne Simpson, Frank Cosentino, and Ron Lappage, eds. *A Concise History of Sport in Canada*. Toronto: Oxford University Press, 1989.
Moss, Stirling. *A Turn at the Wheel*. London: William Kimber, 1961.
Neely, William. *Tire Wars: Racing with Goodyear*. Tucson, AZ: Aztex Corporation, 1993.
Noad, Peter. *VW Beetle in Motorsport: The Illustrated History, 1940s to 1990s*. London: Windrow and Greene, 1992.
Noble, Dudley, ed. *The Jubilee Book of the Royal Automobile Club, 1897–1947*. London: Royal Automobile Club, 1947.
Nye, Doug. *The Autocourse History of the Grand Prix Car, 1966–91*. 2nd ed. Richmond, UK: Hazleton Publishing, 1992.
Offer, Avner. 'The American Automobile Frenzy of the 1950s.' In Kristine Bruland and Patrick O'Brien, eds., *From Family Firms to Corporate Capitalism*, 317–53. Oxford: Clarendon, 1998.
Orr, Frank. *George Eaton: Five Minutes to Green*. Don Mills, ON: Longman Canada, 1970.

Ort, Doug. *The Western Ontario Sports Car Association History.* London, ON: WOSCA, 1980.
Owram, Doug. *Born at the Right Time: A History of the Baby Boom Generation.* Toronto: University of Toronto Press, 1996.
Pappone, Jeff. 'Villeneuve Seeking Job with Former F1 Employer.' *Globe and Mail*, 19 August 2004, at http://www.globeandmail.com.
Parrish, Darla, ed. *Sports Car Club of America: 60 Years in Photos.* Nashville, TN: Turner Publishing Company, 2004.
Partridge, Ken. 'The Moosehead Grand Prix.' *Atlantic Lifestyle Business* 3, no. 4, (1992), 41–4.
Phillips, David. *American Motorsports.* London: Carlton Books, 1997.
Pillsbury, Richard. 'Stock Car Racing.' In Karl B. Raitz, ed., *The Theater of Sport*, 270–95. Baltimore, MD: Johns Hopkins University Press, 1995.
Pope, S.W. 'Amateurism and American Sports Culture: The Invention of an Athletic Sports Tradition in the United States, 1870–1900.' *International Journal of the History of Sport* 13, no. 3 (December 1996), 290–309.
Post, Robert C. *High Performance: The Culture and Technology of Drag Racing, 1950–1990.* Baltimore, MD: Johns Hopkins University Press, 1994.
Powell, Philip Murray. *The Car That Changed the Canadian Road: 40 Years with Volkswagen Canada.* Volkswagen Canada Inc., 1992.
Pritchard, Anthony. *Directory of Classic Prototype and Grand Touring Cars.* Bourne End, UK: Aston Publications, 1988.
– *Directory of Formula One Cars, 1966–1986.* Bourne End, UK: Aston Publications, 1986.
– *Ford vs. Ferrari: The Battle for Le Mans.* Rev. ed. Marina Del Rey, CA: Zuma Marketing, 1984.
– *Specialist British Sports / Racing Cars of the Fifties and Sixties: A Marque-by-Marque Analysis – From AC to Warrior-Bristol.* London: Osprey Publishing, 1986.
Proudfoot, Dan, Gordon Kirby, and Jim Taylor. *Greg Moore: A Legacy of Spirit.* Vancouver: Whitecap Books, 2000.
Radosta, John S. *The New York Times Complete Guide to Auto Racing.* Chicago: Quadrangle Books, 1971.
Rae, John B. *The American Automobile: A Brief History.* Chicago: University of Chicago Press, 1965.
– *The American Automobile Industry.* Boston: Twayne Publishers, 1984.
Rendall, Ivan. *Chequered Flag: 100 Years of Motor Racing.* London: Weidenfeld and Nicolson, 1993.
– *The Power and the Glory: A Century of Motor Racing.* London: BBC Books, 1991.

– *The Power Game: The History of Formula One and the World Championship*. London: Cassell, 2000.
Rhys, D.G. *The Motor Industry: An Economic Survey*. London: Butterworths, 1972.
Richler, Jacob. 'Jacques Attack.' *Saturday Night*, September 1995, 30–5, 84.
Roberts, Randy, and James S. Olson. *Winning Is the Only Thing: Sports in America since 1945*. Baltimore, MD: Johns Hopkins University Press, 1989.
Robson, Graham. *A–Z of Works Rally Cars From the 1940s to the 1990s*. Bideford, UK: Bay View Books, 1994.
Rueter, John C. *The Sports Car Club: How to Join or Organize One*. New York: Sports Car Press, 1960.
Ruiz, Marco. *The History of the Automobile*. New York: Gallery Books, 1985.
St. James, Lyn. *Ride of Your Life: A Race Car Driver's Journey*. New York: Hyperion, 2002.
Sakkis, Tony. *Anatomy and Development of the Indy Car*. Osceola, WI: Motorbooks International, 1994.
Saward, Joe. *The World Atlas of Motor Racing*. London: Hamlyn, 1989.
'SCCA Explain Their Stand on FIA Suspensions.' *Montreal Gazette*, 14 July 1961.
Schnapp, John B. *Corporate Strategies of Automotive Manufacturers*. Toronto: D.C. Heath, 1979.
Scully, Gerald. *The Market Structure of Sports*. Chicago: University of Chicago Press, 1995.
Shaffer, Rick. *CART: The First 20 Years, 1979–1998*. Richmond, UK: Hazleton Publishing, 1999.
Siano, Joseph. 'Al Unser Jr. Barely Beats Goodyear.' *Globe and Mail*, 25 May 1992.
Silk, Gerald. *Automobile and Culture*. New York: Harry N. Abrams, 1984.
Smith, R.P. *Consumer Demand for Cars in the USA*. Cambridge: Cambridge University Press, 1975.
Sobel, Robert. *Car Wars: The Untold Story*. New York: E.P. Dutton, 1984.
Spain, Ronnie. *GT40: An Individual History and Race Record*. London: Osprey Publishing, 1986.
Staudohar, Paul D., and James A. Mangan, eds. *The Business of Professional Sports*. Urbana and Chicago: University of Illinois Press, 1991.
Stein, Jonathan A. *British Sports Cars in America, 1946–1981*. Kutztown, PA: Automobile Quarterly Publications, 1993.
Stone, F. David. 'Grand Prix Racing – North American Style.' *Mosport Competition Magazine*, 1970, 10, 12.
Taylor, Rich. *Modern Classics: The Great Cars of the Postwar Era*. New York: Beekman House, 1988.

Terry, Len, and Alan Baker. *Racing Car Design and Development*. Cambridge, MA: Robert Bentley, 1973.
Todd, Phillip. 'Formula One Bosses Kill '04 Grand Prix.' *Montreal Gazette*, 8 August 2003, at http://www.canada.com.
'Tracy Wins First CART Driver's Crown.' *Globe and Mail*, 26 October 2003, at http://www.theglobeandmail.com.
Tremayne, David, and Mark Hughes. *The Concise Encyclopedia of Formula One*. Bath, UK: Parragon Publishing, 2000.
Valent, Henry. *Road Racing at Watkins Glen*. Watkins Glen, NY: Chamber of Commerce, 1958.
Von Dare, Gregory. *Corvette Racers*. Osceola, WI: Motorbooks International, 1992.
Wallace, Bruce. 'Eyes on the Prize.' *Maclean's*, 16 June 1997, 36–42.
Watson, William G. *National Pastimes: The Economics of Canadian Leisure*. Vancouver: Fraser Institute, 1988.
Weintraub, William. 'Film-Maker Was Dominant Force During NFB's Golden Age.' *Montreal Gazette*, 26 December 2002.
Wenner, Lawrence A., ed. *Media, Sports, and Society*. Newbury Park, CA: Sage Publications, 1989.
Wernick, Andrew. *Promotional Culture: Advertising, Ideology, and Symbolic Expression*. London: Sage Publications, 1991.
West, J. Thomas. 'Automobile Racing.' *The Canadian Encyclopedia*. 2nd ed., 1: 150. Edmonton: Hurtig Publishers, 1988.
Whannel, Garry. *Fields in Vision: Television Sport and Cultural Transformation*. London: Routledge, 1992.
– *Media Sports Stars: Masculinities and Moralities*. London: Routledge, 2002.
Whisler, Timothy R. *At the End of the Road: The Rise and Fall of Austin-Healey, MG, and Triumph Sports Cars*. Greenwich, CT: JAI Press, 1995.
White, Lawrence J. *The Automobile Industry since 1945*. Cambridge, MA: Harvard University Press, 1971.
Wright, Jeff. 'Frank Jobborn: In Memoriam,' *GT Magazine*, August–September 1992, 8.
– 'Moose Loose on Halifax Streets,' *GT Magazine*, November–December 1990.
Wyss, Wallace A. *Shelby's Wildlife: The Cobras, Mustangs, and Dodges*. 2nd ed. Osceola, WI: Motorbooks International, 1987.
Yates, Brock. *The Decline and Fall of the American Automobile Industry*. New York: Empire Books, 1983.
Zbarsky, Ralph. 'Memories of a Great Adventure: Westwood Motorsport Park.' *Sporting Classics*, May–June 1991, 28–9.
Zimmerman, John. *The Atlantic Championship: A Quarter Century on the Road to Stardom*. Indianapolis, IN: USDC Publishing, 1999.

320 Select Bibliography

On-line Sources

Ashley Taws biography. http://www.girl-racers.com/drivers/taws/index.html. Update on post-accident recovery at http:// www.racerchicks.com/news/M_TawsUPD.html.
ASN Canada website. http://www.asncanada.com.
Canadian Autoslalom Championship Official Results, 2004. http://cadl.qc.ca/cac/results/cac2004resultsweb.pdf.
Canadian Motorsport Hall of Fame inductees. http://www.cmhf.ca/execs/inductees.htm.
'The Canadian Road Racing Championship 1969–1970: The Formula "A" Years.' *Canadian Racer*, at http://www.motorsportscentral.com/formula-a.asp (found under feature articles)
Champ Car team drivers site. http://sports.rpm.espn.go.com/rpm/drivers?seriesId=5.
Honda series website (2006). http://www.civicchampionship.com (official Honda series website, 2006).
Indy Car results. http://www.indycar.com/stats/race_results.
'Kathryn "Kat" Teasdale and Katko Racing.' At http://polaris.umuc.edu/~ahuseoni/kat.html.
'Marybeth Harrison's Mach 1 Racing Offical Website.' At http://www.marybethharrison.com.
'Molson Indy History: Getting the Green Flag to Go Racing in Toronto.' At http://www.molsonindy.com/toronto/race/history.html (no longer active).
Pace, Harold. 'Can-Am Racing Part 2: Cultivating Up-and-Coming Champions, 1977–1986.' At http://www.advanceautoparts.com/english/youcan/html (no longer active).
'Shannonville Motorsport Park,' *Canadian Racer*, at http://www.motorsports.central.com/track-display.asp?trackid=smp1&querytype=detail&extra=history.
Shell 4000 rally history site (maintained by Marcel Chichak). http://Shell-4000-rally.org
Targa Newfoundland rally. http://www.targanewfoundland.com.
'Tracy Cashes in on the Gold Coast.' *Champ Car News*, Monday 27 October 2003, at http://www.champcarworldseries.com/news/article.asp?id=7337.

Illustration Credits

Lionel Birnbom: Gilles Villeneuve winning in Montreal (cover); Carling 300 race; genius and talent: Bill Sadler; Heather Wilson and Diana Carter; the home of Canadian racing: Mosport; the cutting edge: the Sadler Mk. V; David vs. Goliath: Clark's Mini vs. Fisher's Pontiac; Peter Broeker; Jacques Duval; ice racing; Canadian Grand Prix, 1967; Trois-Rivières Grand Prix; muscle cars; George Eaton; Formula B; superstar in the making: Villeneuve, 1977

David Brown: airport racing, Abbotsford

Bruce Buntain: Fram and Risley Cobra

Canadian Automobile Sport Club: the CASC's founders

Tom Johnston: MGs racing at Davidson, 1957; Westwood racing circuit; Molson Indy Vancouver

Pete Lyons: Comstock GT40; John Cannon at Laguna Seca, 1968

Shell Canada: Renault Team, 1962 Shell 4000

Index

Abbotsford airport race track, BC, 7, 40, 41, 43
AC cars, 26, 28; Ace-Bristol, 26, 43, 97, 149; Cobra, *see* Shelby cars
accidents. *See* auto sport, accidents in, fatalities in, safety
Adam, Bill, 205
Adams, Nat, 120, 142, 145, 146, 168, 170
advertising. *See* auto sport, advertising in; commercialism; sponsorship
aerodynamics. *See* racing cars, design
airport race tracks. *See* race tracks; *see also tracks by name*
Alary, Phillipe, 214
Alfa Romeo cars, 29, 42, 54, 76, 154, 265n
Alitalia airline, 175
Allard racing cars, 28
Allen, Fred, 38
Allers, Frank, 226
Alpine Rally, 106
amateurism, 8, 22, 38–55, 68, 71, 74, 78, 80, 84, 174, 204
American Indy Car series (AIS), 239–41
American Motors cars, 96, 215
Amon, Chris, 160, 163, 224–5
AMX Javelin. *See* American Motors cars
Andretti, Mario, 6, 240
Andretti, Michael, 42, 240
appearance money. *See under* auto sport
Arundell, Peter, 137
Ash, Vasey, 105
Ashfield, Alvin, 34
ASN (national sporting authority). *See* ASN Canada FIA; Canadian Automobile Sport Clubs; Fédération Internationale de l'Automobile
ASN Canada FIA, 31, 254
l'Association des Coureurs Automobile de Montréal (ACAM), 89, 207, 227
Aston Martin cars, 28, 64
Atlantic Grand Prix company, 241
Atlantic Motorsport Park (AMP), Nova Scotia, 203, 207–9, 211, 225, 233, 241, 247
Atlantic Region. *See* Canadian Automobile Sport Clubs

Atlantic Region Motor Sports, 304n
Atlantic Sports Car Club (ASCC), 55, 61, 88, 207
Attrell, Bob, 177
Austin cars, 26; A-40, 77, 274n; Mini, 26, 95, 103. *See also* British Motor Corporation
Austin-Healey cars, 26, 28, 29, 30, 43, 64, 65, 72, 87, 94, 130, 145, 150, 226, 256; Sprite, 26, 29, 30, 43, 64, 94, 150, 226; 3000, 26, 87, 130, 145
Australia, 102, 210
Auto-Mapic Marathon rally, 110
Automobile Competition Committee for the United States (ACCUS), 92, 165
automobile industry, 26, 27, 75–8, 82, 83, 84, 96, 102, 155, 189, 199, 226, 228; American, *see* 'Big Three' auto makers, *and companies by name*; British, 26, 27, 28, 30, 106, 155, 180, 199; Canadian, 27; Japanese, 199; market, 28, 29, 30, 97, 196, 199, 226, 228; marketing, 77–8, 93, 96, 107, 189, 228
Automobile Manufacturers Association, 96
Automobile Racing Club of America (ARCA), 18, 20
automobiles, 17, 24, 25, 36, 37, 66, 189; American, 27, 28, 33, 95–8, 199, 206, 248, 277n, *see also specific makes by name*; British sports cars, 24, 26, 27, 28, 30, 32, 33, 39, 40, 72, 96, 97, 199, 256, *see also specific makes by name*; compact cars, 107; 'muscle cars,' 29, 95–8, 142, 277n; ownership, 24–5, 26, 36. *See also* automobile industry; car culture
auto slalom. *See* solo racing

auto sport: accidents in, 67, 100, 103, 137, 141, 221; advertising in, 4, 7, 105–6, 107, 181, 182, 188, 215, 218, 232, 239, 241–2, 250, 257, 279n; amateur, 9, 20, 22, 38–73, 77, 78, 84, 93, 94, 113, 118, 131–2, 138, 187, 188, 191, 192, 195–7, 200, 203–20, 225–7, 231–3, 235, 241, 242, 247–9, 251, 253–4, 255, 256, 259; appearance money, 120, 122, 157, 159, 171, 234; audiences, 7, 21, 33, 39, 40, 43, 57, 66, 67, 72, 73, 79–82, 91–4, 97, 119, 121, 122, 124–5, 127, 129, 130, 131, 132, 159, 160, 163, 165, 177, 178, 183, 184, 188, 200, 202–5, 207, 209, 212, 213, 216, 217, 222, 226, 227, 232, 233, 235–6, 239, 241, 248, 250, 251, 253, 257, 259; automobile industry and, 75–8, 84, 204, 226; control of, 83, 87–93, 124, 144, 180, 214, 242–5, 259; costs and funding of, 22, 40, 42–4, 79, 80, 81, 94, 97, 105–6, 118, 122, 123–6, 129, 131, 132, 142, 146, 147, 149, 157–60, 165, 166, 169–72, 174, 176–82, 185–6, 188, 189, 190–2, 199, 200, 206, 208–9, 211–13, 215, 216, 219, 220, 222–3, 224, 226–8, 229, 231–4, 237–8, 241, 242, 249, 251, 253, 256, 258, 286n; decline of, in Canada, 203–20, 231–2; enthusiasts, 7, 8, 19, 24, 25, 26, 33, 49, 73, 75, 78, 79, 81, 84, 94, 127, 163, 217, 226–7, 230, 250, 251, 253, 259; entrepreneurs, 8, 22, 75–8, 251; fatalities in 43, 56–7, 67, 103, 113, 137, 141, 221–2; marketing and, 212, 217, 233, 242, 305n; prize money, 39, 72, 74, 78, 79, 81, 105, 120, 122, 142, 144, 157, 159, 171, 178–85, 189, 200, 201, 204, 214, 219,

Index 325

222, 225, 228, 249; purpose of, 8, 40, 44, 55, 73, 79, 107, 122, 131, 177, 178, 190–1, 197, 235, 239, 242, 251, 254, 257, 258; regulation of, 63–71, 80, 90–3, 252, 253, 254; safety, 40, 43, 48, 56–7, 63, 66–71, 112, 113, 123, 200, 209, 227, 232, 250, 252, 253; spectacle, auto sport as, 7, 8, 79, 81, 118, 119, 122, 132, 176, 184, 188, 239, 241, 250, 252, 257, 258, 259; subculture, 7, 22, 23–37, 93, 132, 209–11, 250, 254, 255, 259; technological change in, 8, 26, 148–55, 157, 170, 171, 251, 252–3; transformation of, 7–10, 83, 132; volunteers in, 39, 68, 80, 81, 229, 239, 244–5, 253; weather, as a factor in, 39, 40, 50–1, 105, 111, 117, 205, 206, 233, 241; women in, 35–7, 39, 94–5, 254–5. *See also* amateurism; amateur sport; Canadian Automobile Sport Clubs; car clubs; commercialism; commercial professionalism; *events by name*; Fédération Internationale de l'Automobile; formula car racing; professionalism; racing; rallying; solo racing; sponsorship

Auto Sport Canada magazine, 199, 222, 226

Auto Union racing cars, 153

Bailey, Phil, 109
Baird, Donald, 26, 29, 30, 32
Bardahl company, 154
Barrell, Bob, 205
Barrell, Les, 76
Bartholemew, Lee, 192–3
Bartling, Rudy, 168, 225
baseball, 5, 6, 8, 21, 259

Bassett, John, Jr, 235–6
Bateman, Doug, 94, 130
Bateman, Lawrence, 59, 60, 84
Baxter Dairies, 247
beer, 253. *See also* breweries; *companies by name*; sponsorship
Belgian Grand Prix, 221
Bellefleur, John, 196, 198, 199, 201
Bell racing helmets, 67
Bennetton clothing company, 9
Bernstein, Kenny, 9
Berthierville, Quebec, 4, 174, 222
Bienvenue, Jacques, 204–5, 225
'Big Three' auto makers, 27, 28, 77, 96, 106; *see also* Chrysler cars, Ford Motor Company, General Motors Corporation
Billes, Dave, 171
Birnbom, Lionel, 173
Bishop, John, 157
Boddy, William, 252
Bon Accord race track, Alberta, 94
Bone, Peter, 24, 31, 34, 47, 104–5, 109, 110, 113–16, 181, 218
Bonnier, Joakim, 119–20, 123, 138, 151
Booth, Percy, 130–1
Booth, Reg, 130–1
Bothwell, Robert, 25
Bowles, Shirley, 95
Boxtrom, Jack, 233
Boyce, Walter, 189, 190, 192, 194, 196–9, 201, 207. *See also* Woods, Doug
Brabham, Jack, 151, 163, 213; Brabham racing cars, 180
Brack, Bill, 3, 65, 94, 100, 167, 170, 172, 177, 180, 181, 183–7, 209
Bradley, Francis, 27, 31, 54, 73, 75, 81, 120, 121, 134, 142, 249
Brand, Peter, 94
Brander, Ross, 76, 103, 123

Breed, Steve, 247
breweries as sponsors, 251. *See also* companies by name
Brezinka, Rainer, 168
Bridgehampton race track, NY, 40, 68, 134, 159
Brighton Speed Trials, Britain, 149
Britain, 16, 19, 20, 28, 30, 31, 32, 53, 136, 137, 146, 147, 149, 154, 157, 208, 255
British American Racing, 258
British Automobile Racing Club – Ontario Centre (BARC-OC), 32, 35
British Columbia, 4, 16, 30, 61–2, 88, 94, 102–3, 110, 114, 115, 141, 145, 168, 178, 182, 199, 200, 205, 206, 208, 212, 225, 255, 256
British Columbia Centennial Car Rally, 117
British Columbia International Trade Fair (BCITF), 102–3, 105. *See also* Shell 4000 rally
British Empire Motor Club (BEMC), 18, 19, 27, 32, 34, 58–60, 76, 87, 103, 123, 125, 131, 165–6, 210; competition activities, 19, 26, 27, 35, 37, 40, 50, 51, 52, 54, 65, 81, 106–8, 120, 164, 191, 192; membership, 58–9, 210. *See also* Canadian Winter Rally; Harewood airport race track; Mosport Park race track
British Grand Prix, 186
British influence on Canadian auto sport, 22, 26–32
British Leyland, 212
British Motor Corporation, 29, 77; Mini, 40, 54, 95, 96, 204, 206, 256
British Petroleum (BP), 128, 129
British sports cars. *See* automobiles, British sports cars

British Standards Institute, 67
BRM, racing cars, 171; racing team, 31, 169, 171
Broadley, Eric, 140
Brocklehurst, George, 94
Broeker, Peter, 76, 77, 98, 100, 138, 169, 176, 177, 180
Brooklands race track, Britain, 31
Brooks, Ralph, 248
Brown, Harold, 146, 286n
Brown, Lloyd, 166
Bryson, Neil, 50
Budd, Alec, 76
Budd and Dyer Ltd, 76, 106
Buffalo Auto Club, NY, 18
Burgess, Tom, 200
Burlington Autosport Club, 87
business, role in auto sport. *See* commercialism; sponsorship
Byatt, Dick, 123
Bytzek, Harry, 168, 204–5
Bytzek, Klaus, 204, 225

Calgary, Alberta, 18, 117, 130, 232, 256
Calgary Sports Car Club (CSCC), 49, 54, 115
Callwood, June, 56–7, 66, 77
Camaro. *See* General Motors
Campbell, Rod, 95, 107, 127, 128, 169, 235
Canada, 27, 28, 29, 30, 33, 56, 60, 64, 73, 75, 98, 99, 100, 105, 106, 108, 117, 147, 155, 163, 165, 167, 169, 180, 182, 198, 203, 215, 227, 243, 256, 257, 258, 259, 260; 'baby boom,' 24, 28, 96; economy, 24, 30, 211–12, 218, 220, 231, 258; immigrants/immigration, 26, 27, 30,

32, 89; middle class, 24, 25, 37, 258; suburbia, 24, 25, 95, 258
Canada Class racing cars, 64, 65, 98–9, 130
Canadair Auto Club (CAC), 23, 31, 32, 46, 49, 106
Canadair company, 23, 24, 31, 32
Canada Touring Trophy endurance race, 140
Canada Track and Traffic (magazine), 41, 42, 76, 77, 78, 79, 80, 81, 82, 95, 115, 119, 121–2, 125, 126, 129, 172, 175, 179, 190, 217–18, 235
Canadian Association of Rallysport, 245, 254
Canadian Automobile Association (CAA), 19
Canadian Automobile Sport Clubs (CASC), 5, 9, 15–22, 24, 31, 34, 35, 37, 38, 39, 43, 45, 48, 49, 52, 53, 55, 57–63, 68, 70, 73, 76, 79–84, 90, 95, 105, 111, 116, 119, 123, 143, 157, 158, 159, 165, 167, 174, 175, 176, 177, 180, 181, 182, 185, 210, 211, 212, 214, 217–19, 221, 222–4, 227, 228, 229, 231, 232, 233, 236, 242–5, 251, 254; annual general meetings, 60, 63, 83, 103, 144, 145, 158, 159, 164, 167, 176, 178, 179, 183, 189, 192, 194, 198, 200, 201, 202, 203, 205, 206, 208, 210, 211, 212, 213, 215, 217, 218, 219, 222, 236; Atlantic Region, 61, 88, 111, 117, 191, 194, 198, 200–1, 204, 206, 207, 208, 225, 241, 247; authority of, 57–8, 63, 67, 71, 84, 87–8, 89–93, 110, 144, 180, 210, 214–15, 222, 236, 242–5; British Columbia Region, 61–3, 88, 117, 179, 198, 204, 207, 212, 219, 223; by-laws and constitution, 90, 92; clubs, 18–19, 23–4, 37, 57, 63, 71, 73, 88–9, 91, 92, 93, 99, 103, 165, 202, 203, 204, 210, 213, 217, 219, 222, 231, 239; communication problems, 217, 222–3, 231; competition committee, 63, 90–1; death of, 222, 242–5; executive director, 76, 189, 198, 211, 229; expansion of, 57–63, 88–9; expulsion from FIA, 243; FIA recognition, 61; finances, 91, 93, 210, 219; founders, 4, 11, 15–17, 19, 21, 22, 38, 47, 52, 84, 119, 164, 173, 251, 259; founding of, 15–22; governance style, 63, 87, 90–3; insurance, 63; licensing, 63, 69–70, 245; loss of national sanctioning authority, 243–5; membership decline, 209–20; national board of directors, 164, 179, 243; national committee, 69, 166; national competition board (NCB), 63, 91–2, 111, 117, 144, 165, 166, 244; national executive, 229; National Karting Committee (NKC), 223–4; Ontario Region, 16, 59, 60, 61, 65, 70, 91–2, 117, 126, 143, 166, 179–81, 192, 204, 206, 210, 217, 219, 225, 255, 304n; Prairie Region, 61, 117, 130, 143, 144, 204, 205, 232; president, 87, 88, 90, 92, 120, 122, 143, 160, 164, 165, 167, 178, 218, 222, 223, 242, 243; professional division, 228–9; Pro Race Board, 229, 244; Quebec Region, 61, 66, 70, 76, 94, 117, 123, 143, 166, 175, 178, 179, 189, 204, 207, 210, 213, 214, 215, 225, 237, *see also* Fédération Auto-Québec; regions, 60, 61, 63, 88–9, 91, 92, 93, 117, 143, 166, 202, 204, 207, 210, 213, 215, 219, 231; regula-

tion of auto sport, 56–71; safety, 66–71, 227
Canadian auto slalom championship, 205–6, 211, 231, 254
Canadian Broadcasting Corporation (CBC), 24, 56, 127, 218, 241, 279n; CBC Car Club, 56
Canadian Comstock Company. *See* Comstock Racing Team; Rathgeb, Charles
Canadian Formula Racing Driver's Association championship, 255
Canadian Grand Prix for Formula One, 4, 5, 76, 100, 163–7, 170, 172, 173, 182, 187, 203, 213, 214, 215, 227, 229, 233, 234, 235, 237–8, 239, 240, 242–4, 249– 50, 254, 256, 257
Canadian Grand Prix for Sports Cars, 58, 59, 91, 119–22, 124, 133–6, 143–4, 154, 164–5
Canadian GT championship, 255
Canadian Karting Federation, 223
Canadian Motor Industries (CMI), 76, 190
Canadian Motorsport Bulletin, 182, 196, 216, 218, 222
Canadian Motorsport Hall of Fame, 3, 6, 17, 259
Canadian National Exhibition (CNE), 18, 235–6, 239
Canadian Race Communications Association (CRCA), 68
Canadian racing championship, 4, 18, 32, 94, 99, 130, 131, 134, 138, 139, 141, 142, 143–7, 169, 170, 173, 175, 176–87, 201, 203; debate over format, 176–80
Canadian Racing Driver's Association (CRDA), 23, 32, 58, 59, 70,
72–6, 78–84, 121, 122, 125, 131, 134, 138, 143, 165–6, 234, 251
Canadian rally championship, 52, 109, 110–18, 188–202, 254, 257; debate over format and purpose, 190–2, 197, 203, 227
Canadian Road Race of Champions (CRRC), 203, 204–5, 211, 232
Canadian Television (CTV) network, 184
Canadian Tire Corporation, 25
Canadian Winter Rally, 27, 29, 34, 36, 50–1, 52, 58, 77, 106, 107, 108, 111, 112, 189, 191, 192, 193, 196, 274n
Can-Am Challenge Cup Series, 3, 58, 59, 76, 99, 121, 129, 142, 147, 148–9, 155, 156–60, 165, 167–72, 182, 203, 213, 214, 224–5, 233, 234; Canadians in, 167–72, 224–5
Canfield, Jack, 208
Cannon, John, 3, 144, 146, 154, 155, 160, 167–8, 171, 172, 178
Cantrack Motor Racing Ltd, 126
Carberry airport race track, Manitoba, 130
car clubs, 15, 18, 21, 22, 23–4, 25, 26, 31, 32–5, 37, 39, 57–63, 72, 73, 80, 81, 82, 88–9, 104, 105, 110, 113, 123, 126, 130, 132, 165–6, 174, 187, 188, 190–1, 193, 195, 206, 208, 209, 213, 215, 218, 219, 223, 234–5, 251, 253, 254, 257; decline of, 209–11, 218–19; legitimizing role of, 33; membership of, 33–4, 88–9, 209–11, 219; social activities of, 34, 38, 39; subcultural features of, 32–4. *See also* auto sport, subculture
'car culture,' 22, 24, 25, 26, 95, 258. *See also* Canada, suburbia; car clubs

Carling Breweries, 48, 72, 122
Carling 300 race, 72, 82, 120
Carlson, Satch, 193
Carp airport race track, Ontario, 41, 67, 68
Carpentier, Patrick, 5, 7, 231
Carrothers, J., 59
CART. *See* Championship Auto Racing Teams
Carter, Diana, 95, 115
Carter, Maurice 'Mo,' 172
Carter, Ray, 30, 72, 73
CASC. *See* Canadian Automobile Sport Clubs
Cassiani, Luigi, 154
Castrol National Rally Championship, 198–9
Castrol Oil company, 182, 198, 199, 201, 207
Cayer, Pierre, 191–2
celebrity, 132, 252, 259. *See also* auto sport, spectacle
Champ Cars, 7, 250, 256
Championship Auto Racing Teams (CART) racing series, 4, 5, 7, 230–1, 239–40, 242–4, 250, 254, 256
Chaparral racing cars, 121, 129, 145, 152, 154. *See also* Hall, Jim
Chapman, Colin, 31, 100, 136, 137, 146, 155. *See also* Lotus
Chapman, George, 24, 41, 144, 145, 146, 217, 218, 222, 223, 230, 242, 286n
Chapman, Pete, 226
Chapman, Stacy, 248
Chappell, Marc, 197
Charters, John, 46, 51, 101–2, 107–9, 113, 190
Chelminski, Les, 24, 32, 47, 52, 106
Chenhall, Martin, 77, 114, 228

Chesnutt, Tim, 248
Chevrolet cars. *See* General Motors Corporation
Chevron racing cars, 180
Chicago, Illinois, 158
Chinetti, Luigi, 59, 120, 123, 137
Chinook racing cars, 155, 160, 180. *See also* Fejer, George and Rudy
Christianson, Peter, 226
Chrysler cars, 96, 105, 109, 116; Plymouth Barracuda, 96; Valiant, 116
Circuit Gilles Villeneuve race track, Montreal, 31, 237–8, 243, 249–50
Citicorp Challenge. *See* Can-Am Challenge Cup series
Citroen cars, 40
CKVL radio, 128
Claresholm airport race track, Alberta, 41
Clark, Grant, 95–6, 120, 135, 152
Clark, Jim, 163–4, 165
Clark, Mary, 114
Clark, Roger, 110
Clements, Ed, 204
Clowater, Tim, 248
Club Auto Sport Laval, 198
Club Autosport Mauricien, 216
Clubine, Oliver, 120
Club de Voitures Sport Cerf-Québec, 89
Coad, Dennis, 143
Coates, Len, 23, 41, 76, 120, 127, 130, 156–9, 164, 177, 235
Collier, Miles, 18
Columbian Canyon Rally, 110
commercialism, 5, 7, 8, 21, 22, 83, 93, 104, 120, 122, 130–1, 132, 155, 165, 166, 181, 187, 188, 241, 251–2, 259. *See also* sponsorship
commercial professionalism, 8, 22,

53, 55, 71–84, 132, 190, 211, 242, 244–5, 252, 256
commodification of auto sport, 8, 9, 181, 242, 251–2, 259. *See also* commercialism
Compagna, Pierre, 243
computers, 253
Comstock Racing Team, 4, 94, 110, 120, 128–9, 133–6, 138–42, 146, 147, 148, 154, 156, 163, 168, 169; cars: Cooper-Ford (King Cobra), 129, 139, 144; EXP, 138, 144, 154; Ford GT40, 141–2, 146, 160, 168; Ford Lotus Cortina, 110, 140; Ford Mustang GT, 140; Lola Formula Junior, 136; Lotus 19, 134, 136; Sadler Mk. V, 120; Shelby Cobra, 139, 169; Shelby Mustang GT 350, 140; members: *see* Clark, Roger; Cooke, Paul; Davies, Brent; Eaton, George; Fisher, Craig; Heimrath, Ludwig; MacLennan, Paul; Mclean, Bob; Ouellete, Jean; Rathgeb, Charles; Ruys de Perez, Stephanie; Sadler, William G.; Taylor, Henry; Wietzes, Eppie; Wilson, John
Concours d'élégance, 34
Confederation Auto Sport Clubs, 304n
Connaught racing car, 73
Connor, Doug, 41
Connor Circuit airport race track, Ontario, 26, 30, 41, 57, 94, 95, 127, 133
Constantine, George, 70
control of auto sport. *See* auto sport, control of; *see also* ASN Canada FIA; Canadian Automobile Sport Clubs; Fédération Internationale de l'Automobile; sponsorship

Cook, Len, 130
Cook-Toledo Motors, 106
Cooke, Paul, 110, 140, 169, 229, 244, 254
Cooper, Charles, 152
Cooper, John, 152
Cooper racing cars, 31, 98, 139, 151, 152
Cordts, John, 160, 167–9, 171, 172
Coristine, Ian, 180
corporate sponsorship. *See* sponsorship
Corvette. *See* General Motors
Cosell, Howard, 9
Cossette, Chris, 205
Cosworth Engineering, 155; engines, 153, 163, 176, 184
Cottenden, Chris, 205
Couture, Jacques, 94, 145, 168, 175–6, 180, 182–3
Cowan, Andrew, 196
CRDA 500 race, 72, 80, 81, 82
Criterium du Québec Rally, 192, 201
Cruickshank, Mark, 248
CTV network. *See* Canadian Television (CTV) network; *see also* media
Cunningham, Briggs, 18, 74
Curta calculator, 46

Dailu racing cars, 144, 154–5. *See also* Greenblatt, Dave
Daimler cars, 54
Dallara racing car, 224
Dancose, Marc, 204–5, 226, 228
Datsun cars, 189–90, 199, 225, 247
Dauphin airport race track, Manitoba, 41
Davidson airport race track, Saskatchewan, 42, 65, 130, 144
Davies, Brent, 110

Daytona 500 stock car race, 6, 184
Daytona race track, Florida, 157
Deacon, David, 225
Debert airport race track, Nova Scotia, 183, 207–8
Delamont, Dean, 90, 164–5, 167, 181
Dempsey, Art, 52, 60, 109
De Palma, Ralph, 18
Department of Transport (federal), 41, 68, 208
Deutscher Automobile Club (DAC), 32
Deux Montagnes race track, Quebec, 216
Devos, Ernie, 94
Dewar, Gordon, 167–8, 205
Dixon, Hugh, 94
DKW cars, 40
do it yourself (DIY), 25–6
Donaldson, Gerald, 163
Donnybrooke race track, Minnesota, 168
Donohue, Mark, 160, 169, 215
Donolo, Louis, 94
Dow Breweries, 106
Dow Quebec Rally, 106
drag racing, 9, 18, 20, 75, 77, 131, 174, 216, 223, 233, 254, 256
Drapeau, Jean, 237
Draper, Dick, 54
Driving magazine, 192
driving skill tests. *See* solo racing
Drouin, Richard, 236
Duval, Jacques, 89, 94, 128, 145, 204
Dyson, Paul, 54

Eagar, Stuart, 206
Earnhardt, Dale, 6
Eastern Zone Endurance (EZE) racing series, 204, 208, 225

Eaton, George, 94, 146, 167–9, 171, 187. *See also* Comstock Racing Team
Ecclestone, Bernie, 234, 242–3, 258
Edenvale airport race track, Ontario, 19, 26, 38, 39, 41, 58, 81, 149
Edmond, Katherine 'Kay,' 190–1
Edmonson, Johnny, 18–19
Edmonton, Alberta, 130–1, 168, 182, 256, 257
Edmonton International Speedway (EIS), 130–1, 232
Edwardes, Robin, 101, 108, 109, 110, 116, 188, 189, 198, 201, 279n
Edwards, Murray, 204, 208
Eglinton-Caledonia Motors, 83
Elkhart Lake, Wisconsin, 68
Ellison, G.J., 103
Elva cars, 26, 28, 181
Empringham, David, 228
energy crisis and auto sport, 211
Entwhistle, Harry, 26, 73, 120
Esaw, Johnny, 184
Esseltine, Bob, 225
Esso Grand Prix ice race, 205
Esso Protec Formula Ford racing series, 241
Europe/European, 17, 20, 22, 27, 29, 30, 32, 40, 47, 72, 74, 77, 98, 100, 106, 108, 109, 110, 114, 118, 123, 133, 136, 146, 164, 172, 173, 185, 189, 194, 199, 201, 202, 208, 224, 226, 235
Evis, R.C. 'Bob,' 63–4, 69, 70, 81
Export 'A' F-2000 racing series, 227
EXP racing car. *See* Comstock Racing Team

fans. *See* auto sport, audiences, enthusiasts
fatalities. *See* auto sport, fatalities in,

safety; *see also* Foster, Billy; Kelly, Wayne; McLean, Bob; Moore, Greg; Pope, Ted; Purdy, Ed; Villeneuve, Gilles

Favreau, François, 94

Fédération Auto-Québec (FAQ), 237, 243, 304n. *See also* Canadian Automobile Sport Clubs, Quebec region

Fédération Internationale de l'Automobile (FIA), 15, 16, 19, 21, 31, 51, 62, 64, 65, 70, 74, 83, 91, 92, 146, 157, 164–5, 167, 181, 201, 214, 215, 234, 236, 242–3, 254, 257; Commission Sportive Internationale (CSI), 90, 166–7, 238; expulsion of CASC, 243; Fédération Internationale Sportive Automobile (FISA), 242–4; International Sporting Code, 67, 146; national sporting authority, 19, 20, 21, 67, 89–90, 243–5; recognition of CASC, 16, 61, 89–90

Fee, Jack, 15, 16

Fejer, George, 155, 160, 168

Fejer, Rudy, 155

Fellows, Ron, 205, 228

Ferguson, Peter, 205

Fergusson, Alice, 35, 94, 114

Fergusson, Jim, 24, 26, 30, 35, 38, 75–6, 78, 125

Fergusson Motors, 75, 106

Ferrari, 6, 29, 59, 64, 97, 120, 121, 129, 137, 141, 144, 154, 156, 163, 173, 187, 197, 221, 241, 250, 256, 266n; *Testa Rossa*, 43, 137; 330P, 144

Ferrari, Enzo, 97, 221

FIA. *See* Fédération Internationale de l'Automobile

Fiat cars, 35, 64, 94, 190, 197, 198, 199, 200, 201

Fidler, Jack, 15, 16, 52

Fineberg, Irwin, 126

Firestone Firehawk Endurance Challenge racing series, 227

Firestone Indy Lights racing series, 255

Fisher, Craig, 95–6, 98, 140, 141–2, 146, 169

Fitch, John, 74, 128, 133

Fittipaldi, Emerson, 240

Folland, Roy, 179

Follmer, George, 160

Ford, Benson, 96

Ford, Don, 196

Ford, Henry, 17

Ford Motor Company, 16, 96, 97, 105–7, 109, 138–42, 156; cars: Anglia, 107; Capri, 176; Falcon Futura Sprint, 108, 109, 115, 140; GT 40, 141–2, 146, 160, 168; Lotus Cortina, 110, 116, 140, 155; Mercury Bobcat, 247; Mercury Cougar, 96, 142; Mustang, 29, 94, 96, 97, 116, 140, 142; Thunderbird, 29; engines: 260-cid V-8, 109; 289-cid V-8, 139, 141; 427-cid V-8, 141; 'Total Performance' marketing theme, 96–7. *See also* Comstock Racing Team; Shelby cars; Shell 4000 rally

formula car racing, 98–100, 170, 176–87, 204–5; named designs and series: Formula A, 169, 176–80, 182, 183, 215, 224; Formula Atlantic, 42, 170, 176, 181, 184–7, 203, 209, 216, 227, 229, 231, 232, 233, 234, 236, 238, 241; Formula B, 98, 176–8, 180, 182–3; Formula C, 176; Formula Ford, 3, 174, 175, 176, 230, 231, 233, 241, 248, 255; Formula Junior (FJ), 98–9, 134, 136, 137, 146,

150–1, 176; Formula Libre, 65, 98, 150, 151; Formula One (F1), 3, 4, 6, 9, 17, 57, 59, 72, 73, 74, 98, 100, 124, 133, 136, 137, 145, 146, 147, 150, 153, 156, 157, 160, 163–7, 169, 170, 172, 180, 181, 184–7, 191, 201, 213, 216, 221, 224, 230, 235, 236, 237, 249–50, 252, 253, 257, 258, 305n; Formula Super Vee, 153; Formula Three, 65; Formula 1200, 255; Formula Two, 4, 98, 138, 241; Formula 2000, 255; Formula Vee, 98–100, 170, 174, 208
Formula One Constructors Association (FOCA), 233–4, 242–3. *See also* Ecclestone, Bernie
Foster, Billy, 4, 57
4×4 (four-wheel drive) clubs, 223
Fox, Tommy, 131
Foyt, A.J., 240
Fram, Dave, 204, 208
francophone competitors, 88–9. *See individuals by name*
Frissbee Can-Am racing car, 225
Fulp, John, 137
funding of auto sport. *See* auto sport, costs and funding of

Gallop, Doug, 109
Gallop, John, 24, 32, 36, 44
Gallop, Nancy, 36
Garnett, Robert, 226
Gazette newspaper (Montreal), 107, 250
Gendebien, Olivier, 72, 73, 115, 119–20, 123, 133, 136, 150, 151
gender and auto sport. *See* women in auto sport
General Motors Corporation (GM), 107; GM Canada, 77, 96, 228; cars:
Camaro, 96, 98, 142, 204, 228, 247, 255; Chevrolet Division, 105, 106, 142, 154; Corvair, 51, 107; Corvette, 27, 29, 30, 43, 64, 72, 78, 95, 97, 145, 150, 154, 204, 206, 228, 247; Pontiac Division, Acadian, 114; Catalina, 95; Firebird, 96, 98, 228; engines, 151, 153, 154. *See also* Player's/GM Racing series
General Tire, 227
Gestion Laurentide Ltd, 130
Gilmour, Tom, 59, 73, 75, 78, 79, 80, 134
Gimli Motorsport Park race track, Manitoba, 183, 186, 225, 232, 254
Ginetta racing cars, 204
Girdler, Allan, 153, 155
Globe and Mail newspaper, 51
go-karts. *See* karting
Golden Triangle Rally, 193
Goldsack, Ron, 140
Good, Jim, 23
Goodhall, Phil, 94, 130
Goodyear, Scott, 5, 205, 230, 240
Gordon, Jeff, 6
Gorries Downtown Chevrolet, 72, 76, 78, 83, 150
Graham, John, 240–1
Grand Prix du Canada Inc., 237
Grand Prix [Molson] de Trois-Rivières, 186–7, 216, 235–6
Grand Prix racing. *See* Canadian Grand Prix for Formula One; Canadian Grand Prix for Sports Cars; formula car racing
Grant, George H., 60
Gray, Stuart, 197
Greenacres airport race track, Ontario, 41, 133

Greenblatt, Dave, 24, 27, 73, 76, 120, 150, 154–5
Gregory, Masten, 74, 121, 154, 160
Grimshaw, Mr, 111
Grinstead, Mike, 60
Groenveld hill climb, 54
Grossman, Bob, 137
Grundy, David, 117
Gulf Canada racing series, 177–9, 182. *See also* Canadian racing championship; formula car racing, Formula A
Gunn, James H. 'Jim,' 5, 15, 16–17, 18, 19, 31, 39, 60, 83, 88, 103, 104–5, 110, 114, 116, 117, 144, 149, 215. *See also* Canadian Automobile Sport Clubs; Shell 4000 rally
Gunn, John, 224
Gurney, Dan, 154, 163
Gurney-Eagle formula racing car, 163
Guthrie, Robert 'Bob,' 208–9, 247
gymkhanas. *See* solo racing

Haas, Carl, 225
Haddow, Don, 54
Hain, Norm, 15, 16
Halda Speedpilot, 46, 107
Halifax, 117, 208, 239–41
Hall, Jim, 121, 145, 153, 154
Hall, John, 94, 145, 204
Hall, Karen, 94
Hamerton, Yvonne, 35
Hamilton, Fran, 94
Hamilton, Joe, 130
Hamilton, Ontario, 18, 30
Hamilton Motor Sport Club, 35
Hamilton Sports Car Club, 210
Hanna, Robert 'Bob,' 26, 38, 54, 59, 66, 75, 76, 125, 164, 178, 182–4, 186, 189, 198, 201, 203, 210, 211, 212, 213, 218, 233, 234, 242
Harbourville hill climb, NS, 207
Hardie, Doug, 196
Hare, Russ, 41
Harewood Acres airport race track, Ontario, 41, 56, 58, 65, 70, 72, 76, 81, 131, 134
Harker, George, 205
Harold Cummings Ltd, 106
Harrington, Robert 'Bob,' 179, 184, 186, 211, 212
Harrison, Marybeth, 255
Harvey, Scott, 116
Hatch, John, 82
Hatter, David, 221
Hawthorn, Mike, 31
Hayes, Fred, 19, 50, 59, 70, 72, 75, 78, 79, 81, 120, 138
Hayes, Peter, 19, 38, 59, 75
Heimrath, Ludwig, 32, 120–1, 128, 134, 138, 139, 143–6, 160, 168, 169, 172, 204–5, 235, 249
Heinonen, Taisto, 200, 201
helmets. *See* safety
Hill, Craig, 72, 145, 178
Hill, Graham, 163, 213
Hill, Phil, 74
hill climbs. *See* solo racing; *see also named events*
Hillary, Reg, 104
Hillis, Brian, 200
Hillman cars, 101, 103, 149
Hoar, Arnold, 225, 247
hockey, 8, 22, 37, 200, 223, 230, 258, 259; hall of fame, 5–6, 259
Hockley Valley hill climb, 54
Hogan, Don, 204, 208
Hogan, John, 186
Holman and Moody, 109

Honda cars, 226, 248
Honda Civic Championship, 254
Honda / B.F. Goodrich / Michelin Challenge Series, 226, 227, 228, 233
Hondorf, Dorothy. *See* Scott, Dorothy
Horne, Donald, 191–8, 219
hot rods, 17–18, 20
Howell, Colin, 262n
Howell, Lloyd, 109
Hudes, Harvey, 126, 224, 233–4
Hughes, Colleen, 195
Hulme, Denis, 163, 169, 213
Hunt, Don, 156–7, 235. *See also* Public Relations Services Limited
Hunt, James, 186

Iacocca, Lee, 96. *See also* Ford Motor Company
ice racing. *See* racing
Île Notre Dame, Montreal, 237
Île St-Hélène, Montreal, 127, 164
Imperial Tobacco, 4, 87, 122, 143, 165, 180, 214, 235; Player's division, 87, 122, 129, 138, 143, 144, 159, 165, 183, 184, 185, 204, 212, 233, 241, 257. *See also* Player's-sponsored races; sponsorship
Indianapolis 500 race, 4, 5, 6, 17, 22, 74, 181, 184, 230, 239, 255
Indian Summer Trophy Races, 58, 81
Indy Car racing series, 172, 187, 205, 209, 213, 224, 227, 230, 235–6, 239, 252, 253, 305n. *See also* Championship Auto Racing Teams; Indy Racing League
Indy racing cars, 153. *See also* Champ cars
Indy Racing League (IRL), 257
International Conference of Northwest Sports Car Clubs (ICNSCC), 62, 65, 94
International Motorsport Association of Canada (IMCAN), 117
International Motor Sports Association (IMSA), 234, 241
Internet, 7, 258
Italy, 6, 175, 201

Jaguar cars, 26, 28, 30, 33, 39, 43, 65, 72, 73, 76, 77, 95, 120, 155, 256; D-Type, 26, 30, 43; 3.4 sedan, 30; XK-120, 26, 39, 65; XKSS, 30, 72, 73, 120
Jaguar Owner's Association (JOA), Montreal, 31, 54, 123, 207
Jamieson, Wayne, 145
Japanese auto industry, 199, 256. *See also car companies by name*
Jeffries, Vern, 26, 39
Jenkins, Jane, 36
Jim Russell International Driver's School. *See* racing, schools
Jobborn, Frank, 208–9
Johnson, Daniel, 165
Johnson, Harry, 60, 125
Johnson, Neale, 31
Johnson's Wax, 159
Jones, Alan, 186
Jones, Terry, 182
Jordan Special race car, 54
journalism, sports. *See* media
Joyce, Les, 225

Kamin, Bernie, 126
karting, 94, 223–4, 230–1, 233, 255, 258
Kaser, Jim, 158
Keck, George, 43
Keith, Peter, 26, 94, 145
Keith, Wendy, 94

Kelly, Wayne, 57, 99–100, 145; Formula Vee racing car, 99–100; Kelly-Porsche racing car, 99
Kelowna, BC, 206
Kennedy, Lou, 41
Kennedy, Ted, 177
Kent, Washington, race track, 158–9
Kingston, Ontario, 15, 16, 19, 21, 48, 59, 226
K & K Insurance, 66, 77
Klausler, Tom, 224
Knap, Muriel, 126, 259
Knox Mountain hill climb. *See* Okanagan hill climb
Kroll, Horst, 32, 99, 145, 205, 224; Formula Vee racing car, 99

Laban, Brian, 252
Labatt Breweries, 128, 216, 233, 234, 236–8, 242–4
Lader, Alan, 183
Ladie's Division Centennial Year Rally, 27
Laguna Seca race track, California, 154, 158, 167–8
Lakeshore Auto Raceway Holdings Limited, 235–6
Lambke, Paul, 225
Lamont, Don, 204–5
Lamont, Tom, 184
Lancia cars, 197
Landar racing cars, 204
Larsen, Tiina, 255
Las Vegas, Nevada, 159
Laurentian Autosport Club, 54, 127
Leathem, Bill, 108
Leavens, Ed, 30, 76, 77, 274n
Leber, Remi, 101–2
Le Circuit St-Jovite race track, Quebec, 89, 91, 100, 126–30, 132, 155, 157, 158, 159, 165, 172, 174, 175, 186, 203, 204, 209, 212, 213–15, 224, 225, 226, 232–6, 277n; closure of, 213–15; financial problems of, 129–30, 214–15
leisure, changing patterns of in Canada, 25, 219–20
Leitch, Corley, 197
Le Mans 24-hour race, France, 17, 30, 97, 137, 140, 141, 154
Lemieux, Red, 114
Leon, Yvon, 242
Lerch, Peter, 94, 126, 160, 168, 286n
Lethbridge Sports Car Club, 130
Letterman, David, 250
Lévesque, René, 222
Lighthall, Peter, 60, 84
Lime Rock Park race track, Connecticut, 74, 128, 133
Lindquist, Bob, 196, 197
Lister Jaguar racing cars, 150
Ljungfeldt, Bo, 109, 115
Lobster Rally, 192, 200
Locke, Graham, 26, 30, 33, 39, 103
Locke, Ron, 204, 208
Lola racing cars, 98, 120, 121, 129, 137, 140, 142, 145, 155, 160, 171, 204, 214, 224–5, 241; Lola-Chev, 214; T70, 121, 145, 160, 171
London Automobile Sport Club (LASC), 23, 131
Long, David, 206
Loop rally, 49, 115
Lotus cars, 28, 31, 43, 64, 73, 98, 100, 120–1, 134, 136, 141, 144, 145, 146, 151, 153, 155, 156, 180, 204; models: Cortina, *see* Ford Motor Company; Elan, 155; XI, 64; Elite, 26; XV, 120; Lotus 19, 120–1, 134, 143;

Lotus 20, 134; Lotus 23, 141, 144, 145, 146; Lotus 49, 163
Lotus racing team, 4, 136, 163
Lowden, Graham, 94
Lower Canada Motor Club, 46
Lowes, Mark Douglas, 239
Luce, Tom, 43
Luck, Jack, 15, 16, 31
Lugar, Derek, 247
Lynn Valley Sports Car Club, 210
Lyons, Pete, 148, 156, 157, 158, 170

McCaig, Roger, 167–9, 171
McCallum, Gordon, 190, 193–5
McCarthy, Frank, 208
McColl, Diana, 94
McConnell, David, 180, 183
McDougall, Donald, 237
MacGregor, Bob, 24, 127, 128, 182, 218
McGuffie, Blake, 212, 223
MacKay, Dale, 247
MacKay, Harold, 240–1
McKee-Ford racing car, 286n
MacKenzie, Lewis, 3, 205, 231
McLaren, Bruce, 100, 121, 159–60, 163
McLaren, Chuck, 125, 126, 196, 200
McLaren racing cars, 99, 121, 129, 142, 145, 146, 155, 160, 167, 170, 171; McLaren-BRM, 163; M1, 167; racing team, 159, 186–7
McLaughlin, Roy, 34, 38, 39, 59, 123, 125, 126
McLean, Bob, 4, 43, 57, 141–2, 145, 147
McLean, Frances, 36
Mclean, Grant, 36, 108, 109
Maclean's magazine, 56, 77
MacLennan, Paul, 109–10, 116
Maddin, Jim, 42, 218

Magill, John, 224
Magwood, Gary, 175–6, 182
Mailloux, Benoit, 237, 243–4
Makins Special racing car, 87
Mallard, Fred, 63, 82
Mallory Park race track, UK, 137
Manson, Paul, 195, 200
March racing cars, 180, 221, 241
Maritime provinces, 38, 61, 88, 199, 248
Marlboro cigarettes, 186
marshals, 39, 68, 70, 244–5, 248–9. *See also* auto sport, safety
Martin, Nicole, 94
Mass, Jochen, 221
Maxwell, Scott, 228
Mayer, Teddy, 159, 186
Mazda cars, 247
Mears, Rick, 239
media coverage of auto sport, 83, 95, 105, 106, 122, 184, 186, 214, 239, 242, 245, 249–50, 252, 253, 259; newspapers, 105, 106, 122, 134, 249; radio, 105, 128; television, 5, 7, 8, 39, 105, 132, 184, 202, 227, 228, 235, 239, 241–2, 249–50, 252, 253, 257
Meecham, Tommy, 244
Mercedes-Benz cars, 29, 30, 105
MG cars, 7, 23, 26, 27, 28, 29, 30, 33, 39, 43, 54, 64, 65, 66, 72, 77, 95, 130, 149, 226, 256; 1500, 66; MGA, 29, 30, 43; MGB, 96; Midget, 206; 1600, 66; TC, 7, 23, 26, 29, 43, 204; TD, 26, 43, 149; twin-cam, 26, 54, 64, 130, 286n
Michigan 500 Indy Car race, 230
Miles, Ken, 139, 284n
Mini, and Mini Cooper. *See* British Motor Corporation

Mission Raceway, BC, 256
Moennick, Peter, 226
Mollison, Don, 103
Molson Breweries, 201, 215, 216, 238–9, 242–3
Molson Indy Toronto, 5, 6, 239, 241, 248
Molson Indy Vancouver (MIV), 5, 6, 7, 239–41, 257
Molyslip Enduro racing series, 225–6, 228, 233
Monaco Grand Prix, 235, 239, 249
Moncton Motor Sport Club, 88
money, as a factor in auto sport. *See* amateurism; auto sport, appearance money, costs and funding, prize money; commercialism; professionalism, sponsorship
Monte Carlo, Monaco, 17, 238, 239
Monte Carlo Rally, 17, 19, 47, 48, 59, 106, 107, 109, 115, 189
Mont Gabriel hill climb, 54, 207
Montgomery airport race track, New York, 149
Montreal, 15, 16, 18, 23, 24, 25, 26, 29, 31, 32, 35, 41, 44, 47, 48, 49, 50, 51, 60, 66, 76, 89, 98, 101, 103, 106, 107, 108, 114, 127, 145, 150, 164, 165, 173, 174, 187, 215, 222, 233, 236–8, 239, 241, 243, 249–50, 266n; race track in, *see* Circuit Gilles Villeneuve
Montreal MG Car Club (MMGCC), 26, 35, 95, 127–8
Montreal Motor Racing Club (MMRC), 128–30, 157, 165
Mont Tremblant, Quebec, 133, 137
Mont Tremblant Circuit Corporation, 128–9
Monza race track, Italy, 208

Moore, Greg, 5, 7, 57, 231
Moorhouse, H.F., 75, 77
Moosehead Breweries, 240–1, 249
Moosehead Grand Prix, 239–41
Moosehead 300 race, 204
Morgan cars, 28, 65
Morrell, Dave, 44
Morris cars, 26, 67
Morton, Barry, 121, 254
Moseley, Arthur 'Art,' 32, 58, 59, 122, 125, 132, 160, 166, 191, 219–20
Mosport Limited, 123–4
Mosport Park race track, Ontario, 56, 59, 91, 92, 109, 119–20, 122–6, 128, 130, 131, 133, 135, 136, 138, 140, 143, 152, 157, 158, 163, 165, 168, 172, 177, 178, 209, 224, 232, 233–4, 235, 236, 248, 254; construction of, 95, 123–5; financial problems of, 123–6, 127. *See also* Hudes, Harvey; Motor Racing Partnership
Moss, Bill, 137
Moss, George, 59, 103, 120, 125, 158, 164–6
Moss, Stirling, 6, 31, 42, 74, 80, 82, 119–20, 122, 124, 133, 136, 150–3
motorcycles, 18–19, 31, 123, 208, 223
Motor Racing Partnership (MRP), 125–6
Motorsport magazine, 31
Motorsport Management company, 241
Motton, Fred, 35
Mountain Trials Rally, 199
Mount Washington hill climb, New Hampshire, 53
Murdoch, Peter, 73
'muscle cars.' *See* automobiles, *and specific models by manufacturer*
Muskoka Motor Sports Club, 40

Mustang. *See* Ford Motor Company; *see also* Shelby cars
Muzzin, Jim, 73, 120, 180

Namao, Canadian Forces Base, Alberta, 254
Namerow, Norm, 89, 126, 127, 128
Napierville drag strip, Quebec, 174
Nassau, Bahamas, racing at, 99, 150, 154, 157
National Association for Stock Car Auto Racing (NASCAR), 20, 74, 181, 252, 257
national auto slalom championship. *See* Canadian auto slalom championship
National Competition Board. *See* Canadian Automobile Sport Clubs
National Hot Rod Association, 20
national racing championship. *See* Canadian racing championship
national sporting authority. *See* Fédération Internationale d'Automobile
National Trust, 125–6
navex/navigational rallies. *See* rallying, navex
Nerriere, Max, 94
Netley airport race track, Manitoba, 41
New Brunswick Sporting Car Club, 88, 248
Newfoundland, 225, 236, 240
Newman, Paul, 240
newspapers. *See* media coverage of auto sport
New York Times, 134
Night Trial Rally, 18
Nilsson, Terry, 94, 145
Nissan cars, 248

Nissonger, Earl, 149
Nordell, Sam, 32, 102, 108–9
North Alberta Sports Car Club, 254
North America/American, 8, 25, 28, 29, 34, 97, 99, 123, 134, 135, 138, 142, 146, 156, 158, 159, 177, 181, 184, 185, 189, 199, 201, 207, 216, 234, 235, 239
North American Racing Team (NART), 59, 120, 121, 137
North American Road Racing Championship. *See* Can-Am Challenge Series
North Toronto Motorsport Club (NTMC), 52, 81, 82
Nova Scotia Highlands Rally, 108, 192–4, 199, 200
NSU cars, 40
Nuffield Organization, 28
Nurburgring race track, Germany, 208

Ogilvy, David, 185, 205
oil companies, 83. *See also* companies by name
Okanagan Auto Sport Club (OASC), 54
Okanagan hill climb, 206–7
O'Keefe Breweries, 205
Oland, Derek, 240
Oldfield, Barney, 18
Oliver, Jackie, 171
O'Neill, Louis, 76, 102, 107, 108
Ontario, 38, 41, 50, 52, 54, 58, 60, 61, 89, 94, 127, 141, 143, 144, 145, 146, 176, 177, 190, 199, 205, 207, 212, 218, 223, 226, 231, 235, 253, 254, 299n
Orr, Frank, 125, 239

Ottawa, 18, 41, 48, 50, 67, 117, 167, 189, 197
Ottawa Light Car Club (OLCC), 19–20, 21, 59, 67, 68
Ouellette, André, 128
Ouellette, Jean, 141
Owram, Doug, 24

Paivarinta, Lauri, 193
Paquin, Maurice, 128
Paradis, Jacqueline, 214–15
Paris, France, 17, 137, 242
Parsons, Chuck, 160
Paterson, Ian, 77
Patrick, Danica, 255
Patterson, Charles, 140
Pau, France, Grand Prix race, 138. *See also* Heimrath, Ludwig
Pearce, John, 194, 207
Pearce, Tom, 15, 16, 19
Peart, Roger, 31, 175, 177, 180, 218, 233, 236–8, 243–4, 254
Pease, Al, 38, 145, 163–4, 167, 187, 286n
Pek K'lona rally, 199
Pengally, Dave, 279n
Pennfield Ridge airport race track, NB, 208, 247–9, 253, 303n
Pennzoil, 207
Penske, Roger, 73, 98, 134, 154, 157, 240
Pepsi Cola, 120, 122, 129, 130, 166
Performance Racing News, 240
Perusse, Jean-Paul, 192, 196, 198–200, 201, 205
Peterborough International stock car race, 125
Petras, Herb, 94
Petro-Canada oil company, 231
Pettipas, Eugene, 247

Petty, Richard, 6
Petura, Vivian, 35
Phippen, Doug, 23
Pike's Peak hill climb, Colorado, 53
Pilkey, Arleigh, 7
Pilon, Jean-Guy, 26, 30, 89
Pinetree airport race track, Alberta, 130
Player's brand. *See* Imperial Tobacco
Player's-sponsored events: Challenge Series, 144, 180, 182–7, 212, 216; Maritime race, 209; Pacific race, 139, 144; Player's/GM Motorsport racing series, 227–8, 232, 233, 241, 255; Quebec race, 91, 129, 144; 200 race, 4, 59, 82, 119–21, 122, 124, 132, 143, 144, 145, 152, 163, 165, 170, 224
Plumley, Jim, 50, 111
Poirier, Guy, 216
police and auto sport, 53, 54, 191
Polivka, Jerry, 26, 38, 54, 70, 73, 95, 126
'pop' culture, 7, 250, 258
Pope, Ted, 56–7, 66, 67
Porsche cars, 27, 29, 43, 65, 73, 95, 99, 120, 133, 134, 138, 143, 170, 171, 204, 225, 241, 256; Carrera, 99; 1500, 65; 550 Spyder, 133; model 917, 170; RS60, 27, 134, 143; RS61, 120; 1600, 99
Posey, Sam, 160
'powder puff' races. *See* racing; *see also* women in auto sport
Powell, John, 175, 180, 185, 199, 205
Prairie provinces, 38, 94, 131, 144, 145, 205, 232, 254. *See also* Canadian Automobile Sport Clubs, Prairie Region

Index   341

Press On Regardless Rally, 47, 194, 197
prize money. *See* auto sport
professionalism in auto sport, 5, 7–10, 53, 55, 56–71, 72–4, 79, 80, 87, 93, 104, 113, 124, 127, 131, 132, 143, 147, 165, 171, 176, 181, 187, 188, 191, 192, 198–200, 202, 209, 213, 217, 223, 224, 226–32, 242, 244, 251, 254–7, 258, 259. *See also* auto sport, costs and funding; commercial professionalism
ProFormance Toyota racing series, 255
Public Relations Services Limited (PRSL), 122, 157, 235. *See also* Hunt, Don
Punshon, Bert, 15, 16, 19, 31, 60, 61–2
Purdy, Ed, 57, 67

Quebec, 30, 38, 50, 52, 54, 58, 60, 61, 88–9, 94, 126, 127, 129, 141, 144, 160, 176, 177, 182, 184, 199, 205, 207, 212, 213–17, 222, 223, 231, 233, 234, 235, 253, 254, 257
Quebec City, 49, 89, 205
Quebecois, 37, 89
Quebec (racing) driver's championship, 150
Quebec Rally, 46, 49, 52, 106, 112, 115, 189
Quebec rally championship, 108
Quinte Auto Sport Club, 210

Race City Motorsport Park [Speedway], Calgary, 232, 256
race tracks, 68, 122, 131, 208, 216, 232, 233, 235, 236–8, 241, 251, 252, 256; airport tracks, 7, 40–1, 43, 68, 72, 79, 122, 127, 130, 131, 133, 147, 183, 207, 208, 232, 235, 241, 247–9, 253; street race tracks, 7, 40, 68, 216, 235–41, 249, 256–7. *See also* Circuit Gilles Villeneuve; Edmonton International Speedway; Le Circuit St-Jovite; Mosport Park; Westwood Motorsport Park; *and other tracks by name or location*
racing, 27, 33, 34, 35, 38, 39, 40, 54, 56, 66, 70, 73, 76 79, 93, 94, 96, 97, 119, 122, 206, 211, 218, 220, 221, 226, 250, 253, 256, 257; cost of, *see* auto sport, costs and funding; driver development, 133–47, 169–70, 173–87, 224, 230–1, 236, 251, 254–5; endurance racing, 81–2, 204, 225–6, 231; ice racing, 39–40, 44, 128, 205; 'powder puff' races, 35, 95; purpose of, 122, 131, 185, 242, 251; schools, 70, 147, 174–6, 187, 208, 230, 231, 254, 255; vintage car racing, 226, 256. *See also* amateurism; auto sport; commercialism; karting; professionalism; sponsorship
racing cars, 9, 83, 181, 242, 249–50; aerodynamics, 152–3; classification of, 64–6; cost of, 40, 66, 139, 147, 155–6, 170–2, 176–7, 180–1, 183; design of, 148–55, 156, 157; engines, 170–1, 176; industry, Canadian, 98–100, 148–56; production sports cars, 73, 131, 144, 145, 176, 204, 226; sedans, 95–8, 131, 140, 142, 176, 204, 226, 241; 'specials,' 72, 73, 120, 145, 147, 150, 156; sports racing cars, 122, 134, 135, 139, 141–8, 153, 157, 158, 187, 224. *See also* automobiles; auto sport, technological change in; formula car racing; *specific makes by name*

342 Index

radio. *See* media coverage of auto sport
Rae, Allan, 205
Rahal, Bobby, 187, 209, 239, 240, 250
Rainville, Marcel, 109, 192
Rainville, Roland, 109
Rallye Des Neiges, 50, 51, 108, 111, 192, 198
rallying, 17, 27, 30, 31, 33, 34, 36, 38, 43–53, 70, 93, 101–18, 188–202, 203, 205, 206, 207, 220, 250, 254, 257, 299n; 'car breakers,' 47, 50, 111–14, 196; commercialization of, 9, 102–3, 104, 105–7, 109, 111, 189, 198–9, 201, 256–7; cost of, 105–6, 118, 188–92; debate over format, 193–5, 197, 200–1; decline of, 190, 195–6, 202, 211, 231; endurance rallies, 46–51, 111–18, 188; factory teams in, 101–2, 105–10, 189, 190, 197, 199, 200, 201, 227; 'map run,' 45; national championship, 52, 109, 110–18, 188–202, 254, 257; navex (navigational), 45, 46, 47, 52, 111, 188, 192, 194, 202, 207, 227, 231, 254, 257, 259; professionalization of, 103–5, 113, 188, 188, 191, 192, 198–200, 202, 229, 254; purpose of, 105, 111, 190–3, 197, 201; regularity trials, 52; selective (speed) stages, 114–16, 189, 192, 193; sponsorship, 103, 105–6, 109–10, 111, 189–92, 198–201, 227; stage rallies, 117, 188, 194, 197, 199, 200, 202, 207, 227, 231, 256, 257; TSD (Time-Speed-Distance) rallies, 44, 47, 256, 257; winter rallies, 43, 47–51. *See also* Canadian Winter Rally; Rallye Des Neiges; Shell 4000; Thousand Islands Rally; World Rally Championship; *and other events by name*
Rally Perce Neige, 198
Rally of the Rideau Lakes, 197–8
Ralt racing car, 42
Ramsey, Stuart, 94
Ramsey, Toni, 94
Randall, Hilda, 94
Randall, John, 94
Randall, Robert 'Bob,' 61
Rankin, John, 247
Rasche, Mr, 111
Rathgeb, Charles 'Chuck,' 4, 133, 134–42, 146, 148, 151, 237
Rattenbury, Jim, 30, 43
Rattlesnake Point Hill Climb, 54
Razelle, John, 94
recreation. *See* leisure
recreational auto sport. *See* auto sport, amateur
Regina, Saskatchewan, 31, 167
regularity trials. *See* rallying
regulation of auto sport. *See* auto sport, control of, regulation of; Canadian Automobile Sport Clubs, authority of; Fédération Internationale de l'Automobile
Renault cars, 40, 76, 101–2, 105, 106, 107–9, 115; Dauphine, 107; Dauphine 1093, 101, 107; Gordini, 115, 117; R-8, 108, 109
Renault rally team, 76, 101–2, 107–9, 113, 200
Rendall, Ivan, 234
Revson, Peter, 169
Rheims, France, 4, 137
Ricard, Edmund, 122
Riley, Mrs G., 35
Riley cars, 31
Rindt, Jochen, 163–4

Ripley, W., 103
risk recreation, 26
Risley, John, 204, 208
Riverside International Raceway, California, 4, 74, 154, 157, 158, 168
Road America race track, Wisconsin, 225
Road Atlanta race track, Georgia, 168
Roberts, Peter, 213
Robertson, Brian, 180, 183
Robson, Graham, 106
Rocky Mountain Rally, 199
Rodriguez, Pedro, 116, 120, 121, 129, 144
Rodriguez, Ricardo, 120, 137
Rogano, Albert, 238
Rogers, Richard, 177
roll bars and cages. *See* auto sport, safety
Rolls Royce cars, 103
Rootes Group car manufacturer, 34, 105, 106
Rosati, Elio, 191
Rosberg, Keke, 209
Roscoe, Bill, 103
Ross, John, 127, 128, 156–60, 177, 213–14
Rothman's Porsche Turbo Cup racing series, 227, 229, 233, 240
Routliffe, 'Slim,' 41
Rowntree, Bryan, 26, 30, 38, 70, 75, 76, 125
Royal Automobile Club, 15, 19, 20, 63, 67, 89, 92, 103, 114, 128, 164–7, 181; General Competition Rules, 63, 67–9
rules. *See* auto sport, regulation of
Rulka, Stu, 206
Russell, Jim, 175. *See also* racing, schools

Ryan, Charles, 166, 179
Ryan, Jean, 216
Ryan, Peter, 4, 24, 27, 56, 57, 120, 121, 128, 133–7, 138, 142, 146, 151, 154, 169, 187, 222
Ruys de Perez, Stephanie, 94

Saab cars, 27, 201
Sadler, George, 149
Sadler Car Company, 150
Sadler racing cars, 73, 76, 120, 135, 136, 138, 148, 149, 150, 151; Formula Ferocious, 151; Formula Junior, 150–1; Mk. II, 149; Mk. III, 149, 150; Mk. IV [Sadler Corvette], 120, 150, 154; Mk. V, 120, 135, 136, 138, 148, 151–2, 157
Sadler, William G. 'Bill,' 4, 26, 38, 39, 54, 65, 70, 73, 76, 120, 135, 138, 148–56
safety. *See* auto sport, safety
Saggars, Mike, 154
St Catharines, Ontario, 4, 135, 149, 150
St Catharines Motor Club, 53, 219
St. Croix, Ross de, 26, 34, 35, 128, 129, 142, 157–9, 164, 249
St-Croix race track, Quebec, 216, 233
St-Eugène, Ontario, 26, 35, 41, 89, 95, 127, 129. *See also* Connor Circuit
St-Félicien race track, Quebec, 216, 233
St John's Motor Club, 88
St John's, Newfoundland, 236, 240
St-Jovite, Quebec, 127, 128, 144
St Lawrence Automobile Club (St LAC), 15, 48, 102
Salvadori, Roy, 151
Sambrook, John, 94, 215–16
Samson, Leo, 127–30

Sanair race track and drag strip, Quebec, 174, 216, 239, 242, 243, 254
Sands, Al, 59, 60, 64, 66, 90
Sangster, Bryan, 243
Saskatoon Sports Car Club (SSCC), 94, 195
Sauber Formula One racing team, 258
Saville-Peck, David, 168
Sayle, Robert, 62,
Scarab racing cars, 150
Schechter, Jody, 237
Schkee Can-Am racing car, 224
Schon, George, 26
Schumacher, Michael, 6, 9, 250, 257
Scott, Carl, 138
Scott, Dorothy (Hondorf), 219
Scott, Dwight, 34, 190–1
Searle, John, 36, 112, 113
Searle, Ruth, 36
seat belts. *See* auto sport, safety
Sebring 12-hour endurance race, Florida, 4, 77, 141, 157
Second World War, 18, 19, 20, 24, 26, 27, 36, 40, 53
sedan. *See* automobiles; *see also* racing cars, sedans
Seitz, Burke, 76
Sellers, Doug, 121
Shannonville race track, Ontario, 231, 233
Sharp, Janet, 94
Shaw, Dave, 216
Shearwater, Canadian Forces Base, 241
Shelby, Carroll, 74
Shelby American Racing team, 139
Shelby cars, Cobra, 97, 139, 141, 146, 149, 169, 204, 208; Cooper-Ford ('King Cobra'), 139; Mustang GT350, 97, 140, 145, 206; *see also* Comstock Racing Team; Ford Motor Company
Shell 4000 rally, 17, 31, 83, 88, 101–6, 108–18, 119, 165, 189, 257; advertising and promotion, 105, 107, 279n; cost of, 105–6; Manufacturer's Team Award for, 101–2, 108–10; organization, 103–5; prize money in, 105
Shell Oil Company, 17, 101–6, 279n
Shelton, Richard 'Dick,' 24, 76, 117, 165
Shelton-Mansell Motors, 76
Short, Tony, 98
Silvera, Bill, 52, 109
Silverstone race track, UK, 155, 208
Simca cars, 111
Singer cars, 26
Smiths Falls, Ontario, 197
Smyth, Phil, 144
Snell, Charlie, 67
Snell Foundation, 67
snowmobile racing, 174
solo racing, 33, 37, 53–5, 66, 203, 205–6, 207, 226–7; auto slalom, 37, 53, 203, 205–6, 259; driving skill tests, 18, 30, 52, 53, 206; gymkhanas, 18, 37, 53, 66; hill climbs, 53, 66, 206–7, 227, 299n
Souris, airport race track, Manitoba, 144
Spa-Francorchamps race track, Belgium, 208
spectacle. *See* auto sport, as spectacle
spectators. *See* auto sport, audience
Spenard, Richard, 205, 228, 244
Spencer-Nairn, John, 94, 128
spoilers. *See* racing cars, aerodynamics

sponsorship, 7–10, 22, 39, 40, 48, 51, 72–3, 74, 75, 78, 83, 87, 91, 94, 97, 101, 103, 104, 105–10, 111, 119, 120, 122, 129, 134, 135, 136, 154, 159, 166, 178–84, 186, 190, 191, 196, 198, 200, 205, 211, 212, 213, 215, 216, 217, 225, 228, 229, 231, 232–3, 235, 239–45, 249–50, 251, 255, 257; influence of, 83, 122, 128, 130, 143–4, 156, 159, 171, 174, 180, 181, 192, 198, 211, 212, 213, 216, 232–3, 236–7, 241–5, 250, 255, 256. *See also* auto sport, advertising in, control of; commercialism; commercial professionalism; commodification; professionalism

sports, 5–6, 8–9, 25, 52, 121, 181, 219–20, 240, 241, 252, 258. *See also named sports*; amateur; commercialism; professionalism

Sports Car Club (SCC) (Toronto), 15, 19, 32, 54, 58, 59, 210

Sports Car Club of America (SCCA), 20, 22, 28, 47, 64, 65, 67, 68, 70, 74, 75, 84, 92, 97, 99, 120, 157–9, 172, 175, 204, 214, 224, 225, 245, 255; amateurism policy, 20, 74–5, 84, 120; Can-Am series and, 157–9, 224–5; Continental Formula A series, 172, 176, 178, 179, 182; Trans-American Sedan Championship, 97–8, 142, 174, 182, 205, 213, 215, 216, 228, 233, 234, 255; United States Road Racing Championship, 75, 157, 158

Sports Car Club of British Columbia (SCCBC), 27, 61–2, 65, 88, 232; competition events, 27, 36, 41, 43, 94; Westwood Motorsport Park race track and, 41–3, 61

Sports Car Club of Saskatchewan (SCCS), 31, 65

sports cars. *See* automobiles; racing cars

sports history, 10, 259–60, 262n

Sports Motor Car Club (SMCC), 15, 16, 18, 19, 32, 33, 35, 36, 50, 51, 108, 112, 113, 195, 198, 219

Sports Motor Cycle Club, 18

stage rallies. *See* rallying

Standard. *See* Triumph cars

Standing, Diane, 247

Stanley, Lester 'Les,' 24, 32, 46, 47, 49, 52, 67, 106

Stebro performance exhaust company, 76; racing cars, 98. *See also* Broeker, Peter

Sterne, G.B., 94

Stewart, Don, 88, 92

Stewart, Jackie, 6, 163–4, 214, 249

Stiles, Vic, 67

stock car racing, 4, 9, 17, 77, 79, 174, 216, 223, 241, 256; tracks, 130, 131, 174, 216, 234, 256. *See also* National Association for Stock Car Auto Racing

Stockey, Chuck, 50

Stone, F. David, 177

street race courses. *See* race tracks; *see also individual cities and tracks by name*

Studebaker cars, 101, 105, 107, 114; Lark, 101, 114

subculture, sports car. *See* auto sport, subculture

Sullivan, Danny, 240

Sunbeam cars, 16; Alpine, 96; Talbot, 23; Tiger, 145

Sundown Grand Prix, 81–2, 134, 140, 169, 204

Surman, Bob, 179
Surtees, John, 3, 121, 137, 145, 159–60, 213
Sutherland, Hugh, 26, 38
Suzuki cars, 248

Tagliani, Alex, 231
Tall Pines Rally, 191, 192, 196, 199
Targa Newfoundland stage rally, 257
Taws, Ashley, 255
Taylor, Henry, 110, 116
Teasdale, Kathryn, 255
technology, auto sport, technological change in. *See also* racing cars
'Teem Atlantic,' 208
Telegram Trophy Indy Car race, 235
television. *See* media coverage of auto sport
Tennant, Walter, 247
Thousand (1000) Islands rally, 29, 36, 47–8, 52, 189, 192
Thuner, Jean-Jacques, 115
Times-Mirror Corporation, 74
Tim Horton's company, 247
tires. *See* racing cars, design of
TNN television network, 241
tobacco, 4, 83, 242, 251, 253, 257, 305n. *See also* advertising; *companies by name*; sponsorship
Tojeiro, John, 149
Toronto, 3, 5, 15, 16, 18, 23, 24, 30, 31–2, 34, 48, 50, 51, 54, 59, 60, 75, 76, 77, 94, 95, 104, 109, 123, 135, 139, 145, 146, 225, 230, 235, 238, 239, 243, 255, 259; street race track in, 235–6, 239, 241. *See also* Molson Indy Toronto
Toronto Star newspaper, 239
Toyota cars, 76, 190, 197, 199, 200, 248

Traco Engineering, 154
Tracy, Paul, 4, 5, 7, 230, 257
Trans-American Sedan Championship (Trans-Am) racing series, 97–8, 142, 174, 182, 205, 213, 215, 216, 228, 233, 234, 255
Trans-Canada rally. *See* Shell 4000 rally
Triskaidekaphobia rally, 46
Triumph cars, 26, 28, 39, 54, 56, 64, 65, 72, 96, 106, 115, 130, 256; Spitfire, 96; TR2, 39; TR3, 26, 56, 64, 130; TR4, 96, 115
Trois-Rivières, Quebec, 89, 216, 235–8. *See also* Grand Prix de Trois-Rivières
Trudeau, Pierre, 213, 222
TSD rallies. *See* rallying
TSN television network, 227, 241
Tugwell, Iain, 192–3, 195, 201, 202, 219
Tuppence Cup Races, 30
TVA network, 184
TVR cars, 28
Twin Lakes Motor Club, 87

United Kingdom (UK). *See* Britain
United States, 17, 18, 20, 28, 29, 40, 43, 48, 53, 74, 105, 115, 121, 133, 140, 152, 157, 158, 184, 204, 226, 232, 254
United States Auto Club (USAC), 74
United States Grand Prix, 98, 136
United States Road Racing Championship (USRRC), 157–8
University of New Brunswick Sports Car Club (UNBSCC), 23, 34, 88, 207, 219
Unser, Al, Jr, 230, 240

Vancouver, 4, 7, 41, 94, 101–3, 114, 145, 239, 241, 249
Vancouver Motor Club, 61
Vandaalen, Blu, 248
Vanderbilt, William K., 18
Vanderbilt Cup race, 18, 134, 136
Van Vliet, Jim, 107
Varley, Les, 39
Vauxhall cars, 109
Victoria, BC, 117
Villeneuve, Gilles, 4, 5, 6, 57, 100, 133, 137, 167, 170, 173–4, 176, 181, 184–7, 205, 209, 216, 221–2, 224–5, 227, 230, 232, 249
Villeneuve, Jacques (brother of Gilles), 225, 226, 230
Villeneuve, Jacques (son of Gilles), 4, 230, 250, 258, 305n
Vintage Automobile Racing Association of Canada (VARAC), 226
vintage car racing. *See* racing, vintage car racing
Volkswagen cars (VW), 27, 29, 34, 40, 47, 53–4, 64, 98–9, 106–8, 134, 247–8, 256
volunteers. *See* auto sport, volunteers in
Volvo cars, 27, 101, 105, 107, 108, 115

Walker Formula 4 racing car, 206
Walsh, Yvon, 205
Watkins Glen race track, NY, 20, 40, 68, 98, 128, 136, 149, 150, 151, 224, 233, 234
Weber, Jim, 226
Weber, Max, 258
Welgan, Ron, 195
Welin, Len, 229
Wenzel, Werner, 190
Werner Ornstein British Motors, 106

Western Canada Motorsport Association, 304n
Western Ontario Sports Car Association (WOSCA), 23, 110, 218
Westwood Motorsport Park, BC, 41–3, 56, 61, 123, 126, 128, 131, 139, 144, 158, 177, 183, 204, 208, 209, 225, 232, 256
Whannel, Gary, 252
Whisler, Timothy, 28
White, Eve, 50
White, Ron, 34
Whitehead, Darrell, 247
Whitmore, (Sir) John, 137
'Wide World of Sports,' 184
Wietzes, Eppie, 3, 32, 110, 139–42, 145, 146, 160, 163–4, 167–9, 172, 178, 179, 182, 187, 205, 228, 284n
Wilden, Kenny, 228
Wilkinson, Charlie, 94
Williams, Stanley, 210, 217
Willis, Elaine, 255
Wilson, Doug, 88, 103–4
Wilson, Heather, 35
Wilson, John, 110, 114, 123, 124
Wingfield, Dudley, 219
Winnipeg, Manitoba, 18, 24, 130, 144, 145, 232
Winnipeg Sports Car Club (WSCC), 195, 232
Winter Carnival Rally, 207
winter rallies. *See* rallying; Canadian Winter Rally; Rallye Des Neiges
Withers, Ken, 103
Wolf, Walter, 224, 237; WR1 racing car, 237
Woloshyn, Roger, 195
women in auto sport, 35–7, 39, 94–5, 254–5. *See also women by name*

Woods, Doug, 189, 190, 192, 194, 196, 197, 199, 207. *See also* Boyce, Walter
Wordham, Bill, 121
World Rally Championship, 114, 194, 197, 198, 201
World Sports Car championship, 140, 146, 241
Worth, Ian, 101–2, 108, 113
Wright, Milton J. 'Milt,' 87, 92, 120, 122, 143, 160, 165, 167, 217, 218–19. *See also* Canadian Automobile Sport Clubs, president

Young, Hugh, 15, 16, 19, 24
Young, Jack, 104

Zerex Special racing car, 157
Zolder race track, Belgium, 4, 221–2